# CD START INSTRUCTIONS

**1** Place the CD-ROM in your CD-ROM drive.

**2** Launch your Web browser*. See below if you do not have a Web browser.

**3** From your Web browser, select Open File from the File menu. Select the CD-ROM (usually drive D for PCs and the desktop for Macs), then select the file called Welcome.htm.

\* We have included the Microsoft Web browser Internet Explorer on this CD in case you do not have a browser or would like to upgrade or change your browser. Please review the CD-ROM appendix of this book for more information on this software, as well as other software on this CD.

## MINIMUM RECOMMENDED SYSTEM REQUIREMENTS

This CD-ROM is designed to work on both Macintosh and Windows operating systems.

### Macintosh System

- Computer: 680x
- Memory: 8MB of RAM
- Software: System 7.0 or higher
- Hardware: 2X CD-ROM drive

### Windows System

- Computer: 386 IBM PC-compatible
- Memory: 8MB of RAM
- Software: Windows 3.1, NT, or 95
- Hardware: 2X CD-ROM drive

# WEB DESIGN
## RESOURCES DIRECTORY

**TOOLS AND TECHNIQUES FOR DESIGNING YOUR WEB PAGES**

# WEB DESIGN
## RESOURCES DIRECTORY

**TOOLS AND TECHNIQUES FOR DESIGNING YOUR WEB PAGES**

## RAY DAVIS

LYCOS PRESS
AN IMPRINT OF MACMILLAN COMPUTER PUBLISHING USA
EMERYVILLE, CALIFORNIA

| | |
|---|---|
| Publisher | Joe Wikert |
| Associate Publisher | Juliet Langley |
| Publishing Director | Cheryl Applewood |
| Acquisitions Editors | Kenyon Brown and Renée Wilmeth |
| Development Editor | Renée Wilmeth |
| CD-ROM Developer | Sarah Ishida |
| Copy Editor | Mitzi Waltz |
| Technical Reviewer | Marinela Miclea |
| Production Editor | Carol Burbo |
| Proofreaders | Carol Burbo and Jeff Barash |
| Cover Illustration and Design | Bay Graphics |
| Book Design and Layout | Bruce Lundquist |

Lycos Press books are developed as a joint effort of Lycos and Que. They are published by Macmillan Computer Publishing USA, a Simon & Schuster Company.

Lycos ™ is a trademark of Carnegie Mellon University.

Lycos Press imprint books are produced on a Macintosh computer system with the following applications: FrameMaker®, Microsoft® Word, QuarkXPress®, Adobe Illustrator®, Adobe Photoshop®, Adobe Streamline™, MacLink®Plus, Aldus® FreeHand™, Collage Plus™.

Lycos Press, an imprint of
Macmillan Computer Publishing USA
5903 Christie Avenue
Emeryville, CA 94608
http://www.mcp.com/lycos

ISBN 0-7897-1060-9

Manufactured in the United States of America
10 9 8 7 6 5 4 3 2 1

**This book is dedicated to my father and mother, John E. Davis, Jr., and Nellie Davis.**

**—Ray**

**FOR THEIR GENERAL CONTRIBUTIONS** to Web authorship, I'd like to thank Joe Lambert and Nina Mullen of the San Francisco Digital Media Center. Web publication may be worldwide, but Web creation needs a local place to develop. Joe and Nina have supplied that local space to a large number of Web authors in the Bay Area.

For her contributions to this book, I'd like to gratefully acknowledge the work of Mitzi Waltz, who dealt with some very painful deadline problems. Much appreciated!

**IN THE BRIEF TIME** since the world has had point-and-click access to the multigraphic, multimedia World Wide Web, the number of people going online has exploded to an estimated 50 million, all roaming around the roughly 35 million different Web sites and hundreds of millions of Web pages in cyberspace. And as the Web makes its way into our everyday lives, the kinds of people logging on are changing.

Today, there are as many Web novices as experts—perhaps more—and all are struggling to get the most from the pockets of information scattered throughout the Web. But while most are in search of useful information, they often stumble aimlessly through cyberspace, using hit-or-miss methods with few results, little substance, and a lot of frustration.

What people need—and what they are increasingly demanding—is a personal guide to the Internet.

In 1994, when the World Wide Web was only just beginning to become popular among the technological elite, the Lycos technology was created by a scientist at Carnegie Mellon University to help people navigate the Web. The company's powerful searching technology is the bedrock underlying a family of information-finding tools that untangle the Internet, offering a simple and intuitive resource for all types of Websters, from "Net vets" to "newbies." And all for free.

Lycos (http://www.lycos.com) is an oasis in cyberspace—an orientation point—with news, views, reviews, and a powerful search engine that all draw on the company's extensive database of nearly 70 million URLs—the better part of the entire Web—that is continuously updated. Lycos delivers more than 6 million page impressions to users each day. Tens of millions of people worldwide use Lycos through its home base in the United States, and through licensing partners. There are nearly 30 companies and online services that power their interactive products with the Lycos technology.

## HOW LYCOS WORKS

The approach to Web navigation is divided into two camps: those who believe that subject-oriented directories (much like the Yellow Pages) are the best way to find information because they are created by humans; and those who believe a powerful search engine which fuels subject-specific queries (type in a word and automatically get back related information) is a superior approach.

In fact, both are necessary, because directories created by humans are incomplete, and search engines that probe the Web's millions of pieces of constantly changing information lack the human intervention that can help users find the most relevant results.

That's why Lycos has created its Navigation Center with a wealth of information-finding tools that combine the best of both approaches. Eighteen subject-oriented Lycos WebGuides group information-finding tools together in categories such as entertainment, business, sports, and more. Each WebGuide offers a number of different tools, like news headlines from all over the Web; Top 10 lists from Lycos's award-winning review service, Top 5% Sites; PowerSearches, which have been constructed by Lycos editors and combine the power of the Lycos search engine with the human touch of a professional Lycos searcher; Pictures & Sounds searches, for access to the Web's multimedia riches; and much, much more.

Tools like PeopleFind can help Web users locate people all over the world that they've lost touch with. City Guides help users research and reach a destination, complete with maps and driving directions, in locations all over the United States and in Canada, the United Kingdom, and Ireland.

The Lycos Navigation Center is everyone's personal guide to the Web. Lycos designed its service on the premise that people want three things from the Web:

First, they want to search or browse or tour the Internet for specific items or subjects; second, they want information with real-world relevance (like company stock information, national Yellow and White Pages, or maps and driving directions); and finally, they want that blend of human touch with a powerful technology engine they can drive themselves.

## SPIDERS ON STEROIDS

The powerful Lycos spider and search technology is the core of the Lycos service. It underpins the spectrum of navigation guides that give Lycos customers a rich Internet experience, whether they are seeking a specific piece of information, or want to rely on the most widely used sites in a given subject category, or whether they are interested in visiting sites that are highly rated by Lycos's dozens of professional editors.

All of these approaches to experiencing the Internet are tightly integrated to create a rewarding and easy-to-use interface that is free and located at the Lycos Navigation Center.

Lycos was originally developed at Carnegie Mellon University by Dr. Michael "Fuzzy" Mauldin, who holds a Ph.D. in conceptual information retrieval. Now chief scientist at Lycos, Dr. Mauldin continues to expand the unique exploration and indexing technology. Utilizing this technology, Lycos has discovered a way to find not just information, but relevant information. Lycos technology has been touted by the Internet community and has been highlighted in several national publications as one of the hottest.

The Lycos database is constantly being refined by dozens of automated software robots, or agents, called "spiders." In fact, the term "Lycos" comes from the Latin for Wolf Spider—*lycosidae lycosa*—a predatory arachnid known for hunting its prey rather than lying in wait.

Hundreds of these spiders roam the Web endlessly, finding and downloading the most important information from Web pages in an abstracted form. Each abstract contains a part of the site: the 100 most important words, the first 20 lines of text, the size of the site (in bytes), and the number of words contained within. Heuristic (self-teaching) software looks at where the words appear in the document, their proximity to other words, their frequency, and other criteria to determine what's most important about the site. In addition, Lycos spiders analyze a site's popularity by the number of hypertext links that point to it from other sites.

Using all this information, Lycos determines how relevant a site is to a user's particular query. When a user enters a search term or phrase, Lycos delivers the results based on their applicability to that query. And *voilá*—the user receives a list of the most likely places in the WWW to find information about the desired subject.

It is this technology that forms the core of Lycos's information-finding tools, giving users a wide variety of ways to find information on the Internet and the WWW and making the Internet a useful tool for the average person.

## THE COMPANY

Lycos, Inc. was incorporated in June 1995 and held its initial public offering ten months later. It was the youngest company in American business history to go public. Now trading on the NASDAQ exchange under the symbol LCOS, Lycos has its corporate headquarters in Framingham, Massachusetts, and other offices in San Francisco, California; New York City; Pittsburgh, Pennsylvania; and Munich, Germany. Contact Lycos at 500 Old Connecticut Path, Framingham, MA, 01701; 508-424-0400. Or send us e-mail at webmaster@lycos.com.

Remember, you can get Lycos, or you can get lost!

**IF THE WEB** were shrunk down to the size of an encyclopedia set, its last three volumes would be entirely devoted to the subject of the Web, with the exception of a few brief paragraphs on the films of Tuesday Weld and bootleg recordings of Neil Young.

The rationale for the book you're holding is that everything needed to publish on the Web can be found on the Web itself. I have good reason to feel comfortable with that assertion. All of my own Web work has been based purely on online resources, and when I teach Web authoring, I rely almost entirely on the Web for texts and tools.

Quite aside from the cheapness and convenience that might lead one to *prefer* the Web as a source, it is in fact *essential* for Web authors to keep turning to the Web itself. Paper publishing and commercially distributed software simply move too slowly to keep up with the field.

Of course, the presence of sufficient information doesn't imply that the information will be easy to track down. The lack of editorial controls—even on large commercial sites—guarantees that a huge proportion of Web pages will be misleadingly full of hype, or so obsolete as to be useful only for a virtual compost heap, or simply innocently clueless.

Even useful references may be embedded in less-than-useful formats, and even the most intelligent newcomer can easily mistake an annoying cliché for an obligatory feature. Experienced Web users will force themselves to live with stylistic flaws if necessary, but that's no reason for the new Web author to spend time learning to *imitate* those flaws.

Unfortunately, most online directories of links have a vested interest in avoiding mention of these problems. To attract advertising dollars, they may try to claim comprehensiveness, as measured in number of entries, which may make them reluctant to do cleanup work. (The last time I used the most famous Web catalog, I found that close to half of the interesting-sounding links were dead.) Similarly, high-tech sites often need to whip up their own flavor of hype to spread on the spongy layers of other people's hype, and would therefore prefer that those layers not collapse.

That's where a book like this one comes in. Here, rather than seeking ads or scratching-your-back-so-you-can-scratch-mine, above all else, I try to save you time, energy, money, and embarrassment.

Tastes differ and pages change, of course; my favored site may be your rank disappointment. But I believe that an honestly stated opinion, even when you disagree with it, tends to be more informative than bland blanket approval.

Have fun disagreeing with me. Most of all, have fun on the Web.

# CHAPTER 1
# WEB AUTHORING IN CONTEXT

**IN THIS CHAPTER YOU WILL FIND:**

☞ **Explanations of URLs and HTML.**

These two concepts transformed the Internet into the Web. Understanding them will make Web authoring more intuitive for you.

☞ **Background on the Web's strengths and limitations.**

As you decide how to focus your time, energy, and money, you must stay firmly grounded in the realities of Web publishing, or face unnecessary disappointment.

☞ **Audience-oriented guidelines.**

If you haven't spent much time on the Web, or simply haven't been in a mood to analyze what you've spent time perusing, this should help you direct your energies wisely. It takes more time to author than it does to browse, and you don't want that time to be wasted.

☞ **Tips for using on-line (and off-line) reference works.**

The written word stays still while the Web moves on. Here's how to deal with the temporal gap.

☞ **Pointers to Web authoring overviews, software, and critiques.**

This book is a useful introduction, but it doesn't have to be your only resource.

## COME IN AND JOIN THE PARTY

I've been excited about the possibilities of the Web since I first encountered the basic ideas behind it, back when it was an experimental project at the CERN laboratory in Europe. I've followed its growth, browsed it, propagandized it, taught courses on it, programmed for it, and authored an outrageous number of Web pages, both professional and personal.

From the beginning, I've held firm to the belief that you have to be on the Web yourself to be able to author for it. Everything I've learned, I've learned from on-line sources; virtually all my Web authoring tools (with a few obvious exceptions, such as Adobe Photoshop) were obtained from on-line sources.

And it's an ongoing process. As a professional, I need to avoid out-of-date approaches and recommendations. Whenever I do any Web project, I always try to get a sweeping view of the state of the art regarding that type of project before I begin designing and coding.

Thus this book. This directory's structure matches the way I myself work and teach. It also matches the way I write Web pages: with links.

### LINKING, NOT TELLING

Laziness is one of the great human survival traits. If hundreds of other people have already covered topics for me (and they have,) why should I duplicate their labor?

Of course, there are many ways to avoid labor: plagiarism and other types of copyright infringement are popular ones. I bring this up to point out one of the great but seldom-acknowledged advantages of Web authoring over print publication:

It's more polite to point than to steal.

The natural human impulse to say "Look at this!," which formerly led to massive photocopying and anonymous cut-paste-and-forwarding in e-mail, can find a more ethical release on the Web. An external link is nothing more than a footnote or citation, which happens to have a trip to the library conveniently built in. Speaking as one Web author to another: please don't erase the original author or quote material out of context, just link.

After all, since you really can't learn Web authoring without going on-line, why shouldn't you take advantage of the opportunities you find there?

### SO WHY WRITE A BOOK AT ALL?

Web browsers aren't well suited to handling hundreds of pages worth of material—flipping through paper is much faster than flipping through downloads. For that matter, accessing directories and software from a CD-ROM is faster than downloading directories and software, even across an ISDN connection. Therefore, our hope is that this book and CD-ROM will be a considerably more effective starting point for you than an on-line search for "Web authoring" would be, even though we expect you to continue your explorations on-line. Books like this one are a balanced diet of fish and fowl, since they do assume that you'll be going on-line to complete the experience, and they even supply you with an HTML version to speed that process along.

There's also a little matter of economics. As we're about to see, it's difficult to make a direct profit in Web distribution...

## WHERE DO WORLD WIDE WEBS COME FROM?

Many of my Web authoring students have been confused about the distinction between "this Internet thing" and "that Web thing." (Let's not even get into "cyberspace.") To answer them, I tell a very simplified story:

The Internet is a loose, world-wide collection of computers that can find each other and exchange messages using something called TCP/IP. Over the decades, many specialized types of message delivery systems (or "protocols") were developed, and a variety of specialized programs and files were developed along with them. Any time we wanted to handle a certain type of message on the Internet, we had to switch to a specialized program that understood the messages, and we also had to know how to handle the outcome of those messages. Usually the outcome was a local copy of a file, which might have come from an entirely different operating system.

After an embarrassingly long time, it was realized that most of this rote decision-making could easily be automated. After all, computers on the Internet had names; the files and users and other resources on those computers had names; and to make it easier to e-mail nontext files, people had already started coming up with names for file types. (These are called "MIME" types, and you can easily find a list of them via the "Helper Applications" setup screen for your browser.) It shouldn't be that hard to come up with names for protocols, we figured. Once we had those, we could then pack everything we needed into one very long, but very useful, name. This name could then be automatically understood by computer programs.

More information about the World Wide Web can be found on The World Wide Web FAQ sheet, shown in Figure 1.1.

## THE URL

These full-featured Internet names are called Uniform Resource Locators (URLs). They're important to understand, because you'll sometimes need to parse them yourself. For example, you might want to manually decide on a specialized program to handle a certain protocol, rather than letting your browser handle the decision automatically. And it's much easier to write links from your own pages if you know what the links mean.

Pointers to full descriptions of URLs will be given in the next chapter. For now, suffice it to say that a URL is usually divided into three parts: the protocol (the type of program that will be receiving specialized messages from your browser), the Internet address of the computer that will be running that program and, finally, the description of what specific item is wanted from that computer. The format is:

**protocol://internetAddress/specific/item/wanted**

For example, FTP is a standard protocol that's used to copy files from one system to another. When you use FTP, you must describe what you want by specifying a directory and file name. So, to fetch a file named "biff.tif" from the file directory "BigPictures" using an FTP server located at the Internet address "ftp.graphixstix.com," you would use the URL "ftp://ftp.graphixstix.com/BigPictures/biff.tif."

Naturally, the "http" protocol in a URL indicates that the link will be connecting with a server that understands HTTP; that is, with a Web server. A protocol that you're likely to only see during testing, and

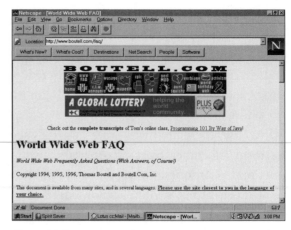

**Figure 1.1**
The World Wide Web FAQ sheet at
http://www.boutell.com/faq/

then only in the address window of your browser, is "file": this indicates that the page is on your local file system. You should never see a URL beginning with "file": in a production Web page!

## THE WORLD WIDE WEB

Once we have a "traffic cop" program that can handle all of this decision-making and traffic-directing, we're suddenly able to list and retrieve all the possible resources of the Internet using one application and one user interface. And if what you retrieve happens to be displayed in the same program from which you requested the retrieval, you'll begin to have the illusion that you're going from one place to another *inside* your program, rather than always being aware that files and messages are being copied to your local computer.

Several years ago, some inspired thinkers at CERN realized that when this illusion was realized, the users would have what's called a *hypertext appli-cation*: that is, displayable information with many possible branches for the users to choose. Even better, since the users at CERN already had the multiple file types and enormous scope of the Internet on their side, they would have a highly distributed multimedia hypertext application! In other words, they (and after they worked a while, we) had the Web.

To sum up, **the World Wide Web is a way to treat the Internet as distributed multimedia hypertext**. This treatment requires a program that can send hypertext messages to you and direct traffic on the Internet side (a "Web server"), and a program that can interpret those hypertext messages and direct traffic on your local machine (a "Web browser"). The special variety of messages exchanged by these two types of software is called the "HyperText Transfer Protocol" (or "HTTP"); the hypertext messages that the browser must interpret are generally in "HyperText Markup Language" (or "HTML").

---

☞ You won't always see all the parts of the URL in a link definition. That's because the missing parts will be automatically filled in from the location of the Web page that has defined the link. Such partial URLs are called "relative" URLs, and they're an essential part of the Web author's life.

A relative URL is assumed to be in the same physical area and to be using the same protocol as the file that is using it. One of the implications is that if you use relative URLs to link your own documents, you can go ahead and test them using the "file:" protocol on your own serverless system. You can then move them to your Web server without changes, and the links will continue to work, even though both their physical location and their access protocol have changed.

For example, the absolute URL for a page as I work on it locally might look something like:

```
file:///HardDrive/Desktop%20Folder/
Web%20Publishing/relativeurls.html
```

If I used an absolute URL to link to this, I would have to change it every time I moved to a new machine. If I moved over to my Windows PC, that local copy would probably have to be linked to using something like:

```
<A HREF="file:///Macintosh%20HD/
Desktop%20Folder/Web%20Publishing/
relativeurls.html">
```

And then when I moved the page to my Web server, I'd have to change the link to:

```
<A HREF="http://www.best.com/~raydavis/
wwwworkshop/relativeurls.html">
```

Instead, using a relative URL, I can link to:

```
<A HREF="relativeurls.html">
```

and nothing has to be changed as I move my files. The same holds true if I have to move the linking file and the linked file to a different directory, or have to move them to a different server altogether.

## HTML

The formatted hypermedia documents that make up the Web are transmitted across the wires using the one data format that is pretty much standard across all computer models: 7-bit ASCII code, which consists of English letters, punctuation, and numerals. The Web would've gotten off to a much slower start if the data format had been anything as complicated as a Quark XPress document!

The word "markup" derives from the practice of marking up a typewritten manuscript with handwritten instructions to the typesetter. A "markup language" puts those formatting instructions in plain-text commands called "tags." The first version of HTML was closely based on a markup language called SGML, which was much used in the early days of computer-based publishing, with the addition of "hypertext" capabilities such as document-linking and image-embedding. Later, new formatting instructions were added to HTML to extend its capabilities. This process is continuing.

## WHY AUTHOR FOR THE WEB?

To judge it by TV ads, the World Wide Web is, in essence, a way of having 3-D stereo-soundtracked movies swoop out at you while you writhe under a handheld camera shouting "Cool!" According to many news magazines, the Web operates essentially as a professional association for pederasts.

I suppose that both of those possibilities are present. But for me, from the very start back in 1992, the Web seemed to be more than anything else a means for low-cost publishing with fast, wide distribution.

A prime example of this is the availability of such works as the Divine Comedy, right on the Web (see Figure 1.2).

Does that sound a little dry? Consider that the last development to reduce prices and improve dissemination time might have been the printing press.

Dry or not, I've found that this formula has served me well since 1992 in understanding the ups and downs of the Web, its explosive growth and disappointing tumbles, and virtually all of its triumphs and absurdities. I pass the formula along to you to help you decide what and how you should *author*—an odd verb that we use instead of "write" since "Web authoring" tasks can include painting, drawing, photography, creating video and audio, programming, or even just repackaging.

Let's examine the implications of that formula bit by bit.

## LOW COST

Think about the costs involved in publishing a pamphlet or magazine. Paper, ink, and typesetting are bad enough, but printing costs go up if graphics are included, and the price soon zooms past the budget limitations of most small presses or amateurs if color graphics are required.

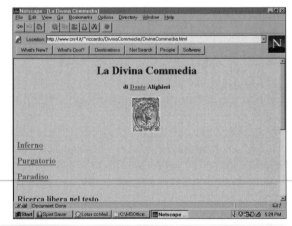

**Figure 1.2**
The complete original text of the Divine Comedy at http://www.crs4.it/~riccardo/DivinaCommedia/ DivinaCommedia.html.

Let's say you just spent your life savings on getting an impressive stack of paper piled up. Now you're faced with the problem of what to do with it. Bookstore and newsstand distribution is extraordinarily difficult to achieve, and even if your work is available to some small segment of the store-browsing public, results are often depressingly hit-and-miss. Subscriptions are much easier for you to deal with economically, but impulse subscribers are a rare breed! You're faced with either spending even more money on advertising, or temporarily reconciling yourself to an audience of family, friends, and rabid collectors.

It's therefore not surprising that the Web is, and always has been, dominated by the sorts of publications that have traditionally only been held in check by cost or distribution worries, such as those listed below (see Figure 1.3):

- **Academic research**

- **Fanzines** and other publications created "for the love of it," including reprints

☞ The tag for a link is "<A>" for "Anchor." Why isn't it called "Link" instead?

Not realizing that HTML would so quickly swamp the fame of its predecessor, the original HTML creators wanted to make as few changes to SGML as possible, and therefore tried to fit everything related to linking into a single new tag.

Now there are two parts to a hyperlink: where you start from (usually called the link), and where you end up (usually called the target). You may want to end up in the middle of a file rather than at the beginning, so there has to be some way of naming the target within the file. This is done with the "anchor" tag, since that's where the hyperlink "rope" is anchored. The name of the anchor inside the document is naturally signaled by the NAME attribute of the anchor tag. Since they now had one hyperlink-related tag, HTML's creators went on to shove the other side of the link into the same tag by adding the HREF ("hypertext reference") attribute to it.

As it turned out, Web authors make many more links than they make anchors, and so we have a case of the tail naming the dog.

- **Ego-driven** essays, diaries, and artwork

- **Small press** fiction and poetry

- **Publicity and advertising**

- **Retail catalogs**

- **Community resource guides**, where "community" might be defined geographically, economically, racially, sexually, politically, professionally, or by several factors put together

- **Public services**, such as transportation reports and weather forecasts

- **Advertisement-driven magazines that are usually distributed for free**, including virtually all computer magazines, which have traditionally given free subscriptions to "professionals"

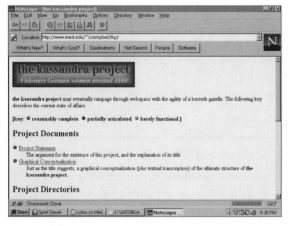

**Figure 1.3**
An example of the sort of information you might not find anywhere else but on the Web: The Kassandra Project, at http://www.reed.edu/~ccampbel/tkp/.

Low cost helps to explain some of the failures of the Web as well. Since the Web is low-cost in its essence, it's very hard for any given publisher to fight against that essence by seeking extra payment from its audience. In other words, gross costs can be reduced by moving to the Web, but gross income is unlikely to appear! Thus, subscription services have only succeeded when they maintain fairly tight control over a much-desired service that could not be gotten elsewhere as easily: the fetishes of stock-market players and pornography addicts have proven particularly ripe for exploitation. On the other hand, a standard newspaper, magazine, game or TV-style sitcom won't have much of a shot at getting bargain-hunting Web surfers' cash.

## FAST DISTRIBUTION

At about the same speed with which your publication can be accessed, you can make it available. That means it can be made available almost immediately after it's created. Despite the best efforts of desktop publishers to create "instant books," the same can't be said of print media!

As a corollary, Web publications can be revised and "reprinted" much more quickly than publications in any other medium. And as a second corollary, the Web is extremely dynamic: not only are additions always being made, but changes to existing material are always being made and, for that matter, existing material is always being lost. Remember the problem with "profit motive" being lost in the low-cost medium of the Web? Just as many of Hollywood's classic films have been lost because there was no economic pressure to keep storing them, Web pages also disappear at the drop of a hat.

We can draw several conclusions from all of this:

1   **There are no standards**. Don't put too much trust in "experts" or zealots (including me, of course). What's successful on the Web is what the market will bear, and it's a close-to-free market.

2   **If you want to play, you have to watch.** You can buy an HTML primer from a few years back and do a decent job of adapting your great-aunt's memoirs for the Web. But if you intend to show off your Web expertise, or to make money showing it off for other people, you're going to have to keep tracking the state of the craft. For that matter, you don't want to unknowingly duplicate someone else's work, or have them unknowingly duplicate yours: you'll both end up with fewer and more irritated viewers. In sum, if you can't afford the time to surf, you probably can't afford the time to do a good job making waves. The only way to understand what you can bring to the Web is to be on it yourself.

3   **Don't put too much trust in particular pages.** For the most part, Web publishers start off fresh and lose interest. Rather than expecting existing pages to be maintained, expect new Web publishers to show up to fill the gap. The exceptions to this painful rule will be obvious and welcome. Please feel free to be one of the exceptions.

4   **Revise and update with a will.** Even the sites which seem most static in nature will sometimes call for updates. Who would've predicted a few years back that the exemplary Jane Austen page would end up being so busy? There's no shame involved in changing things; on the contrary, it's usually a nice treat for old readers.

5   **Don't count on good intentions.** You want to make sure that you actually *have* some old readers. No matter what you make publicly available, you must make sure it's worth

downloading, at least for the audience you have in mind. If you put up and publicize a bunch of empty promises and "Under Construction" signs, your initial viewers will be too disgusted to ever check back again. Test your pages locally until they're ready to go, and don't publicize them till you've looked at them on-line yourself.

## OUT-OF-DATE INFORMATION

This is an even tougher problem than broken links, since obsolete information isn't as explicit about its lack of trustworthiness. When in doubt, check the date. Any Web author worth their salt (and that should include you!) will include page-creation and page-revision dates somewhere on their reference and news pages. A Web-directory site that hasn't been updated in over six months—and, unfortunately, this category includes many star Web-authoring sites of former days—may be useless for your purposes.

## WIDE DISTRIBUTION

The Web is more of a one-time cost than an incremental one. You pay a more-or-less substantial amount for the equipment and a flat fee for the connectivity, and then you can get to everything. What this means is that kids in poor rural areas without a library can get access to a world's worth of information, as long as they have access to a PC and a modem. Once they're connected, it's a level playing field—except for whatever influence that one-time cost had.

In the midst of hyped-up add-ons, plug-ins, and applets, it's important to remember that the Web grew so quickly only because of its cheapness and simplicity. Document formatting and linking were handled by a few instructions in pseudo-English. Virtually everything else was already in place, thanks to existing Internet technology. As a result, Web browsers and Web servers were so easy to write that programmers and students could afford to do the work for free, achieving fast coverage over all computer platforms. Browsers were small and lightweight enough that you could easily run them alongside other applications. Any special file types or messages that came across the Web could be easily routed by the operating system to specialized programs (called "helper applications") that were under your control. HTML itself was simple enough that it could be supported on many low-end computers, and text-only browsers were perfectly usable. In fact, I did most of my own surfing on a text-only browser for a couple of pleasant and economical months.

Those were the days.

When some of the programmers involved with the most popular early browser, NCSA Mosaic, started a commercial company, they had to come up with a way to distinguish themselves and their product. They decided that one such distinguishing mark would be to push work formerly done by external programs into the browser. As a result, the browser became more "integrated," but it also became much larger, much more complicated, and much more like an operating system, since it had to swap between quasi-applications.

Unlike browsers, operating systems are *not* particularly easy to write, and relatively simple browsers soon blossomed into predictable system-crashers. And since users already had an operating system in place before they obtained a browser, a great deal of disk and memory overhead ended up being duplicated, squeezing out users of lower-cost systems.

Things got even wilder with the advent of operating-system-independent compiled programming languages, the best known of which is Java. Not only did this mean that you could download one program that would (theoretically!) run on all comput-

BUILDING BETTER PAGES

# WHEN LINKS GO WRONG

When a URL copied from a printed source or a link from a page doesn't work for you, it doesn't necessarily mean that the information or software you seek has been erased from the Web. Web pages change addresses almost as often as people do, and certainly more often than magazines or books change names. Here's what to do when a link from this book —or any other source, on-line or off-line—fails you:

**1** Unless the error message says something like "Page not found," just try the link again. Errors in resolving domain names are often due to an overloaded local server; errors involving lack of response are often due to an overloaded remote server.

**2** Individual pages sometimes get renamed within a directory on a site, or entire groups of pages may be moved to a different directory altogether. This is especially common in commercial sites, probably due to the bureaucratic overabundance of cooks working on their Web broth. Therefore, look for the missing information by starting from the nearest working URL directory you can find. If the broken URL has a file name after the last slash, try removing the file name: that should lead you to the default introductory page for that file's directory. For example, if "http://www.bozoze.com/shoes/large/floppy.html" doesn't work, try "http://www.bozoze.com/shoes/large/". (If the site's author didn't set up a default page, you'll end up seeing a full directory listing at this point —another fine place to start!)

**3** If the final directory doesn't work or is blank, try deleting the URL up to the next-to-last slash. That will bring you to the next directory up the chain. (In our example, you'll now be looking for "http://www.bozoze.com/shoes/".)

**4** No luck there either? Keep on stripping off directories until you reach the default page for the entire domain; e.g., "http://www.bozoze.com". (This technique is one of the reasons I always configure my browser's preferences to show the "Address" field: it makes editing the current URL easier. It's also one of the reasons I suggest strongly that you always have a default page in your Web directories. More on this subject later.)

**5** If you reach a page that is clueless enough to alert you that this directory-tree crawl won't get you where you want to go, it's time to go outside the URL sequence altogether and do a context search instead. What do you know about the link: Subject matter? Author name? Product name? Try a quick and restricted search in the Yahoo catalog; if that doesn't point to the page's new home, go ahead and use a fuller content-based search using Lycos or another favorite search engine.

**6** Shareware and freeware programmers are often unable to maintain the high cost of stability, and the "author contact" links they include with their work may be broken by the time you've downloaded it and tried it out. If the usual Web searches don't turn them up, try checking for newer versions of their programs in the software archives for the program's platform — Info-Mac sites for the Macintosh, for example, or Windows95.com for Windows.

ers, but it also opened the possibility of letting the browser itself run such downloaded programs, adding another routine to the browser's shaky imitation of an operating system.

Of course, with each new chunk of functionality shoved into the browser, the browser got bigger. More memory was needed, more disk space was needed, and faster CPUs were needed—and if you wanted to take advantage of most non-text sorts of content, a faster Internet connection was needed.

As a result, the level playing field has been trampled into a more complex topography. You want to use Netscape 3.0? You'd better be able to afford something better than a used 386. You can't read a page because the background color makes the text disappear? As Web pundit David Siegel says, you need to upgrade your graphics card—and according to David Siegel, if you can't afford to upgrade your graphics card, you shouldn't be on the Web at all. You want to see Shockwave-animated ads and click on bouncing, squeaking Java mascots? Time to install 32 Megabytes of memory!

It's not surprising that commercial forces have found a way to bring class distinctions to the Web. Some people buy paperback editions of books and cheap dependable cars; others prefer to buy first editions and expensive sports models that break down all the time. The one thing that *has* surprised me is that all the Web browser manufacturers want to build a Masarati—none of them yet has volunteered to build a Mazda.

You, as a Web author, don't necessarily have the same incentives as a commercial software company. Sure, if you do this as a living, you'll have to know how to play the "more is better" game for your clients, many of whom won't mind the idea of restricting themselves to only the wealthiest and most patient segment of the Web audience. If you're doing this for any other reason, though, it would be

> If you need to find useful information in a hurry through the Web (and believe me, if you do this professionally, you'll occasionally be in a hurry!), you can almost strip your fragile-but-sexy Masarati browser down to get a sensible family car. Here's how I do it: Unless I'm specifically researching plug-ins or Java programs, I disable Java and all plug-ins. If I'm visiting a known "danger site," such as HotWired or Project Cool, I'll also disable JavaScript. When I'm in a real hurry, or when other network activity is biting into modem throughput, I'll even turn off image loading. That leaves me with a fairly stable, fairly fast bare-bones browser, as well as a good appreciation of how the other half lives.

wise to reduce your level of "coffee-table technology" to that of your intended audience:

- Remember to set your screen resolution, preferred font, and browser window size to match the systems your audience will be using. Most consumers have much smaller monitors than multimedia developers, and horizontal scrolling is much more cumbersome than vertical scrolling.

- Many ActiveX controls are not likely to show up on UNIX workstations or Macintosh systems for quite some time, so it's a waste of your time to provide them on pages aimed at college students and researchers.

- Newer, more bloated, versions of browsers, particularly those with a full set of plug-ins, will not be able to fit in the constricted memory of low-powered, slightly obsolete systems. If you hope to reach such Poverty Row consumers as public libraries and schools, you'd better cut back on those "advanced" features.

- If you're providing reference material, make sure to keep it available to text-only browsers. I still remember my irritation when a company's technical support site hid the solution for a system-crashing problem behind an imagemap interface. It's easy enough to make sure that a menu of text links is always available, and that text-embedded-in-images is also shown outside the images in some form, even if only as an "ALT" modifier to the "IMG" tag.

In short...

### KNOW YOUR CONTEXT

"My dear young man," Lawrence had said, "everyone is a type. The true mark of social intelligence is how unusual we can make our particular behavior for the particular type we are when we are put under particular pressure."—**Samuel R. Delany,** *Trouble on Triton*

The general approach you take in designing your pages, the basis for all your decisions, depends on the type of content you're presenting: Research-oriented? Artistic? Corporate? Communal? Personal? Educational? Entrepreneurial? Fannish? Playful?

The Web has already evolved a number of recognizable styles, such as the community directory shown in Figure 1.4, with which you should be familiar before publishing your own material. You'll get ideas of what you like from other's pages, and from what you think should have been done differently.

## OVERVIEWS OF WEB AUTHORING

They may be competition, but they're still useful for getting alternative views, and for keeping up with on-line developments. Some of their standout departments may also be mentioned in later, topic-specific chapters, but here are some starting points that I frequently use.

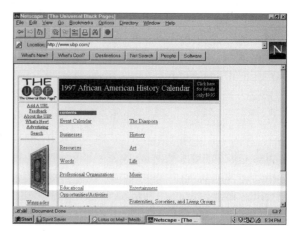

**Figure 1.4**

The Universal Black Pages at "http://www.ubp.com/": a well-designed community directory.

### WebMaster Resources

**http://www.cio.com/WebMaster/wm_notes.html**

This, the main directory area within the highly recommended *WebMaster Magazine* site, is one of my favorite places to catch up on software and tips that I may have missed. But do your readers a favor, and don't copy the site's own super-wide screens and frame-crazy formats.

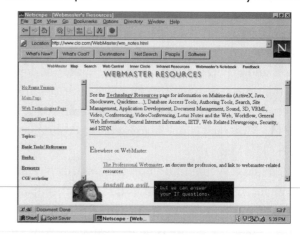

### ServerWatch

**http://serverwatch.iworld.com/**

Although its name implies a strict server-side version of BrowserWatch's client-side news, ServerWatch actually covers a bit more than Web servers per se, including server-side tools and even some client-side authoring aids. A great way to stay in touch.

### ZDNet Whole Web Catalog
http://www5.zdnet.com/zdwebcat/

My favorite of the commercial Web on-line magazines, Ziff-Davis' Whole Web Catalog (actually a collection of links to Web-related material across the company's entire suite of publications) manages to scrape between the Scylla of cluelessness and the Charybdis of sub-adolescent humor to provide some genuinely useful articles, tools, and reviews.

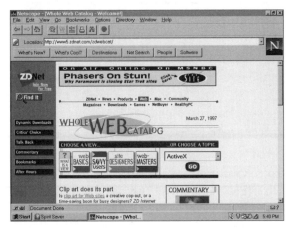

### HotWired's WebMonkey
http://www.webmonkey.com/webmonkey/

WebMonkey is an unusually no-nonsense way to track "cool" (or "coffee-table HTML") technology, since it allows actual negative reviews (a rarity in the dish-it-out-fast Web world). It also includes tutorials on such useful

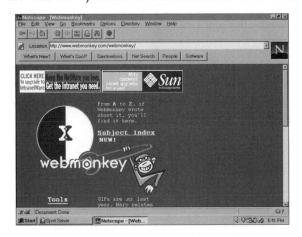

but seldom-mentioned skills as working your way around UNIX. Like many Wired ventures, WebMonkey suffers from a fluctuating attention level and a "too hip to deserve to be so lame" attitude, but it's still well above the average Web-tech site.

### The Web Developer's Virtual Library
http://WWW.Stars.com/

This is a large collection of links and original articles arranged in an exceedingly compact format. The original content may be a little lacking in finesse, but worthy of its own mention is:

### WDVL: The Virtual Library of WWW Development
http://www.charm.net/~web/Vlib/

For a year or two, this was my first stop when looking for authoring resources. Nowadays I have to admit that I tend to go to Yahoo! first. But this "hotlist" of the Web Developer's Virtual Library remains about as compact a starting point as you could find: check out the number of links crammed on that first page, with room for ads.

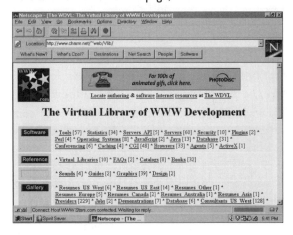

### NetscapeWorld
http://www.netscapeworld.com/

Not an official organ of Netscape, but a general Web-authoring magazine from IDG, publishers of the similarly no-nonsense, high-content magazine **JavaWorld** (http://www.javaworld.com). The crisply dry attitude of the articles contrasts nicely with the fluff often found elsewhere, but don't worry if some of them (particularly those aimed at programmers) go a little over your head when you're first starting out.

### Netscape DevEdge
**http://developer.netscape.com/**

This *is* an official organ of Netscape Communications Corp. Unfortunately, Netscape has been somewhat disappointing in its on-line support outside of those free-beta browser downloads. Netscape has had other business on its corporate mind, and its pages often stress publicity and press releases at the expense of up-to-date documentation. DevEdge, its Web developer site, is a typical hodgepodge, including publicity from old conferences, a bewildering mix of new and obsolete downloads for programmers, and even some useful material. Most of the last is to be found in the "Documentation" area of the "Library" section (http://developer.netscape.com/library/documentation/index.html) . It's worth a visit if only to grab a "preliminary" (don't hold your breath) version of the long-awaited combined documentation for all Netscape-supported HTML tags. (If you want to avoid a long search through frames, you could try going to it directly at http://developer.netscape.com/library/documentation/htmlguid/tags1.htm). After rolling my own for years, it's nice to have someone else finally do the work.

### Microsoft Site Builder Network
**http://www.microsoft.com/sitebuilder/**

Meanwhile, Microsoft has come up with a way to combine developer support and publicity. At its "Site Builder Network," it supplies free software to any Web author who'll explicitly plug Microsoft's Internet Explorer or use Microsoft's alternative plug-in technology, ActiveX (sort of like getting two dozen new socks when you agree to wear a Nike sweatshirt). And we're talking free access to *commercial* software here: I'd already paid for a few of the programs myself. It's true that you don't get user manuals, but if you're on a tight budget and don't mind being part of a Microsoft advertising campaign, check it out. By the way, even aside from the "Site Builder" concept, it's good to keep a close eye on Microsoft's site. After a very slow start, it's become one of the largest sources of Internet freeware around, for both Windows and Macintosh systems.

### CyberAtlas
 **http://www.cyberatlas.com**

The most complete collection of Web statistics, including user population size and demographics, number of sites and servers, and even advertising rates.

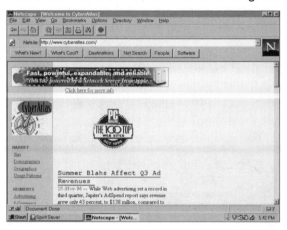

### WebTrends Browser Market Share Report
**http://www.webtrends.com/PRODUCTS/WEBTREND/REPORTS/industry/browser/default.htm**

WebTrends tracks the rough percentages of use for each brand and version of Web browser. How many people are really using that new beta? An invaluable sanity check, particularly for large, commercial Web sites.

## OVERVIEWS OF AUTHORING SOFTWARE

It's essential that you monitor software sites, both to track new versions of the shareware and freeware you'll find on this CD-ROM, and to find out about new software. I tend to do a sweeping search for new software every month or two, and surprisingly often I run into exactly the help I need at the moment.

### Shareware.com
 **http://www.shareware.com/**

This wide-ranging shareware/freeware directory service run by the on-line news-hashers C|Net is one of the only sources to cover both Windows and Macintosh software. Since it offers multiple archives, it's a good first stop when you're looking for a program by name, or when you want to find out what's just been released in a given category. A little creativity may be needed to get hold of the files, though, since the download sites they direct you to are often busy.

## ZDNet Software
http://www.hotfiles.com/

Ziff-Davis' software library has two things going for it: First, it's selective. Since there are often reviews attached to the program descriptions, you don't have to go through as much trial-and-error in deciding whether a given program might be right for you. When you're venturing into an new type of application, this can be a blessed time saver.

Second, it contains site-specific specials. Ziff-Davis' commercial clout sometimes gives it access to software that would otherwise only be available at overloaded company sites.

The site contains both Windows and Macintosh software, though the two camps are kept pretty much apart. Also check the main ZDNet pages for useful reviews of both commercial and shareware programs.

**AUTHOR'S CHOICE**

## The Info-Mac HyperArchive
http://hyperarchive.lcs.mit.edu/
HyperArchive.html

By far the easiest way to use the ubiquitous Info-Mac archive of Macintosh shareware and freeware, this excellent service from MIT lets you search and sort by name or date within categories of software. Its use of the HTTP protocol rather than the less-scaleable FTP protocol makes it much more likely that once you've made a selection, you'll actually be able to start downloading.

## Todd's Macintosh Support Pages
http://www.macshare.com/

This site offers a good personal selection of shareware favorites. The benefit here is selectivity: even if you don't find your dream program, you should at least be able to avoid dogs. As such, it may be your best starting point if you're a Macintosh user.

## Windows95.com
http://www.windows95.com/apps/

Not the largest collection of Windows 95 shareware, but the most convenient, aside from its graphics-only interface. The site's must-picks are marked with a "GET IT" icon. I've never been disappointed with these choices.

> ☞ A big asset of both Windows95.com and ZDNet Software is that within each category, files are listed in chronological order, from most recent to oldest. That's usually the order you'll want to try software in, as well!

## Dave Central
http://www.davecentral.com/

This extensive collection of Windows shareware, with fairly detailed comments, is apparently supplied by the shareware providers. That gives it a helpful Info-Mac feel, except that Info-Mac doesn't include dozens of photos of a stereotypical computer geek hamming it up.

## Macintosh WWW Resource Directory
http://www.comvista.com/net/www/
WWWDirectory.html

Just a warning: You'll still find lots of nostalgic pointers to this formerly very helpful group of pages, but it's been such a long while since it's been maintained that it can't really be recommended any longer.

## Cool Tool of the Day
http://www.cooltool.com/

Entertaining way to check up on Web software you might've missed. The emphasis tends to be on "coffee-table technology," but with so many days to cover, a lot of genuinely useful authoring aids get time in the spotlight as well. As usual with "X of the Day" sites, it's the archive that's most interesting. Unfortunately, at the time of this writing, much of the archive was still off-line after a recent move. Probably the problems will have been fixed by publication time.

### Tucows Shareware

**http://www.tucows.com/**

One of the best-known and most-mirrored shareware sites, this is a good place to check into if Windows95.com's selection is too narrow. Features a primitive (to be exact, a cow-based) rating system. Note that the many mirror sites listed vary wildly in their reliability: you may have to do a bit of clicking around.

### JUMBO!

**http://www.jumbo.com/**

The biggest and least discriminating Windows shareware site, with a token dash of Macintosh shareware on the side. A bit overwhelming, since descriptions are usually not displayed next to the cryptic Windows 3.1-style filenames, but as last resorts go, it's comfortable enough.

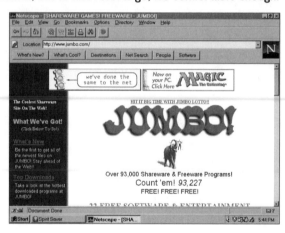

## PUNDITS AND STYLE GUIDES

I'm not the only opinionated Web author out there. If you're in the game, it's a pleasure in itself to look at other authors' opinions and tricks. If you're just learning, it's a great way to pick up inspiration and second-hand experience. Even (or especially) if you sometimes disagree with the opinions so authoritatively pronounced.

### Style Guide for Online Hypertext

**www.w3.org/hypertext/WWW/ Provider/Style/Overview.html**

This is a short and simple Style Guide for on-line hypertext by Tim Berners-Lee, "the inventor of the World Wide Web." A quote from Berners-Lee: "Some of the points made may be influenced by personal preference, and some may be common sense, but a collection of points has been demanded, and so here it is." If I'm too stodgy and conservative for you, you won't like Berners-Lee's advice at all, but it's still my favorite "Elements of Style" for Web publishers.

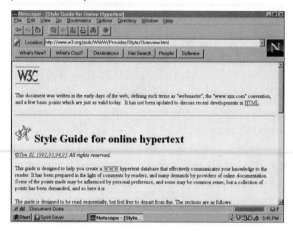

### Yale C/AIM Web Style Manual

**http://info.med.yale.edu/caim/StyleManual_ Top.HTML**

In his "Web Style Manual"— my second-favorite style guide — Patrick J. Lynch ventures into some controversial territory, but makes a convincing case even when I disagree with him. Includes excellent tips on optimizing download times and on managing entire sites, all linked to real examples. This site could've saved me a lot of time when I was starting life as a Webmaster.

### Composing Good HTML

**http://www.cs.cmu.edu/~tilt/cgh/**

Sharp up-to-date observations from Eric Tilton can be found here, based on extensive experience with production Web authoring. It's actually more extensive than its title might indicate: the most uniquely valuable help is to be found in the page's second half, in which Tilton leaves the individual page to consider how (and why!) to manage an entire Web site. The guide is squeezed into one self-contained page, and it's well worth printing out and studying at its considerable length.

## Sun's Guide to Web Style

http://www.sun.com/styleguide/

This common-sense, if slightly out-of-date, style guide is of particular interest for its clean, bite-sized interface.

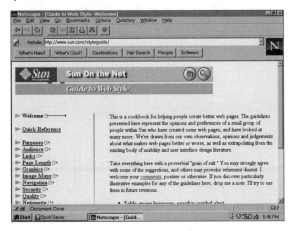

## GENERAL DESIGN GUIDES

The Web might be cheap publishing, but it's still publishing. If you don't come from a commercial graphics background but want to handle some of that work yourself, you should at least get some of the basic terminology down. These sites should help.

## Communication Arts

http://www.commarts.com/index.html

"The World Wide Web site for Communication Arts, the world's largest magazine on creativity for graphic designers, art directors, copywriters, photographers, illustrators and multimedia designers." The site includes online exhibits, discussions of design issues, and databases of (take a breath): clubs and organizations, articles and columns, book reviews, conferences and events, legal issues, and design-related Web sites. Well-designed in its own right, with a surprising emphasis on that good old-fashioned communication art, text.

---

BUILDING BETTER PAGES

## STYLE GUIDE RECOMMENDATIONS

A few favorite style guides of my own:

- **Don't announce a page until actual content is available on it.** No one wants to waste time downloading good intentions.

- **Use hypertext to avoid repetition.** A family of print documents, such as marketing material or press releases, often recaps the same information over and over in only slightly different language. Researchers often have to condense very interesting primary source material in order to present a coherent argument. When adapting such material, take advantage of the opportunity to link rather than rehash or paraphrase.

- **Supply optional downloadable all-on-one-big-page versions of long reference documents.** Bear in mind that network links go down or get swamped. If you're providing a document that many will want to refer to, don't just provide it in bite-sized hypertext form. Give users an option to obtain the whole document at once, either for easy printing or to store on their local systems for quick access.

## Web Page Design for Designers

http://ds.dial.pipex.com/pixelp/wpdesign/wpdintro.htm

This set of pages is specifically aimed at commercial graphic designers with little Web experience. It's mostly well-expressed common sense, but for me a real stand-out section was the one covering cross-platform font issues. Nice design, too.

BUILDING BETTER PAGES

# THE TRUTH ABOUT FONTS

If you do come from a commercial graphics background, as many of my students have, you're going to be frustrated by the lack of tight control in HTML. You may even be tempted to dump it altogether and retreat to the more familiar tight-layout world of, for example, Adobe Acrobat files. Before you do, let me explain why you should consider sticking with HTML, and with the most basic HTML possible:

- It's true that you don't have complete control over fonts. That's because you can't count on a given font being installed on a user's machine: you'd be surprised at the number of computer users out there who lack even Palatino. On the other hand, users *do* have control over which of *their* fonts are used by the browser. If they have eye problems, they can use a large easy-to-read font; if they have limited screen space and need to pack more in, they can use a smaller, tighter font. That's an advantage you shouldn't take away lightly.

- You should also think twice before trying to assert control with HTML font attributes like "FACE" and absolute "SIZE." "FACE," which lets you indicate a preferred font family for text, is particularly dangerous, since it fools you into seeing distinctions on your page that will not be there for the large portion of your audience that doesn't own the font you so carefully chose. (In the on-line examples of "FONT FACE" I've seen, the writers avoid this issue by always choosing standard system fonts — exactly the sort of fonts that would usually be used without the "FONT FACE" tag!)

- It's true that you don't have complete control over layout. Browsers are perfectly capable of relocating graphics and line breaks to match the user's window size—and, frankly, only a graphic designer could believe that this is a problem. It's the only really reasonable approach to on-line reading. In print, there's not much difference in readability between a 5-by-7-inch page layout and an 11-by-14-inch page layout. On a computer screen, there's a huge difference between having to scroll (particularly horizontally, since that breaks the flow of individual lines of text) and not having to scroll. Try reading an Adobe Acrobat document designed for 8.5-by-11-inch paper publication on a 640-by-480-pixel laptop sometime! Save the really tight layout stuff for smaller sections of the document, such as banners and illustrations.

If no one likes underlining, why is it the default? Because color-coding doesn't work very well without color, and users who don't own color monitors still need some way to know where the links are on the page. (For the same reason, I've enabled underlining to make links show up in these black-and-white screen shots.)

By the way, if you're one of the fortunate few who find a screen full of underlines graphically appealing, do remember to keep links color-coded: if all text, including hyperlinked text, is black, those of us who *do* use color monitors might be left in the dark.

## KEEPING UP WITH THE COOL

You need to go on-line to keep up with the states of the art, and probably the fastest way to do so is to occasionally check out what obsessive collectors consider to be the best stuff out there. It's good to use more than one source, though. Otherwise, instead of getting a good overview of current Web expertise, you'll end up only with a good overview of what one person finds appealing.

To emphasize that point, I'd like to start off with an anti-cool site.

- As we'll see later, current HTML gives you much more control over layout than early Web authors had, and few designers nowadays are really forced to resort to a non-HTML-format, sacrificing hyperlinking and download speed (see figure ). In fact, tags such as TABLE give you so much control that you can create the "wide load" problem for your readers almost as easily with HTML as without it! Using even my fairly large high-resolution monitor, I've hit supposedly commercial HTML pages that forced me to scroll my window! Please, before you specify widths using exact measurement in pixels, experiment with using proportional sizing instead. Then resize your browser window to the Netscape default width, and see which approach looks better.

- Do you hate the look of underlined text, and think that color coding is a far more graceful way to indicate hyperlinks? Don't worry, you're not alone. That's why it's easy to turn underlining off in virtually any graphics-capable browser. (I always have it turned off, and so I was taken aback when I first heard a designer complaining about "those intrusive underlines.") In fact, the earliest design-

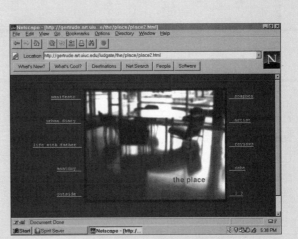

The Place, at http://gertrude.art.uiuc.edu/ludgate/the/place.html.

conscious Web sites, such as The Place, often used their opening screen to explain how to disable underlining.

## Web Pages That Suck
### http://www.webpagesthatsuck .com

Here's a great introduction to the sort of attitude beginning Web authors will get hit with if they jump in cluelessly, waving all the neat toys they've picked up from, well, a book like this one. Vincent Flanders viciously picks apart standard HTML fads, clichés, and pretensions, often ones that were initiated by coverage in the following two sites…

## Project Cool
### http://www.projectcool.com/

Glenn Davis had early success with Project Cool, one of the first "X of the Day" or "Cool Page of the Y" sites. His selections continue to be heavily weighted toward

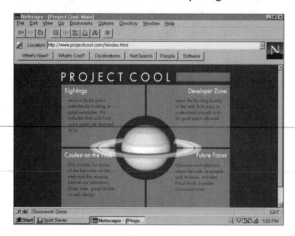

high-bandwidth, memory-intensive, pre-release-browser-specific features, with write-ups in the voice of the perpetually boyish American technophile: coolness, awesomeness, rad rockers and babes rule (or rool) supreme.

## Cool Site of the Day
### http://cool.infi.net/

Different guy; similar "coffee-table HTML" tastes and style.

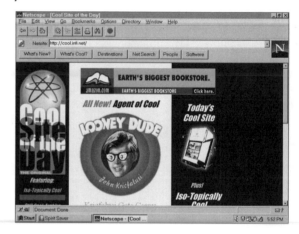

Don't take the "X of the Day" titles literally. When you have time to explore, just go to the archives at the pages (usually called something like "Past Xs of the Day") and sweep through them. Not only is that a better use of your time, it's also a lot easier on the targeted sites: on the "official" day that a site is selected, its servers tend to be completely overwhelmed by new and curious visitors. Wait a week or so, and you'll have a much easier time getting through.

## That's Useful, This Is Cool
http://www.usefulcool.com/

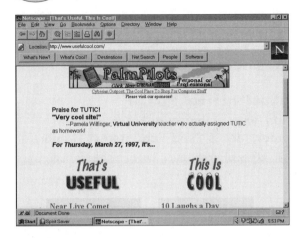

## One Useful Thing and One Cool Thing
http://www.teleport.com/UC/index.shtml

## Yahoo! Internet Life Incredibly Useful Site of the Day
http://www.zdnet.com/yil/content/depts/useful/useful.html

These three offer very pleasant spinach-and-ice-cream meals to remind you of the myriad possibilities of Web authoring—or, if you prefer, to remind you of your competition.

## Yahoo! The Charts
http://www.zdnet.com/yil/content/depts/charts/chcurrent.html

This daily page usually features a half-dozen daily picks, as well as links to other selective indices. Unfortunately, Yahoo!'s more extensive weekly picks (at http://www.yahoo.com/picks/) are almost unreadably marred by weak attempts at humor.

## David Siegel's High Five
http://www.highfive.com/

David Siegel may be the most criticized pundit on the Web, aside from anti-Web writers like Clifford Stoll. I've often joined in the criticism myself: Siegel is unapologetic about his technocrat elitism. But at least his selection criteria are aesthetic rather than simply geeky. His "awards" page (in which his own site won the initial prize!) remains a common first stop for graphics designers on the Web.

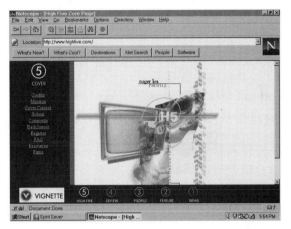

# KEEPING UP WITH THE NOT-SO-COOL

Remember, Web publishing is amazingly cheap. When you publish on the Web, not only can you expect not to please everyone, you don't really have to please anyone at all. The first Web-specific artistic genre to have developed glories in that fact.

I refer, of course, to the genre of "the unnecessary page." And since it's amazingly cheap to look at anything on the Web once you have a connection, these eccentric, obsessive, insane, doltish or just plain incompetent publications can actually find an audience. Creators in other media find this absurd level of freedom to be a horrifying sign of cultural decline, but I enjoy the playfulness of it all, both as an author and as a viewer. I've posted my own share of eccentric-and-so-forth pages, and I've liked looking at others. Nothing wrong with that.

But, as always, stay aware of your context and your intended audience. I once published a rather bizarre (and surprisingly popular) attack on standard Hollywood journalistic styles, and I was downright gleeful when *Entertainment Weekly* pronounced it the "most impenetrable" of the sites they'd surveyed: after all, if they had penetrated it, I would've failed in my anti-*Entertainment Weekly* objectives. On the other hand, if anyone called one of my more corporate projects "impenetrable," I would feel compelled to give the page a thorough makeover.

### Useless Web Pages

**http://www.go2net.com/internet/useless/**

Not critical so much as bemused, this is a great place to get an overview of some of the possibilities for low-impact publishing on the Web.

### Worst of the Web

**http://www.worstoftheweb.com/**

Alas, the two most entertaining of the "America's Funniest Home Pages" sites, "Mirsky's Worst of the Web" and "Mediocre Site of the Day," have both shut down recently due to author burnout. This is the best of the worst-sites sites left.

### Yahoo! Internet Humor

**http://www.yahoo.com/Entertainment/ Humor__Jokes__and_Fun/Internet_Humor/**

A directory of Web satire. Learn or be burned.

# CHAPTER 2
# HTML BASICS

## IN THIS CHAPTER YOU WILL FIND:

☞ **Introductions to HTML.**
These tutorial and overview sites offer a variety of approaches to learning the basics of Web authoring.

☞ **How to begin a Web page.**
Before you even start a document, you should have some idea of what you want to create. Of course, you'll then need to know how to start a document, so we'll walk through that as well.

☞ **HTML references.**
These sites are worth a visit if you need to check the syntax or proper use of a certain HTML tag.

☞ **How to learn HTML tricks.**
Your best sources of professional tips are the Web pages that most impress you.

☞ **Special characters and math expressions.**
Making characters like © or & display correctly on a Web page requires that you enter special character codes; reproducing math equations on-screen can be even more difficult. These sites offer lists of special character codes, or tips for putting math formulas on Web sites.

☞ **HTML standards and specifications.**
HTML has undergone several major revisions over the years. These sites will take you to the official pages for proposed standards, as well as to guides that explain the impact of the varying features and different levels of support that are in popular use.

☞ **HTML validators and link-checkers.**
Even if your pages look fine when you view them on-screen, they may contain improperly used HTML tags or hyperlinks that don't work. These sites can help you proofread your work, and can also help you better serve visitors to your site.

☞ **Browsers.**
While not an exhaustive list, these sites will take you to the home pages of some of the most popular Web browsers for viewing HTML documents. Several sites listed here offer overviews of what features are supported by different Web browsers.

☞ **HTML editors and converters.**
These sites will direct you to authoring tools (mostly freeware or shareware) to simplify the creation of HTML documents, whether you're authoring a site from scratch or working from existing content.

# INTRODUCTIONS TO HTML

The more comfortable you are with understanding and writing HTML, the more adept you'll be at designing good-looking and useful Web pages. Included here are pointers to a number of Web sites that can help, including collections of Web-authoring overviews and step-by-step primers on creating the bare outline of a working document.

## DEVELOPING A WEB PAGE

A *page* is a single HTML document, no matter how long it is. It's what you find on the other side of a link (or, more precisely, what a server has sent to your local system in response to a request from your browser).

For the most part, putting together a Web page is like putting together any other type of communication. The Web's unique benefits lie in your control over the content, and in its ability to facilitate cheap distribution to a very large potential audience. The Web's unique difficulties are your lack of control over the content's presentation, and your lack of influence over any particular audience. To a large extent, you have to trust that the audience will come to you.

Beyond these benefits and detriments, the process for creating a Web site is the same. First, decide on content—that is, what you want to say or show. Second, decide on presentation style—that is, what you want the overall effect to be. You'll waste money, time, and effort if you start fiddling around with formatting nits before these all-important decisions have been made.

The small matters of content and style having been taken care of, what happens next? Here's the course I usually follow, for whatever it's worth:

1  Sketch out materials in a "storyboard" fashion.

2  Reduce and reformat non-text media.

3  Edit (or convert existing text to) HTML-formatted text, adding frequent references to documentation and existing Web pages.

4  Examine the results by dragging the HTML file to a properly set-up Web browser. By the way, when you're starting out you may want to keep two windows open on your browser while you're working: one to hold reference material, and one to view your own work.

5  Experiment with different ways to arrange text and graphical elements.

6  Experiment with breaking up the document in different ways. You may want to use a flow chart as a visual aid.

7  Copy the end products to a publicly accessible place, and test each section of the site with two Web browsers.

8  Revisit and revise as desired.

### How Long Should a Page Be?

A page should be as long as seems reasonable. A set of questions and answers may be very long, but since it's made up of such short, related components, breaking it up would be irritating. In such cases, one should provide easy ways to jump around within the document rather than fragmenting it.

If a long document naturally breaks into interdependent shorter documents (chapters or subchapters, for example) then make them separate Web pages, with easy navigation between them. Sometimes what's originally envisioned as a long, linear document turns out to be most naturally expressed as a cloud of hypertext.

I prefer to rely on direct experimentation rather than on dogmatic dicta such as "no document should be longer than one screen." Try the page out yourself in a properly set-up browser, and see what you find annoying about it. You'll find that it's not that hard to cut and paste your content into new, linked pages if you begin with it all in one place.

## What about Copyright?

This seems a strange question to ask right off, but students always ask it. For some reason, newspapers that give long quotes from interview subjects, magazines that print stills from movies, and TV stations that schedule for the convenience of videotapers all seem to feel that the Web presents special copyright issues.

When it comes to copyrighting material, the law is actually pretty darned simple at this point: Everything created is copyrighted unless the creator explicitly states otherwise. You don't have to photocopy your poems and sketches and sent them to the Library of Congress in a federally insured package sealed with wax and dated by a notary public; you don't have to stick a "C" in a circle on every page; you don't even have to say "Copyright 1997," much less "Copywrite 1997." If you wrote it or drew it, it's yours by law. And if you wrote it or drew it *and* published it—even on the Web—it's *definitely* yours.

It being yours doesn't prevent some legitimate uses of it without your permission. "Fair-use" quoting, satire, and "artistic appropriation" are all historically sanctioned tramplings on intellectual property rights, even if they still result in rather fevered court battles in the present day.

For that matter, your ownership doesn't prevent *illegitimate* use of your material: it just makes such use illegal. Thankfully, most of the bozos out there don't really want to tangle with lawyers any more than you do, and if they think they're running the risk, they'll probably tread a little more carefully around your work.

That's why I tend to stick a "Copyright Ray Davis" at the bottom of every page. It doesn't change

the page's legal status as a copyrighted work, but at least it keeps the bozos from thinking it's not copyrighted. (It also gives me an unobtrusive standard spot from which to link to my home page or my e-mail address.)

What about the copyright problems of hyperlinks? I've tried, but I just can't come up with any argument that giving a link to someone else's page is an infringement of copyright. You might as well say that card catalogs plagiarize books. On the other hand, simply embedding someone else's graphics or other media in your page seems an awful lot like swiping even if you're doing it by pointing the browser back to the original copies. (Note that some sites swipe-by-pointer for satirical purposes—most famously, the electronic magazine Suck, shown in Figure 2.1, which you can find at **http://www.suck.com/**.)

You'll often see me refer to a "properly set up Web browser." What I mean by this is simply a browser whose settings match those of your target audience.

When I browse the Web myself, I'm interested in comfort, and so I customize my browser accordingly. I resize the window to make it fairly large, I change

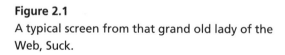

**Figure 2.1**

A typical screen from that grand old lady of the Web, Suck.

the default font from cramped Times to more readable Palatino, and so forth (see Figure 2.2).

But I can be pretty certain that many members of my audience have never touched their browsers' options or preferences. I can also be pretty certain that most of them aren't viewing my page on as large a monitor as I'm using (multimedia developers need *big* monitors,) and so their window size will be smaller (see Figure 2.3). And so when I'm creating new pages, I make sure to check them with default settings, as well as with my own.

> 👉 **By the way, in the most recent versions of Netscape Navigator, you can obtain a window with the default width by requesting a "New Web Browser" from the "File" menu.**

### BASIC HTML

Not only is HTML not rocket science, it's not even computer programming per se—although I can't deny that the title of "Web Programmer" might be useful for salary-inflation purposes!

It's really just desktop publishing: you're describing the layout of text and graphics. The only difference between doing that in, say, Microsoft Word, and doing it in HTML is that in HTML you can see the layout descriptions in quasi-English rather than having them hidden in the binary code. (If you look at a Word document converted to the ASCII-only RTF format, you'll see considerably more complicated layout descriptions than you'll see in HTML.) That's why it's been fairly easy for word processing and desktop publishing software companies to produce HTML converters or editors.

The moral: "Don't be afraid to look at the HTML." Later, when we get to the subject of WYSIWYG HTML editors, I'll add another moral: "You *must* look at the HTML."

### Finding Your Way Around HTML

"Hypertext Markup Language" is a way of mixing the textual content of a document with instructions to a Web browser about how to display that content.

**Figure 2.2**
CNet, as I get to see it.

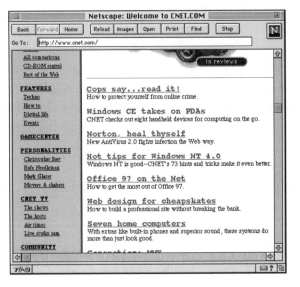

**Figure 2.3**
CNet, as most users probably see it.

The instructions (or *tags*) are distinguished from the text itself by always starting with a "<" and ending with a ">". Yes, these are familiar to most of us as "less than" and "greater than" signs. But since HTML doesn't use them that way, I tend to refer to them as "angle brackets": a left angle bracket and a right angle bracket. You can always separate out the HTML instructions from the text of a document by looking for the angle brackets. (If you're using an HTML editor, the HTML instructions will probably be shown in a different color from the textual content, making it even easier to find your way around.)

Right after the left angle bracket comes the code word for the tag, followed by *attributes* that supply extra information or instructions.

Some instructions are complete in themselves, such as "put a line separator here" or "show a graphic here." These are handled with *standalone tags* like "<HR>" (for "horizontal rule," or, in plainer English, "a line separator").

Other instructions have to be applied to something, such as "put this stretch of text in boldface type" or "make this graphic into a link." These instructions require a pair of tags, one to begin the special treatment (the *opening tag*) and one to stop the special treatment (the *closing tag*); the thing that the instruction is applied to gets stuck between the pair. By convention, the closing tag always consists of a slash ("/") followed by the tag's code name. For example, if you want to put the words "Wholesome Goodness With Every Sugary Bite!" in boldface, you might use the "strong emphasis" tag "<STRONG>", like so: "<STRONG> Wholesome Goodness With Every Sugary Bite!</STRONG>".

(By the way, the main reason I started using an HTML editor rather than writing tags by hand was to avoid the irritatingly mindless work of typing these closing tags.)

### That Which Is Not Explicitly Commanded Is Ignored

If you've ever trained a dog, you know how important it is that commands, such as "Sit!" and "Stay!," are clearly distinguished from speeches, such as "Oh, who's mumsy's sweet little cutesy puppy who's such a good boy?" Well, it's not for nothing that Apple named its Web browser "Cyberdog."

A Web browser considers "real text" to be words and punctuation that aren't included in its command tags. Conversely, it doesn't look for formatting commands in "real text." Spacing and line breaks are considered formatting commands. And so any tabs, multiple spaces, line breaks or blank lines that you throw into your Web document are blithely ignored by the browser—or, to be more exact, they're all treated the same way: as one measly blank space.

If you really want line breaks and blank lines, you have to explicitly ask for them, either by using special HTML formatting commands or by designating a certain chunk of line-broken, spaced-out, blanked-out text as "preformatted" and thus sacrosanct.

Strangely enough, this actually has some benefits. For one thing, it means that Web documents can magically expand or contract to match an individual user's set-up. (The Suck format, in which a very narrow column of very short lines runs down the middle of a page, is enormously irritating when I'm using my laptop, where vertical space is at a premium.) When I'm editing, this capability makes it easy to move between an outline view, which shows the structure of the document, and a text-editing view: I just turn line-wrapping off or on in my HTML editor. After all, it doesn't make any difference to the browser either way.

## Basic Structure

An HTML document should be signaled by opening and closing tags. These tags reassure browsers and editors that it actually *is* HTML.

Inside the HTML document, there are two sections. The first section, the *header*, contains information about the document that does not appear in the document's display. (When you're starting out, the only such information you really need to worry about is the *title* of the document, which will appear as the title of the browser's window when someone's looking at your page. The title is also often used by search engines that may index your Web site.) The second and more interesting section is the *body*, which contains everything that *does* appear in the document's display.

Thus, a minimal Web document should always look something like this (hopefully with something more interesting than "..." included):

```
<HTML>
<HEAD>
<TITLE>...</TITLE>
</HEAD>
<BODY>
...
</BODY>
</HTML>
```

Since these tags are all required, it's a no-brainer time-saver to save a template containing these tags and open it whenever you create a new HTML page. Most HTML editors include a customizable list of sample templates. When you create more complex pages, fancier templates will provide a good way to make sure all the pages in your site share a consistent look. We'll discuss more complicated templates in the next chapter.

## Minimal HTML

We'll offer a much more comprehensive table of HTML code words in the next chapter. But here Table 2.1 provides a reference to the basics: enough tags to let you produce a respectably useful Web page.

> If you're using an HTML editor to make your first pages, you may be offered a bewilderingly vast buffet of options and extras when you create a document and insert tags. Don't worry! Just ignore anything you don't understand. After four years of HTML writing, there are still some tags and attributes I've never had occasion to use!

## AN EASY WALK THROUGH YOUR FIRST WEB PAGE

I always put my Web-authoring students through the same routine: After a broad introduction to the Web, I plop them down in front of their computers, make them start up a pre-configured HTML editor, and walk them through the creation of a bare-bones HTML page. We then save our bare-bones page to a properly named file, drag the file to a Web browser to view it, and then return to the editor to start adding some meat to the bones of the page. Editor to file to browser and back again.

I had originally planned to transcribe that routine in this section. Then, while assembling the links for the book, I found out that Tonya Engst had already done most of the work for me back in 1995. Point your browser to the following link, and enjoy along with me:

### A Do-It-Yourself Web Page
http://web1.zdnet.com/macuser/mu_1195/pub1.html

## Table 2.1: Minimal HTML Reference

| Name | Tag or Tag Pair | Effect |
| --- | --- | --- |
| **Structural Tags** | | |
| HTML Document | <HTML>...</HTML> | Declares that this is a Web document |
| Document Header | <HEADER>...</HEADER> | Undisplayed information about the document |
| Document Title | <TITLE>...</TITLE> | Title of the document; shown by browser above or below the main display |
| Document Body | <BODY>...</BODY> | All displayed portions of the document must appear inside these tags |
| **Text Formatting Tags** | | |
| Top-level heading | <H1>...</H1> | Formats the text as a chapter title, in large bold text with space around it |
| Second-level heading | <H2>...</H2> | Formats text as a sub-chapter title, with slightly smaller type and spaces than H1 |
| Third-level heading | <H3>...</H3> | Formats text as a section title, in bold with a little space around it |
| Citation | <CITE>...</CITE> | Formats text as a book title or foreign word, usually italicized |
| Strong Emphasis | <STRONG>...</STRONG> | Formats text as being very important, usually boldface |
| Block quote | <BLOCKQUOTE>...</BLOCKQUOTE> | Formats text as a self-contained bunch of text, usually with extra space on all sides |
| Preformatted | <PRE>...</PRE> | Leaves the text with line breaks, blank lines, and extra spaces intact; usually with a monospaced font, such as Courier |
| **Text Separation** | | |
| Paragraph Break | <P> | Separates one paragraph from another; usually inserts a double-space |
| Line Break | <BR> | Breaks a line at the given point |
| Horizontal Rule | <HR> | Inserts some space and a horizontal line, nicely breaking up the page |
| **Lists** | | |
| Unordered List | <UL><LI>....</UL> | Sets up a list of items that aren't considered to be in any particular order; usually solid bullets are inserted at the beginning of each item in the list |
| Ordered List | <OL><LI>...</OL> | Sets up a list of items that are considered to have a natural ordering; usually numbers are inserted at the beginning of each item in the list |
| List Item | <LI>... | Marks the beginning of a new item in the list; if it's a numbered list, a new number is generated; if it's a bulleted list, you get a new bullet; you can include paragraph breaks, formatting instructions, and even sublists inside a list item |
| Definition List | <DL><DT>...<DD>...</DL> | A list of pairs of items: see below for an explanation of the pairs |
| Defined Term | <DT>... | Marks the beginning of the first part of a "definition" pair; for example, a term that will be explained or the name of a person; usually left justified |
| Defined Definition (!) | <DD>... | Marks the beginning of the last part of a "definition" pair; for example, the explanation of a term or a description of a person; usually indented |
| **Hyperlinks and Embedded Graphics** | | |
| Link | <A HREF="...">...</A> | Marks the enclosed text as a link to the URL pointed to by the HREF attribute; usually color codes or underlines the linking text |
| Embedded Image | <IMG SRC="..."> | Inserts the contents of the graphics file pointed to by the SRC attribute |

## A "Properly Named File?"

One of the tricky things about Web authoring is that computers other than your own are going to be looking at your files. Another tricky thing about Web authoring is that a computer other than your own is likely going to be *storing* your file. Odds are, in fact, that a Unix machine will be ladling your file out to the masses who are hungry for its wisdom, and therefore that a Unix machine will need to know what to call it.

I suggest following a simple rule: keep your file names in all lowercase letters or numbers, and make the last part of the name either ".html" or ".htm". Don't put spaces in the name, don't put Greek letters in the name, don't even mix uppercase and lowercase letters.

## Andy Carvin's HTML Crash Course for Educators

**http://k12.cnidr.org:90%22/htmlintro.html**

This straightforward tutorial puts together pages of how-to information that are short and to the point. Topics range from header, title, and paragraph tags to embedded images. Each section is followed by a quick quiz designed to test what you've just learned. For example, you can fill out an interactive form that directs you to insert header tags or line breaks in a sample paragraph that's provided; when you submit the form, you'll see the results of your efforts. As the title suggests, the online course was originally designed for teachers, but it should prove useful for anyone who is getting started with HTML coding.

## Beginner's Guide to HTML

**http://www.ncsa.uiuc.edu/General/Internet/ WWW/HTMLPrimer.html**

This good, general-purpose tutorial is offered by the National Center for Supercomputing Applications (NCSA) , where the Mosaic browser was first created, and may even have been originated by Netscape golden boy Marc Andreeson himself. It offers instructions for creating Web documents using HTML, linking between documents, and applying basic formatting. There's a useful glossary, as well of plenty of examples if you just need a cut-and-paste solution. You can view the guide as a single large document, suitable for printing, or in three separate HTML documents that are linked together. Although it could be viewed as a bit out-of-date (having been written before any Netscape-initiated tags existed), for that very reason it makes a very clear starting point.

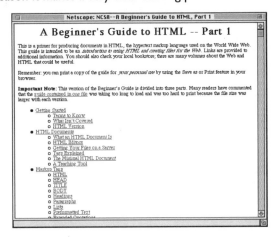

## Classic HTML style at the "Beginner's Guide to HTML." Beginner's Guide to Web Page Creation

**http://members.aol.com/thomasreed/instruct/ web/index.html**

A clearly written and technically adept tutorial by Thomas Reed, which does an especially good job with the difficult subject of how to publish your pages on a Web server. It places the emphasis in these matters, naturally, on AOL. It even provides some "coffee-table HTML" spice, such as an introduction to JavaScript, for dessert.

## Crash Course on Writing Documents for the Web

**http://www.pcweek.com/eamonn/crash_ course.html**

Written in nontechnical language for Web newcomers, this Crash Course is an easy-to-follow tutorial and basic HTML guide. It's targeted at people who want to get started with writing and publishing Web pages, but who care little about the technical details and don't want to read a computer book. Only the most basic tags are

☞ Why shouldn't Macintosh and Windows 95 users make pages with names like "Hot-Tips.html"? After all, Unix allows them.

Well, I once knew a Macintosh-based Web author who decided to put together a set of pages for his corporate site. He made the pages using relative URLs, carefully checked all the links between his pages locally, then moved all the pages *en masse* to the central Web server and went home to sleep. The next day, it turned out that a large portion of the links he'd so carefully checked were now broken.

The reason was that he'd decided to use mixed upper- and lowercase for his file names. The Macintosh file system is case-sensitive when *displaying* file names, but not case-sensitive when *searching* for files by name. In other words, if you ask the Macintosh file system to go get "hottips.html," it'll enthusiastically fetch "Hot-Tips.html" without complaint.

Since mixed case is a bit harder to type and to remember, our unhappy author was occasionally making typos when he created his links: typos such as "hottips.html" instead of "HotTips.html." When he tested locally, he wasn't notified of those errors. But on the Unix Web server, a link to "hottips.html" will *not* successfully retrieve "Hot-Tips.html." *Jamais voilà*; or, as we say in English, broken links.

That's why I try to keep it simple, and in lowercase.

covered, including <HEAD>, <BODY>, headers and paragraphs, lists and hyperlinks, and options for embedding images.

### Creating Net Sites
**http://home.netscape.com/assist/net_sites/index.html**
This thorough beginner's site is hosted by Netscape Communications Corp., creators of the Navigator browser. It's the place to go for summaries of Netscape's extensions to HTML 2.0 and 3.0, as well as a good starting point for information about editing images, tables, and frames. The site also hosts a newsletter called "Off the Net" that offers Web-development news. Other off-site links include pointers to other beginner's tutorials, style guides, and Web-development references.

### The Eight Minute HTML Primer
**http://web66.coled.umn.edu/Cookbook/HTML/MinutePrimer.html**
A Web tutorial for those with really short attention spans. The Eight Minute HTML Primer restricts itself to eight basic HTML directives that are sufficient to build—well, the basic Web page that the Primer has built with them! Simply view or print out the source code of the HTML examples provided, and compare it with what you see on screen. Compact, to be sure, but not exactly a high-powered reference site. PC users (and most Macintosh users) should ignore the cryptic references to "SimpleText" and "TeachText," which are just the simple text editors supplied with the Macintosh OS.

### A Guide to Basic HTML
**http://snowwhite.it.brighton.ac.uk/~mas/mas/courses/html/html1.html**
An excellent tutorial. Tables are used to clearly distinguish HTML code and its outcome in the browser. The user is given a chance to try out HTML tags interactively after each topic, with starter HTML provided.

### HTML: An Interactive Tutorial for Beginners
**http://www.davesite.com/webstation/html/**
OK! GREAT! A completely breathless, exclamation-mark-heavy, frequently-uppercased, not-especially-proofread FULL COLLECTION of WILD WILD tutorials!! You can't fault Dave Kristula's enthusiasm and, if you temper his "SURF'S UP! COWABUNGA!" approach with some more sedate sites, you can find some DARNED FINE information here—although I admit that I soon started thinking fondly of Jonathan Richman's song, "(Someday We'll Be) Dignified and Old."

### HTML Station
AUTHOR'S CHOICE
**http://www.december.com/html/**
From the no-nonsense table grid on the main page onward, this site is home to all manner of HTML reference information. The information here is

broken down into several categories. The "HTML Dem-onstrations" section shows examples of some simple Web pages, tables, forms, framed pages, and client-side imagemaps on-screen, plus the source code for making these effects work. "HTML Specifications" includes good information about the different levels of HTML, plus Netscape and Microsoft extensions. "HTML Entities, Codes, and Types" provides such information as charac-ter entity codes and hexadecimal color codes for choos-ing background and text colors. The "Techniques" section includes some tips and examples of scripts for making it easier to create files with a similar look and feel, as well as the following inspirational words: "Just 'coding HTML' has about as much to do with creating meaning on the Web as changing a typewriter ribbon has to do with writing a novel." Couldn't have said it better myself.

## HTML: The Practical Basics
**http://www.netsurge.com/trillian/htmlbase/**
Notable as the only "practical" Web primer that is print-ed in lavender on a white background, but also notably concise and common-sensible. If you want to just look at a few screens' worth of tutorial, this is a good spot to drop in on.

## HTML Writers Guild List of HTML Resources
**http://www.hwg.org/resources/html/**
This is a collection of links to HTML programming re-sources presented by the HTML Writers Guild, an inter-national organization of Web authors and Internet

publishing professionals. There are several categories, in-cluding lists of HTML elements and attributes, HTML val-idation methods, style guides, and demo pages for testing browser support of different HTML features. Although the site lacks much in the way of original content, you can find a few FAQs, and information about joining the HTML Writers Guild and participating in its mailing lists.

## Introduction to HTML
**http://www.cwru.edu/help/introHTML/ toc.html**
This well-organized tutorial follows a strict outline for-mat, which makes it just as useful for quick referencing. After you have read a chapter, you can click ahead to the next, or take a quiz on what you've learned. The friendly narrative should make this introductory tutorial palatable even to those intimidated by the thought of having to learn HTML coding. The series of lessons shows plenty of examples; the interactive quizzes are well-designed, and help reinforce the basics.

## Introduction to HTML from The WorldWideWeb Handbook
**http://www.ucc.ie/~pflynn/books/ch7-8.html**
This is a very useful excerpt from Peter Flynn's book, covering some of the history of HTML and all of the bare essentials. A little out of date, as any book excerpt is bound to be, but the basics have stayed fairly constant since the Web began.

## Intermediate HTML
**http://www.cwru.edu/help/interHTML/ toc.html**
This guide is a sequel to Introduction to HTML (see pre-vious listing). Here, the pace picks up a little with cover-age of a greater number of style tags, header tags like <BASE> and <META> and Latin-1 character entities, plus extensive information about how to create an interactive form. An HTML tag summary and a glossary are also in-cluded. The tutorial has a search function if you need to look up a specific HTML tag or topic.

## Introduction to HTML and URLs

**http://www.utoronto.ca/webdocs/HTMLdocs/
NewHTML/htmlindex.html**

This is an expansive, educational guide by Dr. Ian Graham, author of *The HTML Sourcebook*. It includes beginner's tutorials, probably the best description of URLs available, details about Netscape and Microsoft extensions to HTML, and a number of essays and other tips for creating well-designed Web documents.

## Microsoft Internet Explorer 3.0 Author's Guide and HTML Reference

**http://www.microsoft.com/workshop/author/
newhtml/htmlr001.htm**

If you needed evidence that Microsoft is serious about colonizing the Web, look no further than this remarkably complete collection of references for Web authors. Even if you're a 100-percent Netscape Navigator fan, this site is worth bookmarking: it's far more coherent than any of Netscape's own authoring pages.

### Project Cool Developer Zone

**http://www.projectcool.com/
developer/**

This site reassures nervous beginners that "This ain't rocket science"! The Project Cool Developer Zone includes both basic and advanced HTML tutorials. The basic one covers basic text and list tags, making links, including images, and adding backgrounds. The advanced one covers imagemaps, tables, creating frames, and client pull features. The frame-enabled site is designed well for an on-screen tutorial, with topics listed in a narrow frame running down the left side of the screen: clicking on a topic updates the contents of the much larger right-hand frame. The advice is written up in a conversational style that makes it easy for readers to get drawn into focusing on how to do accomplish various tasks. On the other hand, it suffers from many of the same design flaws as "Project Cool" itself, and thus, since its advice is sound, it sometimes skirts hypocrisy. For example, its tutorial actually goes a bit overboard by claiming that "you should always include some brief alternate text" with an image. Not necessarily; but you certainly *should* include some alternate text when the image contains nothing but

"nicely formatted" text, and the image provides the only link to another page—which is precisely the case with many of the images which lack "alternate text" on this very site! That's a cardinal sin for a reference page, but I guess this is just one of those "do what I say, not what I do" traps that cool people fall into once they become authority figures...

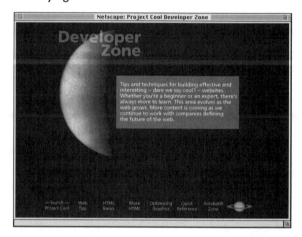

## So, You Want to Make a Web Page!

**http://junior.apk.net/~jbarta/tutor/makapage/
index.html**

If I'm not enough of a redneck for you (hailin' from Braymer, Missouri, population 880), come on down and sit a spell with the overwhelmingly folksy Joe Barta. As Joe says, "this tutorial is geared towards those using Windows 95. It is also shamelessly biased towards Netscape. But rest assured, most of it should work just fine for all you Internet Explorers and users of other (there are other?) operating systems." The advice is sound, the experience is extensive, the exercises are beautifully to the point, and the rhetoric comes as thick and heavy as my Aunt Lucy-May's fried corn mush, if not quite as thick and heavy as Aunt Lucy-May herself.

## Teach Yourself Web Publishing with HTML 3.2

**http://slack.lne.com/Web/Professional/**

OK, it's true that I learned Web publishing strictly from the Web itself. But an overwhelming number of my students and fellow authors have raved about Laura Lemay's one-woman five-foot-shelf-of-HTML, and so I've felt comfortable recommending her introductory texts. Lemay is a terrific writer and a well-known Internet personality from back in the day. And, at least at the time I write this, you can both get Laura Lemay *and* preserve that on-line spirit: the entire text of the latest version of her signature book is available on the Web. Such a bargain! (Note that Lemay's book list and links are in constant flux; if the link above doesn't work for you, start from "http://slack.lne.com/Web/" and see what's new.)

## The Ten Commandments of HTML
**http://www.visdesigns.com/design/
commandments.html**

For those who want a taste of Usenet heat on the comfort of a Web page, Sean Howard has provided this concise summary of some of the most flammable dogma to be seen in the comp.infosystems.www newsgroups. It provides a nice way to read the HTML purist arguments once instead of dozens of times, although actually it's a little more advanced than its name might imply. (Then again, the original Ten Commandments weren't all suitable for minors either.)

## The WDVL: Introduction to HTML
**http://www.stars.com/Authoring/HTML/
Primers/**

This is the first tutorial I've seen that's based from the start upon recent HTML standards rather than those of two years ago. Many useful links are tastefully integrated, and you'll find firm support of the brave new world of coffee-table HTML—all in all, it provides a fine balance to the views of older Web veterans like myself, and it's definitely worth checking out.

## The Web Communications Comprehensive Guide to Publishing on the Web
**http://www.webcom.com/~webcom/html/**

This Web publishing resource is provided by a local Internet service provider for its customers, but anyone will find the tutorials, HTML references, and links to freeware and shareware Web software to be most useful. The site also includes tips and tools for publishing, and for putting your own page on the Web. The coverage

seems mostly limited to the first, pre-Netscape, capabilities of HTML, but it's not necessarily a bad idea to keep it simple when you're starting out.

## The Web Design Group
**http://www.htmlhelp.com/**

"The Web Design Group was founded to promote the creation of nonbrowser-specific, nonresolution-specific, creative and informative sites that are accessible to all users worldwide." For obvious reasons, this is a very refreshing chaser if you've just spent some hours viewing Netscape's or Microsoft's sites, although the writers do occasionally slide into standards-committee finickiness, as in the several-screens-long sermon on proper use of the IMG ALT attribute. Especially recommended: the acerbically sensible FAQ, and the HTML 3.2 reference section mentioned below.

## Webmonkey: Teaching Tool
**http://www.webmonkey.com/teachingtool/**

Part of HotWired's Webmonkey how-to section for Web design and development, this HTML tutorial describes HTML elements such as paragraphs, font tags, and links. Users can explore the examples in either a "learn it" or "do it" mode; that is, they can choose either to just look at an HTML effect and the source code behind it, or to fill in an on-screen form with their own HTML to match a given example. The interface for the test-your-skill portion is that rare thing: a decent use of frames. You can see the desired outcome of each example in a left-hand frame under the heading "Monkey See" (you can view the source code in the same frame any time), and you can submit your own code in a text box in a right-hand frame.

## Writing HTML
**http://www.mcli.dist.maricopa.edu/tut/**

This online tutorial for learning how to use HTML is a project of the Maricopa Center for Learning and Instruction (MCLI). Developed by instructor Alan Levine, it was originally designed to help teachers create learning resources on the Web. But this well-written guide should find a wider audience with its hand-holding steps for writing HTML files and many clear examples.

There's a Basic Level tutorial in 14 lessons and an Advanced Level tutorial consisting of 23 lessons. In these tutorials, you'll learn how to create and modify HTML documents with a simple text editor, compose a series of informative Web pages, and create links to other online documents. You can click a link to see examples of what you'll be able to produce by the end of the tutorial. You can download an archive of all the files used in the tutorial, and complete most of the lessons off-line. Finally, Levine has supplied well-chosen pointers to other tutorials that cover more advanced or more recent topics.

# HTML REFERENCES

Soon enough, you'll become intimately acquainted with the most common HTML tags. You'll probably rely on a specialized HTML editor to help you out with slightly less common ones. But you'll still need a reference work or two (or three, or…) to look into the meaning and syntax of unfamiliar HTML expressions. And if your memory is anything like mine, you'll also want to keep a few local copies of reference works close at hand to help you out with the not-particularly-mnemonic details of even fairly familiar HTML expressions. Luckily, there are a number of convenient reference sources available on-line.

## HOW'D THEY DO THAT?

Hey, how'd they manage to embed text inside the graphic shown in Figure 2.4?

Answer: They split the graphic into three files and glued them around the text in a borderless table (as shown in Figure 2.5).

Start up your Web browser and look at a page. Now go to the browser's menu bar and find a command to "view source" or "view document source." (With Microsoft's Internet Explorer and Netscape Navigator, you'll find this under the "View" menu.) Give it a try.

You can use your browser's source-code view to learn how any particularly enticing page was put together. In most cases, this behind-the-scenes look

should answer your questions. For example, you may discover that an artistically laid-out page was made possible through judiciously placed tables, or that a paragraph indent was achieved not through HTML coding, but with the placement of small, transparent images.

If imitation is the sincerest form of flattery, then there are certainly a lot of sincere Web sites out there. Web designers frequently pick up techniques

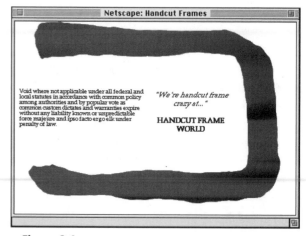

**Figure 2.4**
Text embedded inside a graphic

**Figure 2.5**
The files which generated the graphic in Figure 2.4

from pages they admire for use in creating their own pages. In fact, in the days before Web-mania hit the publishing industry, this was the only way we Web authors *could* learn techniques.

Recycling HTML technique is fair game, but remember that any kind of *programming* code (notably JavaScript, since you'll also see *that* when you "view source") is protected by copyright. Before recycling JavaScript code into your own site, you should check with the code's creator, if named, or the site's Webmaster. And, of course, never copy *visible* content: link to the original page if you want people to see it.

## Bare Bones Guide to HTML

### http://werbach.com/barebones/

Here you'll find an up-to-date list of HTML tags with short summaries of how they function, along with a mention of what version of HTML or what proprietary browser (e.g., Netscape Navigator) supports it. The site, which is maintained by Kevin Werbach, also has more detailed tutorials for beginners, but the main part of the site is extremely concise. You can read the Bare Bones Guide in either a text-only format, which is easy to print and keep around as a reference, or in a more richly formatted version that has links to other introductory ma-

terial. One of the most impressive features of this site is that the Guide is available in so many languages: the last time I stopped in, it was available in twenty languages, including English, Japanese, Dutch, Turkish, Korean, Italian, and, of course, Estonian.

## Compendium of HTML Elements

### http://www.synapse.net/~woodall/html.htm

This detailed reference site created by Ron Woodall has an alphabetical index of HTML tags with the tags and definitions for each letter of the alphabet on a different page. The straightforward descriptions detail what each tag does, which attributes go with it, and which of the leading browsers support it. What really sets this site apart are the working examples of the tags. This lets you quickly see them in action, as well as providing a quick test of the tag-handling capabilities of your own browser set-up. Many sample files are available for testing, including sound files in .MID, .AIF, .AU, and .WAV format. There are interactive forms pages with examples of different attributes and arguments, an extensive frames reference, and miscellaneous useful tips.

## HTML Elements List

### http://www.sandia.gov/sci_compute/ elements.html

Back in 1995, Sandia National Laboratories produced this page with all known and proposed HTML elements of the time, along with their attributes. It's one really big document and, unfortunately, it's quite a bit out of date —but you might want to download a copy for occasional reference. If nothing else, it's an excellent example of how to use internal hyperlinks to navigate within a long reference page.

## Index Dot Html

### http://www.eskimo.com/~bloo/html/

This practical guide provides a comprehensive table of HTML tags supported by Microsoft Internet Explorer, NCSA Mosaic, and Netscape Navigator. The alphabetical tag listings also note in which version of each browser support was added for that tag. Each HTML tag has its own page, which lists browser support, a brief description, all attributes of the tag and what values are permissible, tag examples, and tips and tricks for usage. The site

**Netscape: Bare Bones Guide to HTML**

### BASIC ELEMENTS

| Document Type | <HTML></HTML> | (beginning and end of file) |
| Title | <TITLE></TITLE> | (must be in header) |
| Header | <HEAD></HEAD> | (descriptive info, such as title) |
| Body | <BODY></BODY> | (bulk of the page) |

### STRUCTURAL DEFINITION

| Heading | <H?></H?> | (the spec. defines 6 levels) |
| Align Heading | <H? ALIGN=LEFT|CENTER|RIGHT></H?> [*] | |
| Division | <DIV></DIV> | |
| Align Division | <DIV ALIGN=LEFT|RIGHT|CENTER></DIV> | |
| Block Quote | <BLOCKQUOTE></BLOCKQUOTE> [*] | (usually displayed as indented) |
| Emphasis | <EM></EM> | (usually displayed as italic) |
| Strong Emphasis | <STRONG></STRONG> | (usually displayed as bold) |

also offers brief overviews of HTML 2.0, 3.0, and 3.2, but the emphasis is on comparing tags and features in these popular browsers. There is also an extensive reference to the new specifications for style sheets.

## Microsoft Internet Explorer HTML Reference

http://www.microsoft.com/workshop/author/newhtml/htmlr020.htm

This list of HTML tags and descriptions on Microsoft's site is a good resource when you want to look up what a certain tag is used for, or when you're sneaking a peek at someone else's HTML source and want to find out how they came to write their code the way they did. The information is laid out in a straightforward, reference-only format, but the content is extensive.

## NCSA HyperNews: HyperText Markup Language (HTML)

http://union.ncsa.uiuc.edu/HyperNews/get/www/html.html

Here you'll find a collection of links to HTML reference material in such categories as style guides, authoring tools and converters, and validating tools. Visitors can also submit URLs for other good HTML reference sites to add to the list. This site, like all the others under the HyperNews umbrellas, also includes a user forum where real-time questions on HTML problems are asked and (less often, these days) answered—and which, unfortunately, drags performance to a crawl. I almost always end up interrupting the page download before the years' worth of discussion headers is complete. At least they're at the end of the page rather than the beginning.

## Web Design Group Reference

http://www.htmlhelp.com/reference/

This reference site contains a good cross-section of background information plus many technical details about HTML authoring. Of particular interest is the section on HTML 3.2, also known as Wilbur, which includes several reference approaches (structural, quick reference, overview, and indexed,) available through the Web or as integrated files (in Windows help-file format, as well as HTML). These files can be downloaded and used off-line.

## Web Developer's Virtual Library: Hypertext Markup Language (HTML)

http://www.stars.com/Authoring/HTML/

Alan and Lucy Richmond's Web Developer's Virtual Library is designed to catalog up-to-date information on all kinds of Web reference material and to keep it within arm's reach. Their HTML section goes to great lengths to define the language, and offers links to further information about the various revised specifications. This page sketches out the structure of HTML documents, and distinguishes between elements that fall into the <HEAD> and into the <BODY> portions of a Web document.

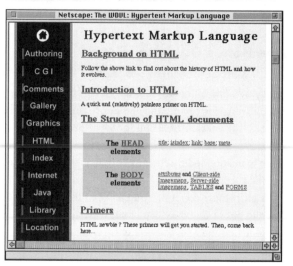

## Willcam's Comprehensive HTML Cross Reference

http://www.willcam.com/cmat/html/tags.html

Excellent reference source which provides a number of views. First, there's a super-compact (on my browser set-up, it fits on one screen!) index of all tags, with links from each tag to a detailed description. Next, there's a long, complete list with descriptions, suitable for downloading and local reference. Finally, and most uniquely, there are indices which group tags by which HTML standards they support—and *don't* support. This is the only site I've found to so conveniently list the Netscape and Internet Explorer extensions that did not make it into the HTML 3.2 standard.

# SPECIAL CHARACTERS AND MATH EXPRESSIONS

In a word processor, when you want to use special characters (i.e., letters and symbols that aren't shown on a standard American keyboard,) you usually use a special key sequence, and the characters are indicated in the document's file with a special code. Unfortunately, different operating systems have developed different standards for which codes stand for which special characters. A "solid bullet" or a "copyright" character made on a Macintosh will not display properly in a Windows program, and vice versa.

Since HTML is cross-platform, it's dependent on plain old ASCII—the standard codes for not-so-special characters——so any special characters must be described using ASCII characters. These HTML descriptions are called "character codes" or "character entities." For example, "&copy;" is the character entity that works as a substitute for the © symbol in ASCII and, therefore, in HTML.

Character entities begin with the ampersand (&) character, which brings in a new problem. If you have an ordinary ampersand in your text—for example, if you make reference to AT&T—your browser will interpret that as the beginning of a special character that's coming up. As a result, you'll have to use the character entity for an ampersand (&amp;) in order for it to display correctly.

Similarly, since the angle brackets that signal an HTML tag are actually less-than and greater-than signs, you can't just type a less-than or greater-than sign into your Web document: when the browser sees the less-than sign, it will assume that it's about to receive a formatting instruction, and it will then get very confused when it doesn't. Instead, you'll have to use the character entity for a less-than sign, "&lt;".

This section includes pointers to sites that list commonly used special characters along with their code equivalents. Don't expect to browse them in a hurry, as most of these pages are *huge*.

Does all this sound unbearably cumbersome? Actually, any decent HTML editor will include tools that can supply character entities more or less automatically. If you're using such an editor, you won't get stuck with looking codes up on a chart and typing them in by hand.

Reproducing math symbols or math equations can pose thornier design problems. Apparently mathematicians and physicists aren't considered a target market by most browser developers! Until the leading Web browsers include more support for the <MATH> tag, you're pretty much on your own. Some common workarounds include serving up math-heavy documents in a portable electronic format, like Adobe Acrobat, or using GIFs embedded in a Web page to represent math symbols or formulas. This section also includes sites that offer tips or workarounds for these display problems.

## ASCII-ISO 8859-1 (Latin-1) Table with HTML Entity Names

### http://bbsinc.com/iso8859.html

This page includes tables of character-entity names, pulled together from a large number of sources that you

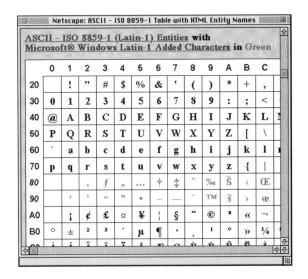

can link to. The charts show you both the entity name (e.g., &lt; for the less-than (<) symbol) and the decimal value for that entity's position in the character set—so, for example, the sequence &#60; could be used in place of &lt; to represent the less-than (<) symbol. You may need to know this when trying to figure out automatically generated HTML source code, since translation programs won't necessarily favor the version most easily understood by humans.

## Character Sets
**http://www.microsoft.com/workshop/author/newhtml/htmlr018.htm**

Another huge collection of special character codes can be found here, courtesy of your friends and mine, Microsoft Corporation.

## Greek Letters, Symbols, Subscripts, and Superscripts
**http://donald.phast.umass.edu/kicons/greek.html**

This site has a nice collection of transparent GIFs of math symbols and Greek letters, created by Karen M. Strom at the Amherst Campus of the University of Massachusetts. She requests a donation if you plan to use the GIFs for commercial sites.

## HTML Special Characters Entity Names
http://www.sandia.gov/sci_compute/symbols.html

This is a reference list of coding information for displaying special characters properly in HTML. For each example, the page displays the entity name on a line by itself, then uses the entity name as an example on the following line, ending with the common term for the character. It reminds readers that these character entities must begin with an ampersand and end with a semicolon. The list has not been kept up to date with recent browser developments, but it may be useful as the most compact of these references.

## ISO 8859-1 Character Set Overview
**http://www.htmlhelp.com/reference/charset/**

This set of pages documents all the characters available in the ISO Latin 1 character set, which is fully supported by standard HTML. You are given the choice of displaying characters in a table or, for older browsers that don't support tables, in GIF files. Each table shows what the actual character looks like, the decimal code for each character (e.g., &#169;), the entity name for the character (e.g., &copy;), and a brief description of the character. This is part of the Web Design Group site, which is dedicated to non-browser-specific Web authoring. Its most distinguishing feature may be its consideration of character-display problems across different browsers and operating systems.

## The LaTeX2HTML Translator
**http://cbl.leeds.ac.uk/nikos/tex2html/doc/latex2html/latex2html.html**

In case you're not familiar with LaTeX, it's a set of macros written in TeX, a software system for typesetting technical documents. LaTeX was designed to simplify the printing of text loaded with math symbols and equations, and this LaTeX-to-HTML utility is designed to convert articles filled with math formulas for publishing on the Web. In doing so, it will convert any math equations or tables into individual inline images. The site includes information about obtaining, installing, and using the translator.

## techexplorer
**http://www.alphaworks.ibm.com/**

IBM's techexplorer is a Windows 95 Netscape plug-in for formatting mathematical expressions found in TeX and LaTeX documents for publication on Web pages. You can find the program by going to the "Download" section of alphaWorks, an experimental research site at IBM that showcases emerging technologies. The techexplorer program is most suited for Web-ifying scientific articles or other technical proofs. The site has online examples you can see after you've installed the plug-in. Links on the page lead to the download area, system requirements, a FAQ, and a feedback page.

# HTML STANDARDS AND SPECIFICATIONS

The official HTML specifications really aren't light reading material, but are worth a look if you're intrigued by how the language has developed over the course of its brief history. Additional related information about Web protocols and specifications is included here as well.

## A Beginner's Guide to URLs

**http://www.ncsa.uiuc.edu/demoweb/url-primer.html**

This probably remains the most "official" introduction to Uniform Resource Locators (URLs). It explains their use as unique addresses for every document and resource available on the Internet, and offers descriptions of pathnames and domain names. Unfortunately, its age is showing: it's a bit out of date, and assumes familiarity with pre-Web Internet protocols. As such, I can't completely recommend it anymore, despite its admirable succinctness. Instead, check out some of the HTML introductions and overviews mentioned earlier.

## URLs: The Names and Addresses of Web Resources

**http://www.w3.org/pub/WWW/Addressing/Addressing.html**

If you just can't get enough of the sizzlingly erotic world of URL specifications, this is the site for you: the official collection of URL-related links from the World Wide Web Consortium itself. Thrill to minutely detailed changes to the official standard! Plunge deep into glossaries and lists of protocols! Speculate wildly about possible new approaches to universal addressing!

## HTML Resources: Official Specifications

**http://www.hwg.org/resources/html/specs.html**

This page on the HTML Writers Guild site briefly describes the status of each HTML version, with links for accessing the official specifications. It makes a good orientation point for use before diving into the formal specs.

There are pointers to the standards in HTML, plain text, PostScript, and TeX.

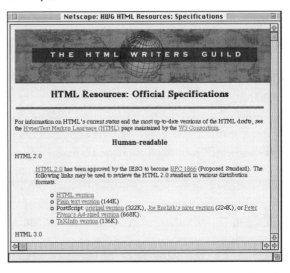

## HTML 3.2 HyperText Markup Language Charter

**http://www.ietf.cnri.reston.va.us/html.charters/html-charter.html**

The HTML Working Group, a loosely organized group under the auspices of the Internet Engineering Task Force, was launched to develop HTML specifications and help create formal standards. This site hosts the charter for the group, including a description of its goals and what it has accomplished so far. There are pointers to current Internet drafts and Request for Comments (RFC) documents, which can define official published standards for Internet technology.

The site directs users to a mailing list covering general discussion about HTML. To subscribe, send mail to www-html@w3.org and in the body of your message type: **subscribe html-wg <your name>**

## HyperText Markup Language: Working and Background Materials

**http://www.w3.org/hypertext/WWW/MarkUp/**

As part of its mission to standardize all Web technology, the World Wide Web Consortium (W3C) is the body charged with defining the open standards of HTML. This home page for the official HTML specifications gives an overview of all HTML-related materials at the W3C.

Although some of the links are to highly technical pages, this is an interesting place to visit if you want to track how HTML has developed and get news about how it may be developing next. Early drafts of proposed new standards show up here first.

## IETF Home Page

**http://www.ietf.org/**

The Internet Engineering Task Force is responsible for managing the development of Internet protocols and technologies. It's split into a number of smaller, specialized working groups (e.g., the HTML Working Group), within which standards are developed through official documents called Requests for Comment (RFCs). Each RFC is given an individual reference number and addresses a specific technology—for example, how IP addresses are allocated or the definition of the MIME e-mail standard. At this site you can learn more about the current status of various RFCs as they are distributed, reviewed, and revised.

## Introducing HTML 3.2

**http://www.w3.org/pub/WWW/MarkUp/ Wilbur/**

This latest version of the HTML specifications was developed by the World Wide Web Consortium (W3C), with heavy and sometimes conflicting input from browser vendors like Microsoft, Netscape, Novell, Spyglass, and Sun Microsystems.

You can read the HTML 3.2 specification (also known as Wilbur) here. This version of HTML added tags for applets, table and math formatting, and text flow around images—most of which have been implemented already in current browser versions from Netscape and Microsoft, although W3C has rationalized their syntax a bit.

## Payment Negotiation: JEPI

**http://www.w3.org/pub/WWW/Payments/**

In October 1996, W3C joined forces with the Internet-industry vendors in CommerceNet to propose JEPI, a mechanism for making electronic payments for online purchases. You can read the specifications on this site, which describe the proposed negotiation protocol and an extension module for enabling such payments.

## W3C—The World Wide Web Consortium

**http://www.w3.org/pub/WWW/**

Working jointly with Internet industry vendors, the W3C aims to promote open standards for Web technology. It is charged with producing specifications and reference software to promote interoperability between all kinds of Web products. At the W3C site, you can find more information about its history and its involvement in areas of Internet development like graphics technology, Web audio and video, security, and electronic commerce.

## World Wide Web FAQ

**http://www.boutell.com/faq/**

Thomas Boutell maintains this FAQ (Frequently Asked Questions) list, a classic starting point for information about the Web. The question-and-answer format gives a good overview of the Web, Web browsers, Web servers, Web authoring, and other resources. Boutell is also the keeper of the FAQs for all the comp.infosystem.www. Usenet newsgroups, and his continually updated documents are always a treasure trove of information.

The FAQ is available from many mirror sites and in several languages. It can also be downloaded as a .ZIP file, as a compressed .tar file for Unix, and as one large text file.

# HTML Validators and Link Checkers

Since even the most eagle-eyed Web designers can mismatch closing tags from time to time, or make poor decisions like failing to nest tags properly, the best way to ensure that your HTML is up to code is to run your files through a validator. While there are C programs and other scripts that'll perform this function, the listings here focus most heavily on places you can go on-line to proof a document or a bit of code.

It's just as important to make sure that all of the links on your pages are valid. Few things frustrate Web visitors and damage their impression of your site more than an abundance of dead links. You should always test every single link on a new page yourself before making it publicly available, to make sure that each link successfully points to the location you intend. After all, no automatic checker can know what your intentions are!

But after your page is up on the Web, it's likely that at least a few of the external pages to which you've linked will eventually move or disappear. Thus you should occasionally check for broken links even on existing pages. The automated validators listed below will help cut back on the tedium of periodic link maintenance.

By the way, many HTML editors also handle validation duties. It's always a good idea for you to check into the capabilities of any generalized HTML and graphics utilities you're using before going through the work of downloading and testing a more specialized utility.

## A Kinder, Gentler Validator

**http://ugweb.cs.ualberta.ca/~gerald/validate/**

This is a very user-friendly HTML validation service, designed to provide easy-to-understand error messages. Unfortunately, it's probably too strict for most Web

> Different HTML validators tend to give different kinds of responses, depending on the philosophy of their writers. Some validators even let you specify different levels of strictness to test against—for example, ensuring compliance with HTML 2.0 versus 3.0, or disallowing Netscape-specific tags. It can be instructive to try several different flavors of validation and work out the differences in their reports, especially when you're starting out.

authors' purposes, flagging almost every Netscape-initiated tag and attribute as a "parsing error!" You'll find ample explanatory links given between the report and the FAQ file. It's developed by Gerald Oskoboiny, who also created lynx-me (see entry below in "Guides to Helper Applications and Browser Capabilities").

### AUTHOR'S CHOICE

### Doctor HTML

**http://imagiware.com/RxHTML.cgi**

This HTML validator, by far the best I've used, can check any URL for spelling errors, form structure, image analysis and syntax, command hierarchy and working hyperlinks. Another great service it offers is an estimate of the time it would take for your page to download over a 14.4 Kbps modem, letting you plan for users with slower modems. The on-line service quickly returns a results page with a brief or detailed report.

Although you can check out individual pages yourself by hand for free, Doctor HTML is a commercial venture. Set up an account, and you're promised more features and streamlined access. Large companies can also look into licensing a local copy of the software.

## Spyglass HTML Validator
**http://www.spyglass.com/products/validator/**
You can download from this site the Spyglass HTML Validator, a standalone program for Windows 95 only that lets Web authors check their documents against one of the HTML specifications for errors. Unlike the on-line validation services, you can run it locally without connecting to the Internet. When the error results have been computed and returned, you can locate specific errors in your document by double-clicking each error message. Unfortunately, Spyglass has let the program go out of date, and you might be better off using a validator that is integrated with an HTML editor.

**AUTHOR'S CHOICE**

## Weblint
**http://www.khoral.com/staff/neilb/weblint.html**
Weblint checks the syntax and style of HTML documents; the name comes from the *lint* program for finding coding errors in C programs. Think of Weblint as attempting to get the fluff off of HTML pages—it can seem a little picky in doing so. The program, written by Neil Bowers, can be downloaded as a Perl script via FTP. This page also has links directing you to Web-based gateways for using Weblint online—that is, pages where you can just type in a URL and have your test results returned to you over the Web.

## WebTechs Validation Service
**http://www.webtechs.com/html-val-svc/**
This is a free on-line HTML validation service. You begin by entering your URL, or just a snippet of HTML code if your page isn't online yet, into an interactive form. Then you choose what standard your document should be graded against—for example, testing compliance with HTML version 2.0, or allowing for a set of Netscape extensions. After you submit your form, the service will return a list of errors (or, depending on your point of view, cluelessly nit-picking suggestions). I don't rate this service as highly as some other Web authors do—I find its standards too restrictive and its messages too cryptic—but I have to acknowledge its popularity.

# WEB BROWSERS

It wasn't long after the original Web browser, Mosaic X for Unix, was publicly released in 1993 for academic use that the commercial browser wars heated up. Dozens of Internet browser technologies engaged each other in fierce competition, each hoping to cash in on the growing Web craze. Netscape Communications had gained the lion's share of the market by the end of 1995, with some 70 to 80 percent of all Web-surfers using Navigator, when Microsoft Corporation posed the first serious threat to Netscape's dominance.

Since then, the two market leaders have vied with each other for position, largely relegating other vendors to second-class citizenship. Their competition has certainly kept prices low. Unfortunately, it's largely been based on publicity-grabbing additions of potentially cool features at the expense of quality, transforming the simple browsers of yesterday into clumsy giants that require fairly high-powered systems (and often crash them).

Anyone who's serious about Web author-ing should have at least two browsers to test their pages on. The worry isn't so much treat-ment of browser-specific-features (those are of-ten easy enough to figure out) as treatment of not-entirely-specified or -supported HTML. Some-thing that looks fine on one version of a browser may be a complete mess on another browser—or even on another version of the *same* browser. Above all, at least one of your test browsers must not be a beta release. Yes, it's true that in the rol-lickin' world of browser development the real dis-tinction between "release quality" and "test quality" is thin, but the PR difference is enough that you can be sure a majority of your potential users will *not* be running beta. By the way, in my experience WYSIWYG HTML editors are especial-ly prone to producing Web pages that only work as expected on one particular version of one par-ticular brand of browser.

## Usenet Newsgroups for Web Browser Discussions

news:comp.infosystems.www.browsers.mac
news:comp.infosystems.www.browsers.
ms-windows

These are the places to go for the latest word on real-life experiences with new Web browsers. As always with Usenet newsgroups, they are also the places to go to be inundated by repetition, immature temper tantrums, and irrelevant noise. I tend to sort the topics by subject and be very selective about which ones I read!

## C|Net's Reviews: Picking the Perfect Web Browser

http://www.cnet.com/Content/Reviews/
Compare/Browsers/products.html

Still mulling over which browser to use? If you're inter-ested in the state of the art pre-Netscape-2.0, check out C|Net's review of 28 Web browsers. The online article includes a link to C|Net's recommendations for buying, as well as links to most of the browsers' accompanying home pages for downloading software or information on

more recent versions. Of course, the browser race has thinned out a bit since late 1995.

## Cyberdog

http://www.cyberdog.apple.com/

Apple's Cyberdog is a Macintosh-only free Web browser based on OpenDoc, IBM, and Apple's OLE-killer for sharing information between applications. Multimedia viewers are built in, replacing separate helper applica-tions. Other features include built-in e-mail and news-group access. By all accounts, it's an interesting technology demonstration but an iffy browser with seri-ous speed and compatibility problems; personally, I'm looking forward to (but not waiting up nights for) the promised Netscape OpenDoc browser component. The problem with both OpenDoc and OLE is that neither one has much of a chance at true cross-platform success so long as the other one exists, which is why cross-plat-form software vendors like Netscape and Macromedia often end up not supporting either.

## HotJava

http://www.javasoft.com:80/products/
HotJava/index.html

This page offers information about HotJava, Sun Micro-systems' free Java-enabled and Java-authored browser. The original versions of HotJava were more convincing as Java demos than as full-featured Web browsers. The upcoming Version 1.0 (!) release looks to be much more interesting, however, since it's based on the considerably more powerful cross-platform support of newer Java li-braries. At the time of this writing, beta versions of Hot-Java were available for Sparc/Solaris and Windows 95/ NT users. At this site you can read about planned fea-tures in upcoming versions, the list of known bugs, and a list of frequently requested features. A HotJava Browser User's Guide offers information about the browser's fea-tures and how to use it. You'll also find links to a FAQ file, the download area, and licensing information here.

## Microsoft Internet Explorer

http://www.microsoft.com/ie/

Microsoft's very impressive Web browser is available for Windows, Windows 95, Windows NT, and Macintosh users. The Internet Explorer site covers a Netscape-wide range of Web topics, including browser developments and new features, resources for ActiveX developers and FTP sites where users can download the latest version of the software. If you're using Windows or a Macintosh, this and Netscape Navigator are pretty much the only games left in town. Other commercial or shareware browsers haven't had much of a chance since Microsoft started focusing a noticeable fraction of its resources on development of free Web software.

## NCSA Mosaic

**http://www.ncsa.uiuc.edu/SDG/Software/ Mosaic/**

One of the earliest Web browsers—and the first supporting inline graphics—NCSA Mosaic was developed for the Macintosh, Windows, and X-Windows platforms, and remained a popular alternative to the commercial browsers, particularly among academics. In early 1997, however, NCSA (a university research center) decided that the time had come to bow out of the browser business, and development ceased as final versions of NCSA Mosaic 3.0 were being completed.

## Netscape Navigator

**http://www.netscape.com/**

One of the most popular and still the most feature-plump of Web browsers, the shareware and commercial (but with free betas) Netscape Navigator is available for the Macintosh, Windows, and Unix platforms. The Netscape browser was initially developed by much of the programming team that created the original NCSA Mosaic browser. In fact, until a rather ugly legal battle with NCSA, the original name of the Netscape Communications company was "Mosaic," which is why you'll still sometimes see references to "Mozilla," an early company monster-mascot, floating around. The Navigator part of Netscape's site includes tutorials for the many Web-page features that Netscape has invented (such as frames and blinking text) or provided early support for, and it's also the place to find downloads of the browser and related files, such as plug-ins.

☞ Whenever you have a very specific question or topic to research, don't bother slogging into Usenet newsgroups with a dedicated newsreader (or, even worse, with Netscape Navigator). All you'll be able to search on are the titles of articles, and even then you'll only get access to the most recent articles, since your news server has to sweep away older articles fairly often.

Instead, make your first stop DejaNews.

## DejaNews

**http://www.dejanews.com/forms/dnq.html**
DejaNews lets you do a surprisingly fast and accurate search across months of stored Usenet articles. For me, it's turned the Usenet from a time-consuming irritation into the most useful reference source I have on the Web. I can't recommend it highly enough.

Nowadays, I only go to Usenet proper to do random browsing on subjects I'm interested in (such as what new HTML authoring systems are being used) ,

to check on time-critical information (such as laser-disk sales) or to add my own articles (such as bug reports and workarounds).

## Spyglass Mosaic

http://www.spyglass.com/products/

Another bit of history: Spyglass obtained the rights for commercial licensing of Mosaic from the NCSA, and for a time was fairly successful marketing its adaptation of NCSA's program to other companies as a bundled browser called "Spyglass Mosaic" or "Enhanced NCSA Mosaic." As Netscape and Microsoft took over the PC and Macintosh markets, however, Spyglass has focused its efforts on providing Web capabilities to other, more specialized platforms, such as handheld devices and set-top boxes. At this point Spyglass Mosaic does not appear to be viable as a general-purpose browser.

## PROPRIETARY BROWSER EXTENSIONS

### BrowserWatch

AUTHOR'S CHOICE

http://browserwatch.iworld.com/

BrowserWatch aims to collect an exhaustive list of available Web browsers and plug-ins, the various computer platforms they support or plan to support, the latest versions of each and the latest statistics on visitors to the site. (Last time I checked, Netscape users had dropped down to 45 percent of the total number, with Microsoft Internet Explorer coming up to 40 percent—quite a change from last year's stats!) Given the accelerated release of new versions of browser beta software, it's a great stopping point to check if your copies are up-to-date. I've bookmarked BrowserWatch's "News Room" section, which pumps out a steady stream of news tidbits and Internet-industry rumors.

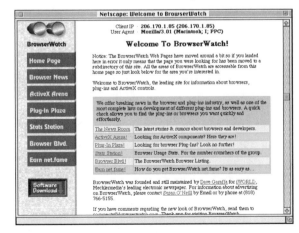

## HTML Tag and Attribute Support by Browser

http://www.browserbydesign.com/resources/appa/apa1.htm

This resource includes eight pages of tables that provide a thorough listing of HTML tags, naming which version of HTML the tag originated in, and providing a comparison of the attributes supported by each browser. At last count, the browsers examined here included: Netscape Navigator 3.0, Microsoft Internet Explorer 3.0 alpha, Oracle PowerBrowser 1.0, HotJava Alpha Release, NCSA Mosaic 2.0, America Online Windows 2.5, CompuServe Spry Mosaic 1.0, Prodigy 2.0d, Apple Cyberdog beta 2, Navigator 2.0, Navigator 1.1, and Internet Explorer 2.0.

## Inline Plug-ins

http://home.netscape.com/comprod/products/navigator/version_2.0/plugins/index.html

This page on Netscape's site provides a list of plug-ins for the Navigator browser—there were over 120 at last count. Plug-ins are platform-specific add-ons that extend Navigator's capabilities without launching a separate helper application—for example, by letting users view movie clips within the browser window or listen to audio. The plug-ins here are arrayed by category: 3D and animation, audio/video, business and utilities, image viewers, and presentations. You can also download software development kits for creating your own plug-ins, and check out other developer resources.

## GUIDES TO HELPER APPLICATIONS AND BROWSER CAPABILITIES

### BrowserCaps

http://www.objarts.com/bc/

This site lets visitors check the capabilities of their browsers by filling out a series of interactive forms. It can be a useful exercise for designers, who often forget that their visitors may be using a less-capable browser than their own. You can run through the tests with more than one browser to see how differently some tags are rendered. At the site, you can review a list of available features, see a to-do list of upcoming future capabilities, and check out related resources.

## Browsers, Viewers and HTML Preparation Resources

**http://www.utoronto.ca/webdocs/HTMLdocs/ intro_tools.html**

This too-seldom-maintained site links to information about browsers, browser helper applications, and HTML editing tools. The links are organized by computer platform, including DOS and Windows, Macintosh, OS/2, and Unix, as well as online services. The browser summaries give details about latest versions (as of 1995, anyway!), system requirements, download size, and licensing terms. The site was created by Ian Graham, but has since fallen woefully out of date. Still, the wide coverage may help you uncover tools not mentioned elsewhere.

## Digital Forms Testing Home Page

**http://www.research.digital.com/nsl/formtest/ home.html**

Do you know how well your browser handles interactive forms? If so, you'll want to take a look at this real-world test suite for trying out your browser's forms-handling capabilities. You can get immediate results on support of features like Netscape cookies, or find out if your browser sends identifying information about its type and version. For the serious Web author, even more interesting than examining your own browser's capabilities is looking at the collective results for all visitors who've completed the tests, which are sorted by browser and type of test. Brief descriptions of the tests themselves are given in the test results section.

## Helper Applications

**http://home.netscape.com/assist/helper_apps/**

Here, Netscape maintains a collection of links to Web-browser helper applications, including video, audio, and graphics programs. There are links from the main page to archive sites, arrayed by platform, where you can download shareware and freeware programs. For novices, there's an introductory page on configuring and launching a helper application, along with a definitive list of media types and their file formats.

## lynx-me

**http://ugweb.cs.ualberta.ca/ ~gerald/lynx-me.cgi**

Web designers who try to show consideration for all users often aim to create pages that will be useful even for text-only browsers. But how many of them ever use a text-based browser to test how their pages actually look? Lynx-me is designed to meet that need. Enter a URL in the single-field form on this page, and lynx-me will show you more or less how that page would display in the text-only browser Lynx. Note that what it shows you is actually a little less than the real thing: on most terminals or terminal emulators, Lynx will be able to use underlines to indicate a link and boldface for emphasis. All you get back from this service is pure unformatted text. With that proviso, still a useful service.

## Rex Swain's HTML Sampler

**http://www.pcnet.com/~rhswain/sampler.html**

Currently, this is probably the best of the combined HTML example/reference pages. The explanations are clear, and for the most part the examples are well-constructed. HTML features not supported by Netscape Navigator are specially called out. The page ends with a list of special character entities. The only problem is the usual one for browser reference sites: it's not kept maniacally up to date. Since a Web author very often goes to such an example site to check up on the effects of new "cool" HTML constructs, this can be a fairly serious flaw. But if

It's usually not hard to try out "real" Lynx for yourself. Many Internet service providers provide Unix accounts as well as pure connectivity. If you Telnet or otherwise connect to a Unix account, you're very likely to find the program already installed: just type "lynx" and hit return. (If you're unfamiliar with Telnet programs or command-line interfaces, you might want to hold off, though.) In fact, when I have difficulties getting a TCP/IP connection to my service provider, I usually dial into my Unix account using a non-Internet program (such as ZTerm for the Macintosh) for a non-TCP/IP, text-only session, and use the "lynx" program to research the problem using the Web.

you're interested in just getting an overview of slightly more established constructs, this is a good resource.

## Web Page Backward Compatibility Viewer

http://www.delorie.com/web/wpbcv.html

Browser vendors vie to ship ever more new-and-improved versions of their software, often with support for new HTML tags, but there's still a large user population that hasn't—or couldn't—keep pace with new updates. Short of hanging on to outdated versions of browser software yourself, how can you envision what your pages will look like to users whose browsers can't display background colors, frames, or Java applets?

This site offers one clever solution. It runs a Perl script (source code available) to let you see what a page looks like when certain tags aren't supported. After you enter a URL to view, you can select which elements should or shouldn't be permitted. The tags in question include those for images, tables, <BLINK>, frames, font changes, background colors or patterns, Java applets, and JavaScript.

### WWW Test Pattern

**AUTHOR'S CHOICE**

http://www.uark.edu/~wrg/

Maybe you've just upgraded to the latest version of your favorite browser, or you're trying out a new browser for the first time. How can you tell at a glance if it can handle special Web features—like Java, for

example—the way you might expect it to? WWW Test Pattern offers one solution: a trial-by-fire test site for checking your browser's capabilities. You can test your browser's support of HTML 2.0 tags, a subset of HTML 3.2 tags, proprietary Netscape and Microsoft extensions, and Java support. (Too bad about the unnecessarily huge graphics files, though.)

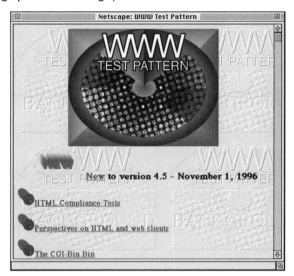

## WWW Viewer Test Page

http://www-dsed.llnl.gov/documents/
WWWtest.html

How many multimedia Web formats is your browser equipped to play? This extremely well-designed page maintained by the Lawrence Livermore National Laboratory can help you ensure that movie viewers and sound players are installed, so you can absorb more of what the Web has to offer.

The tests of your browser's capabilities are simple enough: you push a button to hear a sound or see an MPEG movie play, for example. If you can hear the sound or see the movie display in a separate window, then you're all set with the necessary helper application. If your browser complains that it doesn't know what to do, you can follow a link from the media format's name to learn how to download an appropriate helper application (if any) for your computer platform.

From a Web author's perspective, this page also operates as a nice check on whether your chosen media formats will be available to all users or not, and as a convenient reference for MIME types and their associated applications.

# HTML EDITORS

HTML authoring tools are designed to generate HTML tags automatically for you, rather than making you type each and every character of each and every formatting instruction by hand. If you're creating a Web page from scratch, or making some changes in a Web page, you'll want to use an HTML editor; if you're dealing with a large body of existing material in a different format, you'll probably want to start with an HTML converter and then move to a HTML editor to handle fix-ups.

There are two main classes of HTML editors:

- **Tag-helper** editors, in which the HTML tags remain visible and editable, you choose which tags to use, and the editor program simply helps you by drastically reducing the amount of typing you have to do and by giving you easy access to HTML references and validation. To see what your page will look like when the tags are interpreted, you have to preview your page in a real browser.

- **Quasi-WYSIWYG** editors, in which the editor program attempts to work as most contemporary word processors do, showing you what it thinks the browser will show while you're actually in the process of editing the page. Since browsers don't explicitly show the HTML tags that give them their instructions, in quasi-WYSIWYG editors the tags are invisible, and are automatically generated by the editor.

You can also simply use a normal text editor or word processor, restricting yourself to "plain text" and typing out each tag by hand. Some Web instructors prefer that their students work this way to gain more (painfully more, perhaps) intimacy with HTML. I don't know about you, but personally I've never found drudgery to be as good for the soul as it's often promised to be, and would prefer that the computer cut back on my labor as much as possible. I have to spend enough hours at the keyboard as it is! About the only time I use "plain text" editors (such as SimpleText on the Macintosh or Notepad on Windows) to edit an HTML document is when I have to do a quick fix-up and there's nothing more suitable readily available.

There are many HTML editors out there, all in various stages of maturity or decrepitude. I've tried to cover only a few of the ones I consider the best; for more comprehensive overviews, check out the links below.

---

☞ **Whatever your HTML editor of choice, you'll probably want to set your browsers up to use that editor when they view Web source files. In Netscape, for example, you can go to the "Options/General Preferences" menu and then to the "Applications" submenu. Find the "View Source" line. Press the "Browse" button there to select the application file to use (e.g., BBEdit Lite 3.0). The next time you "View Source" from Netscape, the source HTML for the current Web page will be loaded into your editor for easy cut-and-paste operations.**

---

**Carl Davis's HTML Editor Reviews**
http://homepage.interaccess.com/ ~cdavis/editrev/index2.html

This site has thoughtful, capsule reviews of dozens of Windows-based HTML editors, focusing on how each package excels and where it falls short. Davis deserves special praise for keeping this list so admirably up to date when so many other review sites have fallen silent. Each review displays a screen shot of the software running and lists the platforms supported. Each also notes whether the tool is a standalone product or an add-on, whether the HTML editor is text-based or WYSIWYG or both, and whether HTML syntax-checking is a feature; rates the program's stability; and gives the product an overall score. Also provided is a Java applet to help you make your choice. Davis writes that he welcomes contributed reviews from others.

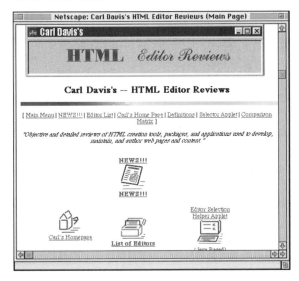

## Macintosh WWW Resource Directory: HTML Editors

http://www.comvista.com/net/www/htmleditor.html

Unfortunately for Macintosh users, the closest equivalent they have to Carl Davis's list is grievously out of date, like all the other pages in the Macintosh WWW Resource Directory. It's a shame, as the page started off as one of the most valuable resources available to Macintosh Web authors. Each product listing included the vendor's home page, availability (commercial, shareware, or freeware), release version, and a product review. For now, you're probably slightly better off checking reviews in the more general Macintosh review sites, such as the Macintosh area of ZDNet (http://www5.zdnet.com/mac/) or Macworld Online (http://www.macworld.com/).

## Mag's Big List of HTML Editors

http://union.ncsa.uiuc.edu/HyperNews/get/www/html/editors.html

This is the NCSA's one-stop shopping resource for HTML editing tools. The opening page also includes one of those patented HyperNews, way-too-long, threaded

discussion forums, this one on topics related to HTML editors. This wonderfully extensive list is arranged according to computer platform; you can also look at editors for languages other than English. Each tool's description includes information about the author, its availability, the current version at time of writing, the URL of the product's home page, and a description of what it does. There are no reviews and it's not kept religiously up to date, but it is impressively comprehensive.

## Stroud's Reviews for HTML Editors

http://www.micro.cc.utah.edu/cws/shtml.html

These in-depth and fairly up-to-date reviews of Windows HTML editors are from the maintainer of The Consummate Winsock Apps List. The coverage of each application not only links to the application's home page and to a download of the application, but also to an on-line discussion forum where you can submit your own opinion.

## Usenet Newsgroup for HTML Authoring

news:comp.infosystems.www.authoring.html

Put on your flameproof suit and your flying-excrement-proof goggles and visit the Usenet newsgroup that discusses (and occasionally froths at the mouth about) HTML authoring. Actually, this newsgroup is the best place to find up-to-date, real-life reviews of new authoring tools, and it's also a pretty good source for tricks, techniques, and melodramatic forecasts of doom. Just try to maintain a thick skin and a skeptical attitude while you're there.

## Windows HTML Editing Tools

http://www.ncsa.uiuc.edu/SDG/Software/mosaic-w/html/editors.html

This resource is a collection of links with descriptions of HTML authoring tools for Windows users. The tools featured include HTML editors, templates, and imagemap editors. Compact and up-to-date, although certainly not comprehensive.

### TAG-HELPER EDITORS

Tag-helper editors are often based on program editors, since programmers share such editing needs with Web authors as easy language reference, automatic creation of "boilerplate" text, use of templates to obtain consistency between new files, color-coded "special words," syntax validation, and global replacement of text across multiple files.

## Arachnophilia

**http://www.arachnoid.com/lutusp/arach.html**

The cost of this "CareWare" Windows HTML editor is hard to beat: if you like the program, you have to stop whining about how tough your life is for a day (price in USA only; non-USA price not specified, though I think things always cost more in Canada). Arachnophilia is mostly oriented toward conversions, doing a great job with text and tables imported from most Windows 95 applications. As an editor it's very promising, although when I tried editing from scratch, it didn't take long before I had to start typing in some tags by hand. If you want to stick to one package for both non-HTML conversions and hand polishing, it's worth the download and may even be worth the lifestyle disruption.

## BBEdit

**http://www.barebones.com/ bbedit.html**

BBEdit is a high-powered, popular, and extensible programming editor for Macintosh users which was early on adapted to HTML editing with the addition of a few extensions. As an HTML editor, it's been a great success, and the current version adds many Web authoring features, including HTML-aware spell-checking, syntax veri-

fication, automatic sizing of inline images, templates, browser previews, and color coding. It has an excellent multi-file search-and-replace function, so you can batch-process routine tasks across large numbers of HTML files. BBEdit is a commercial product, but there are freeware (BBEdit Lite) and demo versions available for downloading. Incidentally, it's what I use myself.

## HomeSite

**http://www.dexnet.com/ homesite.html**

HomeSite is a Windows HTML authoring tool written by Nick Bradbury that's available as both freeware and shareware. It makes use of color-coded HTML tags, a built-in HTML 2.0-compliant browser, drag-and-drop capabilities for inserting documents and images, and a frame wizard. Style sheets and ActiveX controls are also supported. The shareware version includes multiple-file editing, spell-checking, and project-management features. It'll even estimate download times for you. Links from this site point to a question-and-answer page, registration, reviews, the download area, and a showcase section. Even confirmed WYSIWYG seekers seem to be enamored of this program.

Incidentally, Nick Bradbury originally developed HomeSite as a way to speed up the process of moving his old cartoons onto his personal Web site!

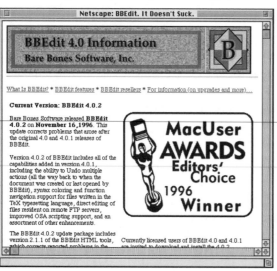

## Horizon Web Text

**http://midusa.net/~bwilken/horizon/**

A no-nonsense $20 shareware HTML editor for Windows 95 with a bare-bones approach that reminds me a bit of, well, BBEdit. It hasn't gotten much publicity and it lacks some of the little amenities we go to an HTML editor for, such as automatic sizing of images. But it's already got a nice assortment of low-overhead features, and author Bryan Wilken seems dedicated to aggressive upgrades. It's probably worth checking in on what he's been up to lately.

## HotDog

**http://www.sausage.com/**

With its gaudy icons and custom sounds, there's no surreptitious way to use this HTML authoring tool. I've always found it too cumbersome to be comfortable, but I can't argue with its popularity, particularly among newer authors. The higher-end version, HotDog Professional 3 for Windows 95, is outfitted with quasi-WYSIWYG views, spell-checking, and HTML syntax validation, among many other features. After you download the software, it's usable for a 30-day evaluation; the full cost is $99.95. There's also a $29.95 Windows 3.1 version of HotDog that lacks the spell-checker, browser view, and some customization features; you can download and use it freely for 30 days as well.

## HTML Assistant Pro

**http://www.brooknorth.com/istar.html**

This site offers a guide to HTML Assistant Pro, a commercial hypertext editor from Brooklyn North Software Works. The full version retails for $99, but a freeware version with documentation is also available here for downloading. The product includes assistant functions for creating tables and forms, as well as a spell-checker. The HTML Assistant Pro site includes details about the product's newest features, ordering information, and a FAQ listing.

## HTMLed and HTMLed Pro

**http://www.ist.ca/**

These $29 and $59 shareware editors from Internet Software Technologies are among the best HTML editors available for Windows. The Pro forms editor has garnered praise from reviewers, but what both versions of the program really have going for them are straightforwardness and customizability. The HTMLed approach is to concentrate on reducing repetitive work for the Web author, rather than on flash. Definitely worth looking into if you're doing this for a living.

## HTML Notepad

**http://www.cranial.com/software/htmlnote/**

This site is the home page for HTML Notepad, an easy-to-use HTML editor that runs under Windows for automatically adding HTML tags to text. There's also a simple interface for constructing tables and forms. The program can automatically add table tags for comma- and tab-delimited table data you insert. Background and text colors can be picked from a color dialog box. Users also have a choice of generating lowercase or uppercase tags, whichever they prefer.

## HTMLpad Pro

**http://www.intermania.com/~imania/
htmlpad.html**

Another nice, straightforward shareware ($20) HTML editor for Windows, distinguished by its emphasis on customizability. (The non-Pro HTMLpad lacks the customizability and is pretty much not distinguished by anything.)

## PageSpinner

**http://www.algonet.se/~optima/
pagespinner.html**

PageSpinner is a $25 shareware HTML editor for Macintosh users, designed to simplify Web-site creation tasks like selecting a background color or creating a table. PageSpinner includes interactive help with AppleGuide, and an HTML Assistant for newcomers. HTML tags can be highlighted in a different size, character style, or color to distinguish them from regular text. The site also includes news updates, mostly listing new features added in each version. Visitors to the site can pay their shareware fees and register PageSpinner online, using either an unsecured or a secure SSL version of the order form. One of the most highly praised HTML editors, with some fanatically devoted users out there.

## World Wide Web Weaver and HTML Web Weaver Lite

**http://www.miracleinc.com/Commercial/W4/**
**http://www.miracleinc.com/SharewareAndFreeware/WWLite/**

The enticingly named Miracle Software appropriately came up with the Macintosh World Wide Web Weaver ($59 direct, with a fully functional demo version available for download), up to date and including the finest table maker I've seen. "W4" gets around the WYSIWYG problem rather brilliantly by tightly coordinating its own operations keystroke-by-keystroke, with a preview displayed in Netscape Navigator or Internet Explorer. It's a very nice program, and if I didn't use BBEdit for other programming needs, I might well be a full-time user. HTML Web Weaver Lite, its precursor, is still available as $25 shareware.

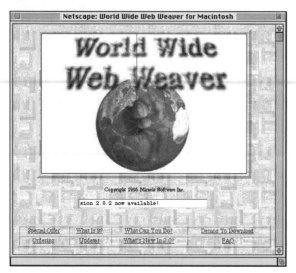

### QUASI-WYSIWYG EDITORS

Quasi-WYSIWYG editors have a number of disadvantages compared to tag-helper editors (see below for a fire-and-brimstone sermon on the subject), primarily their price: Unlike tag-helper editors, which are usually free or cheap shareware, quasi-WYSIWYG editors tend to be commercial software, and are priced like it.

If you're interested in pursuing cheap, quasi-WYSIWYG options, be aware that at any given time at least one of the big commercial programs (Claris Home Page, Adobe SiteMill and PageMill, and Microsoft FrontPage) is likely to have a free beta version available on the Web. As I write this, for example, FrontPage 97 has been officially released and its beta program removed, but SiteMill 2.0 downloads are still possible.

### Why There Is No WYSIWYG Web Editor

Tag-helper editors exist to help you avoid labor. Quasi-WYSIWYG editors exist to help you avoid knowledge.

Now, I don't ascribe to the belief that everyone ought to know everything possible. On the contrary, I'm with Sherlock Holmes in considering useless or uninteresting facts to be a waste of valuable brain storage. I don't know RTF or Postscript, and I don't care: I'm not a laser printer and I'm not a word processor, and for the most part word processors and laser printers seem to do fine without my help. The couple of times they haven't done fine, I preferred asking someone else to interfere, rather than starting to study RTF or Postscript myself.

But when you're dealing with unpredictable, adaptable, shifting, non-standardized standards like HTML, ignorance is not so blissful. I *can't* depend on Web browsers to "do fine without my help." One version of one brand of browser on one platform with one set-up will show a Web page one way; change the version, the brand, the operating system, the user's set-up, or even the window size, and the page will display in a considerably different way. The acronymed phrase "What You See Is What You Get" is meaningless in Web publishing. The best we can hope for is "What You See Might Be What You Get Occasionally" (or "WYSMBWYGO"—pronunciation is left as an exercise for the reader).

Even worse, most quasi-WYSIWYG programs are based on WYSIWYG programs for print publishing rather than on a browser, and thus what they show isn't exactly what will be shown on *any* browser at all.

HTML is not only unpredictable in WYSIWYG terms, it's also *redundant:* on any given display, you can usually create the same effect in a number of different ways.

- Let's say that you have a table that stretches across the width of the browser window. Is it a table that should always be exactly that many pixels wide? Or is it a table that should always stretch across the width of the browser window, no matter how skinny or wide the window is? Or is it not important how wide the table is at the moment—perhaps the table should be allowed to shrink or expand dynamically based on the size of its contents?

- That line of text in big bold print: Is it a first-level header, like a chapter title, which should be displayed in the same way as the browser displays other first-level headers? Or is it text that you would like to appear as being much larger than any surrounding text? Or should it always be shown in exactly that font and at exactly that font size, no matter what the surrounding text looks like? Or is it completely ordinary text that just happens to be displayed this way because you're vision-impaired or have set your monitor to a high resolution?

Only a human being—only the Web author, to be exact—can decide which of these intentions, all of which might lead to the same display in their editing program, is the correct one.

Probably as a result of these inherent difficulties, every version of every quasi-WYSIWYG editor has suffered from similar bugs: bad or non-standard HTML is produced even though the page displays well in the editor (and may even display well in one

or two particularly forgiving or buggy versions of browser), and existing correct but unusual HTML is not accepted by (or displays incorrectly in) the editor. You can fix the first problem, at least, by passing the quasi-WYSIWYG output file through a specialized scrubbing utility or through a tag-helper editor, but doesn't that work against the goal of avoiding HTML?

## Adobe PageMill

**http://www.adobe.com/prodindex/pagemill/main.html**

This product information site for PageMill, Adobe's commercial authoring tool for Macintosh users, promotes it as one of the easiest HTML-less HTML editors on any platform. Designers can drag-and-drop text or images to create body text, links, and embedded graphics. The program can also resize images and convert them from several graphics formats, and helps you create imagemaps. A spell-checker is included. You can download a demo version of the program; registered users can download updates from the site.

This was the first of the big quasi-WYSIWYG editors, and it quickly established the typical benefits (graphic designers were more comfortable avoiding knowledge of HTML) and problems (illegal, unpredictable, or browser-setting-specific HTML was output) of the breed. PageMill 2.0 is, by all accounts, a notable improvement over the first release, including much-praised table- and frames-designers. It also has the ability to see and modify the HTML that the editor automatically generated for you. As a result, the program might be worth purchasing, even if you have some knowledge of HTML.

## AOLpress

**http://www.aolpress.com/**

Like Netscape Navigator Gold, AOLpress can make its "WYSIWYG" claim with a bit more honesty than most editors: it's based on a Web browser. Unfortunately, it's based on the AOL Web browser rather than on one of the market leaders, but still...

As you may have picked up by now, I dislike quasi-WYSIWYG editors, and so AOLpress is the pick of the bunch for me: after all, it's free. To be fair, it's also nice-looking, fast and fairly up-to-date, and it lets you view the generated HTML code, although it doesn't give you much help in changing it. But the usual reluctance to deal with alternative, legal tag forms is there: not only did it refuse to set table-cell alignment options for me, but when I opened an existing page, AOLpress quietly removed all its color settings, apparently because the BODY-tag options were in a different order than it itself would've used. Also as usual with WYSIWYG editors, bizarre HTML constructions, not guaranteed to show properly on all browsers, abound: AOLpress's own introductory page ("Made With AOLpress!") incorrectly embeds a divider within a header.

### Claris Home Page

**http://www.claris.com/products/claris/clarispage/**

This information site for Claris Home Page gives a general overview of this authoring tool for Macintosh, Windows 95, and NT users. The product includes low-stress graphic interfaces and tools for creating forms, tables, and frames. You can store page templates, images, and other frequently used pieces of code using a library feature, and you can switch back and forth between WYSIWYG browsing and plain HTML when you're editing files. The site has links to ordering information, US pricing, and PDF files you can download for more information. There's also a link to a suggestion box for your

comments or bug reports. Its features seem to lag behind PageMill's, but Home Page has its supporters.

### GoLive Pro

**http://www.golive.de/**

Targeted at publishing professionals and graphic artists, GoLive Pro was a commercial Macintosh Web project-management suite with an updatable HTML tag database, a nice drag-and-drop, interface and a much-praised imagemap editor. Generally considered a dark horse in the quasi-WYSIWYG race, GoLive Pro appears to have been superseded by an upcoming product called GoLive CyberStudio. Check the somewhat confusing GoLive site for details.

### HoTMetaL Pro

**http://www.sq.com/products/hotmetal/hmp-org.htm**

SoftQuad has set up this product site for its $159 commercial Web-publishing tool HoTMetaL Pro 3.0, available for both Mac and Windows users, with a free feature-slimmed version available as well. The program has a drag-and-drop interface, optional quasi-WYSIWYG display, templates, labor-saving features, and color wheels for choosing font and background colors. Special editors work with forms, tables, and frames, and there's a built-in graphics editor for creating imagemaps, transparent images and icons. A spell-checker, thesaurus, HTML validator, and many templates are included.

HoTMetaL has consistently been popular as an all-in-one Web authoring tool, particularly among Windows users. It has the usual quasi-WYSIWYG quirks, however: the most recent version still complained about embedded tables and imported files. Also, I often need to use new HTML features which haven't made their way into editor support yet, and HoTMetaL is stubborn about not letting you insert tags and tag attributes by hand; this "you aren't old enough to drive" attitude was enough to ruin the program's usefulness for me.

### InContext Spider 1.2

**http://www.incontext.com/products/spider1.html**

InContext Systems promotes Spider, its commercial HTML authoring tool for Windows users, on this part of its site. The tool aims to let users serve up their pages when ready by pressing a single button. It also automatically converts word processing formats to HTML files, and includes a quasi-WYSIWYG display for envisioning what your finished pages will look like to Web visitors. Automatic HTML validation capabilities are included. The site features a downloadable demo, information on other software, and a gallery of Web page templates, graphics, backgrounds, and multimedia samples.

### Microsoft FrontPage Home Page

**http://www.microsoft.com/frontpage/**

This is the headquarters page for Microsoft's FrontPage Web authoring and site management tool for Windows users. Aiming to give Adobe a run for its PageMill money, Microsoft has gotten overwhelmingly positive reviews for the latest version, FrontPage 97. Like Adobe, it has added the much-needed ability to escape the world of quasi-WYSIWYG to edit HTML directly; it has also received praise for FrontPage's HTML-importing and site-management features.

Links from the main page will take you to a full product overview, program features, sites created with FrontPage, tutorial pages, and developer information. Being Microsoft, there's plenty of marketing material, with links to newspaper and online articles about FrontPage and Microsoft-sponsored contests. The commercial version of FrontPage 97 for Windows 95 and Windows NT costs $149; keep checking back here for possible free betas of new versions.

### Netscape Navigator Gold

**http://home.netscape.com/comprod/products/navigator/gold/**

This is the home page for Navigator Gold, Netscape's Web authoring product. Like the browser-only Navigator, it is distributed as a commercial, shareware, and free-beta product. The tool suite is designed to let users create Web pages automatically with a Page Wizard and document templates, streamline and enhance their e-mail, employ a one-button Web publishing feature, and provide Internet telephony and whiteboard functions. Links from the main page will steer you toward updates on product features (including a demo and a white paper), user guides, plus a FAQ and other support

material. Before its release, many of us looked forward to Navigator Gold as the nearest thing possible to true WYSIWYG authoring for the Web: even if it couldn't account for all possible user set-ups, at least you could be pretty sure that what you saw would match what *some* Netscape users got! As it turned out, a Web browser makes no more of a reasonable foundation for an editor than it does for an operating system. Navigator Gold's interface is awkward, and it lacks some standard editing and Web authoring features. Not much of a contender at present, aside from its ubiquity and some of its site-management tools.

# HTML CONVERTERS AND ADD-ONS

Some people who want to produce Web pages have a bedrock reluctance or inability to deal with explicit HTML. If you simply must avoid that initial scary contact with HTML while creating your first pages, I would recommend that you go back to your current word processing or desktop publishing software, and derive a Web page either through a converter, or, if you own (or can afford to upgrade to) a more recent version of the program, by directly exporting your document to HTML. This approach has two clear advantages over using a quasi-WYSIWYG editor:

1  You don't have to learn new software for a specialized purpose.

2  At least the editor is genuinely WYSIWYG—for printers, if not for browsers!

Actually, the quality of HTML exporters can be very high. You can expect to do some amount of tweaking, but at least it gives you something to start with.

I've heard special praise for the HTML support in Word 97, by the way. If you're an Office 97 user, you'll probably only need to download a HTML tag-helper editor for cleanup duties.

## BeyondPress

**http://www.astrobyte.com**

Astrobyte's BeyondPress is a Quark XPress-to-HTML converter, available for Macintosh users only. The software is available in four different languages.

Users can view and manipulate all text and images in their Quark XPress documents as separate elements for placement in Web pages. All text styles are automatically maintained, and special characters are converted to their HTML equivalents. Quark XPress style sheets can be mapped to HTML styles. It permits the conversion of any image placed in a QuarkXPress document to GIF or JPEG format for Web viewing.

BeyondPress 2.0.4 sells for an official price of $595, though at the time of this writing it was marked down $100. There's a free evaluation version available at the site, where registered users can purchase and download upgraded versions.

## HTML Converters

**http://union.ncsa.uiuc.edu/HyperNews/get/ www/html/converters.html**

This site maintained by the NCSA hosts both an exhaustive list of HTML conversion programs and an exhausting online discussion forum. The list of converters is out of date, but can't be faulted for lack of thoroughness. There are also links to other lists of conversion tools.

## HTML Markup

**http://www.printerport.com/klephacks/ markup.html**

HTML Markup is an excellent $20 shareware Macintosh utility for converting multiple plain-text files into HTML pages, relying on user-tailored instructions for interpreting the text (e.g., "make the first line the title and a top-level header") and adding HTML-specific template items (e.g., "stick a copyright footer on the bottom and make the background color Lisa-Simpson-yellow"). Fully customizable, scriptable, and impressively fast.

## HTML Transit

**http://www.infoaccess.com/**

This Windows conversion tool from InfoAccess is expensive ($495), but it has been praised as the best mass converter around, with easy template management; flexible text, table, and backgrounds formatting; automatic break-up of long documents into linked pages; automatic tables of contents generation; automatic gluing of separate documents into a linked web; and speedy delivery of finished pages. If you have a large library of text to convert, or if you need to keep bringing out text documents with HTML equivalents on the side, HTML Transit might be worth the cost.

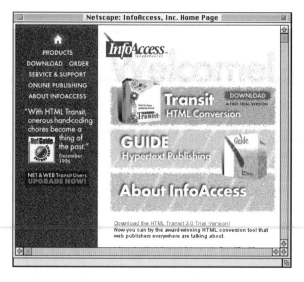

## Internet Assistant for Microsoft Word

**http://www.microsoft.com/msword/internet/ia/**

Microsoft's Internet Assistant is a Word 6 add-on for editing HTML in a WYSIWYG manner. It has some rudimentary browsing capabilities, which are sufficient for helping with the edits. Links from the main page will take you to system requirements, step-by-step instructions, a support and FAQ area, and the page where you can download the add-on.

## RTFtoHTML

**http://www.sunpack.com/RTF/**

Everyone's favorite early HTML converter has only improved with time. RTF (or "Rich Text Format") is a plain-text coding of heavily formatted text, usually used as the lingua franca between word processors (notable Microsoft Word and anybody else) and across operating systems. Virtually every commercial word processor on every computer is able to output RTF. As a result, RTF-to-HTML was a poor man's philosopher's stone, able to turn almost any existing text document into Web gold. Best of all, it was available across Unix, Windows, DOS, and Macintosh systems. It still is, but now it includes special-character translation, table support, newer HTML tags, and splitting of long documents. Maybe I'm just a nostalgic old fool, but I really like this program.

## W3C's HTML Converter List

**http://www.w3.org/pub/WWW/Tools/ Filters.html**

Probably the best current overview of what's available to convert existing files into HTML and to convert HTML files into other document types can be found here. This top-level page contains links to other indices of conversion programs, as well as to the two pages of special interest described below.

## W3C's Word Processor Filters

**http://www.w3.org/pub/WWW/Tools/Word_ proc_filters.html**

This comprehensive reference page on programs that can convert your word processing documents into HTML will point out more filtering tools than you ever knew existed. Currently maintained by Mike Sendall and housed by the W3C.

## W3C's Miscellaneous Filters

**http://www.w3.org/pub/WWW/Tools/Misc_ filters.html**

This page includes dozens of links for converting application files into HTML format. You'll find links to XTND translators, tools for converting Lotus Notes databases directly into HTML, HTML preprocessors, and SGML-to-HTML programs, among others.

# CHAPTER 3
# ADVANCED HTML

IN THIS CHAPTER, WE'LL MOVE ON TO QUESTIONS OF LAYOUT AND WE'LL EXPLORE THE CAPABILITIES AND RESTRICTIONS OF CURRENT HTML AND ITS VARIANTS, VISITING TOPICS LIKE:

## Setting up a web of linked pages.

Although you'll often hear people talk about "a home page," any ambitious publishing project is unlikely to be confined to a single page. We'll look at how to break content up and then link it back together in a reasonable fashion. We'll also cover the art of hyperlinking, and the use of templates.

## Creating tables.

While tables are perhaps the best formatting tool available to the Web author, they can be time-consuming to create. The sites listed here offer shortcuts, as well as design tips for using tables effectively.

## Frames.

Frames are the most controversial of Netscape's additions to HTML, and yet there's no denying their popularity among Web authors. We'll look at how and when to get framed, and at some tools that can make the framer's job easier.

## Style sheets.

The most drastic change in HTML to date is the advent of cascading style sheets, which move the language deep into word processor territory. It's hard to find much worthwhile documentation on this subject in print at this point; we'll see if we can do better on-line.

## An all-in-one HTML 3.2+ reference.

Some things still *do* work better on paper than on a computer monitor: long tables that must be referred to frequently, for example.

## HTML tips, tricks, folklore, and acts of desperation.

Here you'll find collections of practical design tips, and caches of stupid Web tricks. We'll also look at some of the most common real-life formatting problems and their solutions.

## Browser-proof HTML.

After all that heady decadence, we'll take an icy plunge into the problems of browser-proofing your Web pages. It's nice to get fan mail from satisfied users of your pages, but it's also nice to avoid hate mail from those who have been blocked out.

**WITH A COMMAND OF BASIC HTML,** you're already fully capable of publishing worthwhile content on the Web. But it's likely that you'll also be interested in exploring the limits of the medium. (In fact, we Web authors often seem more interested in such exploration than in publishing any content at all.)

## SETTING UP A WEB

Terms relating to the Web often seem to be divided between those that are ambiguous and those that are misleading. What should we call a "set of interrelated semi-self-contained pages?" Sometimes I call it a "site"; sometimes I call it a "web." It needs *some* sort of name—after all, it's rare that anyone accomplishes anything halfway ambitious with just one page. For the present chapter, anyway, let's call this group of pages a lowercase "web" (not to be confused with our medium and our distribution mechanism, the capitalized "Web").

When I'm putting content together for the Web, I generally start out by doing all my work in one huge page. As that file develops, I start to see natural fault lines in the material, and then begin sketching out storyboards for the Web. Don't let the "storyboard" jargon scare you off: at this point, a storyboard may consist of nothing more than circles drawn around paragraphs, or lines drawn between paragraphs, with a blobby doodle on the side. (Please keep in mind that "blobby doodle" is a highly technical, advanced HTML sort of term.)

When I have to adapt existing print material to the Web, I go through the same process—only somewhat faster, of course.

Why look for "fault lines" at all? Just as people are more likely to read books and magazines than to read a 500-foot-long broadsheet, they're more likely to react well to comfortably downloadable and screenable chunks of material that are at least as clearly linked as the pages of a book.

In case you need a nontheoretical reason for avoiding long pages, some Web browsers (Netscape Navigator, for instance) do a poor job of handling large documents. Your users may actually face more delays when jumping back and forth within a 100K file than when jumping back and forth between five 20K files.

There's no need to go overboard, though. The logical breaks (e.g., section changes) of a book exist in uneasy tension with the static, physically ordained breaks of pages. (As William Blake and Susan Howe have pointed out, reading a poem on a well-tailored page is completely different from reading a poem that's been randomly sliced by a cookie-cutter page format.) Computer users are comfortable with a reasonable amount of vertical scrolling, which frees the author to emphasize logical breaks in the material. Take advantage of the opportunity, rather than sticking to a rigid "one page = one screen" formula. Few things look more foolish on the Web than the standard newspaper approach of breaking off an article in the middle of a paragraph and appending a "Continued on Next Page" link.

### DIRECTORY STRUCTURE

I recommend keeping related documents in their own directory, with any graphics files in an "images" subdirectory. This lets you use relative URLs to link tightly associated pages, and thus lets you move them as a group without having to edit their links. For example, I once wrote a web for an on-line magazine that later went "off the air"; it was a fairly easy matter for me to then relocate the entire subdirectory to a different account on a different Web server. It also lets you track text files, which tend to be more volatile, separately from non-text media, which tend to need changing less often.

### Default Pages

As mentioned previously, a Web server is likely to have a default filename that it will use when a reader tries to access a directory. It's usually "index.html" or "default.html." Find out what the default filename is, and make sure that the "home page," "welcome page," or "top page" of each of your webs is named appropriately.

### Navigation Aids

Make it easy for readers to maneuver within your web by providing links to top pages within each document.

If there's a natural sequence to the pages, you can go even further and include a mini table of contents as a navigation bar. No need to get fancy with this by using frames or 3-D metallic embossing: the idea of a navigation bar is to provide a convenience to the readers who need it, not to distract from the content.

Pure sequence can be expressed in a simple line of text at the bottom of a page, as seen in this HTML:

```
<P>
<B>
[
<A HREF="index.html">Index</A> |
<A HREF="part1.html">Previous</A> |
<A HREF="part3.html">Next</A>
]
</B>
```

This translates to the following innocuous display:

```
[ Index | Previous | Next ]
```

As a navigation bar for a long essay on three novels by Samuel R. Delany, I constructed the following table within a table. A background color was used to distinguish the navigation bar from the content, while an inner-table boundary was used to distinguish chapter locations in the essay from the relative commands "forward" and "back." The "button" that would normally point to the current page was left unlinked: the color difference between linked and unlinked text is enough to signal to the user that this unlinked button shows their current place in the essay.

```
<TABLE BORDER="0" BGCOLOR=#ff8888>
<TR ALIGN=CENTER VALIGN=MIDDLE>
<FONT SIZE="-1"><TD><A
    HREF="dd0.html">Previous</
    A></TD>
<TD><TABLE BORDER="1">
<TR>
<TD><A
    HREF="dd0.html">Introduction<
    /A></TD>
<TD>Digression</TD>
<TD><A
    HREF="dd2.html"><CITE>Equinox
    </CITE></A></TD>
<TD><A HREF="dd3.html"><CITE>Hogg</
    CITE></A></TD>
<TD><A HREF="dd4.html"><CITE>The
    Mad Man</CITE></A></TD>
<TD><A HREF="dd5.html">Postscript</
    A></TD>
</TR>
</TABLE>
</TD><TD><A HREF="dd2.html">Next</
    A></TD>
</FONT></TR>
</TABLE>
```

### The Self-Linked Page

If your content's natural form is a long but manageable list of extremely short sections (for example, a questions-and-answers page that takes up more than two screens but fewer than twenty), you'll probably want to use anchor tags to tie links into the middle of the page. When you link to these internal anchors, you'll distinguish them from other URLs by prefixing their names with a "#" symbol.

For example, in a corporate site's Q&A sheet, you might attach anchor names to all the real question-and-answer pairs, like this:

```
<A NAME="price">How much does this
thing cost?</A><BR>
Why, almost nothing!<P>
```

Then you'd collect all the questions at the top of the page:

```
<UL>
<LI>How much does this thing <A
      HREF="#price">cost</A>?
<LI>Are you <A
      HREF="#trustme">absolutely</
      A> sure about that?
</UL>
```

When users first encounter this Q&A page, they'll see the list of questions. They can then either jump immediately to the question they're most interested in, or scroll through the whole list sequentially.

If you'd like to link to an internal link from another document, just stick the name of the internal link (prefixed with the magic "#") to the URL of the document that it's in. For example, you might refer back to a question-and-answer pair from a page transcribing an informal speech presented to stockholders:

```
Some of those dad-blamed competitors
have even had the gosh-darned nerve
to tell the press that we're <A
HREF="qanda.html#price">giving
away</A> our product for free. Well,
I'm here to say that
<STRONG>nothing</STRONG> could be
further from the truth.
```

## TEMPLATES

Pages at most Web sites—even personal Web sites—tend to have some elements in common. Even if every visible aspect of your pages varies, all your Web pages must contain the bare-bones structural elements: "<HTML> <HEAD> </HEAD> <BODY> </BODY> </HTML>." Just as businesses tend to use letterhead stationery and boilerplate salutations, Web authors tend to use template files.

If you use an HTML editor, it's likely to have some templates built in. You can choose from these when you create a new document, and you can customize them for your own purposes. (BBEdit's latest set of HTML templates is so ornate that you'll pretty much *have* to customize them just to slim them down!) If you use an HTML converter, many programs will let you specify a template for automatically custom-formatting HTML output from batch operations. Even if you're just banging out HTML in a plain-text editor, you can still gain a little time by starting new documents off with a template file.

Here are some templative ideas:

- An HTML editor will often let you put dynamic elements in the template: automatically inserting the current date, for example, or automatically re-inserting your page's title into the first top-level heading on the page. Check the documentation.

- When I work on a local web of tightly linked pages, I often use a specialized template containing the local navigation aids.

- If you're doing a reference page, or a page which is likely to be bookmarked by readers, it's good to include the last date it was updated on the page. This will let return visitors know quickly whether there's anything new to see.

- It's a good idea to unobtrusively note authorship on each page, usually in a standard footer.

BUILDING BETTER PAGES

# THE ART OF LINKING
## (OR, KIDS POINT TO THE DARNEDEST THINGS)

The same mechanism that lets users browse your work can also let them find their way to non-print media, or to different works altogether. It's as if opening one book could give you access to an entire library. Of course, reading would be a pretty oppressive experience if books *always* felt it necessary to provide access to an entire library, but you should take advantage of the opportunity when your content supports it.

Some practical suggestions for handling external links follow. I should acknowledge that these are the sort of rules that really are made to be broken: I think I've broken each and every one at various times, usually to try for an effect of violated expectations. But it's good to know what the expectations *are* before you try to violate them.

- **Link to the highest level.** You may remember that when a link is broken, the first thing users try is moving to its directory (that is, to the slash in front of the last part of the link). As an author, you can apply the same principle to reduce the possibility of broken links for your users. The top-level directory is less likely to be reorganized or renamed (and thereby break your link) than a file within that directory. Always "link to the slash" if it ends up at a suitable page.

- **Match the wording of the link with the up-front content of the destination.** If the text (or graphic) of your link has nothing in common with the title or headings of the page you're linking to, your readers may wonder if they really chose the right link—or, worse yet, they may wonder if you really knew what you were linking to.

- **Use links sparingly.** An excess of links gives a chaotic, content-thin appearance to a page—unless, of course, it's a directory page! Find the most crucial leads, link to them from your page, and don't repeat the links.

- **Use external links very, very sparingly.** You should show special restraint with links to pages on external sites (i.e., pages that are completely out of your control). As I can attest from painful experience, external links are a maintenance nightmare. They're always breaking, and you're never notified.

- **Keep links concise.** Embed only the most important word or phrase in your anchor tag rather than the whole sentence. A long, straggling link is not only ugly, it's confusing: the user may well wonder if clicking on the last part of the sentence will take them to a different spot than clicking on the first part of the sentence.

- **Avoid the "click here" syndrome.** Since the reader's eyes will be drawn to linked text anyway, there's no need to announce the fact that you're giving them linked text. By the time they reach your page, they've certainly figured out how to follow a link! (There's also the little matter of browsers that don't use mouse-clicks to follow a link: text-based browsers, for example, or some Windows browsers when used in keyboard-only mode.) Instead, try to embed your links gracefully in a natural context. For sequential arrangements, append a discreet navigation aid to your page instead of imitating a sideshow barker: "For the next exciting step on your fabulous journey, all you have to do is click right this way…"

- **Maintain consistency.** If you use the same icon or phrase on most of your pages to link to the same resource—to an "About the Company" page or an e-mail address, for example—don't change it as you create new pages. You may think that the formula is getting boring, but your readers will appreciate the help. Regular visitors will even expect topographical consistency between related pages. Standard navigation aids should stay in the same relative position from page to page instead of making readers go on a hunt. The easiest way to achieve this sort of structural consistency is to use a template when creating your pages.

Most readers will ignore the aesthetic impact, much as we've learned to ignore barcodes.

- Other information in the standard footer might include links to your home page or to your e-mail address, frighten-the-bozos copyright notices, and any special acknowledgments.

- Corporate logos or, heaven help us, advertisements are typically included in a standard header (not to be confused with the HTML tag called "header").

If you'd like to see an example, here's a template I might use for my personal pages:

```
<HTML>
<HEAD>
<TITLE>#TITLE#</TITLE>
</HEAD>
<BODY>

<H1 ALIGN=CENTER>#TITLE#</H1>

#BODYTEXT#

<HR>
<ADDRESS>Copyright 1997 <A
    HREF="http://www.best.com/
    ~raydavis/">Ray Davis</A></
    ADDRESS>
</BODY>
</HTML>
```

"#TITLE#" and "#BODYTEXT#" are keywords used by my HTML editor to dynamically insert my chosen document title and any plain text that I already have in my editor buffer.

Standardized templates save on labor even *after* the pages are created. Boilerplate information is precisely the sort of thing that requires sweeping changes at a moment's notice. Is your e-mail address included? You'll probably be changing accounts

someday. Do you link to a "Company Information" page? Believe me, someone will eventually decree that the company information file must move to a different directory. If every single one of the hundreds of pages on the site use exactly the same bit of HTML to display the boilerplate information, you can fix them in all in one massive, global search-and-replace operation.

> ☞ Your Web server may be able to dynamically insert the contents of header and footer files into your Web pages as they're being served to your readers. This is more work for the server and will slow things down a bit, but if you need even more dynamic control over boilerplate, it's a good way to go. This approach is often used for advertising headers, for example, which need to be rotated or quickly changed.

# SITES FOR WEB-BUILDING

### Composing Good HTML
**http://www.cs.cmu.edu/~tilt/cgh/**
I referred to this same link back in Chapter 1, but the page actually consists of two parts: one on page style, and one on constructing a web. I wish Eric Tilton had followed his own good advice and split the two chapters into at least two Web pages, allowing me to point you directly to the right place, and preventing me from suffering through a 94K download every time I visit his page. It's worth the wait, just don't use it as a template.

### HTML Grinder
**http://www.matterform.com/grinder/**
One of the few Web authoring tools specifically designed for web-building (as opposed to page editing, site management, or server-side programming), MatterForm's Macintosh-only HTML Grinder is actually a series of task-specific tools, each of which can be purchased separately for $15 each; a full set of 19 tools costs $149. Tools

include global search-and-replace, insertion of text in specially tagged areas (such as "Author"), generation of navigation lists and "Next Page/Previous Page" links, generation of a table of contents that points to internal anchors, date maintenance, and a utility to automatically change links to a file at the same time as you change its name to an "8.3" DOS-type file name from a Macintosh file name.

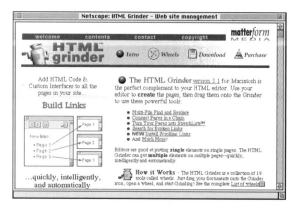

## Perl HTML utilities

**http://www.oac.uci.edu/indiv/ehood/ perlWWW/html/**

This site collects Perl programs that process HTML documents. If you have a lot of Web pages to coordinate and you're comfortable using a Unix account to do it, these programs could save you some time. Besides preprocessors and fillers-in, the list includes a few HTML validators. (By the way, if you're interested in the "processed HTML" route, be sure to check out the list of HTML converters in Chapter 2: "plain text" converters can offer superb template-plus control of the Web pages they produce.)

## A Taxonomy of Tags

**http://www.vuw.ac.nz/~gnat/ideas/html-style.html**

A somewhat dry but worthwhile meditation on how Web authors should handle linking from text.

## Template Technique

**http://www.december.com/html/tech/ template.html**

Part of John December's excellent "HTML Station" site, this page provides the most detailed discussion of HTML templates I've seen. December eventually went from using templates to using programs that automatically generate finished HTML pages, complete with easily changeable standard headers, footers, and formatting, from a directory full of document "bodies." When a template part has to change across his entire site, he simply runs the program and re-generates the finished files.

## Web Development

**http://www.december.com/web/develop.html**

John December walks through his approach to web creation in these pages. Although presented in slide-show-style high-level summaries, his advice is always sound—and given the endless adolescence of most Web advisors, the managerial tone may even seem like a breath of fresh air. The site is itself an excellent example of a tightly linked web. Check out those navigation aids running along the left margin, and see how well the pages adapt to different resolutions and window sizes. Then look at some of the work that went into the site: December uses the development of the "Web Development" web itself as an example of the process it describes! Yes, like the mighty buffalo, every part of this site can be put to good use.

### Yale Style Manual: Site Design

**http://info.med.yale.edu/caim/manual/sites/ site_design.html**

The Yale C/AIM WWW Style Manual previously referenced is undergoing an extensive revision. As this book was being written, this background section was under construction but still apropos. By the way, the full sites of both the original version and the new version of the Yale Style Manual are highly recommended to anyone who wants to understand site and web design: the approach to individual pages is thoroughly informed by sitewide considerations.

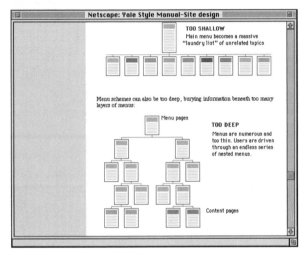

# CREATING TABLES

In the early days of HTML authoring, there was no decent way to deal with tabular data (or, in the vernacular, "rows" and "columns"). We made do either with ugly "preformatted" typewriter-style hand-spaced sections, or with large graphics that contained snapshots of tables from word processor documents.

Thus there was much rejoicing when browsers finally implemented tables as specified in HTML 2.0. But there was an unexpected bonus to this support, a CEO-worth bonus even richer than the bounty it accompanied: HTML tables weren't just a way to look at spreadsheet data. Since they could hold virtually any HTML display element, including graph-

ics, tables could also serve as layout grids. And if you disabled borders on a table, it could serve as an *invisible* layout grid.

But wait, there's more! Despite the best efforts by print-obsessed authors to ignore its capabilities, HTML's peculiar strengths lie in its dynamic adaptability: HTML documents can be adjusted automatically to deal with differences in font, font size, resolution, and window size. The use of relative and percentage-based table measurements brought this same adaptability to table support. For the first time—not just the first time in HTML, but for the first time in any publishing medium—designers had been given a way to handle fairly complex layout tasks in a simple, truly device-independent fashion! Compared to HTML table-based layout, most "portable electronic documents" might as well have been scanned in from paper pages.

Can you tell that I'm a tables fan? I've gotten out of any number of layout jams with their help. I've printed comic strips, indented text, captioned pictures and randomized cut-ups, and built them into billboards, navigation bars, and even actual tables. Of course, nothing's perfect: tables can be a bit cumbersome to make, they don't show up nicely at all on the text-only browser Lynx, not all browsers can handle complicated tables (particularly nested tables), and… well, I guess other than that, they *are* perfect.

Pairing up all the tags that go into a table can be painfully time-consuming, and for complex layout tasks, you'll almost always want to take the HTML reins yourself. Luckily, there are ways to jump-start your table creation: online services for converting tab-delimited or comma-delimited data to HTML tables, HTML editors with built-in table-makers, and downloadable software programs that convert text, spreadsheet or word processing tables to HTML. Editors and some converters were covered in Chapter 2; below I list a few special-purpose tools.

## ANATOMY OF A TABLE

An HTML table is declared by the "<TABLE>" tag and ends, naturally, with the closing tag "</TABLE>." It consists of a series of table rows (declared, naturally, by the "<TR>...</TR>" pair), each of which contains table cells (declared by the "<TD>...</TD>" pair, where "TD" stands, naturally, for "Table Data... uh... cell"). Note that columns are *not* explicitly declared, nor are the numbers of rows and columns. This makes it a lot easier to change tables on the fly, and it also makes it a lot easier to accidentally wreck a table in subtle and mystifying ways.

☞ Probably my favorite personal "stupid Web trick" discovery has been that you can use tables to mimic a variety of comic-strip formats. (I had already seen the table trick that lets you place text within graphics, and that probably tipped me off.) Of course, it's possible that you have no desire to mimic a comic-strip layout in HTML (it takes all kinds, I suppose), but if nothing else, this is an example of how to approach an adventure in adaptable layouts.

The basic comic-strip construct uses one table without visible borders to lay out the artwork and text, and surrounds it with another table that has borders and a caption to supply the comic-strip frame.

A wide variety of dynamically adaptable layouts are possible in the inner table. Generally, I use two rows, with text (or "speech balloons") in the top row and graphics in the bottom row. The graphics always start as one image file, but were cut up into pieces as needed to align the text, and then glued back together by specifying no space between table cells. The text would then be vertically aligned to the bottom of its row, so as to jam against the graphics; each text cell would be horizontally aligned to distinguish it clearly from the other "speech balloons." Variations on this formula might include breaking up a row of graphics with a tall speech balloon, or allowing the graphics and text to spread dynamically to match the width of the window.

Here's a sample of the canonical comic strip layout, with text on top and graphics on the bottom:

```
<TABLE BORDER
CELLSPACING=0><TR><TD>
<TABLE BORDER=0 CELLPADDING=0
     CELLSPACING=0>
<TR VALIGN=BOTTOM>
<TD>"What're <B>you</B> laughing
     at, Peter Pan?"</TD>
```

```
<TD> </TD>
<TD ALIGN=RIGHT><B>"White Power!
     <BR>White Power!"</B></TD>
</TR>
<TR>
<TD><IMG SRC="images/wepeter.gif"
     WIDTH="212" HEIGHT="193"></
     TD>
<TD><IMG SRC="images/
     weslouch.gif" WIDTH="104"
     HEIGHT="200"></TD>
<TD VALIGN=TOP><IMG SRC="images/
     wepower.gif" WIDTH="141"
     HEIGHT="179"></TD>
</TABLE>
</TD></TR><CAPTION
     ALIGN=TOP><B>... & where I
     can find enticingly altered
     echoes of the redneck
     xenophobia which sweetened my
     youth.</B></CAPTION>
</TABLE>
```

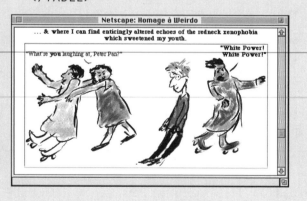

There's also a "<CAPTION>...</CAPTION>" pair, which horizontally centers its contents above or below the table, depending on how you set its "ALIGN" attribute. Finally, there's a "<TH>...</TH>" pair ("TH" for table header), which is nothing but a convenient shortcut to put a centered table cell in boldface.

That's it for the table-specific tags. Not too complicated so far, but the tag attributes *really* dance this mess around. These attributes allow table cells to cross row or column boundaries, and let them direct vertical and horizontal placement of content within a cell, table and cell widths (expressed in number of pixels or as a percentage of available space), borders, spacing, and background colors. Virtually any attribute can be applied to any table tag; virtually anything can be included in a table cell, including another table.

The browser is expected to negotiate all these instructions, plus the widths and heights of the actual table cell contents, and then produce something reasonable —amazingly, the browser usually succeeds.

To find out how you can get in on this deal, check the links below.

## Creating Killer Web Sites: Tables Tutorial

**http://www.killersites.com/tutorial/index.html**
David Siegel's table tutorial is useful and considerably more restrained than much of his Web writing, although his trademark "single pixel" may make a few too many unnecessary appearances and the villainy of borders may be a bit overstated. Given his print background, it's not surprising that Siegel prefers exact positioning of elements on a page—whether the user is set up to see them or not—rather than the user-relative placement favored by myself and other on-line-oriented authors. Despite those caveats, this is a very well-designed introduction.

## Design Ideas for HTML Tables

**http://www.botany.hawaii.edu/tables/**
At this friendly site you'll find a gallery of sample table designs, some icons well-suited to typical table applications, a short and simple tutorial, and a list of table-related links and books.

## Excel 5.0 to HTML Table Converter

**http://rs712b.gsfc.nasa.gov/704/dgd/xl2html.html**
This page's author, Jordan Evans, is distributing his innovative Excel macro for converting Excel spreadsheets to tables for Web pages as freeware. It has been tested on Windows 3.1, Windows 95, and Macintosh systems. Instructions for installing the macro are on the site.

## Instant Tables

**http://www.twoclicks.com/cgi-bin/tabdemo.pl**
This page lets you cut and paste a spreadsheet or tab-delimited data right into an interactive form, which will then convert it into a table for a Web. Save the source, and you're off to a good start. The immensely detailed form lets you specify background colors in cells, text color, table height and width, and a host of other HTML attributes. Another helpful option lets you see what your table will look like to users whose browsers don't support tables.

## Internet Assistant for Microsoft Excel

**http://www.microsoft.com/msexcel/Internet/IA/**
This site is the home page for downloading Internet Assistant for Microsoft Excel, a free add-on for converting data from Excel spreadsheets to tables in Web pages.

## NCSA Mosaic Tables Tutorial

**http://www.ncsa.uiuc.edu/SDG/Software/Mosaic/Tables/tutorial.html**
Despite the title, this tables tutorial is a good starting point for all Web designers, not just Mosaic users. It offers friendly analogies, descriptions of all table tags and attributes, plus good WYSIWYG examples of HTML table coding.

### The Table Sampler
**http://home.netscape.com/assist/net_sites/ table_sample.html**

This tutorial-by-example site is maintained by Netscape. It includes straightforward (if uninspired) examples of the variations achieved by merging cells, changing the border thickness or cell-padding, or tweaking other table attributes. If you're creating an HTML table from scratch for the first time, one of the very simple examples here may be useful as a template.

### Table Tutor
**http://junior.apk.net/~jbarta/tutor/ tables**

This is a low-pressure, down-to-earth set of lessons for creating HTML tables; your teacher is folksy Joe Barta. Excellent examples of layouts more complex than those you'll usually find in a tutorial are joined with much clearer explanations than you'll usually find anywhere. You'll also get plenty of opportunities to be easily amused along with Joe: I especially appreciated the Steven Wright quote. The tutorial is available for downloading in ZIP format. "Learn in the comfort and privacy of your own home. No salesman will visit."

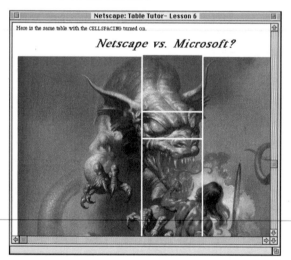

### TableMaker
**http://www.missouri.edu/ ~wwwtools/tablemaker/**

At this site, you'll find a quick-and-easy tool for designing tables online. If you find keeping track of <TR> and <TD> tags a laborious chore, this will likely be a time-saver. There's a comprehensive set of instructions for designing both simple and complex tables. In addition to the Web version, the site makes available a downloadable copy of the program for Macintosh users.

### Tablemaquia
**http://www.absurd.org/absurd/tablemaquia/**

An utterly lunatic parody-*cum*-stress-test of HTML tables, using browsers the same way a cancer researcher uses lab rats. The text is written in a catchy indeterminately-Middle-European mad-scientist tone; the design is surprisingly beautiful. If this site didn't cure me of using tables for layouts, nothing will.

### Testing Tables
**http://www.crc.ricoh.com/~marcush/ tables.html**

Marcus Hennecke's no-nonsense page points out some problems and inconsistencies with the way a variety of browsers handle table layouts. It's an excellent sanity check when you're stymied by a complex format that just isn't showing up right: it might not be your fault; it might be the browser's. (Of course, that's small consolation, since you'll probably have to change your approach to something that *does* work on the browser. But at least you'll have the satisfaction of knowing that it wasn't your fault!)

# FRAMES

*"I think I'm in a frame."*
*"Don't sound like you."*
*"I don't know. All I can see is the frame."*
—*Robert Mitchum and cabbie,*
*"Out of the Past"*

Frames are an HTML construct invented by Netscape. You can employ frames to embed multiple HTML files in a single browser window. Usually the HTML embedded in one frame will have its links directed to fill another frame, so that instead of getting the illusion of traveling from one place to another, you get an illusion of advancing a slide projector.

Very few Web pundits will say a good word about frames. On the other hand, when you actually browse the Web, it's almost impossible to avoid frames: new sites every day seem to be overhauling their interface to jump on the bandwagon. Why the gap between theory and practice?

Simple: *Frames are a bad solution to a real problem.* It doesn't matter how many times someone tells you that a solution is bad. If it's the only solution that's available, you'll take it. I have to admit that another factor may be the deep-rooted human instinct that tells us to jump whenever we see a bandwagon, but there is a legitimate problem that frames are trying to deal with.

For once, the problem was not reproducing print layouts in a computer-oriented display. The problem was one that could only arise on a computer: How do Web authors make self-contained, interdependent displays that are concurrently visible? Or, to put it in more familiar terms, how do Web authors make windows? There was no provision in HTML

for anything other than a "one document = one display" equation, but software engineers and users are used to having a bit more freedom than that.

Netscape came up with a half-assed solution, but at least it tried to come up with a solution. Its programmers decided to take the Microsoft Windows approach, in which an application has one big window but can control multiple sub-windows within its own territory, as opposed to the Macintosh approach of completely free-floating windows.

That was certainly a legitimate decision, but then they didn't follow through. Rather than make "real" windows with help from the operating system, Netscape's engineers reinvented *part* of the functionality of windows all by themselves. Frames are unmovable windows without menu bars or clear resize handles. And here our problems begin.

- It shouldn't have surprised anyone that many window toolbar and menu items actually make reference to the contents of a window. Without that window context, frame users (and Netscape engineers) weren't sure how to move forward and backward, or how to view source, or how to bookmark the current location, or how to examine session history or even how to load images; I notice that image loading on framed pages is still broken in Netscape 3.01.

- Without a button to close frames and without clear resizing handles, layouts cannot be adapted to the user's set-up or to the contents of the page. For example, a horizontal frame that holds an advertisement or a navigation bar will slice a long skinny page in the other frame (such as the text of HotWired's "Flux" column or www.suck.com) down to a mere sliver of content.

- Because all the framed pieces of the browser window must be fixed and rectangular, frames end up squandering display space, and trying to use more than two usually makes your page look like a Mondrian painting, without the color sense. Even if your simple navigation toolbar manages to fill up all of the left-hand side of the browser window instead of just one quarter of the left-hand side, it's still a left-hand side effectively wasted for any reader more interested in the contents of the page than in navigating.

- Since the browser isn't getting help from the windowing operating system to handle all this, there are now *two* pieces of software trying to manage windows on the user's computer—and managing windows is not a terribly simple process. It's no coincidence that the Netscape Navigator started gobbling memory and crashing frequently at around the same time frames were introduced.

---

BUILDING BETTER PAGES

# FRAMES AND THE FRAME-FREE BROWSER

When you do use frames, always provide a no-frames alternative. This used to be important because only one browser supported frames and you didn't want to leave users of all the other browsers staring at a blank screen. Not if you wanted to make friends, anyway. Now that more browsers support frames, it's still important to provide an alternative, since many of us in the Web audience have had time to figure out that we're usually better off without them. (I often end up dragging the page displayed in a frame into a new browser window, just to be able to read it more easily—Microsoft's frame-o-rama Internet Explorer site is a major culprit at the moment.)

Providing a frameless document is easy enough to do:

**1** Append the following HTML to your frames page, between the closing "</FRAMESET>" tag and the closing "</HTML>" tag:

```
<BODY>
</BODY>
```

Frames-aware browsers will ignore any content after the last frame set is closed; non-frames-aware browsers will ignore anything in the frame set. (I do not recommend using the official Netscape mechanism, the "<NOFRAMES>" tag, since it supposedly must be included inside a frame set—and therefore should be ignored by non-frames-aware browsers!)

**2** Copy the contents of the pages that are displayed in the frames. Paste them into the body area of a new frameless HTML document. Arrange nicely. (Since frames provide limited layout control, it's not hard to meet or surpass them in a frameless document!)

**3** Change the links in the frameless document to remove all "TARGET" attributes that refer to frames. You can leave in any that refer to windows, of course.

**4** Test rigorously.

**5** Now that you have your frameless version ready, you can also help out readers who are stuck with older or more HTML-standard browsers: Copy everything in the body of your new document into the post-frames body section of your frames document.

**6** Finally, advertise your frameless version in a suitable spot within your framed version.

Is this a nuisance? Yes, especially if you have to update the top-level framed documents often, since you will have to update three copies: the file that is displayed inside a frame, the frameless file, and the non-frames-browser part of the top-level frames page! But your readers will be grateful.

Incidentally, life for the careful framer should be a little easier as it becomes possible to embed HTML documents *without* using the frames interface—keep your eye on upcoming changes to HTML!

Those are the cons to using frames. Here are the pros:

- There's nothing better available.

Even now, the only other way for a Web author to create a new window is to use JavaScript, which many readers either don't have access to or will have disabled. And JavaScript-created windows are Macintosh-style, not Microsoft-Windows-style; for many purposes, they're too independent, not closely enough tied to the page that created them. For example, I always disable JavaScript before visiting the HotWired site: otherwise I end up with a floating navigation window that is not only useless for me as a reader—I'm almost always going to the site to seek out the newest material rather than to conduct a comprehensive investigation—but that also lingers on long after I've left HotWired behind.

There are some good reasons to avoid frames, and for the most part, I've managed to avoid them, even for navigation aids. (Readers are more likely to navigate out of a page in the first screen and more likely to leave your site entirely than to use a navigation aid—so why permanently sacrifice valuable screen real estate to a special frame?) But the couple of times that I've had "sources" and "destinations" that really did seem to belong on the screen together rather than in different screens, I went ahead and used frames to implement the pages.

Once you understand the pros and cons, you might as well use them, too—but keep on the lookout for them to be replaced by (or to evolve into) something better. Microsoft's recent introduction of "floating frames" at least addresses the Mondrianizing problem, and we might still eventually get access to content-sensitive windows that can be resized and repositioned.

If that sounds naïve, reflect that server-side imagemaps, which we'll get to in a later chapter, were a *horrendously* bad solution to a real problem, and that

their popularity eventually led to their being made obsolete by a much better solution. I'm hoping that will happen again.

In the meantime, here are some sites to help the framer out.

### The Art of Frames

**http://www.spunwebs.com/sites2c/ frmtutor.html**

This is probably the best of the single-page tutorials. Tables are used to illustrate points in a clear but extremely concise way. The page also includes some templates, and a nice collection of examples.

### Frames—An Introduction

**http://home.netscape.com/assist/net_sites/ frames.html**

The official word from Netscape Corporation, although, as usual it hasn't bothered to keep the document up to date: only the frame attributes present in the first release of a frames-knowledgeable browser are mentioned. To learn about later additions, you must rummage through release notes.

### Frames Decoder

**http://www.teleport.com/~cooler/frames/ decoder.html**

Frames Decoder is an on-line service that generates HTML code for a frames-based page, based on your

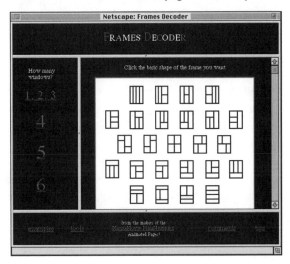

choice of templates. The diagram-based selection goes surprisingly quickly, and the pages are nicely laid out.

### Frames Made Easy

**http://www.ibic.com:80/NIndex/Frames/ EZHome.html**

This unpretentious frames-based page simply steps you through a working example: the creation of the tutorial document itself.

### FrameShop

**http://www.missouri.edu/~wwwtools/ frameshop/**

A slightly overwhelming on-line form that will create the HTML for a frames page. Wildly popular, but I wish it used some sensible default values; as it is, I felt as if I were doing about as much typing as I would have in an HTML editor.

### Framing the Web

**http://www.webreference.com/dev/frames/**

Here you can find an article extensively covering the first version of frames (pre-Netscape-3.0). I especially appreciated the unusually to-the-point use of graphics.

### HTML 3.2 and Netscape 3.0: Frames

**http://webreference.com/html3andns/ frame.html**

This is a nice overview from the Webreference site. Plenty of pointers to working examples are supplied.

### I Hate Frames!

**http://www.projectcool.com/focus/html/sb-09-09-96.html**

Last time I looked, Yahoo! listed eleven sites whose sole purpose was to attack frames, one of which promised to crash my browser. I didn't check that particular link out, but given the amount of venom that frames receive, I would be remiss if I didn't try to expose you to at least one anti-frame statement. This one, by Steve Berlin, gets credit for arguing the point (albeit arguing it loudly), rather than just repeating the words "suck" and "lame" in various font sizes.

### <IFRAME>, I Saw, I Conquered

**http://www.webmonkey.com/webmonkey/ html/96/37/index2a.html**

From HotWired's WebMonkey site, this is one of the few non-Microsoft pages devoted to the floating frames introduced in Internet Explorer 3.0.

### Jumping Out of the Window

**http://www.uni-muenster.de/WiWi/home/ rentmei/html/frames.html**

Presented here is an almost farcically exhaustive list of techniques to keep your HTML from unintentionally embedding a linked page into your frames, perhaps the most common mistake made by frames-using authors.

### THE Netscape Frames Tutorial

**http://www.newbie.net/frames/**

The title is not vainglorious: Charlton Rose has written the best introduction to frames you'll find, beating out the corporate areas of both Netscape and Microsoft. Lessons include basic layouts, the tricky subject of targeting frames and windows, a thorough reference, and even some fairly critical notes on the less useful aspects of Netscape's implementation. My only regret is that it's missing any information on Microsoft's floating frames and embedded objects tags, both of which achieve some of the same benefits as frames and eliminate some of the problems.

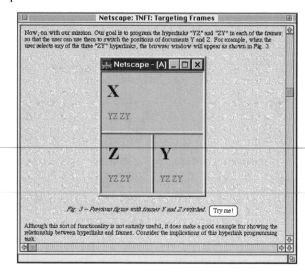

# STYLE SHEETS

Before HTML was anything else, it was a standard. As a standard, it emphasized two factors:

1  **Flexibility.** An HTML document should make sense on any computer platform with any user set-up, including not only text-only displays, but even non-visual displays, i.e., read-outs by speech generators.

2  **Ease of implementation.** It shouldn't be unduly expensive to write a Web browser.

What a difference a little fabulous success can make.

1  As commercial publications, their designers, and their WYSIWYG editing software moved to the Web, flexibility became far less interesting than precise control of layout.

2  As commercial software companies moved to the Web, easy implementation of browsers became far less interesting than establishing a competitive advantage.

Put those two trends together, and you end up with HTML 1997: the original markup language has combined in unpredictable ways with a bizarrely miscellaneous collection of whatever new layout instructions a particular browser manufacturer could come up with at a particular time.

At first, the World Wide Web Consortium (or "W3C," the Web standards organization) tried to maintain a stand-offish stance toward the commercial browsers' tag proliferation. Very much to their credit, its members soon realized that this wasn't going to make their labors particularly useful to real-world Web authors and users, and they re-directed their energies toward reaching two, more practical goals: negotiating a cross-browser standard that incorporated the most popular commercial innovations, and coming up with a long-term solution to the conflict between flexibility and control. The result of the first effort has been the HTML 3.2 standard; the result of the second is called "cascading style sheets."

The new style-sheet standard is an attempt to separate all "tight control" layout features into an integrated set of style properties, eliminating any need for ad hoc HTML tags and attributes such as "<FONT>," "<BIG>," "COLOR," and "SPACER." (As a special enticement, new layout features that no browsers have yet come up with are included as style-sheet properties: for example, "z-levels," the ability to layer one page element on top of another.)

This lets Web authors make their basic HTML truly cross-platform again by maintaining any special formatting instructions both inside and outside the document. Templates that maintain a consistent look across a site are directly and cleanly supported. And since the style-sheet model is well-established in word processing software, the lucrative commercial quasi-WYSIWYG editors should have no trouble adapting to it.

The "cascading" part of cascading style sheets attempts to resolve the continuing battle between Web users who know what they want, and Web authors who assume that users want to (and are able to) see exactly what the Web authors are seeing. Style-sheet properties can be specified by code within the page itself, by a site-wide style sheet outside the page or by the users themselves. The negotiation rules are fairly complex, but at least they're clearly written out! Especially friendly Web authors can even offer their readers a choice of style sheets to apply to the same basic document—although it's easy to picture that feature getting a bit out of control: "Let's see, should I choose the framed page, or the non-framed page, or the framed page optimized for Windows 3.1, or the framed page with corroded typewriter fonts and crumpled paper backgrounds, or…"

In fact, the only real objection that can be raised against style sheets is that they make it so easy to go overboard. Some of the example pages out there make me think of Sandra Bernhard in Scorsese's "King of Comedy": "Don't you want to go crazy? My doctor says I'm not allowed to go crazy, he says I have to stay calm—but *let's just go crazy!*"

Even "restrained" use of style sheets is not necessarily a good idea. I noticed that some of Microsoft's own style-sheet tutorials didn't display properly on Microsoft's own browser, and the larger font sizes looked unpleasantly jaggy as compared to anti-aliased graphics. But W3C didn't *make* the coffee, its members just woke up and smelled it. Given the immense pressure on Web authors to go overboard, style sheets may be the best possible response.

By the way, well-conceived though they are, cascading style sheets don't eliminate *all* the layout problems facing Web authors:

- Templates or dynamically generated pages are still needed to standardize elements displayed on the page, such as headers, footers, and navigation aids. Style sheets only specify how elements should be represented (such as background and font colors); they're incapable of specifying the elements themselves.

- For similar reasons, style sheets do nothing to solve the frames problem.

- Tables are still the easiest way to handle grid layout by hand. (However, I see that there's a pending proposal that would let Web authors use style properties to specify the exact placement of elements on a Web page, and I'd assume that WYSIWYG editing tools would jump at the chance to implement it.)

### Between the Style Sheets
**http://webreview.com/96/11/08/feature/**
From Web Review comes this excellent overview of style sheets, their history, and their place in the browser wars.

### Cascading Style Sheets Gallery
**http://www.microsoft.com/truetype/css/ gallery/entrance.htm**
Boy, give typographers an inch and they'll use it to hang themselves… This "alternative" Microsoft style-sheet gallery, downloadable font collection, and demo depot comes courtesy of the company's digital typography department, whose enthusiasm and ingenuity are more than commendable. If you want to see just how close style-sheet-enhanced Web pages can come to *Mondo 2000*-esque "more illegible than you'll ever be" design, this should be your first stop. And the pages are *really* mind-blowing if you look at them in a browser that *doesn't* support style sheets! Take a look at the figures below for a quick comparison. Just take a few more drags on the blunt and it'll all come into focus…

Sample style sheet page, with style sheets enabled

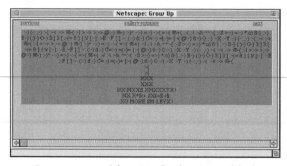

Same page, without style sheets enabled

## Cascading Style Sheets, Level 1

**http://www.w3.org/pub/WWW/TR/REC-CSS1**

The full official documentation of the cascading style sheets standard can be found here. It's a long download, but also absolutely essential at this point. If you're interested in using style sheets, you might as well keep a local copy of this around for reference.

## CSS1 Support in Microsoft Internet Explorer 3.0

**http://www.shadow.net/~braden/nostyle/**

Microsoft deserves credit for providing the first non-Unix browsers with cascading style sheet support, but it brought out its browsers before the standard was complete. As a result, there are some gaps and bugs in Internet Explorer 3.0's handling of style sheets. This valuable site points to documentation of those problems for both the Windows and Macintosh versions of Internet Explorer.

## D.J. Quad's Ultimate Style Sheets Tutorial

**http://www.quadzilla.com/stylesheets/**

I'm usually fairly resistant to D.J. Quad's modem-crushing approach to reference sites, but this is a good one-page overview, with an excellent quick reference table of common style-sheet properties.

## Microsoft Style Sheets Gallery

**http://www.microsoft.com/gallery/files/styles/**

Here, Microsoft supplies a long list of downloadable sample style sheets, illustrated by such typical examples of Web publishing as corporate reports, jeans advertisements, and a UFO newsletter. There's also a list of "showcase sites," non-Microsoft areas that show up well on Internet Explorer.

## Quick Reference to Cascading Style Sheets

**http://www.cwi.nl/~steven/www/css1-qr.html**

The most condensed index of style-sheet properties is this one, though I wish it also included the keywords used to *apply* the properties.

## Style Sheets Guide

**http://www.eskimo.com/~bloo/html/style/css1.htm**

Here's a nice overview and reference from the Index Dot Html site, written with more straightforward common sense than usual. A good FAQ and detailed documentation of tags, attributes, and properties round things off.

## A User's Guide to Style Sheets

**http://www.microsoft.com/workshop/author/howto/css.htm**

Microsoft's own style-sheet guide, oriented toward the beta release of Internet Explorer 3.0. While it's already slightly out of date, it's still one of the most extensive introduction-and-reference combinations available, with an excellent quick reference table of style properties.

## WDG: Cascading Style Sheets

**http://www.htmlhelp.com/reference/css/**

The Web Design Group provides what's probably the best single current source of information on style sheets. This site includes introductory overviews, a tutorial, reference material, and even an article on the misuse of style sheets. (Didn't take long, did it?)

### The WDVL: Cascading Style Sheets for the WWW

**http://WWW.Stars.com/Authoring/Style/Sheets/**

A frothy, enthusiastic introduction, with a few examples and a lightweight tutorial. Not a bad starting place, and the example page is pretty amusing when viewed with a small window or a non-style-sheet browser.

### Web Style Sheets

**http://www.w3.org/pub/WWW/Style/**

The official home page for HTML style sheets is located at the site of their originators, good old W3C (the World Wide Web Consortium). As expected, you get access to official documentation, historical background, and upcoming possible standards (the last time I checked, W3C had just put up a proposal for exact positioning of elements along the x, y *and* z axes of a Web page). But the site also supplies pointers to style sheet news, reviews and other external links.

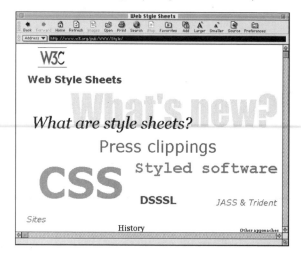

### What's Wrong With FONT?

**http://www.mcsr.olemiss.edu/%7Emudws/font.html**

Convincing arguments are presented herein about why Web authors should use cascading style sheets instead of the <FONT> tag when they want special text effects.

# AN ALL-IN-ONE HTML REFERENCE

Unlike many other references, Table 3.1 segregates those tags included only in the discarded HTML 3.0 standard, most of which were never implemented by any browser and have been replaced by style-sheet properties. Instead, it details only those tags that are in HTML 3.2 or that have recently been added by Netscape or Microsoft.

**Table 3.1: HTML Tag Reference**

| Tag Name | Syntax | Description |
| --- | --- | --- |
| **Structural Tags** | | |
| Color | "#ffffff" or "colorname" | A color, either specified as hexadecimal digits ("00" to "ff") for amounts of red-green-blue, or as one of "Aqua," "Black," "Blue," "Fuchsia," "Gray," "Green,""Lime," "Maroon," "Navy," "Olive," "Purple," "Red," "Silver," "Teal," and "White" |
| Comment | <!-- text --> | Undisplayed text, sometimes used for special purposes by specific servers or browsers |
| Body | <BODY>...</BODY> | Encloses all displayable parts of the document |
| Body Background Color | <BODY BGCOLOR="color">...</BODY> | Sets background color of page |
| Body Background Image | <BODY BACKGROUND="url">...</BODY> | Tiles background with specified image file |

## Table 3.1: HTML Tag Reference (Continued)

| Tag Name | Syntax | Description |
|---|---|---|
| Body Background Watermark | `<BODY BACKGROUND="`*url*`" BGPROPERTIES="FIXED">...</BODY>` | Keeps background image in same screen position as page scrolls (Microsoft only) |
| Body Margins | `<BODY LEFTMARGIN="`*pixels*`" TOPMARGIN="`*pixels*`">...</BODY>` | Sets left and top margins for the page (Microsoft only) |
| Body Text Colors | `<BODY TEXT="`*color*`" LINK="`*color*`" ALINK="`*color*`" VLINK="`*color*`">...</BODY>` | Sets default colors for normal text, unvisited links, active (selected) links and visited links |
| Center | `<CENTER>...</CENTER>` | Horizontally centers the contained material |
| Division | `<DIV ALIGN="`*horizontalAlignment*`" LANG="`*ISOlanguage*`">...</DIV>` | Starts a new section of the document; language can be set using a standard ISO abbreviation |
| Head | `<HEAD>...</HEAD>` | Non-displaying information about the entire document; must precede the body |
| HTML | `<HTML>...</HTML>` | Identifies the document as HTML; should be the first and last lines of the file |
| Marquee | `<MARQUEE ALIGN="`*imgStyleAlignment*`" BEHAVIOR="`*behavior*`" BGCOLOR="`*color*`" DIRECTION="`*LEFTorRIGHT*`" HEIGHT="`*pixelsOrPercentage*`" HSPACE="`*pixels*`" LOOP="`*number*`" SCROLLAMOUNT="`*pixels*`" SCROLLDELAY="`*milliseconds*`" VSPACE="`*pixels*`" WIDTH="`*pixelsOrPercentage*`">`*text*`</MARQUEE>` | Displays an automatically scrolling bar of text; scroll behavior can be "SCROLL" (scroll on and then off screen), "SLIDE" (don't scroll off-screen), or "ALTERNATE" (bounce back and forth); if LOOP is set to "INFINITE" or -1, then the scroll is repeated indefinitely; SCROLLAMOUNT is the distance between repeats of the text; SCROLLDELAY is the delay between repeats (Microsoft only) |
| Multicolumn | `<MULTICOL COLS="`*numberOfColumns*`" GUTTER="`*pixels*`" WIDTH="`*pixels*`">...</MULTICOL>` | Lays out material in multiple columns, all the same width; the gutter between columns usually defaults to 10 |
| Paragraph | `<P ALIGN="`*horizontalAlignment*`" NOWRAP>...</P>` | Formats a paragraph; "NOWRAP" specifies that text should only break when an explicit line-break tag is encountered |

### Undisplayed Non-Body Tags

| Tag Name | Syntax | Description |
|---|---|---|
| Base URL | `<BASE HREF="`*url*`">` | Redefines starting point of relative URLs; must be in document head |
| Is Index | `<ISINDEX PROMPT="`*text*`" HREF="`*url*`">` | Declares that the document is actually a searchable index; any link to this document will prompt the user and then pass the result on to the document again, or to the other URL if one is specified; must be in document head |
| Meta | `<META HTTP-EQUIV="`*HTTPfieldName*`" NAME="`*description*`" CONTENT="`*fieldValue*`">` | Assigns values to special document-wide variables, which will be added to the fields sent by the Web server and can be used by the browser |
| Meta: Content Keywords | `<META NAME="keywords" CONTENT="`*word1,word2...*`">` | Keywords that are often indexed by search engines (Non-3.2) |

**Table 3.1: HTML Tag Reference (Continued)**

| Tag Name | Syntax | Description |
|---|---|---|
| Meta: Character Set | `<META HTTP-EQUIV="Content-type" CONTENT="characterSetDescription">` | Sets character set for document; description is in form "text/html; charset=ISOdescription" (Non-3.2) |
| Meta: Client Refresh | `<META HTTP-EQUIV="Refresh" CONTENT="seconds" URL="linkToGoTo">` | Requests the browser to automatically refresh this document or go to a different URL after a certain number of seconds (Non-3.2) |
| Meta: Document Description | `<META NAME="description" CONTENT="text">` | Describes what the page is about; often passed to readers by search engines (Non-3.2) |
| Meta: Language | `<META HTTP-EQUIV="Content-language" CONTENT="languageCode">` | Gives language and dialect of document for benefit of servers and browsers, which can then negotiate a link on the basis of preferred language (Non-3.2) |
| Special Built-In Links | `<LINK REL="relationship" HREF="url" TITLE="suggestedTitle" TYPE="optionalType" >` | Identifies special links for the document, for example, for navigation-toolbar software; relationships might include "Next," "Previous," and "Home"; previously not much used by browsers, but a particularly important relationship is "StyleSheet," whose URL points to the preferred style sheet for the current document and whose type should be set to "text/css" |
| Special Built-In Links | `<LINK REV="relationshipBeingReversed" HREF="url" TITLE="suggestedTitle">` | The other end of the special document-wide relationships |
| Script | `<SCRIPT LANGUAGE="scriptingLanguage">scriptStatements</SCRIPT>` | Denotes embedded programming code; can be included in the document head rather than the body; code should be embedded in a comment tag so that it does not display as text on browsers that do not interpret the code; the only scripting language accepted by Netscape is "JavaScript;" Microsoft also accepts "VBScript" (Non-3.2) |
| Title | `<TITLE>text</TITLE>` | Title of document; usually displayed with browser window and in history listings; default bookmark name; common search field |

**Text Formatting**

| Tag Name | Syntax | Description |
|---|---|---|
| Address | `<ADDRESS>text</ADDRESS>` | Indicates that text provides an address or contact information; usually the text is italicized |
| Base Font | `<BASEFONT SIZE="number">` | Defines a new base size for relative changes to font size; the default base size is 3 (Non-3.2) |
| Big Text | `<BIG>text</BIG>` | Displays text in a larger font than normal |
| Blink | `<BLINK>text</BLINK>` | Blinks text on and off (Netscape only) |
| Block Quote | `<BLOCKQUOTE>text</BLOCKQUOTE>` | Indicates that a chunk of text is quoted from another source; usually indents on left and right |
| Bold | `<B>text</B>` | Displays text in boldface |
| Citation | `<CITE>text</CITE>` | Indicates that text is a book title or other citation; usually text is italicized |
| Code | `<CODE>text</CODE>` | Indicates that text is programming code or a similarly specialized language; usually uses a fixed-width font |
| Definition | `<DFN>text</DFN>` | Indicates that text defines a term; may italicize the text, but not all browsers respond to the tag |

**Table 3.1: HTML Tag Reference (Continued)**

| Tag Name | Syntax | Description |
|---|---|---|
| Emphasize | <EM>text</EM> | Emphasizes the text; usually italicizes text |
| Example | <XMP>text</XMP> | OBSOLETE: Use preformatted or sample tags instead |
| Font | <FONT SIZE="relativeSize" COLOR="color">text</FONT> | Displays text at the specified size and in the specified color; size can either be an absolute value from 1 to 7, where 3 is normal, or an increment to normal text size, such as "+1" or "-1" |
| Font Typeface | <FONT FACE="firstChoice, secondChoice,...">text</FONT> | Displays the text in the first of the specified typefaces that is available to the browser (Non-3.2) |
| Heading 1 | <H1 ALIGN="horizontal Alignment">text</H1> | Highest level of heading, equivalent to a chapter title; usually displayed as large bold letters with plenty of space above and below; default alignment for all headings is "LEFT" |
| Heading 2 | <H2 ALIGN="horizontal Alignment">text</H2> | Next level of heading, equivalent to a sub-chapter title |
| Heading 3 | <H3 ALIGN="horizontal Alignment">text</H3> | Next level of heading |
| Heading 4 | <H4 ALIGN="horizontal Alignment">text</H4> | ... and the next |
| Heading 5 | <H5 ALIGN="horizontal Alignment">text</H5> | ... and the next |
| Heading 6 | <H6 ALIGN="horizontal Alignment">text</H6> | Lowest level of heading; usually displayed in a font that is smaller than normal text |
| Italics | <I>text</I> | Italicizes text |
| Keyboard | <KBD>text</KBD> | Displays text in a fixed-width font |
| Listing | <LISTING>text</LISTING> | OBSOLETE: Use preformatted or sample tags instead |
| No Break | <NOBR>...</NOBR> | Indicates that text should not be automatically wrapped; line breaks should only occur if specifically indicated by a line-break or word-break tag (Non-3.2) |
| Plain Text | <PLAINTEXT>text</PLAINTEXT> | Displays text in fixed-width font exactly as written, with all white space preserved and no interpretation of HTML tags |
| Preformatted Text | <PRE>text</PRE> | Displays text in a fixed-width font with all spaces and line breaks preserved |
| Sample | <SAMP>text</SAMP> | Displays text in a fixed-width font |
| Small Text | <SMALL>text</SMALL> | Displays text in a smaller font than normal |
| Strikethrough | <STRIKE>text</STRIKE> | Displays text with a horizontal line through it |
| Strong | <STRONG>text</STRONG> | Indicates that the text is very important; usually displays the text in boldface |
| Subscript | <SUB>text</SUB | Displays text lower than normal text and in a small font |
| Superscript | <SUP>text</SUP> | Displays text higher than normal text and in a small font |
| Teletype | <TT>text</TT> | Displays text in a fixed-width font |

**Table 3.1: HTML Tag Reference (Continued)**

| Tag Name | Syntax | Description |
|---|---|---|
| Underlined | <U>*text*</U> | Displays underlined text |
| Variable | <VAR>*text*</VAR> | Indicates that the text is a variable name; usually displayed in italics |

**Breaks**

| | | |
|---|---|---|
| Line Break | <BR> | Inserts a line break in text without starting a new paragraph |
| Horizontal Rule | <HR SIZE="*pixels*" WIDTH="*percentage%*" ALIGN="*horizontalAlignment*" NOSHADE> | Draws a separating line across the browser window; SIZE assigns a thickness; WIDTH assigns a percentage of the total window width; NOSHADE specifies that no 3-D effects should be used |
| Colored Horizontal Rule | <HR COLOR="*color*"> | Sets the color of the separating line (Microsoft only) |
| Paragraph Break | <P> | Inserts a paragraph break; usually a blank line |
| Break Out of Aligned Wrapping | <BR CLEAR="*typeOfWrapping*"> | When room has been left for an aligned object, leaves enough space to become free of the object, and then starts laying out material normally; the arguments to "CLEAR" specify which alignment to finish: "LEFT," "RIGHT" or "ALL" |
| Spacer (Horizontal) | <SPACER TYPE="HORIZONTAL" SIZE="*pixels*" > | Inserts white space into the current line (Netscape only) |
| Spacer (Vertical) | <SPACER TYPE="VERTICAL" SIZE="*pixels*" > | Inserts white space above the next line (Netscape only) |
| Spacer (Image-Style) | <SPACER TYPE="BLOCK" WIDTH="*pixels*" HEIGHT="*pixels*" ALIGN="*imgStyleAlignment*"> | Inserts white space as if a transparent image is taking up space (Netscape only) |
| Word Break | <WBR> | Indicates that the browser is allowed to break the word or line at this point even if within a "no break" area (Non-3.2) |

**Lists**

| | | |
|---|---|---|
| Directory List | <DIR COMPACT>*listItems*</DIR> | Denotes a list without bullets or numbers in front of the items, which may be arranged into multiple columns |
| Definition List | <DL COMPACT>*pairsOfDefined ItemsAndDefinitions*</DL> | Denotes a glossary or other list of paired terms and descriptions; a compact list may result in terms and definitions being placed on the same line |
| Defined Item | <DT>*text* | Item being defined in list |
| Item Definition | <DD>*text* | Definition of item in list; usually indented |
| List Item | <LI TYPE="*bulletOr NumberingStyle*" VALUE="*numberReset*">*text* | Adds an item to a list |
| Menu List | <MENU COMPACT>*listItems* </MENU> | Strictly one-column list that does not have bullets or numbers in front of the items |
| Ordered List | <OL COMPACT START="*number*" TYPE="*numberingStyle*">*listItems*</OL> | Denotes an automatically numbered list; number styles are "1," "A," "a," "I" and "i" |

**Table 3.1: HTML Tag Reference (Continued)**

| Tag Name | Syntax | Description |
|---|---|---|
| Unordered List | `<UL COMPACT TYPE="bulletStyle">` `listItems</UL>` | Denotes a bulleted list; bullet style can be "DISC," "CIRCLE," or "SQUARE"; "DISK" is the default; nested, unordered lists usually are given different default bullet styles |
| **Links** | | |
| Anchor | `<A NAME="name">...</A>` | Internal anchor that can be linked to the URL "#name" |
| Link | `<A HREF="url">...</A>` | Link from page |
| **Embedded Files** | | |
| Background Sound | `<BGSOUND SRC="url"` `LOOP="number">` | Sound to play when page is displayed; the LOOP attribute is optional; a possible loop value is "INFINITE"; the sound file must be WAV, AU, or MIDI format (Microsoft only) |
| Embedded Object | `<OBJECT` `ALIGN="imgStyleAlignment"` `BORDER="pixels"` `CLASSID="implementation"` `CODEBASE="url"` `CODETYPE="codetype"` `DATA="urlOfObjectData"` `DECLARE HEIGHT="pixels"` `HSPACE="pixels"` `NAME="nameForFormSubmission"` `NOTAB SHAPES STANDBY="message"` `TABINDEX="position"` `TITLE="suggestedTitle"` `TYPE="MIMEtype"` `USEMAP="URLofMap"` `VSPACE="pixels" WIDTH="pixels">...</OBJECT>` | Embeds ActiveX control, image, applet, or document (Microsoft only, based on a working draft for a possible new HTML standard; not all attributes or documented capabilities are supported) |
| Horizontal Alignment | `"LEFT", "RIGHT" or "CENTER"` | |
| Image | `<IMG SRC="url"` `ALIGN="imgAlignment"` `ALT="text" BORDER="pixels"` `HEIGHT="pixels" WIDTH="pixels"` `HSPACE="pixels" VSPACE="pixels">` | Embeds an image in the page; if border is set to 0 pixels then no border is drawn around the image; HSPACE and VSPACE specify how much space to leave on the sides of the image |
| Image (Netscape) | `<IMG ALIGN="imgStyleAlignment"` `LOWSRC="url">` | LOWSRC specifies an initial image to display while the main image is being downloaded; other alignment possibilities are "TEXTTOP," "ABSBOTTOM," "ABSMIDDLE," and "BASELINE" (Netscape only) |
| Image with AVI resource (Microsoft) | `<IMG CONTROLS DYNSRC="url"` `LOOP="number"` `START="FILEOPENorMOUSEOVER">` | Dynamic source can be an AVI video or a VRML file; video controls may be included (Microsoft only) |
| Image with Client-Side Imagemap | `<IMG USEMAP="url">` | The URL is usually an internal anchor to the name specified in a MAP tag |
| Image with Server-Side Imagemap | `<IMG ISMAP="url">` | |

**Table 3.1: HTML Tag Reference (Continued)**

| Tag Name | Syntax | Description |
|---|---|---|
| Image Alignment | "LEFT", "RIGHT", "TOP", "MIDDLE" or "BOTTOM" | Standard alignment is "LEFT" or "RIGHT" to put the image against the left or the right side of the page and flow the surrounding material around the image; or "TOP," "MIDDLE," or "BOTTOM" to position one line of text against the image |
| Imagemap Area | <AREA SHAPE="*shape*" CO-ORDS="*listOfPoints*" HREF="*url*" ALT="*alternativeText*"> | Defines linking shapes in imagemap; shape can be "RECT" (coordinates are in the form "leftX, topY, rightX, bottomY"), "POLY" (coordinates are x-y pairs separated by commas), "CIRCLE" (coordinates are in the form "centerX, centerY, radius"), or "DEFAULT" (the link to follow if no defined shape in the image was clicked on) |
| Imagemap Definition | <MAP NAME="*anchorName*> *areaTags*</MAP> | Declares a client-side imagemap |
| Java Applet | <APPLET CODE="*classFileName*" NAME="*nameForApplet Communication*" CODEBASE="*relativeURLbase*" ALIGN="*imgStyleAlignment*" ALT="*nonJavaText*" HEIGHT="*pixels*" WIDTH="*pixels*" HSPACE="*pixels*" VSPACE="*pixels*" TITLE="*suggestedTitle*">*paramsAnd NonJavaDisplay*</APPLET> | Embeds a Java applet on the page; width and height specifications are required |
| Java Applet (Netscape) | <APPLET ARCHIVE="*zipFile*" CODE="*classFileName*" MAYSCRIPT></APPLET> | Get applet class from inside an archive containing many Java applets; MAYSCRIPT allows the applet to access JavaScript |
| Java Applet Parameters | <PARAM NAME="*text*" VALUE="*text*"> | Passes a variable name-value pair to the Java applet whose tags contain it |
| Java Applet Textflow | <TEXTFLOW> | Parser fix: if there are no non-Java tags or content contained in a pair of Java applet tags, insert a TEXTFLOW tag |
| Plug-in | <EMBED SRC="*url*" HEIGHT="*size*" WIDTH="*size*" UNITS="*sizeUnits*" NAME="*objectName*"> | Embeds a plug-in; units can be "pixels" or "en" (or, approximately, characters); special plug-in parameters can also be included in the tag |
| Vertical Alignment | "TOP", "MIDDLE", "BOTTOM", or "BASELINE" | |

**Tables**

| | | |
|---|---|---|
| Caption | <CAPTION ALIGN="*placement*">*text* </CAPTION> | Puts caption on or under the table; placement is "TOP" or "BOTTOM" |
| Caption Microsoft Style | <CAPTION ALIGN="*horizontal Alignment*" VALIGN="*placement*"> *text*</CAPTION> | (Microsoft only) |
| Table | <TABLE ALIGN="*horizontalAlignment*" WIDTH="*pixelsOrPercentage*" BORDER="*pixelsThick*" CELLPADDING="*pixels*" CELLSPACING="*pixels*">*rowsAndCa ption*</TABLE> | Declares a table; setting border to 0 results in a borderless table; padding is the distance between the contents of a table cell and its borders; spacing is the distance maintained between table cells |

**Table 3.1: HTML Tag Reference (Continued)**

| Tag Name | Syntax | Description |
|---|---|---|
| Table Background Colors | <TABLE BGCOLOR="*color*"> or <TR BGCOLOR="*color*"> or <TD BGCOLOR="*color*"> or <TH BGCOLOR="*color*"> | Sets background color for the specified part of the table (Non-3.2) |
| Table Cell | <TD ALIGN="*horizontalAlignment*" COLSPAN="*numberOfColumns*" NOWRAP ROWSPAN="*numberOfRows*" VALIGN="*verticalAlignment*">...</TD> | Adds a cell to the current row of the table; the cell may span more than one row or column |
| Table Header Cell | <TH ALIGN="*horizontalAlignment*" COLSPAN="*numberOfColumns*" NOWRAP ROWSPAN="*numberOfRows*" VALIGN="*verticalAlignment*">...</TH> | Adds a header cell; a regular cell except that by default the text is boldface and centered |
| Table Row | <TR ALIGN="*horizontalAlignment*" VALIGN="*verticalAlignment*">*table Cells*</TR> | Denotes a row of table cells; sets default alignment for cells in row |

**Microsoft Tables**

| Tag Name | Syntax | Description |
|---|---|---|
| Table Body | <TBODY CLASS="*elementName*" ID="*value*" STYLE="*styleProperties*">*rows*</TBODY> | Groups rows to assign styles and place inner borders (Microsoft only) |
| Table Border Colors | <TABLE BORDERCOLOR="*color*" BORDERCOLORLIGHT="*color*" BORDERCOLORDARK="*color*" VALIGN="*TOPorBOTTOM*"> or <TR BORDERCOLOR...> or <TD BORDERCOLOR...> or <TH BORDERCOLOR...> | Sets border normal, highlight and shadow colors; sets vertical alignment (Microsoft only) |
| Table Column Properties | <COL ALIGN="*horizontalAlignment*" SPAN="*numberOfColumnsToSet*"> | Set up new default properties for a particular table column within a column group (Microsoft only) |
| Table Column Group Properties | <COLGROUP ALIGN="*horizontalAlignment*" VALIGN="*verticalAlignment*" HALIGN="*horizontalAlignment*" WIDTH="*pixelsOrPercentage*" SPAN="*numberOfColumnsInGroup*">*cols* | Set defaults for a group of column set-ups (Microsoft only) |
| Table Footer | <TFOOT CLASS="*element*" ID="*value*" STYLE="*styleProperties*"></TFOOT> | (Microsoft only) |
| Table Heading | <THEAD CLASS="*element*" ID="*value*" STYLE="*styleProperties*" ALIGN="*horizontalAlignment*" VALIGN="*verticalAlignment*"> </THEAD> | (Microsoft only) |
| Table Inner Borders | <TABLE RULES="*typeOfInnerBorders*"> | Inner border types are "NONE," "GROUPS," "ROWS," "COLS," and "ALL" (Microsoft only) |

**Table 3.1: HTML Tag Reference (Continued)**

| Tag Name | Syntax | Description |
|---|---|---|
| Table Style Sheet Properties | `<TABLE STYLE="styleSheetProperties">, <TR STYLE="styleSheetProperties">, <TD STYLE="styleSheetProperties">, <TH STYLE="styleSheetProperties">` | Sets up style-sheet properties for the table as a whole, or for individual rows and cells (Microsoft only) |
| **Forms** | | |
| Form | `<FORM ACTION="URLtoSubmitTo" METHOD="typeOfServerCommunication" ENCTYPE="MIMEtype">...</FORM>` | Declares a form; method is either "POST" or "GET"; the default action URL is the document itself; MIME type is for the submission from the browser to the server; the default MIME type is "application/x-www-form-urlencoded" |
| Targeted Form | `<FORM TARGET="targetDisplay">...</FORM>` | Declares where the output of a form should be displayed (Non-3.2) |
| Input Check Box | `<INPUT TYPE="CHECKBOX" NAME="fieldname" VALUE="valueIfChecked" CHECKED>` | Adds a Boolean check-box to the form; CHECKED sets the box on by default |
| Input File | `<INPUT TYPE="FILE" NAME="fieldname" ACCEPT="MIMEtype1,MIMEtype2">` | Lets files be attached to the form submit; the optional list of MIME types specifies what sorts of files are acceptable |
| Input Hidden Field | `<INPUT TYPE="HIDDEN" NAME="fieldname" VALUE="staticValue">` | Adds a constant undisplayed name-value pair to the form submit |
| Input Imagemap | `<INPUT TYPE="IMAGE" NAME="fieldname" SRC="url" ALIGN="imageAlignment">` | Adds the specified image to the form; the field value is set to the x and y coordinates of a mouse-click inside the image |
| Input Multiple Choice | `<SELECT NAME="fieldName" SIZE="numberToDisplay" MULTIPLE>possibleChoices</SELECT>` | Adds a multiple-choice box to the form; if MULTIPLE is not set, then only one of the choices can be selected |
| Input Possible Choice | `<OPTION SELECTED VALUE="fieldValue">text` | Adds a line to a multiple-choice box; if SELECTED is set, then this is the default choice; the default value is the text of the choice |
| Input Multiple Lines | `<TEXTAREA ROWS="numberOfVisibleCharacters" COLS="numberOfVisibleLines" WRAP="code">initialText</TEXTAREA>` | Adds a field with multiple text lines to a form; the area can be scrolled; possible codes for wrapping are "OFF," "SOFT," and "HARD" |
| Input Password | `<INPUT TYPE="PASSWORD" NAME="fieldname" MAXLENGTH="numberOfCharacters" SIZE="numberOfDisplayedCharacters" VALUE="defaultValue">` | Adds a single line of text entry in which typed characters are not displayed; usually the typed characters are replaced with bullet characters |
| Input Radio Button | `<INPUT TYPE="RADIO" NAME="fieldname" VALUE="valueIfPicked" CHECKED>` | Adds a possible choice for a one-choice-of-many field; if no radio button is explicitly checked, the default value is the first choice |
| Input Number Within Range | `<INPUT TYPE="RANGE" NAME="fieldname" MIN="minimumNumber" MAX="maximumValue" VALUE="defaultValue">` | Adds a numeric input field that is restricted to the given range; if minimum or maximum is written without a decimal point, then only whole numbers are acceptable |

**Table 3.1: HTML Tag Reference (Continued)**

| Tag Name | Syntax | Description |
|---|---|---|
| Input Text | `<INPUT TYPE="TEXT" NAME="fieldname" MAXLENGTH="numberOfCharacters" SIZE="numberOfDisplayedCharacters" VALUE="defaultValue">` | Adds a single line of text entry |
| Reset | `<INPUT TYPE="RESET>` | Adds a button that lets the user reset all form fields to their orignal default values |
| Submission | `<INPUT TYPE="SUBMIT" NAME="fieldName" VALUE="label">` | Adds a button for submitting the form; if the optional name is supplied, a final field is submitted with the form; if the value is supplied, it is displayed in the button |

**Frames**

| Tag Name | Syntax | Description |
|---|---|---|
| Area Link Display | `<AREA TARGET="display target"...>` | Requests that the result of the link be displayed in the specified window or frame (Non-3.2) |
| Base Target | `<BASE TARGET="target">` | (In Head) Defines default target display for links from page (Non-3.2) |
| Floating Frame | `<IFRAME SRC="url" ALIGN="imgStyleAlignment" FRAMEBORDER="0or1" HEIGHT="pixels" MARGINHEIGHT="pixels" MARGINWIDTH="pixels" NAME="nameForTargeting" SCROLLING="scrollChoice" WIDTH="pixels"></IFRAME>` | Sets up a frame more or less as you'd set up an embedded image; can be used in normal HTML BODY area without using the FRAMESET construct (Microsoft only) |
| Frame | `<FRAME SRC="url" NAME="nameForTargeting" MARGINWIDTH="pixels" MARGINHEIGHT="pixels" SCROLLING="scrollChoice" NORESIZE ALIGN="imgStyleAlignment">` | Adds a frame to the document frameset; margins are between frames; scroll choice can be "YES," "NO," or "AUTO"; NORESIZE prevents the user from using the frame border as a resize handle (Non-3.2) |
| Frame (Microsoft) | `<FRAME FRAMEBORDER="0or1">`, `<FRAMESET FRAMEBORDER="0or1">` | If FRAMEBORDER is "1," a border is displayed, if "0" no border is displayed; the FRAMESET attribute sets defaults for contained frames (Microsoft only) |
| Frame (Netscape) | `<FRAME FRAMEBORDER="3Dlook" BORDERCOLOR="color">`, `<FRAMESET FRAMEBORDER="3Dlook" BORDER="sizeInPixels" BORDERCOLOR="color">` | If FRAMEBORDER is "YES," then the border is given a 3-D look, if "NO," then the border is a plain line; if border size is set to 0, then no borders are displayed; the FRAMESET attributes set defaults for contained frames (Netscape only) |
| Frame Set | `<FRAMESET ROWS="heightList" COLS="widthList">...</FRAMESET>` | Replaces the BODY pair of tags for a frames document; all content must be derived from pages embedded in individual frames; frame sets can be nested; heights and widths are separated by commas and are expressed as size in pixels (i.e., "200"), or as a percentage of available space ("60%") or as a portion of remaining space ("*" means all remaining space, "2*" means twice as much remaining space as a competitor who specified "*") (Non-3.2) |
| Link to Display | `<A HREF="url" TARGET="targetDisplay">...</A>` | Requests that the result of the link be displayed in the specified window or frame (Non-3.2) |

**Table 3.1: HTML Tag Reference (Continued)**

| Tag Name | Syntax | Description |
|---|---|---|
| No Frames | <NOFRAMES>*alternateHTMLBody*</NOFRAMES> | Specifies HTML to be used when a browser does not recognize frame sets; generally contains a standard HTML BODY section (Non-3.2) |
| Target Display | name of window or frame | Specifies where a link should be displayed; creates a window if there's no matching name; special names are "_blank" (a new blank window), "_self" (the window or frame that holds the link), "_parent" (the window or frame that linked to this page), and "_top" (the main browser window). (Non-3.2) |

**Obsolete "HTML 3.0" tags**

| | | |
|---|---|---|
| Abbreviation | <ABBREV> | |
| Acronym | <ACRONYM> | |
| Author | <AU> | |
| Author | <AUTHOR> | |
| Banner | <BANNER> | |
| Block Quote Plus | <BQ CLEAR="*positioning*" NOWRAP> | |
| Caption | <CAPTION> | |
| Credit | <CREDIT> | |
| Deleted Text | <DEL> | |
| Division Class | <DIV CLASS="*class*" NOWRAP> | |
| Figure | <FIG> | |
| Footnote | <FN> | |
| Inserted Text | <INS> | |
| Language | <LANG> | |
| List Heading | <LH> | |
| Math | <MATH> | |
| Note | <NOTE> | |
| Overlay | <OVERLAY> | |
| Person | <PERSON> | |
| Quote | <Q> | |
| Range | <RANGE> | |
| Spot | <SPOT> | |
| Tab Indent | <TAB> | |
| Table Plus | <TABLE CLEAR="*margin*" NOFLOW COLSPEC="*list*" UNITS="*units*" DP="*decimalPoint*" NOWRAP> | |

# HTML Tips, Tricks, and Acts of Desperation

If you want to grow a fine crop of bizarre misuses, you can't do better than hand a flexible technology to a bunch of students and programmers. Almost from its very beginning, sensible, straightforward HTML was being twisted into the document-mark-up equivalent of balloon animals. HTML has become more complex in an attempt to keep up with the mad scientists, but in doing so it has become an even more tempting experimental subject.

In this section, we'll look at sites that collect not-so-obvious solutions to genuine problems, as well as not-so-useful tricks to astonish or annoy your readers. (Of course, you'll find many of my own favorite deformations of HTML scattered throughout this book as "author's tips.") I'll also be warning you about some of the obsolete advice you'll find as you look into on-line resources. Useful pages sometimes disappear from the Web, but out-of-date pages can live on and on. On the Web as in life, virtue does not guarantee longevity.

Above all, remember what your friends at the Post Office say: the more your packaging pushes the envelope, the less likely it is your message will get delivered.

## Indenting Text

Occasionally over the last four years, it has seemed to me that the most pressing issue facing global civilization was how to indent text in HTML.

In the earliest days of the Web, the user could, at least theoretically, choose between indenting paragraphs and putting spaces between paragraphs. But then too many Web authors became dependent on the paragraph tag as a guaranteed way of inserting vertical space, and the indenting option faded away.

If the most important thing to a Web author was to make sure that one line or an entire paragraph of text was indented, if there was simply no way that anyone would pay attention to the content without that indentation (and you'd be surprised how often I was told that was the case), what was to be done?

Personally (and humbly) speaking, I worked miracles with the block quote and definition list tags, carefully applying line breaks and changes in font style to cover my tracks. The unenticingly named "definition list" is especially well-suited to corporate sites, which always go gaga for hierarchical arrangements: definition lists give you an indefinitely extensible indent-level-within-indent-level mechanism.

There was another option (and remember, we're still talking about pre-HTML-2.0 days!): using "invisible" images to offset text. Those images were called "spacers," and you'll find a special note about them below.

With the first implementations of tables, it became absurdly easy to indent whole chunks of text: you simply made a table with one row and two columns, the first cell of which had a specific width (and no content other than a blank space), and the second cell of which contained the text you wanted to indent.

Vertical spacing and first-line spacing still presented difficulties, however. The most recent developments include a non-breaking-space special-character entity, a typical HTML addition by Netscape (the "SPACER" tag), and, undercutting the Netscape tag's chances for survival, style-sheet properties for margins and padding. Soon the Web will be a paradise of indentation, and we can turn our attention to less serious issues, like war and poverty.

### Spacers Live in Vain

There are a number of Web pages devoted to explaining "spacers," more-or-less transparent graphics that are used to indent and separate text, much as an old-fashioned typesetter would insert lead slugs between characters (see Figure 3.1 for an example of a site that uses this method—and Figure 3.2 for a peek at how it can end up looking). However, this technique has largely been made obsolete by tables and the new HTML features described above.

Graphic spacers have three strikes against them:

- The supposedly invisible graphics become hideously blatant when the user has turned image loading off, since the browser marks their position with a generic icon.

- When users set their browser window or preferred font to an unanticipated size, the careful layout tends to break apart.

- The additional graphics files, even though usually very small, add to downloading and presentation time without adding much visual interest.

## HEADING DOWNHILL

You're reading through someone else's HTML code. There's an "<H1>" tag at the top of the page's body, holding a main title. Then a little bit further on,

there's an "<H2>" to hold the name of a sub-chapter. Then an "<H3>,", then back up to the "<H2>" level… wait, what's this "<H6>" doing here?

Well, in the days before font "SIZE" attributes and "<BIG>" tags, the only way  we Web authors could influence text size was by using the heading tags. If we wanted really big text, we used "<H1>" whether the text was "really" a heading or not. Yeah, we were told not to, but what are you going to do?

That's how we got bigger-than-normal text. But how could we get *smaller*-than-normal text? There wasn't an "<UNASSUMING>" or an "<INESSEN-TIAL>" tag.

Well, let's say that your browser's default set-up is to display text as 12-point Times. Then "<H1>" (or heading level one) text would typically display as bold 24-point Times. Of course, heading level two has to display smaller text than heading level one, and it typically showed up as bold 18-point Times. Heading level three had to be a little smaller still, so it was bold 14-point. And then… and then…

**Figure 3.1**
David Siegel's "Casbah" with image loading

**Figure 3.2**
David Siegel's "Casbah" without image loading

Someone (presumably someone at NCSA, where Mosaic was developed) figured out that the Mosaic browser would run out of ways to differentiate one slightly smaller heading from another by the time you got to heading level four (or normal-sized text). Where was there to go but down?

And so, first in Mosaic and then in Netscape, heading level five actually displayed *smaller* (bold 10-point Times, to be exact) than normal text, and heading level six displayed smallest of all (bold 8-point Times).

Thus it came to pass that any Web authors who wanted that great tiny-print-in-the-insurance-policy effect would put their text into an "<H6>...</H6>" pair.

Then came explicit font sizing, and relative font sizing and style sheets, and the motivation for all this silliness disappeared—but the silliness lingers on.

### David Siegel's Casbah
http://www.dsiegel.com/

### David Siegel's Creating Killer Websites
http://www.killersites.com/core.html

I have to admit these two sites can be fun in a geek-out kind of way—sort of like reading a twenty-four point argument that explains how Batman really *could* beat up Superman. Siegel was a digital font designer before becoming a Web pundit, and the typography and font design sections of the "Casbah" are especially strong. But don't let Siegel's Charlton Heston-like voice of authority fool you into taking these collections of bizarre HTML tricks and control-crazed design theories as pure gospel. Siegel lives in a world in which every computer contains a top-level color graphics card, every browser is the one he's using, and every Internet connection views ISDN as a minimum speed limit. If that describes the only audience *you're* interested in, then by all means follow the sites, buy the books, and live the experience! Otherwise, bring your own salt and don't be shy about using it: the site you kill could be your own.

### Dmitry Kirsanov's Top Ten Web Design Tips
http://www.design.ru/ttt/

An attractively designed and written collection of tutorials and tips from Webreference's St. Petersburg correspondent. The last time I checked in, the top ten list included the BLOCKQUOTE tag as a way to achieve page margins (hate that one, myself, but tastes differ), the joys and sorrows of elastic tables, non-breaking spaces and non-smart quotes, an overview of the games people play with text attributes, and a lovely treatise on white space: how to get it and how to arrange it.

### Dr Clue's HTML Guide [] Meta Tags
http://users.abac.com/cgi-bin/drclue/F1.cgi/
HTML/META/META.html

Excellent coverage of the typical ways that document-wide variables (set with the "<META>" tag) can cooperate with search engines is available here. It deserves a look, if only for its over-the-top video-game layout, including a useful form that will build META tags for most common fields.

### Fred's Dynamic WEB Page Design
http://www.graphic-design.com/Showker/
Web-Design/

What is it about Web tips that puts everyone on a first-name basis? Anyway, this acerbic and oh-so-true response to all those cool Web-design tips out there should be a bracing antidote to the blarney, even though it was only written as a way to attract customers into Fred Showker's commercial workshop. I was particularly pleased to see someone arguing that the point of Web publishing wasn't to put hits on a counter, but to get a response from readers.

## HTML Goodies

http://www.htmlgoodies.com/

This site boxes up a big batch of tips written in a breezy stream-of-consciousness style. Nothing completely unique here, but the large and miscellaneous collection makes for an enjoyable light browse.

## HTML Hot Tips

http://members.aol.com/htmlguru/tips/index.html

## HTML Questions and Answers

http://members.aol.com/htmlguru/qanda/index.html

These are two of a series of pages set up by Chuck Musciano, self-nicknamed "the HTML Guru." I should admit that I haven't been all that impressed by Musciano's guruship: he often repeats material, and the material itself doesn't always seem well thought-out. Perhaps it's just that he doesn't seem interested in tracking down potential flaws in his suggestions, or in posting warnings or alternatives. But if you want an upbeat "I'm OK, Netscape is OK" kind of guru, Musciano may be your chosen master.

## Indenting with HTML

http://www.eskimo.com/~bloo/html/topics/indent.htm

This section of the "other" Brian Wilson's excellent "Index Dot Html" site offers the most thorough coverage of the indentation problem you're ever likely to see, complete with the pros and cons of every possible solution, and summary recommendations. I wish he'd finished it before I'd written my own coverage, but that's no reason for you to miss out.

## META Tag Builder

http://vancouver-webpages.com/VWbot/mk-metas.html

A straightforward forms-based service that can improve your cooperation with search services and other interpreters of the document-wide fields set by "<META>" tags. It has a very useful help page, too.

## The Other HTML FAQ

http://www.stack.nl/%7Egalactus/html/other-faq.html

This unofficial sequel to the WWW FAQ concentrates on commonly requested tricks and techniques. It is probably the most comprehensive and compact collection of its ilk on the Web, although it manages to find time to editorialize shamelessly: "Q: How do I get an audio file to play automatically when someone visits my site? A: Bleh. What if I visit your site at 3am, and there's someone sleeping in the next room?"

## Top 10 Ideas and Hints about Web Design

http://www.tema.ru/top10/

Art Lebedev, a compatriot of Dmitry Kirsanov, offers his own "top ten" at this site. It's fun reading: I especially liked the bit about removing all white space from inside the tags of a linked image. But his advice to insert a space after italicized text is a bit out of date: true, the Macintosh has long had a problem with combinations of italics and plain text, but the latest version of Netscape Navigator

finally compensated for it. On the plus side, that means we can use the "<CITE>" and "<EM>" tags without fear; on the minus side, we have to disregard the years' worth of anti-italics propaganda to be found on the Web.

# BROWSER-PROOF HTML

To close this chapter on a quieter note, let's reflect again on the original intentions of HTML: to be cross-platform and representation-independent. Yes, you sacrifice a lot if you try for those goals. You also sacrifice a lot if you give those goals up.

I can't pretend that I always avoid making that sacrifice. When I produce Web pages for someone else, I usually assume that they want to reach as many readers as possible, and therefore I push for "generic" HTML as much as possible. But in my personal pages, I often experiment with new browser features, or non-browser-safe color combinations, or peculiar layouts, and then I have to reconcile myself to the restricted audience that is reachable when your HTML is tailored to a specific user set-up.

However, I do recommend that you *know* when you're making that sacrifice. Otherwise, you could cost yourself some readers and (if you're doing this for a living) cost your employers some customers.

## Best Viewed With Any Browser
**http://server.berkeley.edu/~cdaveb/ anybrowser.html**
Cari D. Burstein's world-spanning campaign against use (and publicity) of browser-specific features seems to have caught on, despite Microsoft's "we'll give you free software if you put our button on your page" counter-campaign. Maybe it's because, unlike many other supporters of standard HTML, Burstein doesn't make exaggerated claims, and his exclamation marks don't come in clumps. As he quotes from a fellow spirit, Tim Berners-Lee, the creator of the World Wide Web: "Anyone who slaps a 'This page is best viewed with Browser X' label on a Web page appears to be yearning for the bad old days, before the Web, when you had very little chance of read-

ing a document written on another computer, another word processor, or another network."

## Bobby
**http://www.cast.org/bobby/**
Bobby is an on-line service, much like an HTML validator, that checks how accessible a specified Web page is to the disabled.

## Dark Side of the HTML
**http://www.best.com/%7Esem/dark_side/ index.html**
An unusual rant, not about the features browser manufacturers have added to HTML, but about the extent to which browsers *ignore* features inherent in HTML standards. If nothing else, it's another useful warning about trusting the documentation.

## Designing an Accessible Web
**http://www.trace.wisc.edu/world/web/**
The largest index of Web resources for the disabled, including special browsers, guidelines for accessible sites and pages, browser design recommendations, ongoing programs, and even a VRML accessibility project is collected here.

### Designing Web Sites for Multiple Browsers Without Being Bland

http://www1.shore.net/~straub/wprmultb.htm

This guide to being very, very careful is suitably painstaking—more so than I tend to be, certainly, but maybe you're not as lazy. It's notable as the first Web page I've seen that uses cascading style sheets to get a fancy-schmancy appearance with a vanilla HTML document.

### The HTML Terrorist's Handbook

http://www.zikzak.net/~acb/hacks/htmlth.html

Andrew C. Bulhak's list of browser-specific sabotage techniques is, if nothing else, a useful reminder that it is indeed possible to cause discomfort with your HTML. And he doesn't even mention ActiveX or Java!

### Readers with Visual Impairments

http://www.lcc.gatech.edu/gallery/dzine/access/

Here's a low-key introduction to the history of audio-based browsers, with some practical suggestions for improving access to your site for the visually impaired. The author also points to some examples of sites whose authors did the necessary work.

### Which Tags to Use?

http://www.eskimo.com/~bloo/html/misc/whichtags.htm

In a perfect world, Netscape and Microsoft would be pooling a CEO-sized salary for Brian Wilson, whose "Index Dot Html" site is probably the Web's best source for thorough, honest documentation of how each bit of HTML works on each browser. Whenever you're curious about what a tag or attribute *really* does as opposed to what it's *documented* to do, Index Dot Html is the place to go. Wilson is thus in a perfect position to offer advice on how to work around the unstandardized aspects of Web publishing. In this brief page, he explains his point of view.

# CHAPTER 4
# BASIC GRAPHICS

*Fig. 83*

**THIS CHAPTER WILL HELP YOU WITH RESOURCES AND TECHNIQUES COVERING:**

☞ **Graphics in context.**
With images, as with all other elements of your site, you should consider what you wish to express and whom you wish to address before you begin working.

☞ **Web graphics formats and standards.**
These sites explain the differences between popular Web graphics formats like GIF and JPEG, and suggest the kinds of graphics that are best suited to each format.

☞ **Interlaced and transparent graphics.**
Use these tutorial sites and applications as starting-off points for creating these popular graphic effects on your Web site.

☞ **The HTML of Art.**
Introductions, references, and tools to help embed graphics in a Web page, including background images, can be found here.

☞ **Adding color to text.**
These references deal with the use of background and font colors, including those programmer-friendly, artist-hostile hexadecimal specifications.

☞ **Color palettes.**
These sites address Web color-management issues, from the difficulties of cross-platform display to simple matters of taste.

☞ **Imagemaps.**
Here we'll look at the history and art of linking from multiple shapes within a single image file. We'll also cover some applications that can ease imagemap creation.

**THE GRAPHICS** you incorporate into your page design and layout largely determine what readers will think of your site. Whether they come through the front door of your default page or through a direct link elsewhere, visitors will remember if your graphics helped orient them; they'll also remember if they had to wait forever for the page's elements to download. You'll want to set up lively, good-looking graphics that communicate your content's message—even if you're not especially artistic—and you'll want to avoid unexpected display problems.

## GRAPHICS IN CONTEXT

If the pages you're working on have nothing to do with graphics, then don't worry too much about adding extraneous graphics. Readers who are interested in your content won't mind; readers who aren't interested in your content—well, don't worry too much about attracting *their* attention. Directories, search engines, and text-only references are all better off with minimal graphics, perhaps restricted to identity-establishing logos or color choices.

If the pages you're working on are focused on graphics—if, for example, you're showing samples of your artwork or paying tribute to a movie star—then you'd better pay close attention to those graphics. Otherwise, your time and money will have been wasted.

Most graphics contexts are not so straightforward, of course. Usually, images are used in a supporting role, as a more or less important contributor to the overall effect of the site. In that supporting role you might want a polished and professional look, or a scene-stealing attention-getter, or even something playfully unpretentious. For you as a Web author, it's most important to know what role you want your graphics to play. Make sure that your

site doesn't fall victim to miscasting! Remember, just slapping on some "standard" Web graphics achieves nothing—except making your site look "standard."

Sometimes that's really what you want: A cheap corporate site might be perfectly content with being a standard, cheap corporate site, rather than trying to be an unusually useful corporate site or an unusually interesting corporate site. When someone else is paying the bills, it's their call.

But for more personal pages, that standard look is out of place. One of the more remarkable achievements of late twentieth-century capitalism has been the commodification of seemingly resistant notions such as individuality and originality. How do you show you're "cool?" By buying what "cool" people buy and wearing what "cool" people wear. After enough decades of this training, the profit motive isn't even necessary for the behavior to be generated—as has been proven conclusively in the short history of the Web. Alas, using round red buttons instead of standard bullets in a list is *not* enough to make your page uniquely interesting.

Instead, it's precisely the *non-standard* (note that I didn't say "badly produced!") that is likely to work to work well on a personal page:

- I remember when I first encountered typographer David Siegel's site. What impressed me most weren't his Web tips and tricks (most of which I knew already or disagreed with), but the trompe l'oeil coffee ring imprinted beside his text.

- I also remember a high-school cartoonist's site whose table of contents was a scanned-in batch of drawings scrawled on a blue-ruled notebook page. It was (and remains) one of the best uses of navigational imagemaps I've seen.

# WEB GRAPHICS FORMATS AND STANDARDS

Those of us who've had to use a wide variety of computers in our lives will owe one thing to the most highly hyped days of the Web, even if it gets taxed, censored, and extended out of existence: there are finally some truly cross-platform media formats out there.

A few years ago, you might have had to pay for a special (with price to match) program to let you transform the only usable type of file for one set-up into the only usable type of file for another. We don't expect to have to go through that any longer, mostly thanks to the worldwide peer pressure of the Web. No longer does a graphics program on one computer refuse to produce anything that can be read by its opposite number across the Great Operating System Wall; no longer do multimedia developers have to labor to produce semi-identical twins and triplets when an adaptable only child will do.

The trend started with embedded graphics, which were, if not the most important, at least the most blatant advantage of Web browsers and HTML over previous Internet applications. Given the wild number of graphics formats already in common use, the early Web developers tried to make their lives easier by picking formats that were widely supported, non-proprietary, and compressible (remember those download times!) BMP files were too big, TIFF files were too unpredictable, PICT files were too Macintosh-specific. Thus we ended up with GIF and JPEG. (Well, "JPEG" is, strictly speaking, a compression algorithm rather than a file format, but we'll skip that point.)

The GIF format compressed nicely when given the right material to work with, was suitable for 256-colors-or-fewer graphics, and best of all, since it was being pushed by CompuServe as a free standard, it was already cross-platform and associated with the online world. Not surprising that it gained rapid ground.

That ground suffered a frightening quake at the beginning of 1995 when it turned out that CompuServe hadn't had the legal right to push GIF as a free standard, due to its use of a patented compression algorithm. The legalities, being legalities, are far too complicated to get into here. Suffice it to say that we Web authors all ended up pretty much in the same shape we were then. (You'll be able to find more detailed histories on the Web, if you're interested.)

One outcome of the Winter of GIF Discontent was a more urgent push for a better cross-platform graphics format. And I do mean urgent: in only a few months there appeared the first draft of the specification for such a format, called PNG. Unfortunately for the new format, by then the GIF tussle had lost most of its glamour. PNG still doesn't have in-line support from the leading browsers, and at the time I write this, the average Web author still must choose between GIF or JPEG format for embedded images.

## CHOOSING A FORMAT

Before we get to the GIF vs. JPEG decision, just a reminder: Always wait till your graphics are absolutely complete and ready to put on the Web before storing them in either the GIF or the JPEG format. In fact, if you can afford the disk space, store the last version of your graphics in their pre-GIF/pre-JPEG formats. When you translate your pictures into GIF or JPEG, you'll usually suffer a big loss in quality. (To be more precise, you always suffer a loss in quality with JPEG; you'll only suffer a loss with GIF if your image uses more than 256 colors—but if you use a good scanner or paint program, your image probably *does* use more than 256 colors.) Any special effects (blurring, sharpening, coloring, and so on) will work much better on a high-quality image than on a low-quality image. Also, when you re-save the image, which also means re-compressing it, the image will lose even more quality. That's completely unnecessary. Moreover, if you keep a high-quality version of the image in reserve, it will give you the freedom to use that image in different contexts or in different formats later.

When deciding between GIF and JPEG, remember that the goal is the *smallest file size with acceptable quality*. Since it doesn't take much more time to try out four or five conversions than it does to try out one, I often make a couple of samples in both formats, then compare their file sizes and compare their appearance. But there are some simple rules of thumb available for the less obsessive among you:

- **Flat fields of color** are a tip-off that you'll be able to easily reduce the total number of colors, which means that GIF compression will be able to shine. Moreover, the sharp edges usually found around flat color fields are precisely the sort of images that JPEG doesn't handle well: you'll usually end up with a bizarre "halo" or "shimmer," no matter how high you set the JPEG quality settings. Go with GIF.

- **A nonrectangular shape** that you don't want framed on the page—i.e., you'd prefer that it look drawn right onto the page—means you're stuck with GIF, since that format supports transparency.

- **A line drawing in black and white** (or any other pair of colors) is perfect for GIF, since the total number of colors can be reduced.

- **Non-textual imagemaps** should be interlaced to give users faster access to links. Since support for interlaced JPEG files is still shaky, that should sway you toward the GIF format.

- **Heavy 3-D effects or gradients** mean lots and lots of colors. "What?" I hear you protest. "But my amazing floating 'click-here' cube is 100-percent canary yellow, and my radically cool background gradient only goes from dark purple to slightly darker purple!" Sorry, but we're not talking about *variety* of colors; we're talking about *number* of colors, which is a very different thing. Each unnoticeably delicate change in shade or hue is a new color, and so that perfectly smooth transition from dark purple to darker purple can use hundreds of colors without making that fact evident to you. Since GIF compression depends on reducing colors, you'll probably get more satisfactory results from such artwork if you can get away with using JPEG.

- **Photographs** (including photographs of paintings) tend to be easier for JPEG to handle for exactly the same reason: they usually contain lots of gradual changes in shade and hue. (High contrast "artsy" photos are an exception, since they contain flat fields of color and therefore can be GIF-ified without much trouble.)

☞ When you store a file on disk, you almost always end up with wasted space, since disk drives dish out space in standard portions, whether all of it is needed or not. On some large disk drives, the standard portion may be fairly heavy: 17K or more. In such cases, two files may both show up in your file system as 17K, even if one uses only 0.1K while the other uses 16.9K. If you notice a suspicious lack of very small files in your directory listings, and you want to find out how long it will really take to transfer the data over a phone line, check the image file's "properties" (in the Windows world) or "information" (in the Macintosh world). Of course, if the image file shows up as 17K in one format and 116K in the other, there's no need to pursue the matter further!

## Anti-Aliasing Evolves

**http://www.adobemag.com/PDFs/ftrPDF/anti.pdf**

Like most of the Web content from Adobe Systems, this page is only available in the company's proprietary Acrobat format, much as if Microsoft's Web side consisted entirely of Word documents. But even if it's not HTML, this is the best introduction to the topic of anti-aliasing I've seen on the Web. Not only does author Kathleen Tinkel explain the meaning of the term and the justifications for the technique, but she also explains why you don't always want to use it. The article ends with coverage of promising new (as of October 1996) software developments to provide downloading of anti-aliased text that is not embedded in images.

## The Bandwidth Conservation Society

**http://www.infohiway.com/faster/**

The good old Bandwidth Conservation Society has a slightly dissipated air after receiving corporate sponsorship from Netscape and a JavaScript-powered facelift. Thankfully, the top-level page keeps a link to the older version of the site, which remains one of the best overviews of why and how to optimize graphics for the Web without veering into unacceptably low quality. The new version of the site includes a downloadable copy for local reference, interactive comparisons of the images produced by different formats and compression levels, well-

done GIF and JPEG tips, and even an attempt to explain the binary system to non-programmers. It also features an on-line forum, which, miracle of miracles, contains only two postings headed "Isn't there any ladies on this thing" and only one headed "can anyone please tell me how to work this thing! i have no clue." Actually, this is an uncommonly useful on-line Web forum, with many more on-topic articles than one usually finds—but if you have a specific question, you're still probably better off using DejaNews to search the applicable Usenet news groups.

## Buttons for the Web

**http://www.adobemag.com/PDFs/howtoPDF/buttons.pdf**

**http://www.adobemag.com/PDFs/howtoPDF/buttons2.pdf**

**http://www.adobemag.com/PDFs/howtoPDF/buttons3.pdf**

This intensive three-part tutorial walks you through creation of button images (including "pressed" as well as "default" states) using Adobe products, although many of the ideas and techniques apply to other image-editing programs as well. The first document uses photographs as bases for the buttons, the second document uses embossed line drawings and the third uses 3-D text. Well done, though I wish the articles had been supplied in HTML so that we could see the results in action.

## Computer Graphics Techniques Applied to Web Pages

**http://mvassist.pair.com/Graphics.html**

Part of Brazil's "Webling's Cafe" site, this is a nice, if somewhat miscellaneous, directory of links to Web graphics resources, including general overviews, Photoshop tips and plug-ins, clip-art collections, tutorials, and computer color theory.

## Creating Better Graphics for the Web

**http://webreview.com/96/11/22/studio/index2.html**

This anecdotal excerpt from *Designing for the Web* by Jennifer Niederst suggests using a target file size as the focus of your graphics work. Her own target size is a maximum

of 30K for the total of all HTML and embedded graphics. That's a pretty ambitious goal, and it's led to some fruitful experiments in graphics-slimming (Niederst usually restricts herself to 32 colors or fewer), as well as to a "small is beautiful" aesthetic well-suited to the Web. Niederst also tells the all-too-painfully-familiar story of her introduction to system gamma differences.

## Decreasing Download Time Through Effective Color Management

**http://www.microsoft.com/workshop/design/ des-gen/colormg.htm**

This article, from Microsoft's Site Builder Workshop, is more general than its title might imply. It gives a good journalistic introduction to the GIF and JPEG formats, and offers practical advice on how to choose between them. However, the article's GIF tips center, rightly, on color-map issues.

## GIFs and JPEGs

**http://www.widearea.co.uk/designer/ compress.html**

A short introduction to the two formats, with excellent examples of the results obtained from different settings in different browser environments, and a natural branch off into color-palette considerations.

## GRAFICA Obscura

**http://www.sgi.com/grafica/index.html**

This beautiful personal-and-professional (he loves his job) "notebook" from SGI's Paul Haeberli may be more

of an inspirational site than a reference site, but do check in for the inspiration. I've been especially helped by his clear, technically oriented pages on synthetic lighting and matrix operations—and by his odd free-verse page on the properties of light. Consumers beware: his "Image Production for the Web" page is aimed squarely at SGI programmers. Instead, check out the delightful paper-folding pages.

## Graphics File Formats FAQ

**http://www.ora.com/centers/gff/gff-faq/ index.htm**

An extensive (several dozen sections, when divided up for the Web) but far less than definitive list of common Q&As from Usenet, mostly aimed at the world-weary and technically adept. Only a real, honest-to-god programmer who's suffered through an attempt to match a specification would have written something like: "Format specs such as PCX, GIF, JFIF [i.e., JPEG,] and Sun Raster definitely fall into the 'don't let this happen to you' category." To be honest, not all the sections are going to be of direct use to a Web author, but they may give you a better understanding of why that file you downloaded from "alt.binaries.pictures.supermodels.ignatz.mouse" won't display properly. Includes a fine overview of the GIF legal battles of 1995.

## Graphics Formats for the World Wide Web

**http://www.w3.org/pub/WWW/Graphics/**

The nearest thing to an official overview of graphics file formats from the nearest thing to an official authority on the World Wide Web, W3C, this page gives great insights into how GIF and JPEG became the "standard" Web graphics formats, with a few scathing comments as spice.

## Modular Ornament for Web Pages

**http://www.adobemag.com/PDFs/howtoPDF/ modular.pdf**

One of the many annoying Adobe Acrobat documents that Adobe insists on putting out on the Web (these guys charge huge money for an HTML editor, but they refuse to publish HTML themselves?), this is also one of the few designer-oriented Web graphics articles. In it, Janet Ashford uses the often-made parallel between the Web and the early printing press to make a case for ornamental borders and dividers. She also points out that Renaissance-era printing ornaments are in the public domain by now, and thus free for Web appropriation. (I don't blame her for the awful Acrobatization, by the way; the bugs in the display lead me to believe that it was executed long after she'd turned in the article.)

## Not Just Decoration: Quality Graphics for the Web

**http://www.w3.org/pub/Conferences/WWW4/ Papers/53/gq-boston.html**

This paper from the 1995 World Wide Web Conference covers some of the most difficult problems facing Web graphics artists—all of which, sad to say, are still present today. Although academic in tone and mostly aimed at browser manufacturers, its treatment of color issues may be of interest to Web authors in general.

## The On-Line Visual Literacy Project

**http://www.pomona.edu/visual-lit/intro/ intro.html**

Here's a breezy, "art appreciation" introduction to some of the terms and concepts of the working artist, with a good selection (not always perfectly formatted, alas) of illustrations and animations. If you've already had training in the fine arts, you'll likely find it old hat, but for visual illiterates like myself the site is well worth the time.

## Optimizing Web Graphics

**http://www.webreference.com/ dev/graphics/**

From webreference.com comes perhaps the best overview of image-file optimization on the Web. This series of pages touches on virtually all the topics included in this chapter, but is especially strong on GIF techniques. Sensible tips, clear explanations and many examples

make this one of the best Web-graphics introductions I've ever seen.

## Preparing Graphics for the Web

**http://www.servtech.com/public/dougg/ graphics/index.html**

This marvelous introductory site hasn't gotten much publicity yet, and that's a shame. Author Douglas E. Gray has provided a perfect mix of background material and working tips for the Web author, including unusually clear descriptions of the JPEG and GIF formats, dithering approaches, GIF compression, palette problems across browsers, and HTML esoterica. At the end of the "Tips and Tricks" section, you'll find a good selection of Windows shareware and freeware programs.

## Resources for comp.infosystems.www. authoring.images

**http://weblab.research.att.com/phoaks/comp/ infosystems/www/authoring/images/ resources0.html**

This odd but interesting page collects and rebroadcasts the URLs of useful sites recommended by posters in the comp.infosystems.www.authoring.images Usenet newsgroup. Typical URLs might point to FAQ pages for Web graphics, tutorials, or image-editing tools. A project called PHOAKS (People Helping One Another Know Stuff) is behind the URL-collection effort. Probably not quite as useful as regular newsreading or as newsgroup-archive searches, but it's certainly a way to get a different perspective on Usenet resources.

## The Scanning FAQ

http://www.infomedia.net/scan/

Jeff Bone's selection of "frequently asked" scanning questions is not up to the usefulness of Michael J. Sullivan's site (listed below), but since its topics don't overlap many in Sullivan's site, it may make a perfect supplement. Of particular interest to me was the attack on super-high-resolution settings.

## Scanning Photos for the Web

http://photo.net/philg/how-to-scan-photos.html

On this page, Philip Greenspun, an MIT researcher but also one of the first Web photojournalists and still one of the most acidic Web pundits around, shares the Photo-CD-based techniques he's learned through painful experience. Dilettantes like myself and beginners may feel a little lost, but professionals (particularly professionals with access to a Unix box) should appreciate the thoroughly unfluffy approach.

## Scanning Tips

http://www.hsdesign.com/scanning/tipswelcome.html

Whether you're using your own artwork or someone else's, it's unlikely that you'll be relying entirely on computer-generated graphics. Unfortunately, the proper use of a scanner isn't part of the standard training of artists, writers, or even programmers. Moreover, since scanners are expensive, renting time on a scanner is expensive and scanner output is a disk-space glutton, you'll want to avoid trial-and-error as much as possible. A by-product of Michael J. Sullivan's book/CD-ROM, *Sullivan's Scanning Tips & Techniques*, this unique Web resource unveils some of the most troubling mysteries of the scanner. Sullivan explains how to determine proper settings based on your source material and desired outcome, how to use scanner settings and Photoshop to sharpen images, how to "restore" photographs, how to correct color problems, and how to scan objects that aren't flat (i.e., using your scanner like a poor man's digital camera). He also offers ideas for tiled backgrounds, and explains how to purchase and set up your own scanner. He even includes special tips for scanning Polaroid prints. Also on the site are an on-line calculator for estimating scanned file sizes, a directory of businesses and links, and scanner comparison tables for the shopper.

## Usenet Newsgroup for Web Image Authoring

news:comp.infosystems.www.authoring.images

You'll find considerably less heat and considerably more light in this Usenet newsgroup than in many others devoted to the Web. Most questions actually receive serious answers, and it's a great place to look for informal reviews of new graphics software or for browser bugs and workarounds.

## GIF

GIF (for "Graphics Interchange Format") was developed for the cross-platform consumer market some time before consumers had much access to "high end" graphics cards. Understandably, it assumes that 256 would be reasonable as a maximum of displayable colors, and that most computer-suitable graphics would use far fewer colors than that.

Despite its limitations as far as color support goes, the GIF format manages to make room for some special effects that have gained Web-wide popularity, two of which (interlacing and transparent colors) we'll discuss below, and another that we'll save for the video and animation chapter.

It's important be aware of the Web's lack of expiration dates as you research these effects. When transparency and interlacing first became popular several years ago, they weren't supported by any of the leading commercial image-editing tools, and so stop-gap specialized tools and advisory pages were generated. Nowadays, most decent commercial programs will have come up with *some* response to the Web, but many existing pointers may not have been updated accordingly. Before you go searching for the perfect GIF transparency tool on the Web, check the graphics software you've already installed on your system: chances are it'll do the job just fine.

### Reducing Colors

You can think of a GIF file as consisting of two parts. The first is a "color map," a list of all the colors used by the image. The remainder of the file specifies the image itself, using instructions like "Draw 28 pixels of color number 3, then draw 37 pixels of color number 16, then draw…"

For the Web author, there are three important consequences:

1 GIF images cannot handle a wide range of subtle tonal variations. If you're counting on very slight, almost indistinguishable, changes in color (as with gradients or 3-D shading), you're going to end up fighting against the nature of the format.

2 Both parts of the GIF file contribute to the size (and the download time), even though only one part (the image itself) is visible.

3 The easiest way to reduce the size of a GIF file is to restrict the number of colors it contains.

When it comes to GIF color reduction, I usually work by trial-and-error from within my image editor or conversion tool. Virtually any good tool that lets you convert an image from full color to restricted, mapped color will also give you control over how big a color map your final image can use.

Let's assume that I'm working with a full-color (or, in Photoshop terms, an "RBG mode") image—always the best approach when creating artwork. When I'm ready to move the final result to the Web as a GIF file, I have to convert it to a restricted 8-bit (or, in Photoshop terms, an "indexed mode") image with an associated color map—but I'm going to try to use fewer than 8 bits in reality (i.e., fewer than 256 colors).

First, I'll try converting the image using the fewest conceivable number of colors (16 or 32, perhaps). Usually, the result will be pretty horrible: overly speckled, perhaps not even recognizable at all. I'll undo the conversion, and try over again with more colors in the map, repeating as seems required by the awfulness of the results. When I get to something I can bear to live with, I'll save the result as a GIF—or, if I'm now at 256 colors, start looking into using JPEG instead. At this point, I might even go back to the original full-color source image and try simplifying it: for example, by getting rid of some subtle shading that becomes distracting rather than attractive when the image is converted and uses fewer colors.

Be aware that it's possible to paint an image in only three colors, reduce it down to three colors, and yet end up saving it in a GIF file with a 256-color color table, only three of whose entries are actually used. (In fact, not only is that scenario possible, it's the *default* for some tools you might use to create your GIF file.) That invisible color map could account for three-quarters of an image file's size! When you create your GIF file, make sure that you're not only reducing the colors in the image, but also that you're storing the image with a reduced color map.

### Picking a Palette

When you're dealing with GIF files, the file's size mostly depends on the number of colors. But the quality of your image as seen by your readers might also depend on *which* colors you're using.

If your target audience works with full-color (16-bit or better) monitors, you can safely use up the 256 colors of your GIF on a truly breathtaking 256 shades of orange. A color map that has been tailored to the image in this way is called an "adaptive palette," since it's been adapted to the image rather than being set up before the fact. Most of the GIF files in my personal pages are set up with adaptive palettes, since that's the best way to balance file size and image quality.

However, if your target audience is heavily slanted towards users with 8-bit monitors, your 256 color choices will be competing with the 256 colors chosen by the system or by the Web browser. Can you guess who'll win that fight?

If you can't beat them, you can at least join them by forcing your GIF files to use the browser's chosen color map. Most graphics-format converters will let you specify a target palette when you move from full color to restricted, indexed color. Even better, if you're creating original art for the Web (icons, buttons, or background textures, for example) plan to use that color map from the beginning.

We'll get into this subject in more detail later in this chapter, along with other color issues. Don't let all of this weigh too heavily on you at first, though: A lot of artwork and photographs simply aren't well-suited to the arbitrary restrictions enforced by a special color map. It would be silly to ruin your images just so that you can have the satisfaction of having done the "professional" thing. Personally, I only bother using a pre-determined browser palette when I'm dealing with original images that are meant for a professional site. In other circumstances it just doesn't seem worth the constrictions and the extra work to me.

## Interlacing

When you're viewing a image that is stored on your local system, it doesn't much matter how it's stored: it usually gets displayed all at once. But no one likes looking at a blank screen, and so when the file containing an image is slowly coming across a phone line, most Web browsers will try to display what they can *before* the file has been completely copied to your local system—and suddenly the order in which parts of the image are stored becomes visible to the user.

By default, GIF, like many other formats, stores images top-to-bottom, left-to-right. When only half the image has been downloaded, only the top half of the image can be shown. If the file transfer is going slowly and the bottom half of the image contains anything of importance, this process can be fairly suspenseful for the viewer.

The GIF format also allows for interlacing images, however: instead of going strictly top-to-bottom, row-by-row of pixels, an interlaced GIF slices the image up into four top-to-bottom portions. First it stores every eighth row, and then starts filling in the gaps between those rows.

Depending on how the browser decides to display a partial interlaced GIF, the download progress might resemble a rough sketch coming into sharp focus, or a venetian blind being closed. In any case, the viewer gets a rough look at the entire picture sooner.

Since the GIF file is the same size no matter what, why bother to interlace?

- Getting to see the "whole picture" more quickly (even if fuzzily) gives the illusion of a faster download. The viewer doesn't feel as compelled to stare impatiently at a "focusing" process as he or she does to stare at a "curtain drawing" process.

- It's a dreadful thought, but not every viewer *wants* to wait around for all of your graphics to download. Maybe it's a tough day at the Internet hubs and transfers are going slowly; maybe your reader has another file transfer going on in the background, or maybe your reader is simply in a hurry. It's usually easier for a viewer to make a decision to stay around or go away from a rough overall sketch than from the top eighth of the image.

- The ability to interrupt is especially important if your GIF is being used as an imagemap. Nothing is more frustrating than wanting to get to a particular location on a site, but having to wait for an image file to slowly unfold until it reaches the shape that provides a link. Of course, you should always make sure that there's a text-only route to any link that you reach through an imagemap—but if you don't do that, at least make your image interlaced!

## Transparency

The first version of the GIF standard (GIF87a), like many graphics formats, had no concept of transparency. Every image stored in the format had to be rectangular, and every pixel inside that rectangle had a color and would be displayed.

The later GIF89a standard came up with a simple way of handling transparency (or, if you prefer, of storing non-rectangular images) by copping the "blue screen" approach that lets television weather reporters seem to stand in front of a satellite picture. The reporters actually stand in front of a blue screen; all colors in the reporter's picture except for blue are then superimposed over the satellite picture. (Perhaps that's how weather reporters got into the habit of wearing such unbusinesslike attire…)

In the GIF version of blue-screening, you pick one color out of the file's color table, and declare that color to be "invisible." When the browser displays the file, it will skip any pixels whose color is the invisible one. (Draw a cartoon of your favorite weather reporter, stick the cartoon on a blue background, save the image as a GIF with blue defined as the transparent color, and you'll get the full effect.)

Note that the GIF file still stores a rectangle, no matter what convoluted cut-out shape you actually end up showing. You haven't saved any storage space by using transparent GIFs. All you've done is

ask that the browser not display all the pixels that you've stored.

As a Web author, you should know about a couple of problems with the simple blue-screen approach to transparency:

- Once you pick a color to be transparent, it will be transparent anywhere in the image, including places you might not expect. (This one you may have already seen on TV: If the weather reporter is wearing a blue name tag, you'll see clouds from the satellite map showing right through the reporter's body.) This will assuredly trip you up if you, like most sensible artists, create your images on a neutral background like white or light gray. The self-portrait in your GIF file will look great in your image editor, but put it on a red background, and watch those eyes glow.

- Since a monitor's pixels are not infinitely small, anything displayed on a computer has to be mapped onto a rectangular grid. As a result, curved lines tend to look a little jagged in computer graphics unless a technique called "anti-aliasing" is used. An anti-aliased curve will surround the curved line with a few pixels. These mix the line's colors and the background's colors, giving a smoother, more accurately curved look. Most good graphics editors will create anti-aliased lines and characters. The problem is that a blue-screen approach to transparency only allows *one* background color, not a *mix* of a foreground and a background color. Let's say that you've created a text headline image using a white background. Naturally, you want the text to be anti-aliased. Your banner will look fine in your graphics program, but put it on a Web page with a dark background, and the mixed foreground and background colors around the text will form a hideously ugly halo.

To handle the first problem, I try to make sure that the background color I pick is something that's glaringly *not* in the image proper. (Lime green or neon red are typical choices.) Sure, the background looks awfully gaudy in the image editor, but the browsers won't be showing it.

The second problem is a bit more difficult. In fact, it's unsolvable. It's one of the reasons why more advanced image formats (like Photoshop's proprietary format or PNG) take the alpha-channel approach to transparency: by using an alpha channel, you can specify that pixels are "50 percent transparent."

What's the poor Web author to do? We either have to junk anti-aliasing or—at least to some extent—junk transparency. Usually I take the latter approach: I create my "transparent" graphic after I have some idea of the background color for the page that will contain it. The anti-aliased halo won't be so obvious if it's against an appropriate color. Unfortunately, if I ever want to use the image against a drastically different background, I'll have to go back to my original, pre-GIF-ified image file and redo it.

You could also forget about transparency altogether, and try to use exactly the same color on the background of the image and on the background of the page. But to me, that seems like overkill: First, it's actually more difficult than you might think to force the browser to use exactly the same color in both places, especially if the color isn't included in the browser's standard palette. Secondly, the image's canvas will become rather startlingly evident if you end up putting it on a page that uses a background image rather than a flat background color.

Admittedly, my planned-halo approach is not a perfect compromise. But what compromise is?

### Is "GIF" pronounced "Ghiff" or "Jiff"?

Nobody else knows for sure, either, so don't let the other kids make fun of you. Actually, there's an offi-

cial document that specifies "jiff," but, as James D. Murray points out in his graphics format FAQ, that doesn't make much sense: "The 'G' is from the word 'Graphics' and not 'Jraphics'."

### All About GIF89a

**http://member.aol.com/royalef/gifabout.htm**
This is probably the best semi-technical introduction to the inner workings of the format. Royal Frazier, the author of an excellent GIF animation tutorial referenced in a later chapter, also puts the emphasis on animation here, but the structural information is common to both multiple-image and single-image GIF files.

### All the World Reads GIF

**http://www.publish.com/0396/compression/ gif.html**
This page presents a sensible treatment of the GIF format, its benefits and its limitations. I particularly liked the "sock drawer" elucidation of GIF compression.

### Anti-aliasing, Transparency, and the Web

**http://www.lunaloca.com/tutorials/ antialiasing/**
An excellent overview of the anti-aliased transparent GIF problem, with vivid examples. Unfortunately, the "Advanced" sections seem to be permanently "under construction"—that is, they lack any content at all.

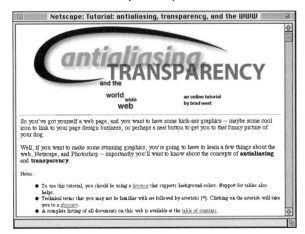

### Creating Transparent GIF Images Using Lview Pro

http://www.iconbazaar.com/tutorials/

Transparency for Dummies: Randy D. Ralph has assembled two remarkably detailed (including screen shots of every applicable menu in action), step-by-step tutorials using the graphics program Lview Pro, one for Windows 3.1 and one for Windows 95. There are also links to download Lview Pro and to other transparency sites.

### DiP: GIF Transparency

http://www.algonet.se/~dip/gif_faq.htm

Part of Thomas Lindström's always entertaining "Digital Pictures" site, this how-to shows the benefits of real working experience more than many other tutorials on the Web. The sections on handling shadows and anti-aliasing are particularly impressive.

### Fefe's Transparency Apparatus

http://www.inf.fu-berlin.de/~leitner/trans/

The Transparency Apparatus is an on-line service for creating transparent GIFs. Select one of thirteen languages from the introductory page, then enter the URL of the GIF you wish to add transparency to. When the image is displayed, click on an area with the color you'd like to make transparent. You'll then be presented with a new page showing the graphic with the selected color knocked out. If all is well, finish up by using your browser's "save" command to store the changed image on your local disk. A nice hack, but as with other on-line image-manipulation services, your image file must already be on the Web, necessitating extra download and upload operations. And since there are free transparency utilities available for virtually every platform, I'd suggest you go with a locally installed program instead.

### GIF Optimization

http://www.nmc.csulb.edu/nmcpages/how/gifoptimize.html

Most optimization guides assume that you've started with an existing image as a given. This page is unusual in guessing that you may be creating images from scratch expressly for publication on the Web—not that unlikely a scenario—and in explaining how you can design source images that will make small GIF files. You should replace all mention of "system palette" colors with "browser palette" instead: the former may have been left over from CD-ROM-based multimedia work. Otherwise, a valuable resource.

### Removing the Kilo From the Byte

http://www.adobemag.com/PDFs/howtoPDF/kilo.pdf

J. Scott Hamlin takes us on an excellent walkthrough of his attempt to turn a photographic image into the smallest possible GIF file, providing a much more realistic notion of the work involved than you'd get from most on-line tutorials. Unlike many Web pundits, Hamlin prefers to use the GIF format, even for photographic material. In his experience, the extra processing time taken up by JPEG decompression makes up for any downloading time that might be shaved off by JPEG compression. That's not my experience, so I may have a faster computer and a slower link than Hamlin does. But I have no quarrels with his main point: that you can make a surprisingly small, surprisingly clear GIF file out of an image as long as you're prepared to work hard at reducing its colors.

### Transparency

http://www.kittenkaboodles.com/main/edu/html/Trans/Trans.html

Now that so many more general graphics utilities can set transparent colors in GIF files, there's probably not much point to downloading this specialized Macintosh program created by Aaron Giles. But I'd still like to pay tribute to its early appearance on the scene, its speed and its classy interface: drag a GIF into the program, click on the color you want to disappear, and that's it. The original author seems to have dropped off the Web, but this page includes the documentation and a step-by-step illustration of the program in action.

### Transparent and Interlaced GIF FAQ

http://www.boutell.com/faq/tinter.htm

This page from Thomas Boutell's World Wide Web FAQ succinctly describes GIF transparency and interlacing, and explains why they're useful on the Web. There are also a few links to applicable utilities, with a special emphasis on freeware.

## Transparent Background Images

http://members.aol.com/htmlguru/
transparent_images.html

Chuck Musciano's introduction to GIF transparency is heavily slanted toward Unix tools, but the section on isolating a background color and the nicely detailed walkthrough example are both usefully platform independent. (Note that the title is a little misleading: this page was written before background images became an optional modifier to the HTML body tag.)

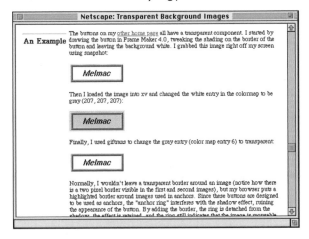

## JPEG

Properly speaking, "JPEG" is not a file format but a standard method of compressing images, originated by the Joint Photographic Experts Group (thus the acronym). But since when do we speak properly on the Web?

The idea behind JPEG compression is that the human eye doesn't necessarily need all the information stored in a full graphics file. Instead, the theory goes, a fair amount of computer-stored data can be thrown away before the eye notices that anything is drastically wrong. The techniques used in JPEG were designed for full-color photographs, and as the source image gets farther away from photographic qualities—in particular, as it approaches sharp, computer-generated shapes or line art—the JPEG methods become less useful.

Note that JPEG compression depends on throwing away exact details of the image. This is why it's called a "lossy" type of compression, and why you should always wait until the very last step of Web image creation before storing your image in the JPEG format. Technically speaking, the GIF format is not lossy: no information is lost when an image is stored as a GIF. Speaking practically, however, since most graphics have to lose some of their colors before they can be squeezed into the GIF format, quality is lost with GIFs as well—sometimes much more quality than would be lost with JPEG.

Since much of the JPEG trickery involves subtle color changes, there's no option for "blue screen" transparency, and there's no way to restrict a JPEG file to use only a particular color palette. On the other hand, JPEG supports the full range of visible colors, and most JPEG viewers on 256-color systems (including Web browsers) manage the color downgrading negotiation fairly gracefully. To put it another way, the GIF format gives you more ways to optimize for a particular set-up; the JPEG format makes it easier for you to make a file that will display adequately.

In fact, probably the only decisions you'll ever have to make when using JPEG compression are whether to make a progressive or baseline JPEG, and how much to try to compress the image—or equivalently, since JPEG compression depends on losing image quality, how high you'd like your quality setting to be.

Although it's doubtful that you'll need them, JPEG compression does support options past the quality settings you're restricted to with most image editors and converters. If you want to experiment with smoothing capabilities or off-the-normal-scale compression, you can try the official "cjpeg" Unix program from the Independent JPEG Group, or search the JPEG FAQ sheet listed below for a heavy-duty conversion program that will run on your own computer system.

### Picking a Compression Level

It's hard to give advice on compression levels (or, if you prefer, "desired quality of image") if only because there's no standard scale for JPEG compression level. Well, actually, there *is* a standard scale, courtesy of the Independent JPEG Group, but very few graphics tools bother to use it. Instead, they all use their own, different scales, which often span different ranges than the Independent JPEG Group's standard.

As I mentioned before, when I'm deciding on a final Web format for a new image, I make a series of samples and then compare their file sizes and their looks. I usually restrict my JPEG tests to one "high quality" file and one "low quality" file, and don't bother with the sort of painstaking experimentation I apply to GIF files.

The reason for this laziness is that, in my experience, JPEG compression settings make astonishingly little difference. All right, a quality setting of 5 percent (assuming your software even allows it) will look awful, and a quality setting of 100 percent will take a lot of file space. But a quality setting of 80 percent usually looks about the same as 100 percent, and a quality setting of 50 percent usually doesn't take much less file space than 80 percent. Only in exceptional cases has it seemed worthwhile to try to find an absolutely optimal JPEG setting: for most images, the distinctions between "pretty good" and "pretty bad" are too slim.

### Progressive vs. Baseline

Depending on how current your graphics editing and conversion software is, you might be given a chance to choose between creating a "baseline" JPEG and a "progressive" JPEG. A baseline JPEG is stored in the usual left-to-right, top-to-bottom way. A progressive JPEG (so called for its more pleasant-looking progress rather than for its political opinions) operates more or less like an interlaced GIF: a rough sketch of the image appears first, and then is brought into focus as more of the JPEG file arrives.

There are a couple of important differences between the GIF and the JPEG ideas of progressiveness, though.

- Back when interlaced GIFs were just coming into fashion, it didn't matter that much if the viewing software didn't understand interlacing: the GIFs would still be displayed top-to-bottom. But software that doesn't understand the progressive JPEG format (and there are still some such programs around) won't be able to display the progressive JPEG file at all.

- GIF files are fairly easy for programs to deal with; JPEG decompression tends to take more noticeable effort. In a progressive JPEG, each one of the "focusing" passes takes just as much effort as displaying the entire JPEG. If the image file is local, or available over a very fast link, this can introduce an unnecessary delay.

Neither of these problems is exactly fatal, but unless I'm dealing with a photographic imagemap, I tend to avoid progressive JPEG.

### JPEG FAQs

http://www.cis.ohio-state.edu/hypertext/faq/usenet/jpeg-faq/top.html

Maintained by the Independent JPEG Group, this collection of frequently asked questions (and their associated frequent answers) is divided into two parts, with a hypertext fan-out of answers. The first part addresses such general issues as how to decide between JPEG and GIF formatting, how to determine an optimal compression level, the difference between "JPEG compression" and "JPEG files," and why there is no transparency in JPEG.

The second part is a remarkably complete cross-platform directory of freeware and shareware programs that display or create JPEG files, including free C source code from the Independent JPEG Group itself.

## JPEG Overview
**http://www.c-cube.com:80../tecno/jpeg.html**
If you're yearning for some straight talk about discrete cosine transforms, come to this technical site, courtesy of the company that cut through the standards committee blockages and provided the JPEG file format we all know and load: C-Cube Microsystems.

## The JPiG Project
**http://www.algonet.se/~dip/jpig_1a.htm**
The Digital Pictures (or DiP) site hosts this proposal (by Ed Scott and site author Thomas Lindström) to add alpha-channel transparency to the JPEG format, loosely based on a proprietary JPEG variant created by Altamira Composer programmers before the product was taken over by Microsoft. Will JPiGs fly? Lack of attention, standards group support, and tools seem like insurmountable wing-trimmers, but the site makes for interesting, even lively, reading.

## Progressive JPEG Information
**http://www.in-touch.com/pjpeg.html**
This heavily framed page was set up to publicize inTouch Technology's shareware progressive JPEG converters. Aside from the download links (and, as always, I recommend checking the capabilities of your current software before downloading specialized programs), you'll also find a side-by-side comparison of normal "baseline" JPEG and the newer "progressive" JPEG format.

## PNG

PNG (for "Portable Network Graphics," or, if you're fond of programmer humor, "PNG's Not GIF") is a graphics format designed from the beginning to overcome many of the problems of cross-platform display. It gained quite a publicity boost when the supposedly free-and-open GIF format turned out to rely on a proprietary compression algorithm. Although that mess has largely been straightened out, on the strengths of its own features PNG has gained plenty of fans from the technical community, most notably the World Wide Web Consortium, W3C, which has officially recommended it as a Web technology.

Previously unattainable graphics features that PNG aims to supply include:

- Real alpha-channel transparency as opposed to GIF's color-coded transparency; this would finally allow anti-aliased graphics to be shown against any background.

- Lossless GIF-or-better compression of images with more than 256 colors: this would let it be used for images with many colors (like JPEG), but would also let the same file format be used across multiple editing sessions (unlike JPEG files, which degrade every time they're saved in the format).

- Non-proprietary compression—and we're promised that there'll be no legal surprises this time.

- Automatic gamma correction to take care of the single most insurmountable problem of Web graphics: the fact that there's no way to create an image that will look the same across different computer systems.

Sounds great, huh? The only obvious strike against PNG is the weight of history, odd though it may seem to speak about the weight of four years of history. If we were back in the early days of the Web and dependent on the free labor of researchers and students, PNG might easily win out. After all, the only reason GIF and JPEG became such popular file formats was the support given them by Web browsers. But nowadays there are plenty of GIF and JPEG files to support and, given the non-proprietary nature of PNG, it's not immediately obvious how a commercial browser company will make lots of money by building in PNG support. Until the most popular browsers support PNG, I would be foolish to use it in my Web pages. (Netscape does have a few PNG plug-ins, but the plug-in format eliminates the benefits of PNG transparency and doesn't support imagemaps.)

To answer the inevitable question: PNG's creators declare that it's pronounced "ping," and even include "unambiguous pronunciation" among the features of the format. I think that's too bold a claim to make for a vowelless acronym; personally, when I first saw it, I imagined it pronounced à la Boris Karloff in "The Old Dark House": "Puh-nhgh-nhgh-hnn…"

### A Better Mousetrap for the Web

**http://www.adobemag.com/PDFs/ftrPDF/mouse.pdf**

Another article in the ever-annoying Acrobat format that *Adobe Magazine* prefers to HTML, this story by J. Scott Hamlin covers the background and probable future of the PNG story.

### PNG (Portable Network Graphics) Home Page

**http://www.wco.com/~png/**

Perhaps the only "official" standards home ever to use the description "turbo-studly," Greg Roelofs's page is simultaneously definitive and informal, not to mention enthusiastic. The site contains everything the PNG student might be looking for: the history behind the format, the features of the format, demos, news, links, applications to create and convert PNG files, and a survey of browser support.

### PNG and Gamma

**http://www.w3.org/pub/WWW/Graphics/PNG/platform.html**

This propaganda piece for the PNG format doubles as one of the best introductions to gamma and color-cast problems I've seen on the Web. The secret? Embedded examples of cross-platform and cross-monitor differences—plus, of course, examples of how PNG solves the problems.

### Portable Network Graphics

**http://www.w3.org/pub/WWW/Graphics/**

W3C has recommended PNG as a perfect replacement for the GIF format on the Web. This is its central page on the format, including links to the "official" PNG home, to press releases, to the PNG standards themselves, to background material on PNG cross-platform benefits, and even to a PNG-handling test for your browser. (Mine failed miserably.)

## THE HTML OF ART

Some of the most confusing aspects of the first versions of HTML were the image-displaying tag attributes, and it shouldn't have been surprising that the first major rift ("BLINK" tag excepted) introduced into the HTML standard by Netscape Corp.

involved images—which is not to say that image-handling became any less confusing. Not only did some of Netscape's additions clash with the intent of the original tag attributes, but soon even the black-on-gray textual environment of Web browsing was under attack by, of all things, hexadecimal numbers. (I always suspected that New Math got a bad rap.)

The basics of embedding an image aren't too ugly, aside from the peculiar abbreviations: "IMG" is the name of the tag, while "SRC" is the URL of the file that contains the images. Past that, we enter murky waters.

## ALTERNATE TEXT

The "ALT" attribute contains text that should be displayed when the image *isn't* displayed for some reason: because the reader has turned off image loading, or because a text-only browser is being used, or because there was a problem downloading the image file.

You should always include an ALT text if the image contains important text that doesn't appear elsewhere (a company logo or a section heading, for example) or if the image operates as a button (i.e., it is a link). If the image is purely decorative, please just let it be: No one will be impressed by seeing a message like "turn on image loading to see my great pics!" or "[Image]" or "yellow dot" or, God help us, "GET A REAL BROWSER." At least I wasn't impressed by any of these messages when I saw them.

It sounds like the ALT attribute might give you a fairly straightforward way to make a page that works equally well with or without images, but don't you believe it. Take a look at Figure 4.1 below for an example of what viewers all too often see.

1  ALT text is supposed to be pure text, as embedded HTML tags have a varying (but always wrong) effect. That means, for example, that you can't make the ALT text for your company logo or big section heading display in an appropriately big, bold way. There are hacks to try to deal with this, but they're all browser-version-specific, and shouldn't be counted on.

2  If you use the WIDTH and HEIGHT attributes in your image tag (and you should), when your page is viewed in a browser with image loading off, the ALT text will be fit into the space reserved for the image. Or, more likely, the ALT text will be cut off and made illegible when it's forced into the space reserved for the image. This seems like a browser bug—after all, if the users say that they want to see text rather than images, why should the browser try to reserve space for the images rather than for the text?—but there's no doubt that it's an extremely *popular* browser bug.

3  Since the ALT text can't contain HTML tags, it can't contain multiple links. Thus it's incapable of replacing an imagemap. If you want to let imageless readers follow your links, you'll have to supply a text-only menu as well as an imagemap.

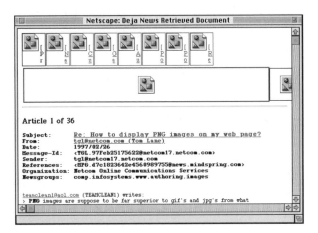

**Figure 4.1**
The amazing truncated ALT text, as found at DejaNews.

The unpleasant moral is that even if you use ALT text in the nicest possible way, you may still have to provide alternative interfaces in your pages. The situation isn't all that nightmarish, however: a compact line of textual links at the bottom of a page can be both very helpful and very inconspicuous.

## ALIGNMENT

I've never been able to understand the intent behind the original HTML "ALIGN" attribute for images. Rather than aligning a picture on a page, it arranges for one (and only one) line of text to either stick out of the top of the image, or out of the middle of the image, or out of the bottom of the image. There just aren't many situations in which those are natural layouts, although heaven knows early Web authors tried to come up with some. If the point was to allow for captions, why not supply a "center above" or a "center below" option instead? I can only guess that the choices arrived at were easy to program.

At any rate, when a young and feisty Netscape Corporation announced that it was adding real image alignment (and centering!) capabilities to HTML, it met with a very enthusiastic reception.

Unfortunately, Netscape chose to use the exact same keyword for *its* alignment (in which text flows around the left or the right of the image) as standard HTML was using, even though the standard idea of alignment (where text should start *vertically* in relation to the image) was completely different. As a result, there's no way to completely control relative alignment of a piece of text and a picture using the "IMG" tag: you can't say that text should start to the right of the image halfway down, for example.

Netscape (and other browser makers) also had problems deciding how to make text flow in a consistent way after it had gotten past its adjoining image. For example, should the first line after a left-aligned image immediately wrap over to the left side of the page, or should it hold off till the end of its paragraph? How about if the line is part of a bulleted list? Even different versions of the same browser handled these layout questions differently, leading Web authors to make frequent use of the "<BR CLEAR=ALL>" tag, which gives us some more predictable control over the end of image-instigated columns, albeit at the cost of unnecessary blank space.

The best solution to these kinds of alignment and layout problems arrived with HTML tables (particularly when their Netscape-instigated extensions are used), and borderless tables are worth pursuing if your layout plans are more complicated than a centered header, text on the left and an image on the right.

## WIDTH AND HEIGHT

The "WIDTH" and "HEIGHT" attributes may not seem particularly useful at first—after all, browsers that don't display images shouldn't care about the size of the images they're not seeing, and browsers that do display images will discover the size soon enough. The question turns out to be, "How soon is soon enough?" A graphical browser can't lay out text properly until the widths and heights of the page's images are known. This can be a fairly long wait and, since the HTML text is already loaded, it's also an unnecessary one. If you give the browser a preview of the images' widths and heights, the text can be laid out before all the images have been fetched.

### How do you get the width and height into the document?

You can do it by hand, by noting the width and height of the image in pixels while it's still in your image editor or conversion software.

If you're working with an existing Web graphic, you can get the width and height from the browser: Just load the image file into the browser as its own page, with no surrounding HTML. In Netscape, for example, you can use the pop-up menu over an embedded image, and pick the "Open This Image" option. The default title given to the bare-image page should include the image's dimensions (e.g., "JPEG image 125x140 pixels").

A few specialized utilities that automate the process of calculating and inserting width and height attributes are listed below.

You might also want to check on the capabilities of your chosen HTML editor. Many will automatically calculate the image's width and height at the moment you insert the "IMG" tag.

Of course, if you change your image after embedding it in the page, you'll have to remember to update the width and height in the HTML accordingly. Forgetting that step is, in fact, how I found the answer to the next question.

### What happens if you use the wrong width or height?

The browser has already laid out the elements of the page, so what should it do when it finds out that it's been lied to? Interestingly enough, both Netscape Navigator and Internet Explorer, trusting creatures that they are, decide to go with what you told them rather than what they see with their own eyes: they'll stretch or squeeze the image to fit the width and height specified in the HTML.

Web authors were quick to exploit this feature for our own ends, of course: We can make a small image to save on download time, and then have the browser expand it into a much larger image. This technique isn't of much use for "normal" GIF files, since it will turn individual pixels into visible squares and produce a blocky, jagged picture. But it can work very well for:

- **Making colored rectangles, horizontal lines, and vertical lines.** Just download one (count

them, one) pixel of the color you want, and set width and height accordingly.

- **Special effects.** Many Web graphics tutorials use the browser-scaling method to zoom in on details of an image file.

> You can also use the width and height attributes to squeeze a large graphic into a smaller space, but that would be a slightly perverse waste of download time. Nevertheless, I've seen Web authors do it! I can only assume that it was a clueless attempt to mimic the "thumbnail" links they'd seen.
>
> A thumbnail is a very small graphics file that links to a large (usually close to full-screen) graphics file. It's usually used to give your readers a fast preview of the larger image, allowing them to decide whether and when to download it. The thumbnail is usually a drastically shrunk and simplified copy of the larger image, or a detail of the larger image.
>
> As you might imagine, thumbnails are extremely useful for museum sites and other collections of artwork. But since the thumbnails are there to give your readers a quick overview of what's available, the entire point is lost if your readers have to download all the huge full-image files before they're able to see the "thumbnail" page.

### GifScan 2.1

**http://www.users.dircon.co.uk/~marcb/ gifscan.html**

GifScan is a Macintosh utility, free for non-commercial use and $10 for money-making ventures. When you drag and drop a group of image or HTML files on the application, it automatically creates appropriate HTML link and image tags, including width and height attributes. Since the generated HTML goes into the cut-and-paste clipboard, you can immediately paste the results into the page you're editing; or, if you prefer, you can edit the results within the utility itself. GifScan doubles as a GIF inspector, providing extensive information about a GIF file's color map, size, and transparency. Biggest problem: It doesn't handle JPEG files or GIF animations.

### html-update-img
**http://pertsserver.cs.uiuc.edu/~hull/html-update-img/**

This page provides access to a Perl program that can calculate width and height for every image in a group of HTML pages, and then automatically insert width and height attributes into the pages' "<IMG>" tags. It's an excellent time-saver if you're dealing with older HTML pages that are already on a Unix server.

### Images in HTML
**http://support.imagiware.com/Images/imagesinhtml.html**

This is another anatomy of the IMG tag, with a few alignment examples. It also contains one of the only "INPUT TYPE=IMAGE" forms examples I've seen.

### The <IMG ALIGN> Extension
**http://tars5.elte.hu/demo/img_net.html**

This hilarious attempt to make Netscape's baroque variations on the "IMG" tag clear by demonstration reminds me of an early Andy Kaufman routine. It's the straightest information you'll ever get, somehow reaching closure with the "(It does not seem to be right.)" aside in small print.

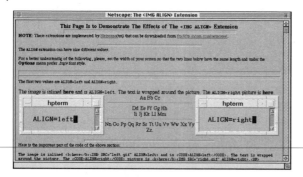

### Jan's Guide to HTML: Images
**http://www.ftech.net/~dutch/guide/images.html**

This page treats the image tag one attribute at a time. Its special strength lies in its heavy use of examples. I was amused to see that the example of old-style alignment exposed a bug in Internet Explorer 3.0—apparently it's not top priority in Redmond!

### WWWimagesize
**http://www.tardis.ed.ac.uk/~ark/wwwis/**

This page points to an unusually powerful Perl script that automatically calculates and inserts image widths and heights. The list of command line options may be a bit overwhelming for the non-Unix-user, but one of them may be just what you need if you're trying to update an older Web site. This is probably the most popular such utility on the Web.

## BACKGROUNDS AND FOREGROUNDS

Black on gray, black on gray; how tired Web authors became of black on gray. But with Version 1.1 of its browser, Netscape introduced color controls for page backgrounds and text, and soon half the Web looked like the opening credits to *Star Trek*. White on black, white on black; how tired Web readers became of white on black.

There are two approaches to page backgrounds: you can specify a background image to tile end-to-end on the back of the page, or you can specify a background color to fill the entire page with.

### Avoiding the Hex

It's fairly common for computer graphics tools to specify colors as a combination of intensities of red, green, and blue. Zero percent of possible red plus 0 percent of possible green plus 0 percent of possible blue makes black; 100 percent of possible red plus 0 percent of the other colors makes bright red; 100 percent of all three colors makes white.

Because computer software is exceedingly fond of 256 (which is how many different numbers fit into an 8-bit piece of memory), it's also fairly common for computer graphics tools to express color intensities as a number between 0 and 255, in which 0 means 0 percent and 255 means 100 percent.

And artists, bless 'em, have learned to live with these peculiarities of computer graphics tools, little suspecting what was in store…

For computer programmers are exceedingly fond of the hexadecimal system, which lets you use one digit for every 4-bit piece of memory, and computer programmers rather than artists ran Netscape Corporation. And so when Netscape added color settings to HTML, they decided that colors could be most easily expressed as a hash mark followed by three pairs of hexadecimal digits (a pair each for red, blue, and green) with no punctuation between pairs. How could they possibly expect that some people would find this confusing?

Luckily, resting directly behind a hexadecimal color specification like "#ffffff" is the decimal equivalent "255, 255, 255" (punctuation added for clarity)—and resting somewhat farther behind both of them are the percentages "100 percent, 100 percent, 100 percent." That makes it easy to ask a computer to translate between the format that your graphics software likes and the format that HTML likes.

Despite my B.A. in math, I usually use a calculator to do these conversions. For you non-calculator types, many image-editing programs now have built-in hexadecimal color displays, but there are also some specialized utilities, which I'll point to below.

### Text and Background Colors

The most essential thing to remember when you decide to modify background and text colors is that text should (in most cases, anyway) be legible.

As my colleagues at Sun Microsystems like to say, "Well, *duh!*" No, I'm not suggesting that you would knowingly put black text on a black background. But remember that not all browsers and not all computers display the "same" colors in at all the same way. Take your carefully modulated, moody combinations, drastically increase their darkness (or, in geek

language, "gamma level,") and strip them of access to thousands of colors, and you'd be amazed at the hideous results.

Much more on this unpleasant subject will be found in the next section, and you should probably read it before partying down with the color-picker applications listed below.

By the way, it's usually a good idea to set a background color even if you've specified a background image. That gives the browser something to show when image loading is off or while image loading is in progress.

### Background Images

Probably the best advice I can offer regarding background images is to avoid them. The cross-platform interaction between text colors and image colors is just too unpredictable to be worth the trouble. Besides, when was the last time you read a newspaper with pictures directly underneath the text? Even comic books usually use plain white speech balloons.

What about those great poem-on-a-sunset effects that you can get on greeting cards? Isn't *that* worth striving for? Well, there's no arguing with aesthetics (at least not in a technical book), but I should point out that Hallmark poets don't usually get stuck with Times as their default font, and that the tiling of your sunset might be disturbing to readers with larger monitors.

If you do decide to have a background image, try for texture rather than illustration, and try to keep the texture bland and light. Light text on a black background can be fairly readable; light text on a varying background is much harder to deal with.

What about those vertically striped pages? You know, the ones with the racing flames down the middle, or the spiral notebook binding down the left hand side, or the ripped paper edge down the right hand side, or the sidesplittingly hilarious "Under

Construction" signs that would be obscuring the text if there was any text to obscure? Well, to answer a question with a question: What about the display space you'll end up having to waste since you don't want to cover up your nifty new vertical stripe?

But if you've come up with a witty and original approach that fits your content, more power to you. Just make sure that the super-long super-thin background image you use to achieve your effect really *is* super-long: users who own large monitors or run with high resolution will not be impressed when your image starts tiling on the right side of the monitor.

One last note: Supposedly, if you use a GIF with transparency as your background image, the background color will show through it. However, you shouldn't count on that particular feature being implemented in many browsers. In fact, both interlaced and transparent GIFs have buggy histories as backgrounds. It's safest to stick with old-fashioned top-to-bottom rectangles as your tiling image. If you really must have a tiling image, that is.

>  **If you want a darker or more complex background pattern on a page but would also like to give your readers an opportunity to read your text, a solution is available, as long as you're willing to use non-standard HTML: Put your text blocks into a table, and use the background color attribute for the table or table cell that the text is in. The table's background color will cover the page's busy background image, and provide a sedately readable setting.**
>
> **This works for Internet Explorer and for Netscape, but it isn't part of HTML 3.2. Speaking editorially, though, table backgrounds are such a great idea that it's hard to believe they won't continue to be supported.**

## Background Colors

**http://colors.infi.net/colorindex.html**

Infi.Net provides this huge list of descriptive color names with associated hexadecimal codes. Click on one, and a document frame is presented that contains a background of the given color and several simply colored squares in the foreground. The approach is especially nice if you've always enjoyed buying house paint, and yearn for an online equivalent. Now you can boot up and relive those happy hours spent deciding between "Dusty Rose" and "Medium Spring Green" while you author for the Web. There's also a brief introduction to color-setting HTML.

## The Background FAQ

**http://www.sci.kun.nl/thalia/guide/color/faq.html**

Here you'll find a breezy introduction to background and foreground color settings, which also includes an extensive collection of links to background textures and color pickers.

## ColorCenter

AUTHOR'S CHOICE **http://www.hidaho.com/colorcenter/cc.html**

Although officially a "beta," this JavaScript-based HTML color picker is my favorite: it's cross-platform, it runs client-side rather than on an over-exercised server, and it compactly combines several approaches to the problem. (I also found it a fairly simple matter to munge a local standalone copy for off-the-air Web authoring.) On the bottom of the page is a large, well-organized color pal-

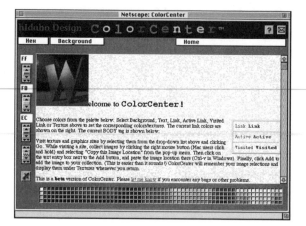

ette (or, if you're in "Texture" mode, a customizable collection of background images); on the left are increment and decrement buttons and numerical inputs to adjust red, blue, and green proportions (or amounts of all colors at once); on the top are menus that let you choose RGB display style (hexadecimal, 0-255 scale, or percentages), what color you're setting (background or any of the text types), as well as direct links to various collections of background images. And in the middle of the page you get to see the results of your current settings.

## Color Conceiver

http://www.wolfenet.com/~monron/
conceiver/

Color Conceiver is a Windows freeware program to help you with colorized HTML. You can pick colors for the background and the usual text variations by using sliders, numerical proportions, or a much-too-limited palette. Previews are clearly shown. You can add custom colors to your palette with hue and luminance maps. The most unique feature of the program is one that I sincerely hope you never use: a tool that attempts to apply a gradient of colors (e.g., a rainbow) to text, using the color attributes of large numbers of "<FONT>" tags. When it comes to doing the basic job, the basic design is fine, and as a proud owner of a 256-color Windows box, I might very well be using this utility if it had shown me the 216-color palette shared by Netscape and Internet Explorer.

## ColorMaker

http://www.missouri.edu/~wwwtools/
colormaker/

This color-picking on-line service is wildly popular, but isn't quite up to the friendliness of some other approaches: The palette you're given to make choices from isn't particularly extensive and, instead of pointing and clicking to choose a color, you have to type in the row and column numbers of your choice. Sheesh, you might as well just use hexadecimal. It has one really nice feature, though: the ability to specify any URL as the document that should be used to display the results, rather than sticking users with a boring sample page. There's also a list of color and background links.

## The Color Manipulation Device

http://www.meat.com/software/cmd.html

The Color Manipulation Device is a Windows utility for choosing Web-page text and background colors. Color selection for red, green, and blue proportions is done purely by sliders; these can get a little frustrating when you're trying to match a sampled shade. A straightforward preview screen is automatically updated.

## ColorServe Pro

http://www.biola.edu/cgi-bin/colorpro/
colorpro.cgi

The best of the server-based on-line color picking services, ColorServe Pro uses a hue and saturation color wheel to obtain your choices. You can switch between brightness levels by loading a different color wheel. What are the benefits of this approach over the usual red-blue-green value settings? Well, for one thing, you can use the intuitive knowledge that the colors at opposite sides of the hue wheel will contrast nicely. For another, Web authors generally do work at two quantized brightness levels: one for the background, and one for the various types of text. (If the background is dark, all the text should be fairly light; if the background is light, all the text should be fairly dark.) This makes the wheel-switching seem natural, rather than a chore. My only reservations about recommending ColorServe Pro are that it's server-based —you'll need a good connection to the site to be able to use it. Also, the results of all the text color selections aren't displayed automatically. Still, it's a great job by last-name-less "Dale of Biola University."

## Color Theory

http://www.contrib.andrew.cmu.edu/usr/
dw4e/color/index.html

As long as you're busy mixing colors, why not check out this elementary color-theory text, which explains some basic terms and some standard approaches to contrasts and harmony? One of the benefits of Web publishing is that color printing is cheaper than on paper, and this free site lets you take advantage of that fact: even the slimmest color-theory books tend to be extravagant buys.

### Decimal <--> HEX Converter

http://www.sci.kun.nl/thalia/guide/color/dec-hex.html

A bare-bones basic form that converts color values from the 0-to-255 RGB ranges used by most image editors into HTML-style hexadecimal form and back again. If you intend to spend much time doing this, you'd probably be happier with a local program, but this page is fine for a one-off.

### Document-Specific Background and Foreground Control

http://home.netscape.com/assist/net_sites/bg/index.html

The official word from Netscape Corporation (at least as of V2.0) can be found here, and it's as compact a treatment as you'll find anywhere, title excepted.

### Hands On: Transparency

http://www.ozones.com/~drozone/handson/transparency/index.html

### Hands On: Transparency 2

http://www.ozones.com/~drozone/handson/dither/index.html

These Doc Ozone tutorials deal with one of the trickier but more popular interactions between transparent GIFs and background images: drop shadows. If you want the object you're picturing to look as if it's casting a shadow against the page, how can you deal with an unaligned background texture? A featureless, dark-gray shadow will look pretty strange pasted over bright yellow wallpaper. (Quick-witted readers might spot this as a special case of the "weird halo around anti-aliased GIFs" problem.) The first tutorial explains how to blend a simple background texture to make a suitable shadow color; the second goes after tougher, more contrasty backgrounds.

### Hex Converter

http://www-personal.usyd.edu.au/~jcj/software.html

Grab ahold of this tidy little Macintosh freeware program, which simply converts between comma-separated decimal numbers and squeezed-together hexadecimal numbers. Perfect for a program of its type.

### Opal

http://www.basta.com/Software.htm

From Basta Computing, this little $10 shareware program is principally a Windows 95 color-palette manager, but it's also the only Windows application I've found that will let you quickly find out the hexadecimal specification for any pixel on the screen. Unfortunately, it's not nearly as well-designed for that purpose as specialized Macintosh applications like Pixel Spy and ColorSieve. Perhaps by the time you read this, some enterprising programming student will have come up with something better…

### Pixel Spy

http://shakti.trincoll.edu/~bhorling/pixelspy/

Pixel Spy, created by Bryan Horling, is probably the best Macintosh color sampler. A color sampler lets you determine the color (in RGB proportions, Netscape-style hexadecimal, hue-saturation-brightness, or other color scales) of any pixel on your screen. It may not sound like much, but a good color sampler will let you match or copy any color on your desktop, in an application or on the Web: just take the color values and run to your image editor, or to your HTML background and text color settings. I use color samplers principally to decide on good matches of background color and embedded image color, but they're also invaluable for debugging 256-color problems: the color sampler will display the color's values *as it's displayed on the monitor* rather than as it's stored in the file—you wouldn't believe how tough it is to get that information otherwise. Truly cheap to license, Pixel Spy sets itself above its freeware competition (ColorSieve, for you foolishly cheap Macintosh owners) by optionally trying to find the nearest match to the sampled color in a specified color table; Web authors are likely to be particularly interested in the "browser safe" color table. And the program only costs five dollars. When I say "truly cheap," I mean it.

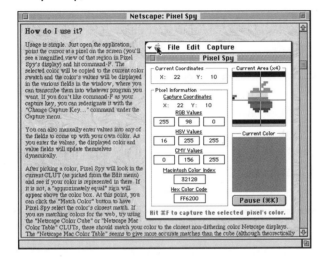

## Rex Swain's Zoomable RGB Color Sampler

**http://www.pcnet.com/cgi-bin/cgiwrap/ ~rhswain/colors.cgi**

A CGI-based background- and text-color picker that gets its "zoomable" name by letting you narrow in on exactly the right color (or, more accurately, exactly the right color for the monitor you're using at the moment). If you pick a greenish blue from the palettes on the first page, you'll go to a page with a range of greenish blues; if you then pick a light greenish blue, you'll go to a page with a range of light greenish blues... then you can start doing similar niddling comparisons for text colors against the background. Sort of fun, in the same way that trying out pens in a stationery store can be fun.

## RGBtoHex

**http://www.lne.com/rgb.html**

About as straightforward a little form as you could find, this on-line converter takes red, green, and blue values

from the standard 0-to-255 scale and displays the HTML-style hexadecimal outcome in the very color you've specified. The Perl script used by the page is free and downloadable.

## 216 Color Guide from Great Wave & Electron Co

**http://itd.rrpc.com/clrguide/index.ssi**

This site lets you choose a background color and then check how 216 different colors of text would look against it, or choose a foreground text color and then check how 216 different colors of background would look behind it. How does it choose the 216 colors? Wait for the next section. For now, suffice it to say that GW&E have provided an on-line service that could easily save you some trial-and-error.

## Using Named Colors in Internet Explorer

**http://www.microsoft.com/workshop/design/ colors/colornames.htm**

More coverage of the long list of "named colors" supported without much official documentation by both Netscape Navigator and Internet Explorer can be found here. This site at least bothers to explain where the names came from and how they ended up in the browsers. It also distinguishes itself by showing all 140 named colors sorted in four different ways: by hue, by brightness, by saturation, and by name.

## The Visca Colored Table Borders Pages

**http://www.visca.com/color/tab-bord.html**

A slightly obsessive examination of the fact that the 3-D edges on table borders are based on the background color of the page. The formula used to make the highlight and shadow colors of the borders is described, and three large image files containing 216 variations of background color, showing their effects on table borders. It takes all kinds; personally, I was much more amused when I saw the table border 3-D effect applied to a background *image*.

### WebColor

**http://ourworld.compuserve.com/homepages/jyigdall/netscape/webcolor.htm**

This flexible Windows freeware program by Michael Yigdall lets you choose background and text colors by using sliders, direct RGB values, sampling of an image, or a customized collection of favorite colors. Its biggest problem is the lack of a built-in preview.

## COLOR CHOICES AND PALETTES

The output of a black pencil is noticeably unlike that of black oil paint, which in turn is noticeably unlike black watercolor paint or black chalk. But the reassuring numerical quality of computer art can fool us into thinking that we've reached some sort of pure ideal of color in our images.

No such luck. It only takes a year or two for history to assert unquestioned sovereignty over rationality. Computer manufacturers have had decades to diverge, and so the color I see on my AV-enhanced Macintosh has little in common with the "same" color as seen on a 8-bit Windows laptop. There are two villains at work to ensure that we can't get along:

- **Color palette differences** between systems
- **Gamma level differences** between monitors

Between them, those two factors mean that the colors you use in your images may not be the same colors your readers get—and even when the colors *are* the same, they're *still* not the same.

Pretty depressing, huh? Cheer up: Leonardo da Vinci and Rembrandt had to go through a lot worse with their artwork, and yet people are still willing to look at their paintings.

And if that's not reassurance enough, delve into the sources below.

### COLOR PALETTE DIFFERENCES

The number of colors that can be displayed at once depends on the graphics card and graphics memory of your reader's computer. What happens if there aren't enough colors to go around?

How that limited supply of colors will be parceled out depends on the program that's running. A graphics program will usually bend over backwards to give the top-level image the colors it wants. (That's one reason that sending a downloaded JPEG to an external specialized viewer will often give you a nicer picture than looking at it as it's embedded in the browser.)

But since browsers generally show several top-level images at once, browser programmers decided to make their lives a little easier by using a standard set of colors for every image on every system. Thus, on 256-color systems, Netscape Navigator and Internet Explorer both use a special cross-platform 216-color palette. The good news is that these colors look more or less the same between Windows and Macintosh (gamma levels excepted). The bad news is that the browsers won't pay any attention to your image's own preferred color choices.

When an embedded image wants to use a color that the system isn't willing to give, the browser has to try to mimic the missing color as best it can. It usually does so with a technique known by the quaint name of "dithering": it speckles several other colors together in a pointillist fashion, much as skin tones are approximated on the Sunday comics page by mixing dots of pink and white. The effect isn't exactly gorgeous, but it's usually better than nothing.

Sometimes, however, it's worse than nothing, and in *those* cases, you as the Web author should probably consider specially tailoring your images to the cross-platform 216-color palette.

## GAMMA LEVEL DIFFERENCES

Even the exact same color using the exact same palette will show up differently on different systems with different monitors.

The reason is a problem in video electronics that you'll usually see referred to as *gamma level*. It turns out that when you pump more energy into a video monitor (for example, by asking for more juice to a white phosphor dot), you don't get *exactly* that much more brightness in return. Throwing the power to 100 percent makes the dot white, all right, and turning the power down to 0 percent makes it black. In between those two extremes, however, the dot will tend to be a little darker than expected.

Some computers (e.g., the Macintosh and, to an even greater extent, SGI workstations) attempt to fix up the gamma curve in software to make the monitor's display match the theoretical requested brightness more closely. Other computers (most Windows PCs, for instance) leave the monitors alone and assume that computer artwork will be designed to match electronic reality.

The result is that any picture, other than a black and white line drawing, that looks fine on a Macintosh will usually look too light on an SGI workstation and too dark on a Windows PC. Not only that, but if you try to correct for the darkness problem by just twiddling the brightness and contrast controls of your monitor, then the *hues* will probably differ noticeably.

There's no real solution to the gamma problem, I'm afraid, although there are software utilities that let Macintosh users adjust their gamma settings. When creating their images, many Web authors use that capability hoping to achieve a *compromise* gamma level halfway between that preferred on PC compatibles and that preferred on the standard Macintosh. After image editing is complete, they'll then reset gamma back to normal.

Why don't savvy Macintosh users just permanently set their gamma levels to match the PC's? Well, if all you're doing with your computer is looking at cross-platform graphics (Web TV, anyone?), that might not be a bad idea. But if you ever do anything *else* on your Macintosh, you'll be taking images that expect Macintosh-level gamma and turning them into murk.

☞ This is more of a true confession than a tip, but it might make you feel better: I once created a personal page in which, for reasons we don't need to go into, I wanted to restrict myself to the colors of mud, volcanic rock, and lava. In other words, dark brown, black, and dark red. It's an impossible situation: I had the choice of washed-out ashy colors on one platform, or black-on-black illegibility on another. If I'd been making the page for someone else, I would've tried to talk them out of the idea. But since it wasn't being done professionally, I gritted my teeth, remembered the example of Andy Warhol's cover design for "White Light, White Heat," and lived with the knowledge that many of my readers got the black-on-black effect.

## The Browser Safe Color Palette
http://www.lynda.com/hex.html

One of the most linked-to pages on the Web is Lynda Weinman's treatment of the 216 colors that are guaranteed to show up in both Netscape Navigator and Internet Explorer on both Windows and Macintosh systems. The full set of colors is supplied in two gigantic GIF files, one arranged by hue and the other by brightness. (It's too bad that she hasn't turned these into tables with colored cells to cut back on the download time...) More useful still is the link to Weinman's FTP site, where you'll find a "browser safe" color table in a form suitable for loading into Photoshop and some other image-creation programs.

## CGSD: Gamma Correction Home Page

**http://www.cgsd.com/papers/gamma.html**

Welcome to Gamma World. This is a model reference site: introductions and detailed articles are all clearly written, graphics are efficiently designed and to the point, and there's a nice balance between original content and external links.

## Color Tables

**http://mrlxp2.mrl.uiuc.edu/~www/rgbtbl.html**

It may not look fancy and it may not be jumping with interactivity, but Gernot Metze has provided something useful with this page. First presented are the 16 colors that were deemed worthy of names by Windows and the HTML standard. Then there's a theoretical introduction to the 216 "browser safe" colors. Finally, and most notably, tables containing the colors themselves are shown. Now, plenty of sites supply the browser-safe colors. And plenty of sites supply easy-to-read palettes of colors including hexadecimal codes, as we saw in the previous section. But here you get both, which makes it much more likely that something resembling your color choices will show up on your reader's monitor. It's a worthwhile addendum to Victor Engel's browser palette site.

## The Discriminating Color Palette

**http://www.adobe.com/newsfeatures/palette/main.html**

In this article reprinted from *Adobe Magazine*, author Lisa Lopuck explains how to use Photoshop to create dither-free images. You don't need to use Photoshop for the contextualizing remarks and techniques to be useful to you, but the article doesn't bother to emphasize just how low a GIF color table can go. Don't make this your only stop, though it's fine as an introduction or a refresher course.

## DMS Guide to Color for the Web

**http://www.oit.itd.umich.edu/projects/DMS/answers/colorguide/**

This is one of the best introductions to GIF color issues, with a good collection of realistic examples and some coverage of the decision we all have to make between adaptive and browser palettes. Note to the baffled: what this page refers to as "diffusion" is what most references call "dithering": mixing up dots of two different colors to give the (not always very convincing) illusion of a third color.

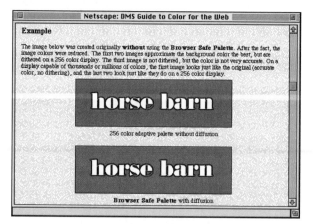

## Hands On: 216 Colors

**http://www.ozones.com/~drozone/handson/gifpallette/index.html**

Cheers to Doc Ozone for expressing what most of us have thought at one point or another while viewing the "browser-safe" palette: "Really now, how many shades of fluorescent green do we really need?" Besides the salutary grumpiness, this succinct page offers both a Photoshop-ready color table *and* an Illustrator-ready color table.

## Hue and Cry

**http://www.mediacentral.com/Magazines/DCMag/dcoct/f3.htm/534782#a**

We Web authors may moan about color inconsistencies between monitors, but that's nothing compared to the problems that graphic artists producing for print have dealt with for years: ink has considerably less in common with a monitor than Windows 95 has in common with the Macintosh OS. This article from *Media Central* magazine is a lively introduction to the ongoing difficulties of color coordination, and to some possible future solutions.

## I Am Curious Yellow

http://www.upenn.edu/newmedia/colors/

Ignore the creepy graphics (at least there's no link to "1000 Pictures of Pamela Anderson") and you'll find one of the best introductions to color differences between computer platforms, with historical background, technical information, jargon definitions, color scales, useful tips, and loads of well-integrated (if not always up-to-date) links. Deserves extra credit for the easy to remember formula "bit depth x resolution = $$".

## In Design School, They Promised No Math

http://webreview.com/96/03/15/tag/index.html

This article from *Web Review* explores palette differences (with a noticeably pro-Mac slant), nicely positioning the Netscape compromise palette. It even makes a valiant attempt at explaining hexadecimal. Luckily, author Bob Schmitt provides links to some excellent on-line tools to handle the hex thing automatically, as well as a link to a Photoshop-loadable version of the Netscape palette.

## Pantone Home Page

http://www.pantone.com/

Pantone is a company dedicated to defining colors consistently, so it's not surprising that it has begun to get involved with the Web. Pantone offers a commercial package called ColorWeb, which seems to be a printed version of the same "browser-safe" palette information available on the Web for free. More interesting in the long run may be its attempts to automatically adjust for gamma level in downloaded image files; currently, its Web-oriented software seems restricted in scope (and damned hard to download), but it certainly has the motivation to improve it.

## Poynton's Colour FAQ

http://www.inforamp.net/~poynton/notes/colour_and_gamma/ColorFAQ.html

A nutritious mixed bag of questions and answers, which range from the slightly theoretical ("What is color?") to engineering esoterica ("How do I transform between CIE XYZ and a particular set of RGB primaries?") with a range of interesting facts and useful definitions scattered along the way.

## Poynton's Gamma FAQ

http://www.inforamp.net/~poynton/notes/colour_and_gamma/GammaFAQ.html

Poynton's back, and gamma's got him. Another fine mix of physics, physiology and practical advice can be found on this gamma-level page. Among the practical items, you'll find brief guides to adjusting your monitor and to handling murky or high-contrast images.

## The Safety Palette

http://www.microsoft.com/workshop/design/safety/safetypalette.htm

An excellent introduction to GIF palette issues from Microsoft—and only to GIF palette issues: its treatment of JPEG is so perfunctory that I wonder why the company even bothered. Not surprisingly, it's better than most at dealing with the Windows system palette.

## The 256, Oops, 216 Colors of Netscape

http://www.connect.hawaii.com/hc/webmasters/Netscape.colors.html

This site picks up where Netscape's own extremely terse description of its 8-bit palette (basically just a list of all 216 RGB combinations) leaves off. The evolution of the palette is covered well, and the page's treatment of the missing 40 colors (colors that aren't missing on the Macintosh) is the clearest I've seen.

## 216 Colors of the Web

http://www.netscapeworld.com/common/nw.color.html

Netscape World supplied this good introduction to browser and system palette issues. A wider variety of approaches to color management than usual is described, and the real-world examples are a welcome touch.

### Victor Engel's No Dither Netscape Color Palette

http://the-light.com/netcol.html

This site is not only the definitive word on the components of the cross-platform cross-browser palette, it's also one of the most remarkable experiments in visualization on the Web, right up there with the virtual frog-dissection kit. The color map is displayed as a split-open cube, as an imagemap with no links (you move your cursor above a color and look at the browser's status line for the color's hexadecimal code), as a spinning animation, as a super-small GIF that can be scaled up using width and height attributes, and as separate red, green, and blue components. That still doesn't exhaust all the images: there are also GIFs that show the 40 extra colors available on 256-color Macintosh systems, others that show dithering grays, and so on.

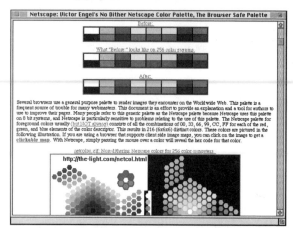

### Why Do Images Appear Darker on Some Displays?: An Explanation of Monitor Gamma

http://www.cs.cmu.edu/afs/cs.cmu.edu/user/rwb/www/gamma.html

An excellent technical overview of gamma that goes well beyond the usual "Macintoshes are brighter" is published here. Alongside the expositions, which make me wish that I'd had this guy teaching me physics, author Robert W. Berger includes some useful images that will let you determine the gamma of your own system, if you're willing to step back six feet and squint.

## IMAGEMAPS

In HTML, as we all know by now, you link from a piece of text by putting it inside a pair of anchor tags.

You can link from an embedded image in the same way: by putting the image tag inside a pair of anchor tags. Unlike text, an embedded image file can't be color-coded or underlined to show that it's a link. By default, it will be given a text-colored rectangular border, and that border will be color-coded if the image is a link. (Images that are self-evidently links, like buttons, can safely lose the borders: just throw the "BORDER=0" attribute into the image tag.)

This assumes that an individual image is like a word: that it's a complete and single entity that naturally only leads to one (at most) other place. However, as you've probably heard before, a picture is actually worth a thousand words —or at least it takes as long to download as a thousand words. What if you want to use a large picture that contains *many* distinct entities? Each one of those objects in the picture might naturally link to a different place.

Thus the need for imagemaps: they provide a way of breaking a picture up into separate links, rather than making everything in the picture link to the same place.

### SERVER-SIDE IMAGEMAPS

It's a mark of how desperately Web authors wanted multiple links from an image that such a horrendously poor idea as server-side imagemaps became not only possible, but popular.

The whole idea of hypertext is to build pointers leading to other content into a file with content, rather than having to jump back and forth between a dull directory and individual self-contained documents of interest. HTML used this idea to make the Internet feel more efficient by letting the "traffic cop" functions go into the browser on the user's own computer: the browser shows content to you, and also knows where to direct you when you select hyperlinked content.

Well, if the image file is on the reader's own computer, and the HTML text is on the reader's own computer, and the links from the text are on the reader's own computer, wouldn't it make sense for the links from the image file to be on the reader's own computer?

It would make sense, but there was no way to do it using the first versions of HTML. And since in those pre-Java, pre-Netscape-extension days the only way to add functionality to the Web was to have the Web server do extra work on its end, the Web servers got stuck with the job. The image and the HTML were on the client machine, but when the reader clicked on an imagemap, the server needed to run a special program and find a special matching file on *its* machine. After finding the file, it would then have to find a link that matched where the reader had clicked, and then whisk that link back to the reader as if it had never gotten involved at all.

This Rube Goldberg contraption could break down in all sorts of ways, of course. First, you had to make sure that your server had the special program and that you had access to it. Then you had to make your special image *links* file (separate from both your image file and your HTML file), and put it some place that your server could find it—often a different directory than your own. Then you had to keep all three files coordinated for the rest of their lives. (Did I say three files? Actually, you often had to keep *four* files coordinated: many server imagemap programs required you to put a pointer to your image links file into a special system-wide directory file—assuming you could get permission!)

And then there was the problem of testing. The Web author has the responsibility of testing all documents and all links locally before making files accessible worldwide. But how could we test imagemaps on our local machines, since they required a server to run? We ended up having to install and maintain local Web servers (not the simplest programs in the world) solely for the purpose of testing imagemaps.

The Web author wasn't the only one with problems; the Web reader had to contend with slower and more broken links (because of the server's intervention), and had to live with an unpleasant amount of mystery: Where exactly on this image should I click? Where exactly will I *go* when I click on it? Since the browser program had no way to know the shapes that were linked or what URLs they were linked to, there was no way for it to tell the reader.

Life is better now. We have client-side imagemaps, and there's no need to worry about the server-side problems anymore. So why am I even bothering to complain?

Because most of the imagemap material that you'll find while you browse the Web was written some time *before* client-side imagemaps took over. (That's the reason that the directory for this section is a little bare.) Some other pages, written during the transition period, may sound a little distrustful of these newfangled client-side contraptions; when they mention "new browsers," they're probably referring to Netscape 2.0. Don't let out-of-date pages throw you off. Especially don't let them convince you that you'd be better off using server-side imagemaps.

## CLIENT-SIDE IMAGEMAPS

Every browser company seems to get at least one shot at adding a genuinely useful HTML extension. Spyglass, the company that officially got the NCSA Mosaic program after Netscape got most of NCSA

Mosaic's programmers, had its moment of glory when it moved imagemaps into the browsers, where they belonged.

An embedded image is declared to be an imagemap by pointing its "USEMAP" attribute to a named anchor inside the HTML file (i.e., a URL of the form "#name"). The standard actually allows the URL to point anywhere, but browsers have varying reactions to being directed outside the current page. (Oh, let's name names: Netscape didn't bother to implement that feature.)

That named anchor should point to a "MAP" tag, which contains definitions of all the linked shapes in the image.

Each link is defined by an "AREA" tag, which describes the type of shape (rectangle, circle, or polygon), the coordinates defining the shape inside the image, and the URL to link to.

Perhaps an example is in order. Let's say that you have a painting of a sad clown, and want to link to the "Pagliacci" home page when your reader clicks on his heartbreakingly red rubber nose. First, you need to determine where the nose is within the clown image. A circle shape is defined by the coordinates of its center and the distance from the center to the edge. Bring the clown file into your favorite image-editing program (or into a specialized imagemap application), point at the center of the nose, and note the "X" and "Y" coordinates—they'll usually be listed in a status line or information display. Go in a straight horizontal line to the edge of the circle and see what the difference in "X" coordinates is: that'll give you the nose's radius.

For the sake of this example, we'll assume that the center of the nose is 80 pixels from the left of the picture and 175 pixels down from the top of the picture, and that the nose is a respectable 20 pixels wide (i.e., there are 10 pixels from the center to the edge). Our complete client-side imagemap might look something like this:

```
<MAP NAME="bigred">
<AREA SHAPE="CIRCLE"
      COORDS="80,175,10"
      HREF="http://
      www.classical.net/music/
      comp.lst/works/leoncavallo/
      pagliacci.html">
</MAP>
<IMG SRC="images/emmettkelly.gif"
USEMAP="#bigred" ALT="[Laugh,
clown, laugh]">
```

The syntax used to define client-side imagemap links is not that far removed from the approach used for server-side map files (the files on the server's system that contained the links for an image). This made it possible for programmers to write conversion programs. If you're stuck with existing server-side maps (or with programs that produce server-side maps), you should check them out. Just remember that the one thing lost by the move to client-side imagemaps was the ability to define oval shapes: instead, you have to use polygons or perfect circles.

## Generating Maps

You might think that defining shapes by writing down X and Y positions is a ridiculous waste of time—after all, the shapes are right there on the screen! And you'd be right to think so.

There are two approaches to creating imagemaps in software:

1 Use a specialized imagemap program that lets you trace the outlines of each linked shape using a mouse or graphic tablet, and that then automatically generates map coordinates.

2 Create your graphic using an imagemap-savvy image editor, assign links to the separate

graphic entities contained in a compound image, and then export the compound image as a Web image file with associated HTML.

I include some pointers to both types of software below.

As with other Web-specialized shareware, be aware that the capabilities you need may already be built into any commercial program you're using. Many quasi-WYSIWYG HTML editors feature some sort of support for imagemap creation. I myself got by on the server-side imagemap capabilities of Fractal Design Painter for quite a while, despite its typically murky interface.

## ALTERNATIVES TO IMAGEMAPS

Let's revisit the motivation behind imagemaps:

A large image file might actually be made up of many shapes, each with its own meaning and, therefore, its own natural link.

So why can't each shape be its own image file? Then we could link from them by using the anchor tag, just as we do with pieces of text, which would be much easier than fussing around with all those coordinates. We could also take advantage of the "ALT" text attributes to let non-image-viewing readers follow our links.

That used to seem like a ridiculously naïve idea. After all, if all the shapes were separate image files, then we'd have to count on the browser to arrange them nicely on the page—which was something like counting on the government to spend your taxes wisely.

However, as we've seen, HTML and browsers have gained quite a bit of layout expertise since the early days of the Web, and it's sometimes possible to avoid the development overhead of imagemaps.

- Tiling background images and background colors can establish a mood or site identity: you don't need to paste graphic elements into a large graphic just to get a background.

- Menu buttons can be pushed close together by specifying no border and no extra margin space: they don't have to reside in a single large image.

- Almost any rectangular grid can be implemented by tables. And since the transparent areas of linked GIF images aren't displayed and also can't be clicked on, it doesn't always have to be glaringly apparent that the linked images have been placed in a rectangular grid.

- Style sheets have finally introduced the notion of layered page elements. If the trend continues, we may expect to see multiple layers of graphics eventually show up as well. (Right now the closest thing we have is an embedded image over a background image.) Similarly, many images are created only so that text can be displayed in a special font. But there are several current proposals that would let users download font definitions instead.

The fact that there are alternatives to imagemaps doesn't mean that you have to use them. If you're dealing with a genuinely integrated source image, imagemaps will probably remain your best option. And eventually the sheer number of "small" graphical objects being downloaded will be more of a performance clog than one larger download would be. But it's always nice to have alternatives!

### Convert Server-side Imagemaps to Netscape Client-side Imagemaps
http://www.popco.com/popco/
convertmaps.html
This page is a forms interface to on-line service that converts a server-side map file to client-side imagemap HTML. You copy and paste the contents of the server-side file into the form, fill out a few extra HTML details as desired, and get back something to copy and paste into an updated document. As an interactive on-line service, this is unfortunately useless for batch operations, but it'll

do the trick if you only have a few old server-side maps to dispose of.

## Current and Cool
**http://www.adobemag.com/PDFs/ftrPDF/current.pdf**

This state-of-the-art overview from *Adobe Magazine*, presented in Adobe's usual anti-HTML file format, Acrobat, could have been listed in several directory sections. After all, it gathers information from Web authors concerning HTML tricks, pre-loaded graphics, JavaScript mouseovers, and use of background images. But I decided to put it here since the article begins by considering a couple of table-imagemap hybrids.

## Imagemap Authoring Guide and Tutorial Sites
**http://www.cris.com/~automata/tutorial.shtml**

Written to accompany the Web Hotspots application, this is a brief, two-page overview, one page of which is dedicated to showing the same imagemap implemented three ways. It's pleasantly designed, however, and includes a good collection of links.

## ImageMapper
**http://www.dcs.gla.ac.uk/~snaddosg/help/about.html**

At long last, Macintosh-based Web authors have a replacement for the late WebMap (an application that gave the Macintosh an early boost for Web authoring and which you'll find many out-of-date references to on the Web, but which also, trust me, is very much *late*). Glasgow University undergrad Stuart Snaddon's $10 shareware program handles all the basics blessedly well, including client-side imagemaps. It's no Map This, but it's better than anything else.

## MapConvert
**http://hyperarchive.lcs.mit.edu/cgi-bin/NewSearch?key=mapconvert**

Alas, Jeff Barnum, the author of MapConvert, doesn't maintain his own home page, and so I'm forced to direct you to the Info-Mac archive for the latest version of his

AppleScript (i.e., Macintosh-only) application to turn old server-side imagemap files into client-side HTML maps.

## Mapedit
**http://www.boutell.com/mapedit/**

This $25 Windows shareware program may be second only to Map This in quality. But since Map This is free, you can probably figure out what to do.

## Map This
**http://www.ecaetc.ohio-state.edu/tc/mt/**

The top imagemap editor for Windows-based Web authors is Map This, an amazingly powerful piece of freeware that has been awarded, co-opted, and incorporated worldwide. Map This supports both client-side and server-side maps; it also supports drag-and-drop links, zooming and snap-to grids, and checks for common errors. The program's author, Todd C. Wilson, has gone on to develop an improved shareware imagemap creation program, LiveImage, but he's established some tough competition.

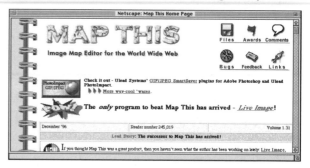

## A Proposed Extension to HTML: Client-Side Image Maps
**http://www.ics.uci.edu/pub/ietf/html/draft-seidman-clientsideimagemap-02.txt**

A little slice of Web history that is still linked to from all over (including Netscape's site!), this is James L. Seidman's proposal to extend HTML to handle client-side imagemaps. Since client-side image mapping ended up being implemented pretty much as he proposed it, the document has continued to work as a reference page long after the proposal's official lifespan ended.

## Spyglass: Client-Side Image Map Tutorial

**http://www.spyglass.com/techspec/tutorial/img_maps.html**

This is the official tutorial from Spyglass, the browser company that originated client-side imagemaps. It's probably the best introduction available, although it understandably assumes that the reader has some previous knowledge of server-side imagemaps. The reasons for client-side imagemaps are explained, and both syntax and examples are supplied.

## Web Hotspots

**http://www.cris.com/~automata/hotspots.shtml**

Web Hotspots is a high-powered imagemap creator, with a $49 price tag to match. Sensibly, its designers began with the assumption that imagemaps are not indivisible units, but instead a layered collection or collage of smaller images. What they've produced is therefore a collage-management program, in which images associated with links can easily be moved, layered, and scaled. Web Hotspots also includes support for background patterning, text buttons, and transparency.

## WebSoc Primer: Imagemaps

**http://www.gla.ac.uk/Clubs/WebSoc/primer/imagemaps.html**

This page is a good, solid introduction to both client-side and server-side imagemaps, only marred by its out-of-date references to HTML 3.0's competing (and now completely discarded) approach to the problem. In retrospect, it's a little touching to see how optimistic the author was that the alternative approach's obvious superiority would ensure its victory over established practice.

# CHAPTER 5
# FURTHER INTO GRAPHICS

*Fig. 83*

## IN THIS CHAPTER YOU'LL FIND:

### ☞ Converters and optimizers.

These references and shareware applications will help you to translate one type of graphics file into another, and help you slim down those files to avoid alienating your audience on the Web.

### ☞ Image editors.

The downloadable shareware and freeware graphics tools on these sites will let you create your own images and save them in graphics formats suitable for the Web.

### ☞ Image libraries and collections.

Whether you're idly browsing for ideas to spruce up your bullets and navigational icons, or looking for a very specific background tiling image, here are dozens of sites to help you out.

### ☞ Fonts.

Probably the most common types of original graphics on the Web are images of text in a special typeface. Here are introductions to the art of typography, collections of fonts and tips on how to handle fonts.

### ☞ Special effects and Photoshop resources.

A huge amount of original graphical work on the Web is actually generated by software, usually through add-ons to Photoshop and other commercial image editors. There are many on-line sites dedicated to the topic, including tutorials, and collections of freeware and shareware graphics filters.

### ☞ 3-D graphics.

These resources will show you how to dress up your site with 3-D logos and text just like the ones you see in the opening credits of local talk shows! (Or not.)

### ☞ Other electronic document formats.

When HTML just won't do—and I suppose that such circumstances might occur somewhere—here are some alternative image and text formats as well as formatters, most of which come along with Netscape plug-ins or Internet Explorer ActiveX controls.

**NOW THAT WE'VE COVERED** what kinds of graphics files are available to Web authors and how those graphics can be used, we can move on to the actual graphics themselves. Whether you're planning to use your own computer-generated artwork, to scan in print or photographed material, or to re-use existing graphics files, you should find the resources in this chapter helpful.

# CONVERTERS AND OPTIMIZERS

As already noted, the GIF and JPEG formats largely gained their current popularity due to their use on the Web, so it's not surprising that creators of pre-Web graphics programs had not exactly made those two formats their top priorities. As with other Web technology, freeware and shareware programmers stepped in to fill the gap, providing a number of ways to convert existing image formats to the Web.

More recent versions of most commercial and shareware graphics software packages include built-in support for the preferred Web formats, and that level of support may well be sufficient for your needs. But given the pressure on the Web author to balance quality with file size, and the difficulty of achieving that balance by hand or with more general software, specialized tools continue to be used by many Web professionals.

Two very different types of software are used to output GIF and JPEG files: standalone programs and plug-in filters.

## STANDALONE PROGRAMS
A few of the most popular standalone graphics converters also serve as image viewers or primitive image editors, and if you look at a lot of graphics on the Internet, you might weigh viewer functionality when you're trying to decide on a purchase: JPEGs, especially, can often look better in a specialized program than they do in the browser.

Most standalone converters or optimizers are designed to support batch conversions. After deciding on default settings for the output files, you can simply drag and drop multiple image files onto the program icon.

## PLUG-IN FILTERS
Plug-in filters are pieces of software that aren't able to run on their own, but that might add conversion capabilities to an existing image-editing or conversion program. Most plug-ins are produced for Adobe Photoshop, since it's the most popular image-editing program, but many other image editors (Fractal Design Painter, Macromedia XRes, and the Windows shareware program Paint Shop Pro, for example) are able to take advantage of the plug-in filter industry by declaring compatible support of Photoshop filters. Equilibrium's expensive DeBabelizer program also supports third-party plug-ins.

General support of "Adobe Photoshop-compatible plug-ins" is no guarantee that an image-editing program will actually manage to work with a particular plug-in. Many add-on filters were only tested thoroughly on Photoshop, and may not work as expected for other programs. You could end up crashing your system, so proceed cautiously while experimenting with any new combination of program and plug-in, even if the plug-in worked for you in another image editor.

## clip2gif
**http://iawww.epfl.ch/Staff/Yves.Piguet/clip2gif-home/**
I'm enamored of this free Macintosh conversion utility from the estimable Yves Piguet (also author of the freeware animation program GIFBuilder). Specifically designed to handle image-format conversions in batch mode or programmatically, it does that one thing beautifully well. For batch conversion, you simply set up your output

preferences and then drag-and-drop to your heart's content. Unlike other graphics programs, its scripting interface supports everything you get at the user level (accepting commands like "save file as GIF scale 50 depth 4 with interlacing transparency first pixel"). In fact, it supports even more functionality than there's a UI for: the programmer can use clip2gif to do some primitive drawing into the output image, even though there are no drawing tools in the program. Calls from both AppleScript (the Macintosh's standard command language) and C are supported. The sensibly chosen supported formats are PICT, GIF, TIFF,  and JPEG. Sure, its GIF options aren't the greatest in the world (there's no access to the "browser-safe" palette, for example), and its JPEG compression is just adequate, but the price and convenience are hard to beat. Although I have plenty of commercial graphics software on my Macintosh system, clip2gif is what I usually turn to for conversions.

## Demystifying DeBabelizer

**http://webreview.com/96/11/22/feature/ index2.html**

Even before the Web, graphic artists were being given headaches by the constrictions of cross-platform display: multimedia CD-ROM content has to look fabulous (or stomach-churning, depending on the project) on a variety of Macintosh systems and 256-colors-or-fewer home PCs. DeBabelizer, a commercial software program from Equilibrium, has long been the favorite graphics conversion and optimization tool for laborers in professional multimedia. Since DeBabelizer does an unequaled job of optimizing shared color palettes, it was natural to put the program to use for producing Web GIF files. Powerful and expensive, DeBabelizer can also be fairly described as having one of the most arcane user interfaces to be found in graphics software, making this extensive tutorial from *Web Review* not only useful, but close to necessary: If you're renting time on a machine with DeBabelizer, you don't want to have to spend much time learning the ins and outs of the program.

## GIFConverter

**http://www.kamit.com/gifconverter.html**

Good old GIFConverter, which got many Macintosh users onto the Web in the early days, is starting to show

its age a bit when compared to commercial products or to Windows-based shareware. Its image manipulation tools overlap with GraphicConverter's, but GIFConverter doesn't handle nearly as many file formats. On the other hand, it does quite a decent job with GIF transparency and with JPEG compression, and has just added scriptability and PNG support. Is it worth the $30 fee? Depends on what else you have on your system, but you always download it for a free trial to help you make your decision.

## GIF Wizard

**http://www.raspberryhill.com/ gifwizard.html**

GIF Wizard is a free online service that optimizes any GIF file you specify. You'll note I didn't write, "that attempts to optimize..." I think I'm pretty good at reducing image file sizes by hand. The way I figure it, it may take a while, but the results are worth it if you add up all the time saved by all the readers of my pages. But GIF Wizard makes me feel like I'm trying to carve a toothpick from a tree trunk with a hunk of rock—and a soft hunk of rock, at that. I've never once fed it an image that it couldn't improve. This is an amazing program, especially when you consider the inherent difficulty of trying to GIF-optimize an image that is already stored in the GIF format: once a full-color image has been stripped down to 256 colors, most of the damage has been done. You should always be able to get better results starting from a full color source. But GIF Wizard makes that inherent limitation seem purely theoretical. Moreover, the program is constantly being improved. At the time of this writing, the site just took advantage of an HTML 3.2 feature, and now lets you optimize a file on your local drive, rather than insisting that the image already be on the Web. GIF Wizard's only problem lies in its implementation as a strictly online service. You can only handle one file at a time, and you can't even do that if you're unable to get a connection to the GIF Wizard site. (Raspberry Hill Publishing, the sponsor of GIF Wizard, is promising to make a commercial version available soon for Sun-based Web servers, but unless you own a SPARCstation, that doesn't count as local access to the program!) As a result, it's really only usable for spot work, not for projects that require you to generate dozens or hundreds of graphics. (Again, Raspberry

Hill is promising that a commercial version will handle directory-wide optimizations.) But if you're just doing a picture here and there, you'd be crazy not to take advantage of the service.

## Graphic Converter
http://www.goldinc.com/Lemke/gc.html

A sturdy Macintosh shareware workhorse, Graphic Converter continues to keep up to date with virtually every image file format, including GIF, JPEG, and PNG, along with a basic set of image manipulation functions such as cropping, scaling, and rotating. It doesn't play favorites, though, and its JPEG and GIF handling isn't as good as you'll get with a specialized tool—or even as good as the built-in capabilities of Photoshop. But if you have to deal with many esoteric image types, chances are that you'll have Graphic Converter on your system anyway. It may be enough for you to get by with.

## Graphics Workshop
http://www.mindworkshop.com/alchemy/gww.html

Another piece of impressive graphics shareware for Windows 95, Graphics Workshop handles virtually any graphics format imaginable (with the odd exception of Photoshop's), image management, screen capture, and image clean-up tools. It costs $40, but you can download an evaluation copy and get a free comparison against the rather crowded field of competitors.

## HiJaak Pro
http://www.quarterdeck.com/qdeck/products/hjpro/

Like Graphic Converter on the Macintosh, the point of this venerable Windows commercial program is universal viewing of and conversion between image file formats. In HiJaak's case, the formats include PostScript, VRML 1, and 3-D models, as well as the Web favorites, GIF and JPEG. Screen capture, font management, image catalogs, and a nice selection of image cleanup tools (smooth, crop, gamma correction, and so on) are thrown in for good measure. HiJaak Pro can't compete with more specialized shareware when it comes to optimizing files for the Web, but if you need the program for other reasons, you may find its GIF and JPEG handling perfectly adequate. Currently no demo version is available for downloading: it's "buy and try" for $100.

## HVS Color and HVS WebFocus
http://www2.interaccess.com/dfrontiers/

HVS Color is Digital Frontiers' bread and butter: a $100 Photoshop plug-in, available for both Macintosh and Windows, that uses a patented algorithm to boil down full-color images to get shockingly good-looking 256-color images without dithering. 256 colors or fewer, no dithering, lots of flat color... Hmm, sounds like a good start to GIF-making. Digital Frontiers must've had the same thought, because it followed HVS Color up with HVS WebFocus, a Macintosh-only GIF and JPEG "Web image factory" plug-in. HVS WebFocus is available for $130, or in a bundle with HVS for $160. Although an impressive demo version of HVS Color is available, currently the only way to take a look at HVS WebFocus (a lesser-known and -reviewed program) is to order it.

## ImageMagick
http://www.wizards.dupont.com/cristy/ImageMagick.html

This is an impressive (and free) image manipulation and conversion program, distributed with C source code. Originally written for Unix systems which use the X library, the program has been successfully ported to Windows NT (and thus Windows 95), and partially ported to the Macintosh. However, if you'd rather not deal with its

Unix-style interface, you might prefer the Imaging Machine incarnation referenced below.

### Imaging Machine
**http://www.vrl.com/Imaging/**

Visioneering Research Laboratory's Imaging Machine is one of the most interesting free services available on the Web. It's basically just a forms interface to the image-manipulation program ImageMagick referenced above, but a forms interface is easier for most Web authors to negotiate than the program's original command line interface. And the program is an impressive one, handling format conversions, image overlaying, GIF animation building, and a wide array of filtering options, including transparency, interlacing, equalizing, and the ever-popular implosion.

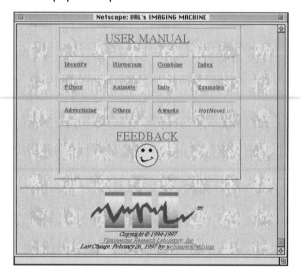

### Jasc Image Robot
**http://www.jasc.com/irobot.html**

Image Robot ($50 shareware for Windows 95) is designed to handle batch image processing, but it goes considerably further than the "BMP-to-GIF" functionality of most such processors. The commands that can be automatically applied to your input image files include brightness and contrast adjustments, adding borders, resizing—in fact, most of the commands from Paint Shop Pro. Rather than having to become a programmer to create scripts, you simply apply commands from a menu to a sample image. When the preview looks like what you're after, save the script and go to work. Also included is a "poor man's DeBabelizer" optimized palette calculator, which puts together the best 256-color palette for a range of input images.

### JPEG Comparison
**http://webreference.com/jpeg/**

The Webreference site is responsible for this much-needed comparison of the results of various JPEG outputs. The JPEG standard allows quite a bit of flexibility, and both the visual quality and the size of an output image can vary drastically from one compression program to another. This web reviews the JPEG chops of standard Photoshop, DeBabelizer, and two Photoshop plug-ins, ProJPEG and Transmogrifier. It also includes an interesting interview with Independent JPEG Group kingpin Tom Lane regarding the probable causes of the very variable quality we find in competing JPEG outputs. Since the pages haven't been updated in a while, you should take the final recommendations with a pinch of salt, but the bulk of the text is still worthwhile.

### JPEG Transmogrifier
**http://www.in-touch.com/giftshop.html**

I can't say much in praise of the interface, and I can say even less about the pointlessly obfuscatory design of the inTouch Web site (actually, I could say quite a bit about it, but this isn't the place). Still, this unassuming $12 piece of shareware did a better job of JPEG creation than any other Macintosh tool I've tried—and it's also the cheapest Macintosh tool I've tried. There are no sliders, no preview screen, and no expert advice; just good-looking, extremely compact JPEG files quickly produced, with the only spice being the option for progressive (or "interlaced") JPEGs. Highly recommended, with bemusement.

### PhotoGIF
**http://enlil.boxtopsoft.com/PhotoGIF/**

This highly praised Macintosh Photoshop plug-in from BoxTop Software converts full-color images into optimized GIF files. Transparency-handling includes a brush to easily remove any intrusive speckling. Unlike some other GIF-conversion tools, PhotoGIF can create and optimize GIF animations. However, the filter is missing a preview function, which makes it difficult to try out different color-palette options, especially since the plug-in itself doesn't venture to make any suggestions. The filter takes advantage of its Macintosh-only status by using the metadata portion of the output GIF file to store icons and other information—the downside, of course, is that the Web author must remember to strip the file back to basic GIF data before transferring it to the server. (Most Macintosh-based Web authors will have already set up their file-transfer program to do this automatically.) The cost of the filter is $45 by itself. or $70 bundled with PhotoJPEG. Unfortunately for us penny-pinching types, the demo version is save-disabled, which means we can't really get a good idea of how well its output compares to that of other tools or find out what the final image will look like across multiple browsers until coughing up the registration fee.

## PhotoImpact GIF/JPEG SmartSaver

### http://www.ulead.com/products/noslip.htm

This Windows tool distinguishes itself from other converter-optimizers by providing immediate feedback and a long memory, both big time savers in the trial-and-error-and-go-back-again world of Web graphics optimization. As you experiment with different palettes or compression levels, the image itself stays visible in the window, avoiding the laborious "save, re-open, close and throw away" cycle. You can save even more time by setting up a batch comparison, which puts a single source image through a number of pre-set conversions and lets you view the contrasting results. Meanwhile, a history list of

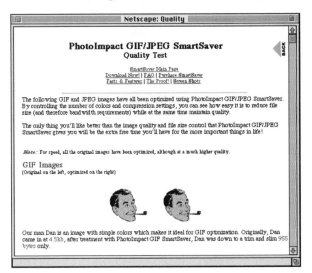

past settings is being saved on the side, letting you quickly go back to re-check your memory of what worked best. A smoothing function helps you replace murky areas (these often wreck both the look and the size of GIF conversions) with flatter colors. Standard transparency and interlacing support are supplied. SmartSaver is supplied by Ulead as both a standalone application and a selection-savvy Adobe Photoshop export plug-in. A bargain at $30, it's also included in the full PhotoImpact image-editing package. (One limitation on the standalone package: You'll have to go to a different tool to optimize GIF animations; Ulead has positioned its GIF-animation optimizing within a different member of PhotoImpact suite, GIF Animator.)

## PhotoImpact GIF Optimizer

### http://www.ulead.com/products/go_main.htm

For a less-hands-on experience, you might want to try this $30 piece of shareware intended for batch operations. Batching optimizations is usually an iffy idea: the trade-off of quality for size is not one most of us want to leave up to a machine. But GIF Optimizer restricts itself entirely to non-destructive changes. By going after redundant or unnecessary components of the file, it attempts to speed up GIF downloading without reducing the image's visible colors—indeed, without changing the image visibly in any way. As such, it's no substitute for the careful color-selection process that must precede GIF-file creation, but it does provide an excellent final polish for the GIF file after it's made.

## ProJPEG

### http://www.boxtopsoft.com/ProJPEG

ProJPEG is a Macintosh Photoshop plug-in from BoxTop Software. The good news is that it provides a preview of the final result along with its quality-compression setting bar. The bad news is that the preview is restricted to a tiny portion of the screen, with no zoom, and with scroll-bars as the only positioning aid. Since most Web authors reserve the JPEG format for larger images, this seriously compromises the usefulness of previewing. Like its sibling, PhotoGIF, the downloadable demo version cannot save to disk—but at least it estimates what its output file size would be if it could save to disk. It costs $35 by itself, and is bundled with PhotoGIF for $70.

## Stroud's Reviews for Graphics Viewers

**http://www.supernet.net/cwsapps/ simage.html**

The title may not promise much, but this reviews section of The Consummate Winsock Apps List covers shareware image-editors and converters as well as viewers. The reviews are among the best and most up-to-date that you'll find on the Web, but be sure to check the sibling site "for Web Graphics Tools," as the division is somewhat arbitrary: you'll find tools of both types in both areas.

## ThumbsPlus

**http://www.cerious.com/**

A Windows program that puts the emphasis on image-management rather than on painting or drawing, which makes sense given the percentage of Web graphics that are based on existing computer art or scanned images. It maintains a window showing thumbnails of all images in the collection you're working on—very useful when working on a suite of pages whose graphic elements are shared. The support of varying graphics formats is superb. A Macintosh version is in beta test as I write.

## Web Graphics Tools

**http://www.pcmag.com/features/webgraph/_ open.htm**

*PC Magazine* put together this excellent comparative review of Windows-based tools for Web image handling, including sections on format optimization (editor's choice: DeBabelizer Pro for Windows 95/NT—although I should note that the most expensive "competitor" to this $600 program is only $130!), imagemap creation (editor's choice: Web Hotspots), and GIF animation (editor's choices: WebImage and PhotoImpact GIF Animator).

## WebImage

**http://www.group42.com/webimage.htm**

At first it's tough to categorize this $40 Windows program from Group 42. The list of features might seem a little miscellaneous to a traditional graphic artist: there's GIF animation, image management using thumbnails, format conversion (including PNG), border and button ef-fects, transparent and interlaced GIFs, imagemap creation, and automatic file encoding (for Usenet groups, for example). What holds the elements together is their common usefulness for Web authoring.

# IMAGE EDITORS

Personally speaking, I haven't had that much difficulty in getting text printed on paper, but the Web has been wonderful for letting me show off overly conceptual photographs and horrifically crude artwork that no publisher in its right mind would ever have touched (see Figure 5.1).

In the next section, we'll point to libraries of existing image files that you can plunder at your ease, but you might also be considering taking advantage of the medium by putting some original content on your original page. Just in case you're one of those rebels, here are some shareware and freeware applications to help you scan your photos or oil-paint-encrusted canvases into digital form, or to let you scrawl directly into a computer file.

On Windows 95, Paint Shop Pro is just one of many shareware programs powerful enough to handle small

**Figure 5.1**
See what I mean? When you're publishing your own work, it doesn't have to be totally polished.

online productions. But if you work on a Macintosh and you're at all serious about putting artwork on the Web, you're almost certainly going to wind up using Photoshop. Your local photocopying business may rent out time on a scanner and a Photoshop-equipped Macintosh or PC. If you go that route and are reluctant to shell out additional cash for a home copy of the program, or if your home system just isn't powerful enough to run it, there are a few freeware programs that, combined with graphics-conversion shareware, may be enough to get you by. But I don't guarantee it…

 Even if the planned outcome of your image creating session is a GIF with 16 colors, strive with all your might to do your work on a full-color system rather than on your good old 256-color clone. Most image editors refuse to do their most interesting tasks with 8-bit graphics cards. When they don't refuse, you'll still encounter some peculiar experiences, such as watching an area seem to become lighter while you're darkening it. Even worse, unless you're very careful to restrict your GIF file to the "safe" browser palette, the end results you see may have very little in common with the "real colors" of your image, and very little in common with what your readers will see online.

I don't hold with some pundits' notion that all Web users should run out and upgrade their systems, but Web authors who create graphics really should consider it—or at least consider renting time on a higher-end system.

## Adobe Photoshop

http://www.adobe.com/prodindex/photoshop/

Photoshop's official corporate site isn't just a repository for advertising brochures and press releases. Adobe's "Tips & Techniques" area features more tips for Photoshop than for any other product (about 30 links at last count), easily downloadable updates, and a thoroughly annotated directory of add-on products from Adobe and from third parties.

## BME

http://www.softlogik.com/freestuf.html #anchor54064

As an enticement for Macintosh owners to try its full-featured Web-authoring system, PageStream, SoftLogik has made this free image editor available for downloading. It doesn't handle JPEG, but can save GIF, PICT, or BMP formats. There's a good selection of effects filters, and you can pick up even more for $25; the minimal set of image manipulations (cropping, resizing, and so on) is also included. The most obvious problem when using BME to do touch-ups is the brush. And I do mean *the* brush: there's only one, it's rectangular and it's ugly as sin.

## DiP presents Microsoft Image Composer

AUTHOR'S CHOICE

http://www.algonet.se/~dip/MSIC_1a.htm

As far as I know, this is the only non-Microsoft page devoted to Image Composer to date, but luckily it's from Thomas Lindström's site of sophisticated boom-boom, Digital Pictures. Lindström was an admirer of the Composer program when it was first developed by Altamira, before that company was purchased by Microsoft. Image Composer takes a unique approach to image editing, and this extensive two-part tutorial from a hard-working user makes an invaluable introduction.

### Fractal Design Online

**http://www.fractal.com/**

Fractal Design is the maker of Painter, my (and several other Web authors') favorite image-editing program for producing original graphics; it's also the distributor of Ray Dream Designer (one of the most popular 3-D programs) and Expression (a very cool vector-based painting tool). Like the company's products, the Web site interface is slightly busy and memory-hungry; unlike the products, the Web site lacks content. Outside of a gallery of computer-generated art, it's only worth checking for press releases and software updates.

### How a Digitoil Is Made

**http://home.sprynet.com/sprynet/websedge/howdo.htm**

This unique page walks through the creation of an original landscape using Paint Shop Pro. I found it considerably more illuminating than the artificially simple examples used in most tutorials.

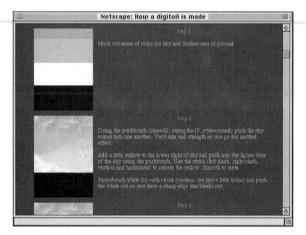

### Image Is Everything

**http://www.hyperstand.com/NewMedia/96/15/td/Photoshop_Live_Picture.html**

From *New Media* magazine comes this comparative review of four top commercial image-editing programs: Adobe Photoshop 4, Fractal Design Painter 4, Live Picture 2.5.1, and Macromedia xRes 2.0. Speaking as a user of three of the programs, I found Chuck Henderson's overviews fair and to the point, although I probably would've found time to grouse a bit more about Painter's interface.

### LView Pro

**http://world.std.com/~mmedia/lviewp.html**

Another in a series of impressive shareware image editors for Windows, LView Pro is a little simpler and a little cheaper ($30) than Paint Shop Pro, but it still handles conversion of a wide range of file formats, screen capturing, and Web-imaging basics like transparent GIFs. As you can probably guess by its name, LView Pro developed from a graphics viewer; it continues to offer slide-show and other display-friendly capabilities. It's also available on a CD-ROM (with over 800 image files filling up the "bonus tracks" space) for $40.

### Macromedia xRes

**http://www.macromedia.com/software/xres/**

Of the commercial competitors to Adobe Photoshop, xRes seems to have the best shot at success: it's designed to handle memory better, it can use Photoshop-compatible plug-ins, it's cheaply bundled in with some other Macromedia products, and Macromedia seems determined to maintain alternatives to Adobe's software suites. Although the program is not as powerful or as mature as Photoshop, if you're planning to buy another Macromedia program anyway, you should take advantage of the bundling deals to check it out.

### Microsoft Image Composer

**http://www.microsoft.com/imagecomposer/**

Image Composer is marketed in conjunction with Front Page 97, but it's a full-featured and highly recommended image editor in its own right, putting the emphasis on the manipulation of existing images rather than on naturalistic painting or drawing tools—although even the tools for creating original art are a cut above those in most shareware programs. The list of special-effects filters and clean-up options (including gamma-setting) is impressively long, but what gives Image Composer an edge over competitors like Paint Shop Pro is its ability to manipulate non-rectangular shapes within a larger canvas, giving the artist some of the same possibilities offered by Photoshop's wonderful layers feature. Image Composer's "sprites" may be less powerful than layers, but they're also more intuitive. The program can take advantage of 32-bit Adobe Photoshop filter plug-ins, such as Kai's Power Tools. Special Web-authoring features include simultaneous full-color and GIF or JPEG views of the image you're working on. At the time of this writing, a free beta was still available for download at Microsoft's site, probably constituting the best bargain in the graphics-software world; the program is also bundled with Front Page 97 and Visual Interdev.

## NetSketch
**http://www.vegasfx.com/netsktch.html**

NetSketch is a $69 Windows shareware program that attempts to help its users create Web-ready artwork as quickly as possible. To that end, the company's efforts have been concentrated on a simplified interface, which has gained much praise for its intuitive simplicity, and bells and whistles are restricted to those most popular among Web authors (drop shadows, anti-aliasing, text effects, and transparency, for example—although it doesn't export transparent GIFs). The program is designed for original work rather than for editing existing images, but its efficiency and friendliness might make it a good match for your personal pages.

## NIH Image
**http://128.231.98.16/nih-image/Default.html**

The Macintosh freeware image editor NIHImage may be mysterious (it was written by scientists for scientists—scientists from the National Institute of Mental Health, appropriately enough…). It may be picky (it seems to only really understand PICT and uncompressed TIFF files). It may feel oddly constricting on a well-stocked system, too, as it assumes a world of 256 colors, and its palette handling isn't the most intuitive. That said, it does at least use round brushes, have access to inks other than basic black, and run on a Macintosh, which makes it the best deal I've found. You'll have to get another program to convert the PICT files it creates to JPEG or GIF format, of course. Note that this may be the only image editor for which "Is there any help in understanding densitometry and/or gel analysis?" counts as a frequently asked question.

## Paint Shop Pro
**http://www.jasc.com/psp.html**

One of the most powerful and extensively used pieces of shareware ever produced, Paint Shop Pro is generally acknowledged as the No. 1 image-editing tool for slim-walleted Windows users. A full list of features would take up most of the page, but among the highlights are full GIF, JPEG, and PNG support; screen capture; image-management with thumbnails; batch format conversions; textures and gradients; seamless tiling and support for 32-bit Photoshop plug-in filters. Most of the Web graphics produced on the Macintosh were done using Adobe Photoshop, but most of the Web graphics produced on Windows were done using this program, which costs $500 less.

## PhotoImpact with WebExtensions
**http://www.ulead.com/webex/we.htm**

PhotoImpact is a very impressive suite of integrated Windows tools from Ulead Systems. Unlike most low-priced image editors, PhotoImpact includes layering (or "object-based composition") functionality, and deserves a look if only for that. Other features of special interest to Web authors include a button designer, a background tile maker, an imagemap editor, gradient and texture editors, and 3-D effects filters. Ulead's much-acclaimed specialized tools, GIF Animator and GIF/JPEG SmartSaver, are bundled into the deal and closely integrated with the program. (Note that, unlike most entries in this section, and unlike the separate specialized tools which begin with the "PhotoImpact" name, the full PhotoImpact image-editing suite is strictly commercial software, not available for downloading.)

## StreetGraphics

**http://www.odyssee.net/~hugow/menue.html**

The rare shareware image editor based on resolution-independent vector graphics (like commercial programs such as Freehand and Illustrator) rather than on bitmap graphics (like Photoshop or Painter), StreetGraphics is a very promising entry in the crowded Windows shareware field. Like Fractal Design Expressions and recent releases of commercial vector-based programs, StreetGraphics attempts to mimic the output of "natural" tools, such as brushes, airbrushes, and calligraphic pens. Also like commercial vector-based programs, StreetGraphics shines at text-based effects. But unlike commercial vector-based programs, StreetGraphics costs only $95 and can be freely demoed.

## Stroud's Reviews for Web Graphics Tools

**http://www.supernet.net/cwsapps/ swebimg.html**

Another superb collection of reviews associated with a shareware directory, The Consummate Winsock Apps List, this one including GIF-animation tools and image editors that have been  marketed as especially for Web authors. More image editors and image-format converters can be found in the undifferentiated collection of reviews "for Graphics Viewers."

## WebPaint

**http://www.barentsnett.no/webpaint/**

WebPaint is the only Windows 95 shareware image editor that puts equal stress on image creation (with extensive brush, drawing, anti-aliasing, and eraser tools) and on Web image formatting (with special features like 3-D button-makers, and full GIF and JPEG support, including GIF animations). This is also the only image-editing program I've found that assumes you'd like to do your work in 256 colors (rather than in full-color mode). Depending on your system, that may make this program either a must-have or a so-what. At the Web site, you can download a slightly hobbled copy of the software, register it

for $45, or simply try out your Norwegian while the program's author tries out his English.

# IMAGE LIBRARIES AND COLLECTIONS

I don't have much in the way of personal tips with which to introduce these collections of icons, backgrounds and other clip art. When I put images on my personal pages, it's because I made them personally. When images went on the professional pages I've worked on, professional artists created them, even if I boiled them down into Web format. If images are for their own sake, why turn to generic images? If images are to establish a special identity, don't you need special images?

Well, obviously I'm swimming against the tide here. Perhaps the best analogy to clip art is the three-piece business suit with tie (or, depending on which coast you work on, the black T-shirt and jeans with obligatory piercing): it's not a declaration of individuality so much as a declaration of unity. For whatever it's worth, here's a guide to the tides, the ties, and the piercings of reusable Web images.

As you browse, you'll undoubtedly encounter what may look like confusion as to the proper use of these online images. Icons and background tiles are just as popular for users who are customizing their computer desktops as they are for Web authors, and many "icon" and "background" sites were first set up for the former. But the needs of the two types of consumers for tiny pictures and seamless backgrounds are close enough that we can live with the ambiguity. Just be aware that the desktop-customizing images will generally work with the chosen desktop's system color palette, rather than a "browser safe" palette, and that the desktop-customizing backgrounds will not stress small size and legibility as much as Web page backgrounds should.

Note that any seamlessly tiling background image can also be used as a surface texture to be applied to 3-D objects. Most commercial CD-ROMs of textures are sold for that purpose, but "desktop patterns" are likely to be a cheaper source.

☞ **The caveat regarding cross-platform visibility applies even more strongly with background images than with background colors, since even under optimal conditions, visibility of text against an image is slightly impaired. Most of the clip art you'll find on the Web has not been forced into the "browser safe" palette, and of course none of it has been made gamma independent.**

**As a result, the best background images try for low contrast and low saturation—which makes some of them vanish entirely when viewed on a 256-color system.**

## Aaron's Graphic Archive

**http://hoohoo.ncsa.uiuc.edu/Public/AGA/**

I love the background tiles on this site: jazzy, colorful, but still practical images that remind me of UPA's most stylized cartoons. Perfect for donning a beret and growing a goatee. Unfortunately, they aren't seamless tiles, and the grid look in itself can be distracting. The rest of the works here are typical boiled-down photos, and whether you find anything of use will depend entirely on the chance overlap of your interests with Aaron's.

## Andy's Art Attack!

**http://www.andyart.com/noframe.htm**

This site holds collections of Andy Evans's original artwork for animations, arrows, backgrounds, bars, bullets, buttons, and counters. It also contains graphics tips, HTML tutorials, and links to other graphics sites. Evans works in the glossy semi-3-D mode typical of buttons on the Web. In fact, he's produced so many buttons that he's set aside a pay-to-enter area of his site for them, The Button Vault, which he promises to add to at the rate of 150 a month. Let's see, in two years that'll come to 3600 buttons.... As Thomas Disch asked Samuel R. Delany when they visited the British Museum's library, "Why are you and I making more books?"

## Anthony's Icon Library

**http://www.sct.gu.edu.au/~anthony/icons/**

This directory started way back in 1991, when the trendiest thing around was X Windows on Unix systems, and its chief focus remains X Windows. After the earlier sections of the chapter, you should have some conversion tools lying around, but if you don't, compiler Anthony Thyssen has done the work to convert many Unix bitmaps into GIF format. (The page that attempts to explain the process is a sad reminder of how balkanized the software world still is.) The icons themselves are on the clunky side and untouched by anti-aliasing tools, but what do you want from a free academic site? Note that the oxymoronic Large Icons might make good starting points for your own work: you can customize them and then shrink them down to working size. At the home site, icons are only available for batched downloading, but the mirror sites often display the images on their pages.

## A+ Art

**http://aplusart.simplenet.com/aplusart/index.html**

This attractive collection of free art by Wyatt Lehmenkuler ranges from strictly middle-of-the-road to the sort of patterns you'd find in a kid's bedroom. It includes the biggest set of cartooned interactions with the horizontal dividing line you're ever likely to see.

### Archive Directory of Decorative Lettering
http://www.ist.net/clipart/uwa/
**iconsfnt.html**

The Clip Art Connection hosts this set of pointers to some beautiful letter-illustrations well-suited for use as initial caps or for special banners. Alphabet blocks, two sets of initial caps from 19th-century publishers Cheswick Press, beautiful illuminated initials snagged from a 1490 printed book, and some over-the-top Victorian illustrated capitals—it's all enough to make you want to re-write *Le Morte d'Arthur*.

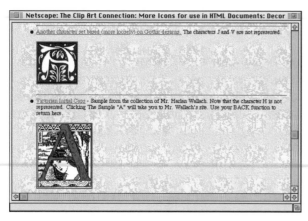

### Artbeats WebTools
http://www.artbeatswebtools.com/

Not to get all elitist or anything, but there are two audiences for clip art: the enthusiastic but clueless, and the grizzled professional. (Let me hasten to add that there is often no quicker route to grizzled professionalism than enthusiastic cluelessness.) If you're a stogie-chomping, bourbon-belting member of the grizzled camp, what you want out of clip art is easy access: you know what your clients want, and you want to give it to them with as little fuss as possible before making it out to the racetrack. Once you've reached grizzlehood, you know that the Internet has proven itself incapable of defense against fuss, and that the grizzled professional Web author might be better off turning to a CD-ROM for her clip art. If you happen to be that grizzled professional, you can't do much better than the WebTools CD-ROM from Adobe darlings Artbeats Inc.

### The Art Machine
http://www.TheArtMachine.com/

If you'd like a quick refresher on the difficulties of anti-aliasing, the opening splash page of this "GRAPHICS INTENSIVE!" site supplies a vivid example of how bad 3-D-styled text looks when it's not anti-aliased, and how bad the light-colored haloes around anti-aliased pictures look when they're placed on a dark background. Once you get into the site proper, you'll find a series of huge, perspective-defying 3-D computer-generated scenes, whose insistent unreality seems doubly disturbing given the basic blandness of their elements. The site periodically switches to a new series of images, making the contents of the old series available on CD-ROM, so if you're interested in the work, it's worth checking back in. Every week, a small background image and a large background image are singled out and made available in various size and palette combinations. A form lets you request that the weekly background image be mailed to you automatically, or you can simply ask to be notified by e-mail when it's ready for downloading. Considered as a whole, the Art Machine is an impractical but perversely entertaining artifact that could probably only come into being on the Web.

### Axem Textures
http://axem2.simplenet.com/

A specialist in natural photographic backgrounds, Axem has made over 800 textures (leathers, papers, woods, wallpapers, and so on) available for downloading here. The ones specifically designated as Web backgrounds are sensibly made, with low contrast and brightness settings kept at the end of the scale. Axem also hires its texture-making services out, if you're in a contracting mood.

### Background Images Archive
http://www.ist.net/clipart/uwa/bkgs/bkg_
**menu.html**

Despite its title, my favorite images in this collection are the rope and metal horizontal rules—but the genuinely classy left-hand-graphics backgrounds and the Australia-on-a-platter icon also impressed me. Judging by Usenet requests, the site's spinning-globe collection can expect to attain widespread popularity.

## Background Paradise

**http://desktopPublishing.com/
backgrounds.html**

If you were wondering where good backgrounds go when their creators are finished with them, you'll find them enjoying the afterlife here at the *Desktop Publishing* magazine site. Several on-line sets of attractive, original backgrounds (the left-margin ones are particularly nice) spend eternity hobnobbing here with links to background tips, utilities, commercial sources, and other free or shareware libraries.

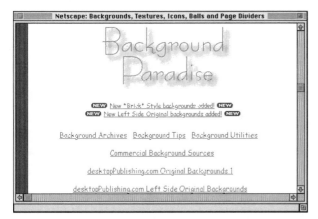

## The Backgrounds Archive

**http://the-tech.mit.edu/KPT/bgs.html**

This collection of seamlessly tiling background textures, part of the Pixel Foundry, was one of the earlier such sites on the Web, and the interface is simpler than you'll find at some other collections, with no sample pages. A bigger problem is that the site's navigation is based on CGI scripts, and perhaps as a result, individual pages can be very difficult to access, even at non-peak times. Of the samples I did manage to download, the "stucco" backgrounds looked more like blobby marble to me, but lived up to their pledge to avoid undue visual distraction.

## The Ball Boutique

**http://www.octagamm.com/boutique/**

"Your source for orbs, spheres and round things" also contains some nice display alphabets. The spheres themselves have been doused just a bit too heavily with computer-generated-F/X perfume for my taste, though. After

all, there's only so much shiny metal with intricate runnels that one eye can take.

## Barry's Clip Art Server

**http://www.barrysclipart.com/**

One of several collections of collections in this section, Barry Pase's site isn't distinguished for its size or its clear organization, but it does contain some unusually pleasant artwork that I haven't encountered elsewhere. You'll find more of the average bullets and backgrounds in a more specialized Web-graphics site; if you're looking for more traditional (or less average) clip-art illustrations, check in here.

## Boersma, J. Page, Web, GIFs

**http://www.ecn.bgu.edu/users/gas52r0/Jay/
gifs.html**

Jay Boersma, like Jeffrey Zeldman below, revels in the challenge of creating desktop-icon-sized (32 by 32 pixels) artwork, and the 200 obsessive miniatures (many based on famous fine art pieces) in his GIFs-4-Us page are enough reason to visit this site. You'll also find downloadable archives of 250 polished horizontal separators (I loved the screw), a huge collection of decorative and button images, and 40 faux-paper backgrounds. A larger collection of background images (categorized as "Representational," "Mild-mannered," "Hyperactive," and my favorite, "MiniGIFs") are intelligently displayed and demonstrated using frames and tables. Note that Boersma's work is shareware, not free: if used for commercial purposes, a fee of $10 or $20 should be paid for each category; otherwise, he asks for whatever you can afford.

## Bruce's Web Page Graphics

**http://www.hypercon.com/babeard/
graphics.html**

The leather-jacketed Bruce icon, extremely annoying MIDI samples in tow, presents the flags of these United States (including the US Virgin Islands and American Samoa), 200 flags from around the world (occasionally looking a little roughed up by their iconization), an array of spheres in various colors and tiny sizes, some more or less gaudy GIF animations (actually, the blue lava lamp is sort of realistic and the red warning light is sort of ominous), rotating metallic 3-D letters (wait an hour after eating before going in), background tiles (including wallpaper, stucco, and, the specialty of the house, rumpled satin sheets), and a dozen of those wide, thin background images for authors who don't want to put anything into the left-hand sides of their pages. You can also hire Bruce to produce a text banner (your choice of text) in one of an extensive set of font-and-effects combinations (iced-over Cooper Heavy or flaming Impact Bold appear to be two of the more popular).

### The Clip Art Connection
**http://www.ist.net/clipart/**
This is an overwhelming compilation of clip-art collections, presented by Eric H. Force and his disk-space-heavy Internet service provider. With thousands of solidly professional samples to go through, it makes a great starting place for image-scroungers. I treat the largest of the incorporated collections separately, but other items you'll find at this page include pointers to FTP-site search engines, a huge listing of theme-specific collections (themes include horses, human fossils, and cigars), a directory of artists and cartoonists available for hire, and a directory of commercial clip-art vendors, with special mention of the sites that offer downloadable free samples. Many of the collections are "bound" into large Acrobat files, suitable for downloading and local perusal at your leisure: a great convenience if you have to use a lot of clip art professionally.

### The Copyright Website
**http://www.benedict.com/ homepage.htm**
While you're going around snagging images and distributing audio samples, you might start to become curious

about intellectual property laws. Even if you don't use clip art, you might find much of interest in this site, which thoroughly and entertainingly covers international copyright issues—at least as of 1995, which is when the "late breaking news" page was last updated. Benedict O'Mahoney, an intellectual-property lawyer, knows his material well, and includes practical information, as well as a list of famous folk who weren't successful arguing "fair use" (Robert Rauschenberg was once busted for a collage—bad news for pretentious artist types) and a clear definition of "public domain."

### Dr. Zeus' Textures
**http://www.best.com/~drzeus/Art/Textures/ Textures.html**
Dr. Zeus (normally disguised as mild-mannered Harold Poskanzer) has managed to come up with a new approach to wild-but-seamless textures. Rather than simply hitting a Kai's Power Tools button and taking a nap, he uses Photoshop's smudging tools to warp and smooth complex photographic images past the point of intelligibility. The end result is both uncommonly beautiful and subtly nightmarish. It's an idea that's definitely worth checking out, at least until the new technique becomes its own cliché. In a clever twist, the sample page for each background displays the original photographic source in the foreground.

### Free Art @ Solarflare
**http://www.solarflare.com/freeart/index.html**
Amber Lamperti is obviously not your average kid-with-Kai's-Power-Tools Web artist: the work at this site is

about as professional (*not* the same as stodgy) as it gets. Some beautifully photographic backgrounds are available here, but the most impressive part of the site may be its bundled "theme sets": downloadable archives containing a background image, at least one bullet image and a horizontal separator image, all designed to work together in mood and color.

## Free Backgrounds
http://wctravel.com/web/freestuf.htm

The biggest attraction here is the utilitarian set of 29 scanned-in and very mellowed-out wallpaper images. There are also a few color-and-effects coordinated sets of left-margined background images, horizontal separators, button backgrounds, and decorative elements.

## IconBAZAAR
http://www.iconbazaar.com/

Randy D. Ralph's huge collection (and huge collection of pointers to other huge collections) is a common starting point for image hunters. It's unfortunate that he doesn't include descriptive names or put fewer icons on a page: looking around a bit here will give your browser a thorough workout. The images themselves tend toward a rather clunky, cartoonish look, which seems especially popular in Windows-oriented sites. Graphics in each category are available for bundled downloading as .zip archives. Categories include animals, animated icons, arrows, flowers, fractals, cartoons, and symbols.

## Image Paradise
http://desktopPublishing.com/cliplist.html

What's paradise without images? This superset of *Desktop Publishing* magazine's "Background Paradise" is a large collection of links to clip-art sources on the Web grouped into reasonably sized categories, with more commercial clip art, stock photography, and fine-art collections than you're likely to find elsewhere. The two- or three-line descriptions and the site-search function are helpful time-savers.

## Images are Free . . . Not!
http://www.adobemag.com/PDFs/ftrPDF/images.pdf

A more seamless introduction to intellectual property law and Web images than can be found at Benedict O'Mahoney's site, this Acrobat-formatted file also gives you the déjà vu thrill of watching the same damned Illustrator graphic draw itself over again in layers on every bite-sized screen. The text is fine, though at points it seems a little too alarmist to match the current reality of the Web.

## Infinite Fish Seamless Textures
http://infinitefish.com/texture.html

Welcome to Kai's Power Tools country. The 165 textures here are about as KPTed out as they come, complete with KPT-like "evocative" names like "failed honeycomb," "gloomy desert, " and "ensign meat." It's hard to imagine what font color would be able to stand up to this sort of treatment, but you could always do what the site itself does, and use a table with background colors to shield the text from excessive radiation. The samples are kind of trippy if you're in the mood, but the usual question arises: Since it takes about as much time to create a KPT effect as it does to download it, and since it's always much more fun to create a KPT effect yourself than it is to look at someone else's, why wouldn't anyone that likes this type of graphic simply go out and buy KPT? Infinite Fish deserves credit for the HTML designs, though; showing a wide variety of different font colors against the background is a nice idea (even if it is wasted labor with these backgrounds), and I'm sure that someday soon I'll swipe its "window through a table" technique.

## Julianne's Background Textures
http://www.sfsu.edu/~jtolson/textures/textures.htm

Julianne Tolson has arranged this free collection of 500 background tiles in a useful color-to-color-range-to-design-approach organization which makes it easier to match the artwork or foreground colors you've chosen already. As always with any fairly large collection, the quality and usefulness of the images vary wildly, but some are among the best I've seen. Take Tolson's dynamic client-side-pull tour for a quick look at the highlights.

### The Lemay Collection

**http://www.ist.net/clipart/marcel.html**

Marcel Lemay supplied this set of over 1,000 black-and-white GIF files to the Clip Art Collection archives. Images are from commercial clip art of the 1950s, and have that much-sought-after cheap retro look. For the most part, they're too large and raw to use as is, but they might make good starting points for your own artwork. If you find yourself downloading Lemay images in the hundreds, you might want to give your modem a rest and purchase the full set on diskette for $15, shipped priority mail.

### Pardon My Icons

**http://www.zeldman.com/ icon.html**

Now you're cooking with gas! Jeffrey Zeldman, the co-creator of the first great Hollywood publicity success on the Web, the *Batman Forever* site, has provided several hundred tiny images that are completely unusable as "visual grace notes to ornament your next annual report." Although they seem to have been originally intended for desktop icons, a little color touchup should make them at home in the less-stringent environment of the Web. Disturbing, amusing, barely recognizable, wide-eyed, tawdry, bestial, slack-jawed, or starring in an Edward D. Wood Jr., movie, these images may be just what you need on your genealogy page—or they may just serve as reassurance that you're allowed to do something original with decorative graphics. If you desire the full experience, Zeldman offers a set of background tiles ("Disturbing Patterns") built in somewhat the same spirit. Icons and background images are both available for batched

downloads on the Mac Daddy page. While you're strolling around Zeldman's space, check out his "Ask Dr. Web" series, which contains some of the most sensible (if not necessarily the most restrained) Web-authoring and graphics-creation advice I've seen.

### The Pino Cartoon Icons

**http://www.tornado.be/~pino/cartoons.html**

Snagging animated and comic-strip images is a common pastime on the Web, but Robbie Ceulemans' icons win out for their size vs. quality high-wire act. The Bulwinkle images alone were enough to win his site a mention.

### Planet Earth Images

**http://www.nosc.mil/planet_earth/ images.html**

This page is an unusually well-organized directory of image collections on the Web, with special attention paid to flags, maps, and space photographs. Links are only displayed by page title; no descriptions are given. But as long as you're dealing with titles like "Victorian Art For Mother" and "Byrd Polar Research Center," you can't go too far wrong.

### Public Domain Images

**http://www.PDImages.com/**

This site, whose principal purpose is to publicize a multimedia location service in Washington DC, also offers a semi-random selection of historical and natural images for downloading as JPEG files. Included on the download page when I looked were a photo of Lincoln, Shakespeare's signature, a Monte Verde toad, 14th century daggers, and a sperm cozying up to an egg. Just as advertised, a mixed bag. If you're interested in purchasing video or film clips, you should check out the page of "Unusual Finds," which include a firing-squad execution, dogs being inducted into the US Army, a nine-year-old lion tamer, and Richard Nixon making use of the White House bowling alley.

### Realm Graphics

**http://www.ender-design.com/rg/**

Over 300 textures, over 300 bullet styles, and slightly saner numbers of horizontal separators and icons can be downloaded from this site. The background textures are especially worthy of note; they cover a nice range from tastefully natural to tastefully artificial, with only a few lapses into lazily computer-generated "psychedelia." Actually, even some of the textures *labeled* as psychedelic don't look like lazily computer-generated psychedelia! The test pages are beautifully handled, not only showing the usual white and black text against the chosen background, but also showing table boundaries and a reasonable assortment of graphic elements. Most of the graphics files on this site are available for downloading as .zip archives, bundled by type (icons, arrows, and so on).

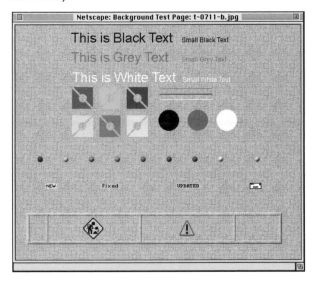

### The Rocket Shop Library
**http://www.rocketshop.holowww.com/ library.html**
The Rocket Shop has supplied a royalty-free collection of professionally fun graphics here, divided between glossy cartoons and glossy 3-D images, most with a colorful retro look, heavy on bulbous appliances and, well, rocket ships. The page of GIF animations would look right at home on a children's CD-ROM.

### Texture Land
**http://www.meat.com/textures/**
I've always thought that Meat was a gorgeous site, and that the FLUX group responsible for it had great taste.

That's probably why it avoids using any of the textures assembled in this massive collection on its site, most of which look as if they've just dropped out of Kai's Power Tools and couldn't find their way back home. A great disappointment, but take a look around the rest of the pages. (By the way, if you're looking for the very nice background behind the "Texture Land" logo, you might find something similar at the Realm Graphics site.)

### The Truth Shall Set You Back
**http://www.publish.com/0397/royaltyfree/**
From the excellent on-line magazine *Publish RGB* comes this dire warning against the unspoken limits of "royalty free" clip art—where royalty-free means, among other things, not wanting to pay Princess Di a modeling fee. Most royalty-free collections aren't license-free. (I can't pretend to fully understand the distinction, but if you're a rock band that wants to put something on an album cover, you'd better be careful.) Even once you pay the license fee, you may still be threatened with a lawsuit (at least in a litigious democracy like the United States) if you show the back of a man's head in a context he disapproves of, or if you show a trademarked landmark like the Hollywood sign or Rockefeller Center.

# FONTS

Sometimes Times Roman just doesn't cut it.

If you're not a commercial artist already, you'll probably be surprised at how many of the images you create for the Web merely display text, but it's just business as usual in the publishing world. Many of the effects that embedded graphics are typically used to achieve—giving a consistent feel to a site, asserting corporate or personal identities, setting an emotional or social context—also traditionally involve choosing a typeface. And since you can't easily, at the moment, deliver a new computer font along with your page, you'll probably end up taking a picture of your text as displayed with your typeface, and then delivering that picture.

> ☞ **Just remember two things:**
> **Don't overdo it.** Files that contain text can usually be made very small, but opening and closing huge numbers of small files adds an appreciable amount of overhead, and increases the chances of an ugly "broken link" icon.
>
> Always make sure that important text also shows up somewhere in plain-text form, either in the "ALT" option of the IMG tag, or in the document proper. Otherwise that important information will be unavailable to users who aren't loading graphics or who can't load graphics. I once saw a commercial company's home page in which the name of the company was nowhere to be seen. The company's well-paid but under-experienced Web designer had decided that since the name was included in the logo (which, of course, I couldn't see), there was no need for it to show up anywhere else.

By the way, if you're interested in using trendy handwritten or grunge fonts but only need them for a page or two, here's a seriously rad and, like, sincere suggestion: borrow a scanner or a pressure-sensitive tablet and try drawing your own letters. The text is going to be distributed as an image file anyway, and at least this way you end up with some of the quirky variability of real hand-scrawling. Who knows? Maybe that big agent from ITC or Adobe will spot you and make you an offer.

## Chank Diesel: "I Don't Talk to Strangers."

**http://www.chank.com/**

Mr. Diesel is one of the great success stories in the current wave of hand-scrawled typographers, moving from humble—well, "self-abasing" might be more accurate—punk 'zine roots to completely digitized fame and fortune. His site still maintains a 'zine attitude, albeit a rich kid's 'zine. Even the font names are pure poetry to an old punk's ears. (Although, come to think of it, an old punk's ears may not be the most discriminating instruments around.) Hangin' in the 'hood here are at least one new

free font every week, a collection of old free fonts, a slightly larger collection of commercial and shareware fonts, and pointers to all the admiring essays ever devoted to Diesel himself.

## The comp.fonts Home Page

**http://www.ora.com/homepages/ comp.fonts/**

Would that all Usenet groups had found such cozy nests on the Web. This spin-off from the comp.fonts newsgroup not only points to the FAQ sheet (supplied in an admirable variety of formats), but serves as a central directory to font-related Internet resources. Most spectacularly, it serves as home to the Internet Font Archives, the Web's most comprehensive source of downloadable freeware and shareware fonts.

## The Dingbat Page

**http://members.aol.com/aborigins/ding.htm**

A small but unique Windows-only (TrueType format) directory of historically or anthropologically slanted alphabets, miscellaneous dingbats (with an extensive directory of dingbat links), and some novelty fonts arranged by season (e.g., the Bunny font for March). This should be your first stop when looking for music tablature, a set of hieroglyphs, or the Prince symbol.

## Disappearing Inc

http://www.disappear.com/rockin.html

If "The Future of the Word" essay below is a little sedate for your tastes, check out the "Disappearing Discourse" area of this commercial site, which demonstrates available fonts with intentionally inane "typography debate" conversation-droppers. Although incidentally serving as home to some very nice display fonts, the site is first and foremost one of the best of the many ego-puffing "CD-game-in-black" Web experiments I've seen. Expect dropped graphics along the way, enjoy the pretty pictures that make it through, try to ignore self-made comparisons to Marcel Duchamp and "The Future Belongs to Us!" battle cries (funny, I thought the future belonged to Bill Gates... ), and don't be surprised if your browser cracks under the load.

## Fontaholics Anonymous

http://home1.gte.net/tiaralyn/Fontaholics_ Anonymous.htm

This site reminds me of the old joke: "What drinking problem? I have plenty to drink." Fontaholics Anonymous is the largest annotated directory of shareware and freeware font sources, and the annotations are overwhelmingly enthusiastic. All links are on a single long page, a perfect arrangement for launching new browser windows. If you're as cheap as I am and want lots of display fonts to play with, this is your spot. Just don't expect it to save you from having to buy a commercial Helvetica and Palatino.

## FontHaus

http://www.digitalthread.com/fonthaus/ index.html

FontHaus is an annotated directory of what the site's authors consider the best Web resources for digital typographers. Commercial type foundries, shareware collections, and state-of-the-art sites all get well-rounded coverage—though the final section, "Links," looks a little underfed.

## Fontographer

http://www.macromedia.com/software/ fontographer/

Macromedia Fontographer is by far the most popular font-designing software for the consumer market (professional type foundries use more expensive software-and-hardware combinations). The latest versions of Fontographer have gotten mixed reviews (to put it kindly) from comp.font users, and the program is a little expensive unless you obtain it through one of Macromedia's excellent software bundles. Still, it's practically the only game in town for Macintosh users, and was also the only semi-professional program on Windows until Pyrus released FontLab Composer.

## Font Source Paradise

http://desktopPublishing.com/fonts.html

Here we are at another sphere of Paradiso, courtesy of those latter-day Beatrices, *Desktop Publishing*. Font Source Paradise is a categorized collection of typographic links with clear descriptions, kept up-to-date more scrupulously than most Web directories. There are the usual links to commercial designers and to freeware and shareware font libraries, but I noticed that the "Specialty Type" and "Utilities" listings were both considerably stronger than I found at any other typography site.

## The Future of the Word

http://www.adobemag.com/PDFs/ftrPDF/ future.html

A quick overview of the jump in use of "stressed," handwritten, corroded, or otherwise untraditional fonts and layouts, presented in a "some people say, but some other people say" journalistic style. It's not a bad way to get acquainted with the basics of the debate, and for once the use of Adobe's Acrobat format makes sense, given the material: obsessive control over typeface and layout is precisely where Acrobat PDF wins out over system-independent formats like HTML.

### Graphion's Online Type Museum

**http://www.slip.net/~graphion/ museum.html**

This site isn't a museum so much as a well-chosen collection of Web essays on the history and practice of typesetting. The "Typographic Visionaries" page points to biographies of (and lovely samples of work from) ten typographers, starting with Gutenberg and ending with Jan Tschichold. Basic concepts and vocabulary are covered in "Elements of Typography" and a glossary. The least graphically intense page, "Old Phototypesetter Tales," is also the most invaluably unique: a fascinating (and even moving) industry-insider history of typesetting in the twentieth century, with eyewitness accounts of the change from lead typesetting to phototypesetting, the more recent change to laser printing, and the even more recent change to completely electronic publishing. All in all, this makes an easy, attractive starting place for picking up typographic background.

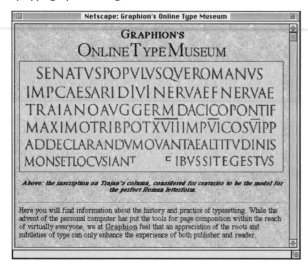

### The Internet Type Foundry Index

**http://members.aol.com/ TypeIndex/index.html**

The ITFI maintains a definitive (and blessedly annotated) directory of links to typeface producers, distributors, and designers, from the most established of commercial concerns to the most tentative of student essays. The

only criterion for entry is that the linked-to party must not have a reputation for stealing font designs. (Font piracy is a serious problem in the typographic world, and in sponsoring this project, PenUltimate Type Foundry gives consumers a guaranteed way to boycott the pirates.) The directory itself is kept scrupulously up to date, with a busy "What's New" section and with broken links noted. The page of miscellaneous type resources includes more on-line magazines than you'll find in "Yahoo!," as well as professional organizations, companies that specialize in customized (or "signature") fonts, type-designing software, and a brief but worthwhile list of other typographic centers on the Web. Those in search of font-creation utilities should note that the "Microsoft Typography" links directory maintains a more extensive selection of software providers; those in search of outré typefaces should note that the "Internet Font Archives" is the biggest directory devoted to downloadable freeware and shareware fonts; otherwise, you can safely make this your first stop. Unexpected pleasures at ITFI include the reviews section (maybe it's just because I don't have cable TV, but I haven't encountered many font reviews in my life), and a series of guided "Web Tours": ITFI has arranged to put its tour icon on the pages of an interestingly varied set of type designers, and you just go browsing via the icon, eventually ending up back at the ITFI site.

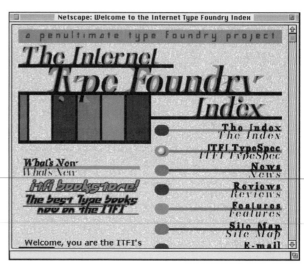

## Make Your Own Fonts with Chank!

**http://www.tripod.com/triteca/eyesite/chank/970114.html**

You know you're learning from a working professional rather than from a teaching professional when you hear things like "We have to finish this part quickly before the machine crashes" and "I don't know why you have to do it that way, you just do." From TriTeca's Eye Site comes this handy guide to the exciting work of digital font design, courtesy of typographer to the stars, Mr. Chank Diesel. Perhaps a little Macintosh-centric (in the first paragraph, he instructs PC users to "go away"), but still one of the most thoroughly practical hands-on walk-throughs you'll find anywhere.

## Microsoft Typography

**http://www.microsoft.com/truetype/**

I may have mixed feelings about Microsoft's decision to take over the Web, but I can't quarrel with its corporate strategy: give away lots of free stuff. The typography department is no exception, with a home page built to support frequent raids for high-quality TrueType fonts and related software. The page also includes propaganda and technical information on style sheets and the TrueType font format, and a surprisingly extensive links directory.

## Not-So Distant-Cousins

**http://www.adobemag.com/PDFs/ftrPDF/cousins.pdf**

This well-written and informative article comparing the use of type on-screen and on-paper comes from *Adobe Magazine*, which should certainly be in a position to know a thing or two about the subject. User readability studies are cited, the serif-vs.-sans-serif debate is explained, and even the proper uses of colored text and backgrounds are covered.

## ParaType Internet Font Fair

**http://www.paratype.com/**

As Mr. L. Bloom (late of Dublin) once pointed out, Italian is "*Bella Poetria*" even when used to haggle over money, and the position of Italian among European spoken languages is, I think, held by Cyrillic among European alphabets. ParaType is the world leader when it comes to designing typefaces for gorgeous Cyrillic, and also designs typefaces for the Arabic, Greek, Georgian, and Hebrew alphabets. At its site, a selection of Cyrillic typefaces is displayed in repose; many are also displayed in action, being used in real-life contexts such as Russian advertisements and banknotes. As special bonuses, you get the Web's classiest use of 3-D GIF animation in a logo, and a view of current highway conditions in Moscow. (Looked cold and wet to me.)

## Pixel Fonts

**http://www.dineros.se/**

This set of unusually good-looking display alphabets is specially designed for use on the Web. Letters are in large sizes, and supplied with a range of backgrounds blended into the anti-aliased edges—an extremely useful service that is skipped all too often by clip-art suppliers on the Web. Alphabets include "Bender" (bent wire), "Woody" (nailed-together slats) and "Copper" (complete with polished rivets). One alphabet is available for free downloading; the others must be purchased, for $10 each, or $40 for the full set of ten.

## Poptics Fonts

**http://www.knownet.net/users/plillie/Shareware.html**

These $10 shareware display fonts for Windows and Macintosh, from Patricia Lillie, are in a commercially light-hearted vein well-suited for party announcements and such. Fifty well-drawn cartoon dingbats (including snails, dinosaurs, and the ever popular cow-with-sunglasses) are included with each set.

## Pyrus Digital Typography

**http://www.pyrus.com/index.html**

Pyrus's Windows-based font-designing software is well on its way to providing much-needed competition to Fontographer (having already eliminated the only other competition, Type Designer, by buying its company), but its Web site wasn't doing so well the last time I checked in. Press releases for unreleased software mention nothing but ship dates that have since been missed, and what's available isn't clearly distinguished from what's not, even on the order forms! Maybe we can blame it on the language barrier: most Pyrus programmers work in St.

Petersburg, Russia. Luckily for the company, happy beta testers in the comp.fonts newsgroups have been supplying their own publicity. Pyrus is planning to provide font-design tools at every price level: SigMaker for $30 is a little convenience tool to let you store a graphic as a character in an existing font. At $200, ScanFont may be of most interest to beginning font makers: it's built to streamline the usual "amateur font" process of scanning in existing material, doing some vector-based cleanup, and spitting out a TrueType font. At the top of the line is FontLab Composer ($800), a fully equipped double-byte-character font-designer complete with vector editor. Promised to come are FontLab Composer at $300 and TypeTool at $100. Also promised to come are Macintosh versions of all these programs, but I wouldn't bet the farm on it.

## TrueType Typography
**http://www.truetype.demon.co.uk/**

TrueType is the format used to describe most Windows and Macintosh fonts nowadays. In one of the rare Apple and Microsoft joint operations, the companies banded together to avoid mutual dependence on Adobe's Post-Script format (which was at that point completely proprietary). TrueType is also pretty complicated stuff. If you decide that you'd like to try to understand it a bit better, come here, to the major non-Apple, non-Microsoft site devoted to the technology. It covers TrueType (and not-so-TrueType) software utilities and format specifications, answers readers' questions, and even carries an interview with one of the inventors of TrueType.

## Type Designer
**http://www.dsdesign.com/td.htm**

This low-cost (about $100) Windows font-design program has garnered much praise, particularly for its production of TrueType fonts, but its days appear to be numbered now that Pyrus Digital Technology (makers of rival product FontLab) has merged with DS Design.

## *Typofile* Magazine
**http://www.will-harris.com/type.htm**

Daniel Will-Harris's lively, well-designed site is dedicated to the use of type on monitors, rather than on paper. That emphasis is unusual in the typographic world, and it

makes this site of special interest to Web authors. Web-and-font news is reported, interactive guidelines on font selection are given, guest articles are invited (and quite well-written, judging from the examples I saw), and new typefaces from all over are demonstrated. This is the sort of Web zine that gives vanity publishing a good name.

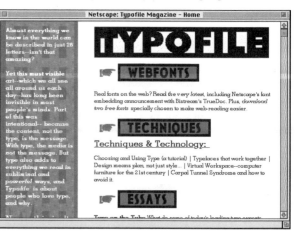

## typoGRAPHIC
**http://www.razorfish.com/bluedot/typo/**

This suitably gorgeous site, graphics-heavy but fast-loading, contains a history of the alphabet, a typographic timeline, a gallery, a set of graphics-intensive essays, a glossary, and one of the better uses of Shockwave: a tutorial on font anatomy. typoGraphic is probably the Web's best introduction to typography—if you can read it, that is! From top to bottom, the site (unnecessarily) relies on JavaScript, and empty black pages are all you'll see if you use a non-Netscape-browser, which makes typoGraphic not only a good example of a beautifully laid-out site, but a good example of how otherwise skilled authors can use "cool" technology to shoot themselves in the foot.

## Using Text in WWW Graphics
**http://the-tech.mit.edu/KPT/Toms/Text/index.html**

This thorough and well-written essay covers the practical basics of embedded text. The emphasis here is on readability rather than slap-dash self-expression, and such often-abused techniques as drop shadows and embossing are treated in that light. Such often-ignored techniques as kerning and spacing are also brought into the picture. The very different issues raised by large type and by small type are reasonably treated in separate sections. Another great tutorial from Tom Karlo.

# SPECIAL EFFECTS AND IMAGE-EDITING RESOURCES

The Macintosh platform used to be the only possible choice for serious graphics work. It also used to be the best source (after Unix, of course) of freeware and shareware alternatives to commercial programs. But the computer world has been through some changes lately. Software development under Windows 95 is easier than software development for the Macintosh—not to mention easier than MS-DOS!—and nowadays, not only are all the major commercial Macintosh-based multimedia tools available (with varying levels of quality) for Windows 95, but worthwhile freeware and shareware alternatives to those tools are much more easily found on Windows 95.

Perhaps the situation will have changed by the time you read this, but for now, a Macintosh user who wishes to create images has little choice but to go with a commercial program (usually Adobe Photoshop), and sometimes with more than one (but one of them will usually be Adobe Photoshop). Cheapskate that I am, I've tried my best, but even I eventually had to resort to commercial software to find adequate Macintosh graphics and multimedia tools.

For that reason, I've had to be a little less pushy about my pro-shareware slant in this chapter of the directory. But you'll find plenty of Paint Shop Pro pages to balance things out.

## LAYERING

In many software reviews, you'll find that image editors with support for "layering" are singled out for special praise. Layering gives you a way of maintaining separate components of an image in a single graphics file; the classic real-world analogy is that of laying a clear sheet over a background to draw animated objects without permanent damage to the background. Layers are enormously helpful for collage work, for fool-proof experimentation, for computer-generated effects and for animation, but they have a special use for Web-graphics production: eliminating the anti-aliasing halo that afflicts so many transparent GIFs.

As you may recall, anti-aliasing attempts to make curved or angled edges look smoother by gradually shading the edge colors away, rather than abruptly cutting them off. These extra border pixels are (theoretically) partly transparent, since only part of the edge color is used. Unfortunately, since GIF has no notion of partial transparency, when they are converted to GIF files anti-aliased pixels can only imply semi-transparency by being blended with a background color. If you put those GIF-formatted images against a different background color, the pixels that were originally intended to be semi-transparent are instead mixed with a color that isn't the edge color and also isn't the background color. Thus, a halo—and the need to produce variations on the same site-wide icons to avoid haloing when you (or your client) decide that a new background color is needed for a page.

Layering à la Photoshop gives the Web author an easy way to produce those variations. When you export an image, the result is based only on what's visible in your file; unseen layers aren't included. It's an easy matter in a layered graphic to turn layer visibility off, or to reorder layers. And so you can store all the backgrounds of interest in the same image file, as separate layers. Create and store your original icon as a full-color image, with true transparency, in a layer on top of the backgrounds. Whenever you need a new, un-haloed GIF, turn off all layers except the icon's layer and the selected background's layer, and then export the image.

If you need to add a new background color later, just add a new background layer to the file and have your new, un-haloed GIF file in seconds. If you need to change the icon, just edit the top layer's image, and you can generate a full set of un-haloed GIF replacements in minutes rather than hours.

## The Action XChange
**http://jmc.mit.edu/photoshp/gamma.htm**

Photoshop 4.0 introduced application-specific macros called "actions," and they immediately became popular as a way for non-programmers to combine information on techniques (since actions are editable by the user) and filter functionality (since they can be run with a single key-click). This on-line archive of freely available Photoshop actions was put together in a hurry by MIT undergrad Joe Cheng, but he's groomed it into one of the premiere Photoshop resources on the Web—even if he does occasionally have to take a break for fraternity initiation week or other emergencies. On-site tutorials include the basics of setting up and using a downloaded action file, debugging and troubleshooting tips, and advice on how to improve the quality of a new action.

## Alien Skin Eye Candy
**http://www.alienskin.com/alienskin/ eyecandy.html**

Second only to Kai's Power Tools in popularity among Web authors, Alien Skin's set of Photoshop-compatible plug-in filters is demonstrated on-line at the company's Web site. Most of the filters are specialized to create a specific effect, but some of the effects are pretty amazing. (I was particularly taken by "weave" and "perspective shadow.") If you'd like to try them out locally, Macintosh and Windows demo versions of the filters are available for downloading. Cheapskates beware: list price is $200.

## Andy's Photoshop Tips!
**http://www.andyart.com/photoshop/**

For the basics, you should stick to the Photoshop Web Reference site below. But for "stupid Photoshop tricks," this site is the best around for balancing quantity and qual-

ity. I was especially taken by the rounded inset 3-D button, the fuzzed background tiles, and the de-colorized photos, but the standard Web clichés are well-covered, too.

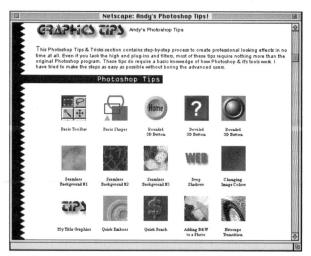

## Bruce's PaintShop Pro Tips
**http://www.hypercon.com/babeard/ psptips.html**

From Bruce's Web Page Help comes this set of techniques that will let you produce the same sort of graphics you'll find on sites like Bruce's Web Page Help. The effects themselves are pretty standard stuff (neon glow, beveled buttons, marbled text, and so on), but the walk-throughs are friendlier than most, with some thought given to the sorts of things that tend to go wrong when you're just starting out.

## The Button Maker Duo
**http://www.hsv.tis.net/~puon/photoshop/ buttonMaker.html**

If you desire pseudo-3-D buttons and happen to be lazy, cheap, and a Photoshop owner, you might avoid walking through any of the many tutorials on the subject by simply downloading one of these free (although the author notes that "a fruit basket" would be welcome) plug-in filters. One makes round beveled buttons, the other makes rectangular beveled buttons; both are available for Windows and Macintosh systems. The filter versions I tried seemed to have some problems on my Power Macintosh, but given the price, why not give them a try yourself? (A free Macintosh alternative is the DekoBoko filter, which can be found in the SuckingFish Filters package available at various plug-in archives.)

## Colleen's Photoshop Plug-in Page
**http://www-leland.stanford.edu/~kawahara/ photoshop.html**

Although they're Macintosh-only (and not native Power-Mac, at that), I had to put in my own plug for these too-little-known filters from Hugh Kawahara, since they're my favorites after Kai's Power Tools. In fact, they're more generally useful than Kai's Power Tools. They're so useful that you end up wondering why Adobe didn't make them in the first place. This set provides the Photoshop user with full control over adjustments to color saturation levels, reduction of color images to black-and-white, selections based on pixel color, and color modulation. Since no filter set is complete without something to get your images psychedelicized, a color rotator is also provided. Kawahara also comes up with an interface innovation that leaves MetaTools and Adobe filters in the dust: instead of using the original image as a preview window or restricting the preview to a tiny unresizeable square, these filters create a new preview window in which the progress of each modification to the effect's options can be clearly seen. I hope some smart company gives this guy a cushy job soon. These filters won't be enough to make him rich, since they're charity-ware: If you like them, Kawahara asks that you make a donation of some kind.

## CoolType
**http://www.binary.net/cooltype/**

As the title implies, this site began as a repository for text effects. However, it's since fattened into a hefty directory of all varieties of Photoshop tricks (or, if you're in a bad mood, Photoshop clichés). The less-overused effects include burning paper, reflected lights, and letters made out of such unusual materials as mercury, chrome and glass. Recipes tend to be concise no-nonsense lists of option settings, but intermediate results are usually pictured. By the way, unlike some other sites, most of the pages on the CoolType site assume that you're using Photoshop 3.0 rather than Photoshop 4.0. Version 3.0 users should rejoice, but 4.0 users might prefer to go elsewhere; though it's true that 4.0 can achieve anything

that 3.0 could, the interface has changed enough with the new version that older walkthroughs are of limited value.

## digital showbiz
**http://www.dsb.com/products/products.html**

Some of the best Photoshop add-ons I've seen are from digital showbiz ltd., and this is also one of the most amusing playground sites on the Web. Its "flux" collection of Windows plug-in filters covers some of the same overtly computer-generated ground already psychedelicized by Kai's Power Tools and Photoshop's own bundled filters, but the company really shines with the virtual props of "cracks and drops and dabs and scraps" and the rusty, decayed backgrounds of "ruff stuff." Free samples from each collection are available for download, and Macintosh users can at least get a kick out of the on-line, forms-driven interactive test drives, and the anecdotal backgrounds behind the backgrounds.

 ## DiP—The Photoshop Index Page
**http://www.algonet.se/~dip/ photoshop/PS_index.htm**

Photoshop tips made up the original centerpiece of Thomas Lindström's Swedish delight, Digital Pictures, and the Photoshop section is still a great place to get lost. Good thing, too, since getting lost is pretty much the only way to stumble across all the content hidden away in the rainforest-like proliferation and debris of Lindström's site. (One hint for the newcomer: the "Images" gallery section sometimes contains links to more software tips than can be found in the "Tips" sections.) There are a few

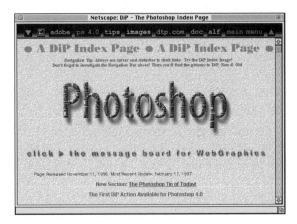

"stupid Photoshop tricks" here, but there is more emphasis on genuinely useful time-saving techniques for the Photoshop pro or semi-pro. Find your way to one of several "central" pages and you'll get access to pages devoted to Fractal Design Painter, Microsoft Image Composer, Kai's Power Tools, and Goo. It's too bad that Lindström felt compelled to use a JavaScript-only interface for some of his pages, though, as it imposes unnecessary restrictions on his audience.

## The Filter Factory Compendium
http://pluginhead.eyecandy.com/ffc.htm

Although the filters most often used in Photoshop are platform-dependent executables written in C, Adobe made it possible for non-programmers (as long as they know fairly advanced math!) to create cross-platform filters using a special plug-in called the Filter Factory. A small cult has built around that capability, and you can follow its achievements at this site. After a brief introduction, a helpful Q&A and an extensive directory of Filter-Factory-created filters are given.

## GrafX Design Web Graphics Tutorials
http://www.grafx-design.com/tutorials.html

This page branches off into two sets of tutorials on the standard basic effects, one for Paint Shop Pro and one for Photoshop. Nothing much outside the norm here: just 3-D buttons, beveled text, chrome, and the other familiar friends; the "raised label text" effect was the most exotic thing that I noticed. But the walkthroughs themselves are carefully written and exceptionally well-illustrated. A few of the walkthroughs assume that you've obtained Alien Skin plug-in filters.

## Graphic's Plus Filters!
http://www.hypercon.com/babeard/filters.htm

A free package of Windows filters for Photoshop and Paint Shop Pro, including a beveler to make rectangular buttons, a "starlight" creator (or, less poetically, a white-speckler), an "old photo" imitator that colorizes towards sepia (I wonder if the authors of Web favorite The Beige Page know about this), and simple embossing, spotlighting and border-fading filters. A free apostrophe comes with every download.

## Hands On Training by Doc Ozone
http://www.ozones.com/~drozone/handson/index.html

A CD-ROM-styled site with beautifully illustrated coverage of Photoshop techniques for 3-D stylings and lighting effects, including drop shadows, beveled buttons, rounded metallic objects, and inset bars. Dr. Ozone does sometimes assume that you own a Macintosh and some commercial plug-in filters, but for the most part his techniques apply across platforms. If you like his approach, you might want to save on image-downloading time by grabbing the full archive (in .zip or StuffIt format) as $20 shareware.

## How to Make Seamless Backgrounds
http://the-tech.mit.edu/KPT/Makeback/makeback.html

This is the standard reference pointed to when new Web authors ask how to make nice-looking tiles for their page backgrounds, a carefully detailed walk through the process of turning an innocuous bit of painting into a rectangle that seamlessly tiles. Although Photoshop is the tool used for the demonstration, author Tom Karlo points out that the same process can be followed using any image editor, as long as it can offset images and wrap them around.

## Jasc Web Developers Forum
http://www.jasc.com/webdev.html

Paint Shop Pro has become wildly popular as a tool for Web graphics, and its maker, Jasc. Inc., has responded by setting up this excellent central launching point, replacing other Paint Shop Pro directories. Links to tutorials, tips and techniques, impressive sites that used Paint Shop Pro to produce graphics, and plug-in filters are all supplied. (There are also links to more general Web resources, but it's hard to see why Jasc bothered to add to that crowded field.) On-site content includes advice on scanning, an illustrated overview of some of the leading third-party plug-ins, introductions to GIF transparency and palette reduction, and a few special effects walkthroughs.

## Jeff's Paint Shop Pro Tips

http://www.geocities.com/SoHo/2365/grab_
bag_page.html

This is one of several sites that offer genially loquacious Paint Shop Pro walks through some standard Web graphics effects. Jeff Burton also covers a few more practical points, such as how to get rid of background speckles in an anti-aliased GIF and how to use the 216-color "browser safe" palette in Paint Shop Pro. Burton sometimes misses the subtler points—in the speckles-eliminator, he doesn't mention that you'll bite something from your graphic's edges each time you use the technique; in the browser-safe tutorial, he doesn't appear to notice that his graphic's embedded text became illegible after he applied his technique—but I love his attempt to prove that you don't need to spend a lot of money to learn graphics techniques. "I didn't have to buy a Rolls Royce to learn how to drive."

## Laurie McCanna's Photoshop and Corel Tips

http://www.mccannas.com/pshop/menu.htm

Dozens of well-written original graphics techniques can be found here in a compact text-only list. Most of the write-ups are slanted towards Web graphics (transparent background, GIF animations, paper texture backgrounds, little colored balls, and so on), and many include Paint Shop Pro or Fractal Design Painter variants. Unlike many tip-writers, McCanna is a Windows user, which may make her pages seem a bit friendlier to many of my readers. However, the techniques are as cross-platform as the image editors she uses.

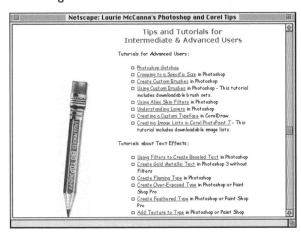

## Making Your Own Bevelled Buttons

http://the-tech.mit.edu/KPT/Toms/Bevel/
index.html

A beveled button has that slightly raised, flat on top but 3-D sliding off the sides look that is so ubiquitous on the Web. There are plenty of filters to automatically generate beveled buttons out there—in fact, there are plenty of beveled buttons already made and available for the taking. But if you want to understand the process of making them, or want to get your hands virtually dirty by virtually carving your own, you can't go wrong with this Photoshop-oriented walkthrough by Tom Karlo.

## MetaTools

http://www.hsc.com/

The best known of the Photoshop plug-in specialists, MetaTools produces Kai's Power Tools, KPT Bryce, KPT Actions, KPT Convolver, and our friend Goo. The MetaTools corporate site doubles as an impressive collection of FAQs, tips, example images, and even Web clip art. Many's the Photoshop guru who cut her teeth on the original set of power tips by Kai Krause, head of MetaTools development. (At the time of this writing, MetaTools had just announced that it was merging with Fractal Design. The two companies' products complement each other nicely, but you can expect to see some changes to their Web sites.)

## PaintEngine

http://mars.ark.com/~gschorno/machine/

There are a number of Photoshop plug-in filters that automatically apply painterly effects (soft brush strokes, pastel chalks, angular expressionism, and so on) to photographic material, but this is the best free one I've encountered. (Author Greg Schorno says that he'll be glad to take contributions to support further development, though.) Windows only, I'm afraid, but since it's 16-bit, it should work with Paint Shop Pro 3.12.

## Paint Shop Pro Web Graphics

http://www.pspro.ml.org/

Once you've got Paint Shop Pro, plan to stop by this collection of tips and techniques, most involving text and button effects. The tutorials are linked to examples of the end results, which is a nice help to those who haven't become comfortable with graphics jargon yet. On-site tutorials cover file optimization, use of masks, anti-aliasing (beginners beware: "you should use it on every image you make" is a bit of an exaggeration), and transparency. Directories of Paint Shop Pro sites and font libraries lurk at the bottom of the page. Even the "quick tip" one-liners are genuinely useful here.

### PC Resources for Photoshop
**http://www.netins.net/showcase/wolf359/ adobepc.htm**

Most older graphics tutorials and directories assume that computer graphics work will most likely be done on a Macintosh. Windows users might want to bookmark this site, which stays focused on the problems and benefits of Photoshop on the Windows platform. Generic Photoshop tips and tutorials are better handled elsewhere, but for more operating-system-dependent issues (like plug-in management, keyboard shortcuts, and thumbnail previewing) or operating-system-dependent executables (like 3-D programs or the plug-ins themselves), this is the place to go. The links directories include unusually detailed descriptions, which should save the harried tips- or filters-seeker quite a bit of time. (Unfortunately, the links also contain a lot of deadwood, which should waste some of that saved time.) One of the most important areas of the site also applies to Macintosh users (at least those Macintosh users who are comfortable with Adobe's Filter Factory): a huge gallery illustrating the results of 240 (and counting) of the filters at the Filter Factory Compendium.

### The Photoshop Action Cornucopia
**http://pac.skyline.net/**

The Action Cornucopia seems slightly larger and better organized than its rival, the Action XChange mentioned above—though that may be an illusion due to the number of one-entry categories. At any rate, the true action collector will want to visit both sites. Like many Photoshop collections, this one is particularly strong on text effects.

### Photoshop Paradise
**http://www.desktoppublishing.com/ photoshop.html**

From *Desktop Publishing*'s wide world of paradises comes this definitive collection of links to Photoshop books, Photoshop plug-in filters, Photoshop tips and techniques, and other Photoshop focus-points on the Web. No original material, though.

### Photoshop PlugPage
**http://www.boxtopsoft.com/plugpage**

Although it was in the middle of a re-design when I last visited, the PlugPage maintained by BoxTop Software remained the most extensive collection of Photoshop-compatible plug-ins on the Internet. If you see a reference to a Macintosh or Windows image-editing plug-in but don't know where to find it, chances are good that it's available here.

### Photoshop Web Reference
AUTHOR'S CHOICE
**http://www.adscape.com/ eyedesign/photoshop/four/**

The pick of the independent Photoshop-specialist sites is Austin Chang's extensive reference work, currently approaching book-like scope. Chang explicitly decided against turning it into a collection of what he calls "stupid Photoshop tricks." Instead, he explains the fundamentals of the program, helping his readers to find their own original applications. He may have done a better job than Adobe's own "Quick Start Guide." On most pages, links are based on imagemaps using the application's own interface; the filters page is distinguished by a click-to-try-

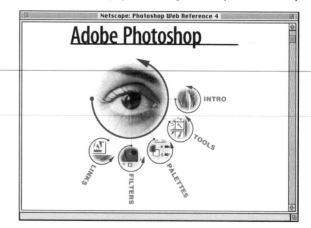

it-out interface. (Since the serial-imagemap approach can slow down a search for a specific topic, after strolling around for a bit, you'll probably want to bookmark the site's well-made index page for quicker access.) The confusing array of blending modes (or, as Chang calls them, "layer glues") is more clearly explained here than in any other reference I've read. Even as a fairly grizzled Photoshop user, I found the succinct references to keyboard shortcuts and modifiers to be helpful. There's even a practical page on color theory.

## The Plug-in Head
http://pluginhead.eyecandy.com/

Home of the "Filter Factory Compendium," Alfredo Mateus's site has more to offer Photoshop users—particularly Photoshop users on Windows: pointers to and information about add-ons such as plug-in filters, custom brushes, and special maps to use when applying Photoshop effects; image-editing news; a select list of favorite sites; and, best of all, a few tutorials on the truly advanced topic of displacement maps.

## PSP Web Graphics: Filters
http://www.pspro.ml.org/filters.html

This plug-in directory from the Paint Shop Pro Web Graphics site deserves special mention for restricting its coverage to those Adobe Photoshop-compatible plug-in filters that the author has tested for himself in Paint Shop Pro. There shouldn't be any compatibility surprises if you start from here.

## Selecting Like a Pro in Photoshop
http://www.adobemag.com/PDFs/howtoPDF/select.pdf

Adobe Photoshop's basic image-selection tools are the best I've ever used, and this is an excellent tutorial on Photoshop's advanced selection techniques. It's in the Acrobat format common to all content at the *Adobe Magazine* site, but any Photoshop user will want to download a copy for local reference anyway. Now if only someone would explain how to handle image-selection in Fractal Design Painter, I'd be all set up…

## Ticks on Trips
http://www.iserv.net/~rtideas/

Here's a bundle of rather terse recipes for Photoshop textures and text effects. Although the text effects are on the hackneyed side (ice and flames and so on), the computer-generated textures impressed me; they include raindrops, rough stone, long grass, and a surprisingly convincing burlap.

## TipLinx
http://desktoppublishing.com/tips.html

Not everyone is using Photoshop or Paint Shop Pro. (Well, actually, virtually everyone *is*, but those aren't the *only* programs that everyone is using.) Here's a more general directory to image-editing tips, including sections on Fractal Design Painter, Illustrator, PageMaker, Corel Draw, and Quark XPress. Oh, and also Photoshop and Paint Shop Pro.

## Ultimate Photoshop
http://www.sas.upenn.edu/~pitharat/photoshop/main.html

Given the occasional drops into under-construction areas, a better title for this site would be "Penultimate Photoshop," but it's still very promising. The directories of filters, plug-ins, and brushes are among the largest I've seen, and they're helpfully divided between commercial products and free downloads.

## Web Style Photoshop and HTML Tips
http://www.geocities.com/SiliconValley/Pines/6070/tips.htm

As the indulgent reader may have discovered, I lean towards skepticism as regards "stupid Photoshop tricks" and the pages that love them, but this site charms even me. Maybe it's because the author doesn't like what he calls "Photoshop monkeys" artwork, or maybe it's his sense of style in both image and text (where there's nary a "Voila!" to be found), or maybe it's just because he finds new and interesting angles on some of the most hackneyed topics. There are drop-shadow walkthroughs (and plug-in filters) all over the Web, but this is the place you'll learn about making your drop shadows interact realistically with your background texture. (Okay, the page on reducing GIF size isn't the best in the world, but at least he had the good taste to name its source file "dumdown.htm.")

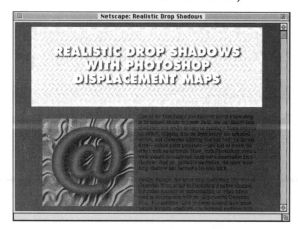

## WebWeaver XXI: Paint Shop Pro Tips and Tricks

**http://www.webweaverxxi.com/psp40/**

And the techniques come a-tumblin' down! One of a number of similarly titled pages, this one immediately distinguishes itself by its scattered but somehow enticing layout. One could say much the same of the techniques themselves. Although the graphics that result won't ever be mistaken for William Morris, they're still sort of fun: smudging a basic tree shape, making silly text effects, creating gold mirrors with gold frames, and so on. Adding to the clubhouse feeling, many pages here have been supplied by the site's regular readers.

# 3-D GRAPHICS

3-D graphics are a special case in the world of computer-generated art. It's a special case that's gotten a lot of attention, but it still has to struggle against the problems typical of any computer-generated art.

- **Lack of meaning.** Although I get the impression that many Web 3-D artists are hoping for the sort of response that cigarette lighters and soda bottles get from Hollywood versions of "primitive cultures," or that computer punchcards got from science-fiction movie audiences

in the 1960s, the mere fact that something is manufactured isn't enough to make that thing interesting to most viewers. An image that has no reason for existence doesn't magically gain a reason by virtue of being generated.

- **Lack of unique interest.** If you created your image by buying a piece of software and pushing a few buttons, it's pretty likely that several thousand other people are doing the same thing. (If they aren't, then that piece of software won't be updated very often!)

On the other hand, like other computer-generated art, 3-D offers the possibility of acceptable results without training in the fine arts or overly intensive labor—at least not intensive labor from you. (Your computer may be occupied for quite awhile, though.) And, as with every artistic technology from mud puddles on up, playing with the tools can generate new ideas.

There are two completely different approaches to achieving a 3-D look: overlaid effects and 3-D modeling.

## OVERLAID EFFECTS

Starting from a 2-D graphic—a painting, an image, text, or a vector-based drawing, for example—you can add such effects as perspective and shadows to gain the illusion of depth, in what is basically just a machine-aided version of what painters and engravers normally learn to do by hand. In the previous section, you found sites that walked you through some recipes for 3-D effects and 2-D image-editor add-ons that can automatically take care of much of the work.

Since most people have an easier time understanding the basics of drawing, typing, and photography than understanding the wire-frame world of 3-D modeling, this approach is usually quicker to learn. It also tends to be less costly in time, and in hardware and software requirements. Best of all, the look of the final work isn't subject to the limitations of low-cost 3-D modeling or texture-applying software.

On the other hand, there are serious limits to how well a piece of software can guess at depth when it's given just rows of pixels with no other information; correspondingly, there are serious limits to automatically applying 3-D effects to 2-D graphic input. And no matter what tools you use, you'll need at least a little background knowledge about what rules "real" artists use to fool the eye.

Note that vector-based 2-D drawings give much more information to the computer than bitmap art does, and can therefore produce more "intelligent" 3-D effects. (One reason that 3-D effects are so often applied to text is that most fonts are vector-based.) But if you want original artwork, vector-based drawing starts to bring in some of the same hassles as 3-D modeling, and at that point you're probably better off making the jump.

## 3-D MODELING

When most people talk about "3-D graphics," they're thinking of art that is completely derived from computer-stored, geometrically defined structures called models. Two-dimensional patterns with abstractly defined textures and reflectivity are draped over the structures. These structures are positioned within an abstractly defined space with abstractly defined light sources. In a process called rendering, all of this information is used to calculate the final image.

There's no theoretical limit to how exactly a computer can model the real world (or an imaginary one), but each step of the 3-D graphics process outlined above imposes serious practical barriers in terms of CPU, disk, and memory requirements. As a result of these practical limitations, 3-D graphics

tend to have an instantly recognizable "look," heavy on plastics and light on animal or human life. (Ironically, the failure of most 3-D graphics to achieve verisimilitude has given such failures a certain cachet: we recognize them as "high tech" and therefore we feel they must be worthy of special respect, no matter how incompetent they may be as images—or even as high tech. As Paul Muni says in Howard Hawks's *Scarface*, "Expensive, huh?")

The great benefit of computer-generated 3-D is that you can re-use the models. If one image was all that resulted from a 3-D model, the expense couldn't possibly be justified. But even though the first image can be more easily done by a human artist, the image that results from moving everything just a little costs just about as much of a human artist's time; move everything just a little bit more, and it's the same amount again—whereas once you've constructed your set of plastic models it's not that much more work to reposition them. Thus, 3-D graphics have proven most useful in manufacturing design, where frequent revisions and accurate measurements are important; and in animation and multimedia games, where objects, lighting, and the point of view all frequently shift positions.

## 3-D ON THE WEB

Web applications that play on the theme-and-variation strengths of 3-D graphics—VRML and Quick-Time VR—will be treated with other animation and video techniques.

Unfortunately, there's not much to say in favor of 3-D applications as a way to produce still images for the Web. The JPEG format works poorly on images with sharp edges, GIF works poorly on images with subtle variations in shade, and computer-generated 3-D images tend to have sharp edges *and* subtle color variations. As a result, even when produced with a great deal of labor and pride, 3-D images tend to look jagged and muddy once embedded in a Web page. To reproduce well on the Web, computer-generated 3-D either needs to be of the sort of photographic quality that is outside the consumer price range, or needs to be so simple that there's little point to the graphic other than satire. (The latter can be effective, though: witness the beautiful use of 3-D graphics in the Spatula City site at http://www.wam.umd.edu/~twoflowr/spatula.html.) Most of the computer-generated 3-D you'll find on the Web comes from repurposed models—still shots from animations or games, outputs from school or self-paced learning projects, or simple re-use of the models that came with a commercial 3-D graphics application or of models downloaded from the Web.

Keeping all that in mind, if you'd like to join the saw-toothed plastic party without spending a lifetime or a fortune, the following links should help.

I don't attempt to point to every available commercial program in this section. Instead, I restrict these listings to general overviews and the cheapest entry-level software. The commercial 3-D graphics arena is fairly crowded at present, and promising new programs are still being developed; given the system requirements and expense of most good 3-D graphics generators, you'd be better off checking the most current reviews possible. One thing to bear in mind when you do go shopping: major manufacturers like Macromedia and Fractal Design often give great deals on bundled software, and if you're planning to buy another program from them, you may discover that a fairly expensive 3-D package has suddenly dropped to an additional expense of less than a hundred dollars.

## ActiveArt

**http://www.3d-active.com/**

One of the few non-game, non-VRML attempts to bring 3-D graphics onto the Web in true 3-D format is the ActiveArt project by Plastic Thought Inc. ActiveArt viewers

and plug-ins can rotate, zoom, and otherwise treat 3-D images as 3-D objects. Unfortunately, since ActiveArt is based on Apple's QuickDraw 3D technology, it's currently only usable on Macintosh systems.

## Amapi

**http://www.yonowat.com/Products/ Products.html**

Yonowat's Amapi 3-D graphics applications are well-regarded, relatively inexpensive, and usually cross-platform. The Web site offers downloadable demos of the commercial programs but, at least at the time of this writing, one of the most intriguing programs was downloadable for free: Amapi Web. Amapi Web's interface is designed around the assumption that beginners will want to edit existing models rather than having to make their own models from scratch or being stuck with already manufactured models. That seems like a reasonable assumption, and this seems like an excellent deal.

## Asymetrix Web 3D

**http://www.asymetrix.com/products/web3d/**

Like Micrografx's Instant 3D and Simply 3D products, Web 3D is a Windows 3-D graphics generator that gets new users off to a quick start by relieving them of any need (or opportunity) to define their own objects. As the name indicates, Web 3D's distinguishing feature is its focus on Web graphics: its pre-built 3-D object library includes such Web graphic clichés as banners and beveled buttons, and it exports directly to GIF or JPEG format.

## Avalon

**http://avalon1.viewpoint.com/cgi-bin/ setmirror.pl?site=vp**

This site provides a rather clumsy interface to one of the most important early FTP collections of 3-D graphics models, textures, utilities, and FAQs. At this point, the 3D Cafe site might make a better starting point, particularly for models. However, there doesn't seem to be complete overlap between the sites, so you might want to keep Avalon on your search list, if only for the FAQs and pointers.

## Breeze Designer

http://www.povray.org/ftp/pub/povray/
modellers/breeze/BreezeDesigner.html

Breeze Designer is a Windows freeware 3-D model editor built to accompany the Windows freeware rendering program POV-Ray. Newcomers beware, though: the interface and documentation are left as exercises to the reader. You could also try 3-D-game-oriented model editors like MedDLe and QMET, or the shareware POV-LAB, but if you can afford one of the cheaper commercial programs, you might be better off buying it.

## Bryce Age

http://pluginhead.eyecandy.com/bryceage.htm

The maintainer of the Photoshop Filter Factory Compendium site, Alfredo Mateus is also a fan of the Meta-Tools 3-D landscape generator, KPT Bryce. This page includes original tips, usually involving interaction with Photoshop, and links to other Bryce-dedicated sites. The tips are few but choice; when I checked in, they included this all-too-common 3-D complaint: "This picture looks much better when rendered with full quality and with all the colors and gradients preserved. But that would take a lot more time to download..."

## Busting Out All Over

http://home.dti.net/shadow/imagesoup/
articles/dimension.html

From the ImageSoup site comes this brief overview of various 3-D effects, aimed at Web authors. Its tone is considerably more enthusiastic (e.g., "[artificial 3-D] models, by their very nature, reek of depth and realism") than my own, and I recommend it not only as an introduction but as an alternative point of view.

## Computer Graphics World

http://www.cgw.com/

*CGW* is one of the leading magazines in the field of 3-D graphics. Its Web site includes a small selection of articles and reviews from each issue. On-line content includes news, an image gallery, and directories of vendors, design studios, schools, industry events, and jobs. The annotated links list is unusually strong.

## Font F/X

http://www.dcsifx.com/

Font F/X is one of several specialized 3-D programs that take advantage of the fact that the shapes of letters in most fonts (unlike the shapes of your cats in a photograph, say) are defined in a computer-friendly way. I can't pretend that their sample images are all that appealing, but since it's only $30 and free demo copies are available for downloading, Windows users should check it out.

## KPT Bryce Tips

http://www.halcyon.com/alrives/brycetips/

Alexander Rives has put together the most impressive KPT Bryce site around—at least while the old Terraformers Guild site wanders in limbo looking for a new home on the Web—with dozens of technique walkthroughs, tutorials, and "stupid Bryce tricks." One particularly valuable page documents some previously undocumented features of the program.

## The Mac's 3-D Edge

http://www.macworld.com/pages/august.96/
Feature.2267.html

This mid-1996 overview of Apple's QuickDraw 3D technology is from the site of *Macworld* magazine. Although the practical implementations of QD3D have not yet triggered deafening applause, the ideas behind the technology are interesting, and this article is a good introduction. It also includes a section on 3-D accelerator cards, but this market is moving so quickly that you'd be better off seeking a more recent source of information. By the way, you'll find more reviews of commercial 3-D graphics programs at the *Macworld* site than at other consumer computer magazine sites; it's a great place for Macintosh shoppers to start their research.

## Micrografx

http://www.micrografx.com/

Micrografx is best known for two budget 3-D programs for Windows, Simply 3D, and Instant 3D. Both are reasonably priced tools that don't let you create new 3-D models, but do let you position and apply effects to existing objects, including typefaces. Both have gotten favorable reviews for their intuitive interfaces in their budget categories; libraries of pre-made objects are supplied with both applications. At the time of this writing, Micrografx was selling its software only in a somewhat bewildering variety of bundles, so you might have to do a bit of searching to find the applications you're interested in.

## MINOS

**http://www.mygale.org/08/rlb/minos.htm**

MINOS for Windows is advertised as "the first 3D Solid CAD system in freeware." If you want to bring your visions of plastic pipes and gears to the Web, this is your program.

## PC 3D Accelerators FAQ

**http://www.cs.columbia.edu/~bm/3dcards/3d-cards1.html**

This frequently-asked-questions sheet offers an unmatched wealth of detail on 3-D graphics accelerator cards and manufacturers as of early 1996. It's been a year since the list was changed, and so it's already slightly out of date; I recommend using it as a reference rather than a buying guide.

## POV-Ray

**http://www.povray.org/**

The Persistence of Vision Ray Tracer is free. Not only that, but its source code is free, which means that it's fairly easy to compile new run-time versions for new computer platforms. Is it any wonder that it's the most popular renderer in the 3-D graphics world? The official Persistence of Vision home site contains introductions to and FAQ sheets about ray-tracing and POV-Ray, downloadable archives for each available platform, and full documentation, as well as a pointer to the

Macintosh POV-Ray site, a great source of Macintosh 3-D graphics information.

## Ray-tracing in Photoshop?

**http://www.rahul.net/natpix/RayPS.html**

Ray-tracing is one of the techniques used in the final "rendering" stages of 3-D graphics generation, named for its emphasis on lighting effects like reflection and refraction. The glossiest (and most expensive-looking) 3-D graphics tend to be ray-traced. On the one hand, it's very accurate mathematically (and very hungry for CPU power); on the other hand, it tends to produce unrealistically mathematical results. In this meaty article, animator/photographer Kevin Björke points out that the intervention of a human being and a bitmap medium (in this case, Photoshop) can sometimes achieve results that are as good as or better than a ray-tracing program can, which will come as no surprise to anyone who's seen a Vermeer painting. It makes a great introduction to the possibilities of advanced Photoshop techniques, such as displacement maps.

## Terrainman

**http://www.users.interport.net/~jashear/shareware.html**

Terrainman is $10 Macintosh shareware that creates topographic 3-D models (DXF format) from 2-D bitmaps (PICT files, to be exact). Like many bitmap-based 3-D effects filters, it's guided by the brightness of the pixels in the bitmap. A light pixel is considered higher than a dark pixel. Terrainman differs from a simple bump-map filter in giving you interactive control over the extent of calculated depth, full rotation and other variables. It's a great idea, and the program sports a very nice interface as well.

## Terrain Forge

**http://www.geocities.com/SiliconValley/Park/7425/terrain.htm**

Terrain Forge is more or less the Windows 95 freeware equivalent to Terrainman, although more restrictive and with a less interactive interface; it's a program that generates 3-D height data from a small (250 by 250 pixels) grayscale image. Its users say that it makes a nice addition to their graphics suites.

## 3-D Animation Software: Ideas Taking Shape

http://www.pcmag.com/features/software/1519/_open.htm

This group review of 3-D animation products for Windows users (with a special focus, understandably, on powerful Windows NT systems) comes from *PC Magazine*. The reviewed software ranges in price from $300 to $7,000, making this one of the most extensive overviews available, and it comes complete with tabular feature summaries for each product. The informative sidebars include an overview of the 3-D graphics generation process, notes on text-only and other specialized 3-D graphics utilities, and a glossary of 3-D terms; the pages are extensively illustrated with Shockwave animations.

## 3D Artist Magazine

http://www.3dartist.com/

The Web site for *3D Artist* features excerpts from (and corrections to) articles and reviews in the print magazine, a directory of on-line 3-D artists available for work, 3-D news and announcements, and classified ads. Most imposingly, it serves as home to the *3D Artist Handbook*, a huge directory of software and hardware companies, commercial sources for 3-D models and textures, hardware manufacturers, print publishers, video companies, service bureaus, and user groups. Special sections cover plug-ins, utility applications, books, news, and on-line tutorials for 3D Studio Max and LightWave 3D.

## 3D Cafe

http://www.3dcafe.com/asp/default.asp

It's hard to believe that Windows 3-D graphics generation could continue at its current pace if this site ever went off the air. The locally maintained collections include plug-ins for 3D Studio and LightWave, format converters, 1500 True Type fonts (a 69M download, even compressed), 700 textures, a handful of full (and large) 3-D environments and, most impressively of all, innumerable 3-D models arranged in categories such as "Anatomy," "Horror," "Plants," and "Toys." If you can't deal with the download times (frankly, even I was put off by the size of that fonts collection), you can always shell out

$100 for the site's CD-ROM, guaranteed to be made fresh on the day you order.

## 3D Design Online

http://www.3d-design.com/

The Web site for *3D Design* magazine includes Windows-oriented reviews and articles, an archive of free background textures, an annotated directory of cheap Windows shareware, and an annotated archive of free plug-ins for 3D Studio MAX.

## 3D Engines List

http://cg.cs.tu-berlin.de/~ki/engines.html

The extremely well-maintained 3D Engines List describes features of and provides links for virtually every piece of 3-D-handling and virtual-reality-handling software on virtually every platform. Unless you're a programmer, you probably won't use the list enough to bookmark it, since it only covers "engines," not authoring tools, but it's a terrific reference work.

## 3-D Graphics for the World Wide Web: THE BASICS

http://WWW.Stars.com/Authoring/Graphics/3d/

"Web graphics are getting hotter and hotter every day... and 3D is the way to go!" This 1995 tutorial for the Web Developers Virtual Library site bounces enthusiastically through the vocabulary and workflow of 3-D graphics as practiced without creation of original 3-D models. Besides effectively demonstrating "the basics," the site also demonstrates the hype and some of the pitfalls of 3-D:

the standard text effects produced by the author's budget 3-D graphics program don't look nearly as appealing as those that would have been produced by a 2-D image editor or plug-in filter; not making his own 3-D models, the author is stuck with text and a limited set of inanimate objects for content; the colors and lines of the rendered images seem garish or murky when forced into standard Web graphics formats.

### 3D Object File Formats

**http://www.cica.indiana.edu/graphics/3D.objects.html**

3-D artists seem to thirst for heavenly cities and towering views, and so it's not surprising that they've ended up with Babel. This invaluable page covers almost forty different Unix 3-D modeling formats, giving the typical file extensions for the format and pointing to the software that produces it. Most formats are concisely described; many are linked to their on-line specifications. Seven VRML formats are also covered. The page was last updated in 1994 and it's restricted to Unix, but even so, it's the best reference available.

### 3DSite

**http://www.3dsite.com/3dsite/**

You have to scroll past a large screen's worth of ads to get to the content here, but it's worth doing. A well-annotated archive of Macintosh graphics freeware and shareware is maintained on a local FTP site. Probably the highlight of 3DSite is the "Model Market": a collection of pointers to free and shareware 3-D objects, model archives, textures, and VRML files. It's fairly easy to submit new objects and links with a combination of an HTML form and FTP. Skip the classifieds (unless you like seeing job-seekers categorizing their resumes as "Hardware") and the humor section (unless you think mothers-in-law are hilarious). The good stuff is rounded off by the reference links at the very bottom of the page: exhaustive lists of 3-D FAQ sheets, references, research labs, Usenet newsgroups, books, and magazines.

### Wire Frame University

**http://www.mindspring.com/~maw01/school/unv_main.htm**

Part of Mark Willis's Wire Frame Studio site, WFU provides a series of introductions to 3-D graphics, starting with "Form and Color," and moving on to "Fundamentals of 3D," "3D Modeling," "Model Attributes," "Rendering," and "Post-Production." A lab section walks you through the use of POV-Ray. Elsewhere on the site, you'll find shareware programs and artwork by Willis.

### Xaos TypeCaster: The 3D Type Plug-In

**http://www.xaostools.com/desk/products/typecaster/typecaster.html**

Xaos, specialist in plug-in filters, has garnered praise recently for this Macintosh Photoshop add-on, which adds 3-D effects to text with easy control over color, transparency, texture, beveling, and lighting. A demo version is available for downloading.

## OTHER ELECTRONIC DOCUMENT FORMATS

HTML gives the typical benefits of a non-proprietary standard—cheapness and wide accessibility—but HTML also has the typical problems of a non-proprietary standard: slowness to change and the inability to make a huge profit. Netscape Corporation may have done its level best to convert HTML into a proprietary format, but it has been somewhat hobbled by its non-proprietary history.

The Web was designed with HTML more or less in mind, but to an even greater extent, it was designed with the flexibility to handle new formats. Software companies therefore have the opportunity to push alternative (and usually proprietary) approaches to hypermedia. These non-HTML formats are handled by browser plug-ins or helper applications, and therefore tend to cause a break in the user interface, even when they've been adapted to handle URL-based linking.

We'll be covering some of the HTML alternatives (Macromedia Shockwave and VRML, for example) in later, more specialized chapters. But even in the realm of general document layout, there are a couple of direct competitors to HTML, virtually all of them courtesy of traditional, print-oriented software companies.

That historically based slant towards paper publication is both the strength and weakness of most proprietary formats. On the one hand, they usually promise more precise layout and greater control than can be gained with HTML; on the other hand, the types of precision and control they're speaking of (exact placement on a medium with known dimensions; use of special fonts from a well-stocked system) are much better suited to sheets of paper than to the varied world of computer monitors.

### ADOBE ACROBAT PDF

Seeking to establish the sort of domination over the Web that it's had over print publishing for many years, Adobe has been pushing its proprietary PDF electronic document format hard. It has managed to get a lot of converts, especially among print publishers and graphics designers, and most especially among the subset of publishers and designers who never try to read documents on-line.

David Siegel-like designers who absolutely insist on the illusion of precise control may be much better off using Adobe Acrobat than spending hours fiddling around with HTML tricks that are likely to fizzle on "wrongly" configured Web browsers. Personally, I've always found the PDF format to be considerably more painful than straight text would be, much less HTML. The promise of precise layout is utterly mendacious in on-line publishing. Only if you've got a color 8.5-by-11-inch monitor with 133-pixels-per-inch resolution might you may actually get to see a document that resembles what its author

intended—and even then don't expect to flip the pages as quickly as you can with paper.

The most recent release of Adobe Acrobat offers much improved performance. On the UI side, Adobe has finally come up with a way to avoid the disruptive (and carpal-tunneling) zoom-scroll-and-page labor of earlier PDF documents: the Acrobat reader can now automatically zoom a document's page to match the current window size. This makes it work much more naturally on a computer screen; for the first time ever, I've actually been able to read Acrobat documents with relative ease rather than with a stream of invective. Acrobat page breaks are still arbitrary, however, and graphics and fonts that were originally intended to be dealt with off-line on a high resolution printer often don't behave nicely in an on-line, 72-pixels-per-inch setting.

### Adobe Acrobat Overview
**http://www.adobe.com/prodindex/acrobat/**
This is the official word on Acrobat production software (a cool $300 for Windows, Macintosh, or Unix systems). A $900 Windows-only package is designed to handle mass conversions from paper documents. A free Acrobat standalone viewer and Netscape plug-in are available for downloading. Other downloadable products include an Acrobat OLE server, and third-party Acrobat plug-ins that enable red-lining and other functions.

### Common Ground
**http://www.hummingbird.com/cg/commonground/**
DigitalPaper is an electronic document format invented by Hummingbird Communications; Common Ground is the name of a suite of products that helps meld DigitalPaper to the Web. Documents are richly formatted and can contain hyperlinks. Annotation support is built in. Available for free downloading are the usual Netscape plug-in (Windows only) and standalone viewer, as well as an evaluation copy of DigitalPaper publishing software; a Java-based viewer was in beta release at the time of this writing.

## CyberLinks

http://www.pioneersys.com/di/cl

CyberLinks is a bundle of OLE-based, Windows-only software that adds URL hyperlinking to any OLE-aware application, most obviously to the Microsoft Office components (Word, Excel, and PowerPoint). The theory is that as long as your readers have the proper OLE-aware software and CyberLinks installed on their local systems, you won't have to convert OLE application-created documents to HTML. (Of course, this level of homogeneity is much more likely in a corporate Intranet than on the World Wide Web!) Microsoft's own Office 97 now has much of this capability built in, so do a features comparison before you buy.

## Envoy

http://www.twcorp.com/products.htm

Tumbleweed Software, creators of the Novell Envoy electronic document format, continue to plug away at providing viable competition to Adobe. Magazine reviewers have supported Tumbleweed's claims that its format produces smaller, richly formatted, embedded-font text documents (complete with outlines, indices, annotations, and hyperlinks) faster and more cheaply, and that you can display Novell Envoy documents with less RAM. However, Acrobat continues to have an edge as far as embedded graphics go; not surprising, given Adobe's extensive experience in graphics-software development. The Tumbleweed site provides documentation, free Envoy plug-ins and standalone viewers, an ActiveX control, evaluation copies of its $80 extended viewer and $250 Envoy publishing package, and pointers to enthusiastic reviews.

## On the Road

http://www.adobemag.com/PDFs/howtoPDF/pmpdf.pdf

## Packing Light With PDF

http://www.adobemag.com/PDFs/howtoPDF/packing.pdf

## Remarkable Linking Bookmarks

http://www.adobemag.com/PDFs/howtoPDF/bookmark.pdf

## Not a Byte to Spare!

http://www.adobemag.com/PDFs/howtoPDF/spare.pdf

These four tutorials by Teri Patrick first appeared in *Adobe Magazine*. Although it's assumed that you're using PageMaker to produce your documents, these remain the best guide to Web-oriented Adobe Acrobat formatting. (You can expect the *Adobe Magazine* site to continue to post articles about the PDF format, and if you're interested in Acrobat, you should check in every month or so.)

# CHAPTER 6
# SOUND

Fig. 83

**IN THIS CHAPTER YOU WILL LEARN:**

☞ **Audio in context.**
When should you create downloadable sound files?
How can you decide what format and delivery
mechanism to use?

☞ **Sound-file formats and standards.**
These references describe the features and opera-
tion of leading digital file formats like AIFF, AU,
MIDI, and MOD.

☞ **Web-specific sound technologies.**
Many new audio formats have been developed specifically to get around the latency problem of Web
downloads.

☞ **Producing original Web audio.**
Ready to make your own sound clips, or to adapt
someone else's? These recording and conversion
utilities, mostly freeware or shareware, will let you
reach a tolerable quality level without renting a professional sound studio.

☞ **Sound clips.**
Free and shareware archives of digital sound files
abound on the Internet. Although most are meant
for local use, they can sometimes give a boost to
your own Web soundtracks.

DIGITAL AUDIO doesn't compress as easily as text or still images do, and so, despite its importance in other multimedia applications, it got off to a slow start on the Web. New compression and browser technologies have made sound much easier to encounter, if not always easier to deal with.

The resources in this chapter should make your sound bites a bit less painful for both you and your listeners.

## AUDIO IN CONTEXT

As with any other medium of communication, sound content either exists for its own sake or is used as "spice." The latter use of audio is a hallmark of multimedia applications, from pinball games to corporate presentations, and recently some Web authors have been using it in the same way. It may be worth pointing out, however, that the Web is a unique multimedia application.

- On the Web, there's no guarantee of the end user's system capabilities, or of the state of Internet transmission. What's a mild and easily overlookable delay for you might be interminable for a given user. Even if the sound comes across correctly and on time, the transmission of the file could clog up access to what your readers are really looking for on your site.

- Sound is much more intrusive than image, and the Web is used for work and for reference as well as for sport. Your audience isn't captive, and you have no control over its current circumstances. Speaking personally, if I'm in circumstances that permit any background noise, I'll probably be playing my own choice of music—very likely I'll be playing it through my computer's own speakers, in fact—and I won't be pleased if a Windows software archive belts out a distorted rendition of "The Beer Barrel

Polka" without warning every time I load a page. Of course if I'm in circumstances that *don't* permit noise, an unexpected soundtrack will be even less welcome.

- Many audio-clip archives were originally set up for people who wanted to personally customize the system sounds on their own computers. However, putting audio on the Web is publishing, rather than personal or one-shot use, and entirely different copyright considerations come into play. Record companies aren't known for their friendly live-and-let-live attitudes. I've hit *reference* sites on the Web that play sub-transistor-radio copies of "Super Sounds of the Seventies." Quite aside from their unpleasant effect on me, I wonder about their effect on Bob Segar's lawyers.

## DIGITAL SOUND FORMATS

Sound is a complex analog signal that relies on continuous time, and is thus fairly resistant to digital compression. Quality audio either requires analog formats (e.g., LPs or cassette tapes) or massive amounts of storage, such as CD-ROMs.

If the complexity of the signal is reduced, compression has more of a chance, but only at the cost of blatantly low quality. Although advances have been made in compressed digital audio over the past few years, the basic formula still applies: digital recorded sound can only achieve realistic quality by taking up a huge amount of space.

Since the amount of digital space taken up translates directly into the time it takes to download, one would think that audio wouldn't have much of a chance on the download-conscious Web, but there are three loopholes left open:

1  **Realistic quality may not be necessary.**
   If the audio content can survive reduction

BUILDING BETTER PAGES

# AUDIO ON THE WEB

On the Web, audio spice is likely to overpower the meal. For the most part, you'll be better off reserving your labor and your server disk-space for sound whose *content* is important to your site.

The most obvious example of audio-friendly content would be a page devoted to particular musicians. But there are quite a few other possibilities:

- The highly compressed formats that are easiest for Web authors and users to deal with are best suited for speech, and when tone of voice is important to the content, these formats are the best delivery mechanism. Storytelling, joke-telling, or reminiscences can all make fascinating audio clips. Indeed, the interview highlights distributed through oral-history sites have probably been my favorite genre in Web audio. This *doesn't* mean that your audience will necessarily be impressed by a chance to listen to your company CEO's speech to the stockholders! The more artificial and staged the situation, the less likely that a non-actor will come up with anything the Web audience is interested in hearing. The usual "Welcome to my home page!" audio clip is a notably clichéd example of what not to do with speech.

- Short audio clips are great for learning to distinguish between sounds. Your auto-repair page might associate knocks, pings, and thumps with diagnoses. Or you might want to provide instructions for dealing with the wide varieties of sounds emitted by household pets, or by the French. One of my favorite audio sites is a page of comparative heartbeats. I'm not a doctor, but they're interesting as background noises, and they make great starting points for soundtracks.

- Some sounds are just plain interesting or novel. I've spent an outrageous amount of time downloading insect sounds from an entomology site. (Did you know that there's a bee species that actually *trumpets*? Hear for yourself at the Carl Hayden Bee Research Center site, shown in the illustration below.) As another popular example, the Tupperware corporate site helpfully supplied an anthology of Tupperware-lid burps. Perhaps your cat, like mine, does a remarkably accurate Slim Pickens impersonation; or perhaps your job gives you easy access to the noise of collapsing buildings.

The Carl Hayden Bee Research Center ("http://gears.tucson.ars.ag.gov/") is a great source of apiarian multimedia.

to phone-call levels or lower, one of several approaches to "spoken word" compression can be taken. The resulting files will still be large, but at least they won't be *impossibly* large. The digital sound-clip files you find in Internet archives often use this type of compression.

2  **Sound may start playing before the download is finished.** If we had to wait for a phonograph needle to traverse an entire LP before any sound was heard, recorded music wouldn't have become much of an industry. Similarly, it may not matter so much that a digital sound file takes a total of five minutes to download, as long as most of that five minutes is spent listening, rather than waiting. The special Web formats designed for early starts are called streaming audio, of which the most famous example is RealAudio.

3  **Sound doesn't have to be recorded to be played.** Just as plain text takes up much less digital space than a photograph of printed text does, musical notation can take up much less space than a recording of a performance of that music. If you can count on your listener's computer to perform according to your specifications (and if you're capable of making those specifications), downloads could be made very small. MIDI is the most popular type of "musical score" in the computer world.

Of course, these loopholes can be combined. To take an all-too-familiar example, the only way to obtain a streaming effect across telephone modems is to reduce the quality of the streaming sound to spoken-word levels.

## CONTROLLING DIGITAL AUDIO SIZE

As we all know from seeing those wonderful oscilloscope-like graphs, sound consists of waves. The distance between waves is the *frequency* of the sound, which is the same as the pitch; the size of the waves gives the *amplitude* of the sound, which is the same as the volume. Right?

Well, not quite. Not unless you're dealing with pure, piercing electronic tones. Natural sounds have extremely complex wave patterns that are considerably harder to sort out. Complex waves can always be broken down mathematically into combinations of simple regular waves, but that's not a simple task. (Synthesizers have an easier time of it, since they go in the other direction, combining pure electronic tones in hopes of approximating the complex wave patterns of natural sounds.) In practice, sound waves are unpredictable and highly convoluted continuously across time.

It's the combination of complexity and continuity that causes most of our problems with digital audio. An analog medium, like the varying magnetic signals on a cassette tape or the hills and valleys of an LP surface, can straightforwardly mimic the varying waves of sound. But by its very nature, a digital medium is non-continuous: it has to keep discrete elements in separate little boxes.

A digital storage medium like computer memory can only approximate a continuous signal like sound by storing a sequence of static slices in time, in somewhat the same way that a movie approximates motion by storing a sequence of still images. The number of slices per second is measured by the *sampling rate*. The *bit rate* (sometimes called the *resolution*) measures the quality (equivalent to the amount of description) of the sound contained in each slice. In practice, digital audio approximates a sound wave by storing a series of amplitudes. The bit rate determines how many possible amplitudes can be stored, while the sampling rate determines how finely detailed the wave portrait is (or, more mathematically, what the highest recordable frequency is).

Unfortunately, there's no audio equivalent to the video world's persistence of vision, and so sampling rates have to be considerably higher than the 15 frames per second that we can get away with in video—in fact, they have to be at least *five thousand* slices higher for us to obtain even barely recognizable sound. On the other end of the scale, CD-quality audio uses 44,100 samples per second.

For any given format, the easiest way to decrease file size is to lower the bit rate and the sampling rate. In fact, for the "traditional" audio formats, which are the easiest files for you to make and which will reach the largest number of users, lowering bit rate and sampling rate are pretty much the *only* way to decrease file size: There are various compression schemes around, but they're fairly limited in what they can do and they increase the odds that your file won't play properly on your users' systems. Unfortunately, lowering the bit rate tends to introduce unpleasant noise, and lowering the sampling rate tends to destroy the distinctive timbre of natural sounds.

Oh, and if you know what's good for you, avoid stereo: two channels of sound take exactly as much space as two copies of one channel of sound. Given the constraints of Web-delivered audio, you're almost always better off using bandwidth to improve the quality of one monophonic signal instead of supplying two channels of murk.

### Choosing Digital Audio Settings

Opinions differ on how to handle sampling rate and bit resolution.

One school of thought draws an analogy to the digital graphics world, and says that you should record and work with audio in the highest-quality format that you can deal with, waiting till the final export to reduce its sampling rate and resolution—otherwise, you'll be worsening the signal with each new change. Unfortunately, it's even more difficult and expensive to create high-quality audio than to create high-quality images, and most of us have to work within painfully noticeable limitations.

Another school points out that many of the cheaper audio programs have trouble converting to lower rates (much like a GIF-conversion program that chooses horrendously bad color mappings), and that it may therefore make more sense to work in the lower-end target sampling rate and resolution from the very beginning. If only because of the difficulties of obtaining high-quality recording on normal consumer hardware, this may be the best approach.

Table 6.1 provides a guide to the most common sampling rates and bit rates and their uses.

### AUDIO OVERVIEWS

#### Audio FAQ

**http://www.cis.ohio-state.edu/hypertext/faq/ usenet/AudioFAQ/top.html**

Life must be complex in the rec.audio Usenet newsgroups. Answers to frequently asked questions take up 15 separate text files. Most of the questions and answers revolve around consumer high-fidelity equipment (e.g., "What is surround sound?"), but depending on how you create your own sound samples, you might get the answers to your own questions in the rec.audio.pro FAQ or the "Recording" section of the rec.audio FAQ. You'll find the latest versions of all the FAQ sheets at this site. (Beware the "Web version," which the FAQ itself points you to; it hasn't been updated for two years.)

**Table 6.1: Common Sampling Rates and Resolutions**

| Sampling Rate | Bit Rate | Use |
|---|---|---|
| 48 kHz | 16-bit | Typically used for DAT recording. |
| 44.1 kHz | 16-bit | CD audio. At 44,100 samples per second, frequencies up to 22.05 kHz can be reproduced, reaching the upper end of audibility. 16-bit resolution lets the recording cover 96 dB of volume changes. When you grab a sample from an audio CD, it'll be in this format. But you'd better have a big, fast disk if you intend to record in it: even a monophonic signal eats up over 5MB a minute! |
| 22.05 kHz | 16-bit | The usual top-of-the-line standard rate for contemporary computer digital audio. Note that it is exactly half the CD audio rate. 16-bit resolution makes a huge difference to audio quality, but note that older systems' hardware was usually restricted to 8-bit resolution: some portion of your potential audience may be left out if you use the higher rate. |
| 22.05 kHz | 8-bit | The most standard rate around, although the lower resolution adds hissing and other noise. If you're feeling conservative, this is probably the safest single setting; older hardware or badly written software may only understand this combination of sampling rate and resolution. |
| 22.254 kHz | 8-bit | The Macintosh was the first PC with built-in audio, and this was the old top-of-the-line audio format for Macintosh systems, based on the computer's own hardware. The preferred Macintosh sampling rate is now 22.05 kHz rather than 22.254 kHz, to make for easier cohabitation with other platforms and with CD audio. You'll still find the older rate in many archived files. (Note that in newer Macintosh systems, files in either rate will show up as "22 kHz" and both will be played at 22.05 kHz, but the playback change to older files exacts a significant cost in quality. If you're editing audio files, keep track of the difference.) |
| 11.025 kHz | 8-bit | A lower-end standard rate. Note that it's exactly one quarter of the CD audio rate. |
| 11.124 kHz | 8-bit | Again, a standard used on older Macintosh systems; again, on current Macintosh systems, this rate and its successor will both be displayed as simply "11 kHz." |
| 8 kHz | 8-bit | Almost matches the quality of a conversation on an Italian public phone. Common for highly compressed speech; not so common for symphony orchestras. |

## Audio for the Masses

**http://www.webmonkey.com/webmonkey/ geektalk/96/42/index3a.html**

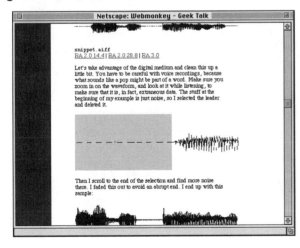

From HotWired's Webmonkey site, Adam Powell walks through creation of a simple Web sound clip, from selecting a shareware editor, through clean-up of the recording, to final conversion to streaming audio.

## Audio Unplugged

**http://www.adobemag.com/PDFs/howtoPDF/ unplug.pdf**

This article from *Adobe Magazine* walks through some simple sound effects produced with Adobe's QuickTime video editor, Premiere. Since no effects plug-ins are used, the ideas behind the techniques are applicable to any sound editor. Flanging (a popular "whoosh" effect), thickening, pseudo-stereo, and motion effects can all be achieved by manipulating multiple copies of a single audio track. (I would suggest resisting the temptation to click on the links to the sound-clip example here: this file is in

Adobe Acrobat format and, at the time of this writing, Acrobat audio links were a quick route to reboot.)

## A Comparison of Internet Audio Compression Formats

http://xanadu.com.au/sc/audio.html

This page presents a table comparing the outcomes of various approaches to audio, including uncompressed WAVE and AIFF, AU u-law encoding, MPEG-1, TrueSpeech, ToolVox, and RealAudio. Although such comparisons are somewhat artificial in the real world (ToolVox and other highly compressed formats aren't suitable for musical content), it's nice to have the bare numbers so clearly displayed.

## comp.speech Frequently Asked Questions

http://www.speech.cs.cmu.edu/comp.speech/

This enormous directory of speech technology is the Web site corresponding to the comp.speech Usenet newsgroup. Speech compression, synthesis, coding, and recognition are all covered, with over 500 links to Internet resources. A link to the comp.speech FTP site gives access to newsgroup archives, phonetic dictionaries, and software.

## Computer Music Journal

http://www-mitpress.mit.edu/Computer-Music-Journal/

This is the Web home for MIT's *Computer Music Journal*, a quarterly print magazine that covers a wide range of topics relating to digital audio-processing and music. The heart of the site is the interface to *CMJ*'s FTP archive, including a few articles from the magazine, sound files, source code, author contacts, and reference lists. Special Web-only pages include a great set of links for the computer-music novice, and directories of sound-clip archives, research centers, and many other music-related categories.

## Digital Audio Software For Multimedia

http://www.hyperstand.com/NewMedia/96/02/td/audio/Digital_Audio_Software.html

If you're serious enough about original music production to be interested in high-end, high-cost recording software, you should look into this review from *New Media* of professional audio editors for the Macintosh and Windows platforms.

## Dolby Laboratories

http://www.dolby.com/

Although this is predominantly a no-nonsense corporate propaganda site, it does include a glossary of film sound, a great deal of technical information on noise reduction, and pointers for consumers who want to set up their own surround-sound systems.

## Electronic Music Interactive

http://nmc.uoregon.edu/emi/emi.html

This page takes you to a remarkably informative embedded Shockwave application that introduces the viewer (and listener) to the theory and practice of electronic audio and music, beginning from the basics of sound and sine waves, and continuing through concepts like amplitude, phase, and harmonics and signal transformations like envelope generators and band-pass filters, all the way to MIDI data and sequencers. Despite the ambitiously wide range of topics, the text and diagrams remain clear, and the replayable animations and sound examples are extremely helpful when dealing with such material. The

content more than makes up for the occasional Shock-wave glitch. (Hint: *Always* pick "Continue," *never* pick "Stop.") The author, Jeffrey Stolet, writes that he was unable to find a "true beginning electronic music text" for his music-theory classes; in rectifying that, he's provided a top-rate example of educational multimedia.

## FAQ: Audio File Formats

ftp://ftp.cwi.nl/pub/audio/AudioFormats.part1
ftp://ftp.cwi.nl/pub/audio/AudioFormats.part2

These two text files may not be the prettiest looking or most up-to-date documents on the Internet, but the first part remains the best general introduction to sound formats as of 1995—no streaming audio here! The second part is more miscellaneous, dropping into sometimes useful and sometimes painfully detailed notes on specific formats.

## Graphics and Sound File Formats

http://www.nlc-bnc.ca/publications/netnotes/
notes24.htm

Skip down to the last third of this page and you'll find the most concise and comprehensible introduction to the formats, vocabulary, and problems of digital audio available on the Web. The effects of sampling rate, bits per sample, and number of channels are all clearly described; covered sound formats include such popular file extensions as AU, AIFF, WAV, MOD, SND (lots of SNDs, it turns out), and VOC.

## Internet Underground Music Archive

http://www.iuma.com/

This well-known vanity publishing venture for unsigned musicians may be slightly easier than setting up your own site, particularly if you don't have access to a RealAudio server. It's less selective than the average music-industry showcase, but a lot cheaper, too. For non-musician Web authors, the site may still be of interest for its support of multiple audio formats and hosting of various Web 'zines.

## IRCAM

http://www.ircam.fr/index-e.html

IRCAM, funded by the French government, is one of the leading music laboratories in the world. Its Web site includes summaries of IRCAM's research and development work, and information about hardware and software products produced by the organization.

## Mac Sound Utilities

http://www.wavenet.com/~axgrindr/
quimby4.html

This page seemed a little more complete and up to date than its sibling, "PC Sound Utilities"—or perhaps it simply has less competition. At any rate, it's a fine collection of annotated links to Macintosh audio applications. (The editor's picks? Sound Hack for conversions; SoundEffects for editing.) Specialized pages on the site contain links for Macintosh CD players, MIDI applications, mods applications, and useless (if not annoying) novelty programs. By the way, most of these links go directly to a download-able executable rather than to an application's home page, and so you may not always end up with the latest versions. With this, as with other software archives, if you find a program you like it's almost always worth a search for a dedicated site.

## Make Some Noise

http://www.cnet.com/Content/Features/
Howto/Audio/

C|Net's introduction to Web audio is inoffensively optimistic in the usual C|Net fashion, but keep paging and you'll encounter some good (if somewhat dated) information regarding file sizes, embedded audio, and streaming formats. The pages include a Shockwave toy that lets you try out various combinations of sampling rate and bit rate on a pre-made sound sample.

## Making a Recording with Sound Effects

http://www.mcs.csuhayward.edu/~tebo/
Classes/4850/Audio/UsingSE.html

All Macintosh users have simple sound recording and playback capabilities, courtesy of their system's microphone and basic software. For impatient low-end Macintosh owners, this page offers a step-by-step guide to making a recording using the SoundEffects utility.

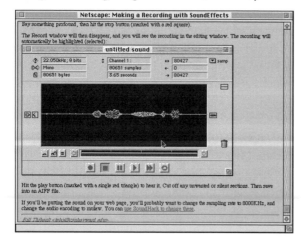

### MPEG FAQ

**http://www.powerweb.de/mpeg/mpegfaq/**

MPEG (a product of the Moving Pictures Experts Group) may be best known as a set of video-compression standards, but thanks to the success of *The Jazz Singer*, audio-compression formats are a major part of this group's work. Part of the wide-ranging MPEG Archive site maintained by Frank Gadegast, this FAQ (and the site as a whole) is particularly strong on MPEG audio. The ideas behind the compression formats are explained with humor but without nonsense, and pointers to MPEG audio commercial and freeware utilities are supplied for every major computer platform. Elsewhere on the site you'll find MPEG-related links, an extensive directory of MPEG playback utilities, and a CD-ROM containing MPEG sound samples and utilities, the contents of which are also available online.

### Overview of Digital Sound

**http://www.sfoundry.com/pages/tech/sndovw.htm**

Sonic Foundry has provided this useful overview of digital sound on its Web site, covering the most important concepts and basic vocabulary items such as "quantization" and "sampling rate."

### Shareware Music Machine

**http://www.hitsquad.com/smm/edit/index.html**

The Shareware Music Machine site contains software for writing, editing, and playing music across Windows 95, Windows 3.1, Macintosh, and other systems. Files are categorized as "real-time audio" (i.e., streaming players), "players and editors" (which could more accurately be called "miscellaneous," since it contains many other programs of interest to the on-line composer), MIDI tools, and mods tools. Unlike shareware archives that give the hapless searcher only a file name to interpret, the Shareware Music Machine provides an informational page about each program. Although not complete by any means, the Shareware Music Machine makes a very useful supplement to platform-specific and topic-specific directories.

### TechTools—Web Audio

**http://www.techweb.com/tools/multimedia/audio/audio.html**

Speaking of *The Jazz Singer*, this page lost a lot of credibility for me when it referred to Al Jolson as the man "who amazed the world when he appeared on a new invention called television." (As we all know, it was actually a product called Myst that first made television popular.) Well, the site is called "Tech Tools," not "Cultural Allusion Tools," and if you ignore the rough surface, you may find just the basic introduction you've been looking for.

### The Web Multimedia Tour—Audio

**http://ftp.digital.com/webmm/audio.html**

The rare overview to be based squarely on professional experience, this page of John Faherty's Web Multimedia Tour covers a wide range of audio formats and Windows software, annotated with personal impressions: the Real-Audio format is "the one I've had to put the most work into to make the recording sound reasonable after compression," and DSP's TrueSpeech offers "probably the best compromise between quality and compression." The section on how to handle audio broadcasting shouldn't be missed by anyone planning a live Web event.

## World Forum for Acoustic Ecology
http://interact.uoregon.edu/MediaLit/
WFAEHomePage

A site devoted to the sounds that surround us (not to be confused with "surround sound"), WFAE also includes annotated directories of links to music-related Web resources. The "Internet Audio Software and Programming" and "Technical Information: Sounds, Resources, and Applications" pages are likely to be of special interest to Web authors; the latter page includes general information on sound recording and pointers to sound-editing utilities.

# SAMPLED SOUND EDITORS AND CONVERTERS

"Sampled sound" is basically computer jargon for a recording which is stored digitally. As mentioned before, there are serious limitations to how much real-world audio can be compressed, and the differences between the major "traditional" digital sound formats are not all that noticeable, in either file size or sound quality. Historically, each operating system has developed its own favorite audio file formats. In practice, standard audio players are now available for all platforms for each format, and so it really doesn't matter much to your listeners which you use. I advise going by convenience: use whatever format your favorite sound editor on your favorite platform seems most comfortable with.

## AUDIO FILE FORMATS

For convenient reference, here's a list of the digitized audio file-formats you're most likely to come across.

## WAV

Whether you call them "WAV," "WAVE," or "RIFF WAVE," files with the ".wav" extension are in the standard sound format for Microsoft Windows and IBM OS/2. WAV supports virtually any sampling rate up to 44 kHz, and both 8-bit and 16-bit resolution.

☞ Although for any given platform some application can almost always be found to play an uncompressed audio file, be aware that a particular audio application, especially one that's in its early stages of development, may turn out to be painfully finicky. For one of my own multimedia projects, I ended up going through more than a dozen combinations of software and option settings before managing to produce a file that my libraries were capable of playing. If your target application is in beta, do some early tests to make sure that your editing set-up can integrate with it.

Compression is its own can of tightly packed worms. Many audio file-format specifications allow a wide variety of compression algorithms to be applied. In theory, this is a good thing: it keeps the formats from going "out of date." In practice, however, something needs to decompress the file's data before it can be heard. An audio player can honestly claim to support a given audio file format without being able to interpret all possible compression formats stored in the file. The result can be massive user confusion, and even a fair amount of Web-author confusion. Either be extremely conservative about your compression choices, or use an audio-file format that wears its compression algorithm on its sleeve, like RealAudio or TrueSpeech. And bear in mind that all audio compression is lossy: Once you've compressed a sound, there's no turning back, so you'd better make sure that you've done all the editing you intend to before starting to compress.

The safest compression to apply to WAV files is probably Microsoft's own ADPCM, which can manage a 4-to-1 compression rate on spoken-word material.

## AIFF and AIFC

Both the Apple Interchange File Format and the Apple Interchange Format Compressed use the file extension ".aiff" or ".aif." As you may have gathered already, these formats are commonly used on Macintosh systems, though they're also popular on SGI workstations. The most common compression algorithms applied to the files are the Apple-proprietary MACE 3-to-1 and MACE 6-to-1, where "MACE" stands for Macintosh Audio Compression and Expansion. As you also may have gathered already, the 6-to-1 format compresses more thoroughly, but with a larger reduction in quality.

### AU

You'll see the native audio-file format for Sun and NeXT called all sorts of things, since those wacky engineering types insisted on using a Greek letter ("μ") to name its most frequently used encoding scheme, "μ-law." Because the letter resembles the Latin letter "U," you'll often see the terms "u-law" or "U-law;" because it's pronounced "mu," you'll also see the term "mu-law." It's a lot of fuss for such a limited format. Originally designed for telephone systems, u-law is monophonic, is most commonly recorded at a low-quality 8 kHz sampling rate, and is restricted to 8-bit storage, although the special encoding scheme results in almost 12 bits worth of real (if noisy) dynamic range. (A similar encoding scheme used by European telephone systems is called "a-law"; Sun and NeXT audio files with that encoding often have the extension ".al" rather than ".au.") Despite the limitations, the Unix roots of the Internet guarantee that you'll bump into plenty of AU files as you browse on-line archives.

### QuickTime

QuickTime for audio? Well, it's actually one of the more dependable multimedia file formats out there: the player doesn't take much space, and it handles MIDI as well as sampled audio. On the Macintosh, audio CD tracks can easily be converted to QuickTime files for further editing. As a result, you will sometimes see audio-only QuickTime files, often

produced by people who own video-editing software but no audio-editing software.

### MPEG Audio

MPEG audio compression is designed to drastically shrink high-quality (typically 44.1 kHz, 16-bit) sound without causing noticeable distortion. MPEG algorithms come in three flavors, with Level 1 being easiest to decompress (and doing the worst job) and Level 3 being hardest to decompress (but achieving beautiful audio quality). Due to the demands made on computer processors by the compression schemes, there aren't many software MPEG players out there yet, especially for MPEG-3, and the ones that exist usually only work with special audio hardware, or on Pentium or PowerPC systems.

### VOC

The proprietary VOC format was developed by Creative Labs for its SoundBlaster sound cards. Since these are the most popular sound cards in the PC marketplace, the format is fairly common, despite its focus on specific hardware and its relative lack of flexibility.

### Sound Designer II

Digidesign, the originators of this format, has created some of the most popular sound editing tools on the Macintosh, and as a result, Sound Designer II has become a bit of a de facto standard for sound-editing software, much like Photoshop image files.

### The Ambiguous "snd"

The file extension ".snd" is used by at least four different audio formats: NeXT "AU"-style u-law files, Macintosh system sounds, Amiga audio, and Tandy audio. Although most of the ones you'll find on the Web are AU-formatted files, be sure of the context before downloading a "snd" file!

## KEEPING TRACK OF AUDIO FORMATS

With all the potential for confusion, it's important that you name your sound files unambiguously and make sure that your Web server associates the correct MIME type to them. Table 6.2 should help with that, as well as help you assign plug-ins and helper applications for your own Web listening.

### Awave

**http://hem.passagen.se/fmj/fmjsoft.html**

Awave, a remarkable piece of Windows 95 shareware from Frank Markus Jönsson, plays and converts audio in over a hundred different digital formats, making it a perfect helper application for your Web browser. It also functions well as a sound editor for both MIDI and sampled audio, displaying the elements of a sound file graphically as a tree whose leaves are waveforms.

### ConvertMachine

**http://www.kagi.com/rod/convertmachine/moreinfo.html**

This versatile Macintosh sound-format conversion program by Rod Kennedy is a companion to his popular SoundMachine sound-playing program. Simply set up your format, compression, and sampling-rate options, and start dragging files into the conversion chute. Stereo can be mixed down to mono, audio CD tracks can be compressed, and translations can be made between AIFF, AU, WAV, MacOS Finder sound files, QuickTime movies, and Sound Designer II files. On a personal note, I'm grateful to ConvertMachine for being the only Macintosh audio software to reliably produce sound files playable by early-issue Java applications.

### Cool Edit

**http://www.syntrillium.com/**

Syntrillium Software's Cool Edit is the Paint Shop Pro of audio: a shareware program as powerful as lower-level commercial programs at a fraction of the cost ($25 to $50, depending on what features you need). Cool Edit users can record in mono or stereo from a CD, keyboard, or microphone, can merge and trim files, can clean up or add effects to sound samples, and can read and write virtually every digital audio format in common use. The application is scriptable, and can be used for batch conversions. The most recent version, Cool Edit 96, can export to the RealAudio format. At the time of this writing, the company was preparing to release a

**Table 6.2: Audio Formats**

| Audio Format | Filename Extensions | MIME Types |
|---|---|---|
| AIFF | .aiff, .aif | audio/x-aiff |
| AU | .au, .snd, .al | audio/basic |
| MIDI | .mid, .midi | audio/midi, audio/x-midi, application/x-midi, audio/x-mid |
| MOD | .mod | |
| MPEG-3 | .m3u | audio/x-mpegurl |
| MPEG-3 | .mp3, .l3, .bit | audio/x-mpeg3 |
| RealAudio | .ra, .ram | audio/x-pn-realaudio |
| RealAudio plug-in | .rpm | audio/x-pn-realaudio-plugin |
| Shockwave | dcr,dir,dxr | application/x-director |
| TrueSpeech | .tsp | application/dsptype |
| WAV | .wav | audio/x-wav |

commercial version of the program, Cool Edit Pro, with a suggested retail price of $400

### Gold Wave

**http://web.cs.mun.ca/~chris3/goldwave/**

This shareware digital audio player and editor for Windows may be Cool Edit's best competition. Gold Wave includes multi-threading recording and playback, a 10-band equalizer, many effects filters, and direct sound manipulation using the mouse. Registration is $30. The site includes download locations, an order form, and a very helpful FAQ.

### How Sound Sampling Works

**http://www2.heidsite.com/heidsite/audio/ soundprimer.html**

This excerpt by Jim Heid from *The Macworld New Complete Mac Handbook* provides an excellent practical introduction to sampling rate and bit resolution. Heid explains how to choose rates and resolution, and how to make optimal recordings within the bounds of your choices. Although the sound-editing software he mentions is all Macintosh-based, the ideas and techniques are thoroughly cross-platform.

### Pro Tools by Digidesign

**http://www.digidesign.com/Newdigiweb/ Digiprod/pt_software/index.html**

Digidesign is known for its professional audio-production hardware and software tools. It's packaged a software-only (but still professionally priced) Pro Tools system for Power Macintosh owners, including multiple record tracks, simultaneous editing of recorded audio and MIDI tracks, and many mixdown features. Elsewhere on the Digidesign site, you'll find upgrades, information on cross-product compatibility, a software library, and customer profiles.

### QUACK Sound Effects Studio

**http://morello.wildnet.co.uk/quack.html**

This amusing piece of Windows 95 shareware lets non-musicians create somewhat random sound effects by connecting various wave patterns and filter icons together into trees. Is it worth $35? That probably depends on just how amusing you find it; the feature-crippled download should help you decide.

### SoundApp

**http://www-cs-students.stanford.edu/~franke/ SoundApp/**

Norman Franke's freeware Macintosh application, SoundApp, can play and convert a large number of formats (including MIDI and some varieties of mods and MPEG audio), and also supports playlists (with shuffle play, yet). Unlike other old-time freeware authors, Franke has kept SoundApp up to date, making frequent improvements and bug fixes. As an added service, his "SoundApp Formats" page is one of the best references to audio file-formats on the Web, packed with detailed practical information. There are no streaming audio formats, though, as SoundApp doesn't support them.

### SoundEdit 16 and Deck II

**http://www.macromedia.com/software/ sound/**

SoundEdit 16, a mature Macintosh sound-editing package from Macromedia, lets you edit 16-bit 44-kHz sound—although you'll probably want to tighten up that audio a bit before putting it on the Web! Although available for stand-alone purchase, most owners obtain it packaged with Macromedia's authoring bundles. The program's feature set includes CD audio-capture, multi-track mixing, special effects, advanced synchronization, batch file-processing, and a range of sampling rates and compression algorithms. The installation CD-ROM includes hundreds of royalty-free clip sounds. Standard SoundEdit 16 can produce files in such common formats as AIFF, AU, and WAVE; a plug-in from Progressive Networks allows export to RealAudio format, and a plug-in from Macromedia lets you use the streaming Shockwave audio format. The more complex multitrack recording and mixing program Deck II was acquired by Macromedia in 1995: it makes a youthfully strange bedfellow for SoundEdit 16, but it's gotten excellent reviews. Deck II is suitable for working with CD-quality audio, and integrates well with MIDI files and video work.

## SoundEffects

**ftp://ftp.alpcom.it/software/mac/Ricci/html/sfx.html**

SoundEffects is a popular $15 shareware sound editor for the Macintosh. As its name indicates, it emphasizes digital effects, and it's helped along by a plug-in architecture that eases the addition of new effects: you just add a new effects module when it's ready. Unfortunately, author Alberto Ricci was lured away to the world of commercial software before even being able to reach Version 1.0! He suggests that we, like him, concentrate on the SoundMaker program. In case you choose the cheaper route, however, this page supplies pointers to download sites and reviews.

## Sound Forge

**http://www.sfoundry.com/**

Sonic Foundry helped put Windows on the digital-audio map with its Sound Forge program, production software that handles recording, editing, processing, and a wide range of effects. Sound Forge is still going strong at Version 4.0, with support added for multi-level undo, direct edit mode and many Web-friendly formats. For $150, you can pick up the less powerful budget version, Sound Forge XP. The Sonic Foundry Web site points to feature lists, product FAQ sheets, and blurb-ripe reviews; on the less directly commercial side, you can find an introduction to digital sound and its jargon, and downloadable save-disabled, limited-time demo programs.

## SoundHack

**http://shoko.calarts.edu/~tre/SndHckDoc/**

SoundHack is a shareware Macintosh sound editor by Tom Erbe. Although it plays and converts the usual as-

sortment of digital audio formats, its strength rests in sound-processing functions such as time-stretching, pitch-shifting, spatializing, and noise reduction. To register, you can send Erbe either $30, or a piece of music or art that you've made; only registered users have access to the PowerPC-native version of the program.

## SoundMaker

**http://www.allegiant.com/soundmaker/**

SoundMaker is a new but already much-praised addition to the small list of low-end ($100, in this case) commercial Macintosh sound editors. The interface is intuitive, but the truly distinguishing feature of the program is its emphasis on sound effects, dear to the hearts of audio amateurs everywhere. Dozens of effects are supplied with the program and, taking a page from Alberto Ricci's SoundEffects shareware, a modular architecture allows easy creation and storage of new sound effects. The program is unfashionably fast and slim, making it usable on older Macintosh systems and, perhaps more importantly, making it useful as a helper application with a QuickTime video-editor or a multitrack recording system like Deck II. A save-disabled demo version is available for downloading, but at this time final purchase must be made by mail or phone.

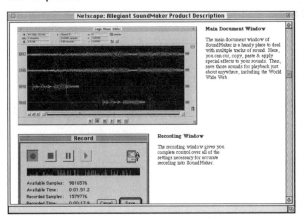

# STREAMING SOUND FORMATS

Audio and video are stored in large files that take a noticeable time to download even on fast connections; on modem-based connections, the wait can be excruciating. Streaming audio and video formats are designed to start playing before a file is completely copied to the user's local computer. This is more satisfying from a UI point of view, and also gives the user a chance to determine the value of the download earlier in the process.

For most audio applications, a streaming format makes a lot of sense, but the following less attractive features should be kept in mind.

- A quicker start doesn't translate into better quality. In fact, since the amount of information contained in the file has to be restricted to what can be transmitted across the wires in the time it takes the sound to play, the quality is usually considerably less than you could get by waiting for a differently formatted file to be fully copied. It's as if an interlaced GIF stopped loading after the first pass was drawn. At 28.8 modem speeds, about the best that can be achieved is AM radio quality. One workaround often taken by Web authors is to offer users a choice of files, making more complete audio files available for faster connections.

- Glitches in transmission ("Unreliable performance on the Internet? Say it ain't so!") usually result in noticeable gaps and jumps in sound. Especially with musical content, this sort of glitch can be even more irritating than a long startup wait.

- Streaming audio formats often require more of a financial investment than traditional non-streaming formats. RealAudio only works if there's a special (and costly) program running on the Web server; Shockwave requires Macromedia authoring software.

- Since streaming formats rely on a direct connection between the user's machine and a Web server, each new format tends to require a new browser plug-in. This introduces an extra delay and platform-dependency issues. Moreover, users quickly learn that adding plug-ins increases their memory requirements and decreases the stability of their browsers, and so a large proportion of those users who *can* download an appropriate plug-in will choose not to do so.

To deal with this last point, alternatives to browser plug-ins try to *force* a download of the executable, either via Internet Explorer's ActiveX controls or via a Java applet. But these approaches have their own problems.

With ActiveX, the audience is effectively restricted to Windows Internet Explorer users—and many of us will have turned ActiveX controls off, for reasons I'll get into later.

With Java applets, there's the promise of cross-platform support, but only for users with working Java support: a problematic assumption, for reasons I'll get into in the same chapter. Also, since Java applets are temporarily cached rather than permanently stored, the delay in loading the executable code will almost always be added to the delay of loading the audio.

The end result is that non-streaming audio formats still have a place, especially if your file is fairly small, or if you're working with a restricted budget, or if you want to deliver the highest possible quality to the highest number of users.

And when it comes to plug-ins, nothing succeeds like success for the Web author. We're best off if we restrict ourselves to the most popular types of sound files (RealAudio, Shockwave, and the non-streaming formats supported by default plug-ins), since that greatly increases the chance that our users will be able to hear our work.

## A/V Streaming Brings the Web to Life... Almost

**http://www.hyperstand.com/NewMedia/96/ 14/td/AV_Streaming_Web.html**

Although written before the release of RealAudio 3.0, this article from *New Media* magazine remains the most thorough and thoughtful review of the many competing audio-streaming formats. Don't miss the sidebar on "pseudo-streaming" formats like QuickTime and Active-Movie, which can start playing files before they're completely loaded, even if they can't get off to quite as quick a start as "true streaming" formats can.

## Crescendo PLUS

**http://www.liveupdate.com/proddes.html**

The excitement over LiveUpdate's MIDI-playing plug-in, Crescendo, has dampened since Apple's QuickTime and Netscape's LiveAudio have made MIDI a standard browser feature. Perhaps in response, the company has issued a streaming MIDI plug-in, Crescendo PLUS, for $20. The question, of course, is whether consumers are willing to pay to start playing MIDI files in "one second or less," given that most MIDI files on the Web are already fairly small. (I note that an additional "feature" of the newer plug-in is that Webmasters can prevent users from saving a local copy of the MIDI file—seems like a hard sale to make!)

## Echo Speech

**http://www.echospeech.com/**

Echo Speech Corporation is the maker of streaming sound utilities optimized for speech. The vanilla Echospeech plug-in doesn't require special server software, but the company also sells a variant, EchoCast, which uses a Windows NT or Windows 95 real-time encoder to handle live broadcasts. The authoring software is free for non-commercial Internet use; businesses and Intranets must pay a $99 licensing fee.

## Layer3—Streaming MPEG Audio

**http://www.powerweb.de/mpeg/layer3.html**

This page from the MPEG Archive site is devoted to the MPEG Level 3 format, which can provide both streaming and very high quality, but which is not widely supported at present. It points to downloadable MPEG 3 samples and players of varying stability and, most interestingly, lets you compare the quality of an MPEG3 sound to the same sound in RealAudio format.

## MPEG 3 on Macs!

**http://www.rust.net/~rosenblu/mp3.html**

As author Aaron Rosenblum says, most of the Web pages devoted to MPEG Layer 3 are also devoted to Windows or Unix platforms. He's remedied the situation with this straightforward page pointing to MPEG 3 players and utilities for the Macintosh. He also provides a page explaining how Power Macintosh and Sound Edit 16 owners can create their own MPEG 3 audio files.

## Netscape Media Server

**http://home.netscape.com/comprod/server_ central/product/media/index.html**

The Netscape Media Player is a plug-in designed for streaming audio and live multicasting, with synchronized multimedia possible by using Netscape's LiveConnect Java-based technology. As with Progressive Networks' RealMedia product line, the money is expected to come from purchases of the required server program, the $1,000 Netscape Media Server, available for Unix and Windows NT systems.

## RealAudio

**http://www.realaudio.com/**

Version 3.0 of RealAudio introduced much-needed improvements in sound quality and, after facing some serious competition, Progressive Networks still seems to rule the streaming media format world. At this site, named after its flagship product, you'll find downloadable plug-ins and encoders, plenty of corporate propaganda, pointers to samples and to third-party applications, and a long list of commercial products, including the "deluxe" RealPlayer Plus plug-in and a full menu of streaming servers with prices starting from $300 for an audio-only server that can handle 10 simultaneous customers and ending at $20,000 for 400 streams on an unlimited number of CPUs. (The budget-minded should note that RealAudio files support "pseudo-streaming" without any extra server software; another possibility is using an Internet service provider that gives access to its own site-wide media servers.) If you decide to use RealAudio for your Web pages, don't miss the "DevZone" area of this site: hidden away in the innocuous-sounding "Tip of the Week Archives" are extensive and essential tutorials on encoding clips, improving sound quality, handling live broadcasts, and properly configuring sites.

## Shockwave Streamed Audio

**http://www.macromedia.com/support/soundedit/how/shock/**

As part of improving its Shockwave format for Web-delivered multimedia applications, Macromedia independently developed its own approach to streaming audio, one that doesn't require special servers (although it does require ownership of a Macromedia authoring product: Shockwave Audio, or "SWA"). Even though it was originally conceived as an add-on, Shockwave audio won praise for the high quality of its MPEG compression when compared to sound clips encoded in the RealAudio 2.0 format, and Shockwave soon became popular as an audio-only format. However, RealAudio 3.0 closed some of the quality gap, and Macromedia itself chose to use the RealAudio format for one of the newest Shockwave products, Flash. At the time of this writing it was rather difficult to find any Shockwave streamed-audio information on the Macromedia Web site; the best starting page

seemed to be this one, which explained the then-new format to existing users of the SoundEdit 16 program. It's possible that the company is de-emphasizing its streaming audio development. If that turns out to be the case, it's too bad.

## ToolVox

**http://www.voxware.com/toolvox/moretoolvox.html**

Voxware is a software company that specializes in compressing recordings of speech, mostly for telephone-like applications. Voxware has developed the ToolVox plug-in to apply the same technology to one-way downloaded audio. ToolVox audio streams without need of a special server, and can contain MIDI data as well as sampled analog sound. The ToolVox plug-in and a basic encoder are free for downloading; an enhanced ToolVox Gold encoder must be purchased by phone.

## TrueSpeech

**http://www.dspg.com/internet.htm**

The DSP Group's TrueSpeech speech-compression algorithms provide what is probably the best possible real-time digital audio over a 14.4-Kbps modem. They have been licensed by many other companies, including Microsoft: TrueSpeech compression and decompression (optimized for an 8-kHz sampling rate and 16-bit resolution) is built into the Windows 95 Sound Recorder. The company's Web site houses a free TrueSpeech player to stream WAVE files that use TrueSpeech compression; there's also a free TrueSpeech encoder for Windows 3.1 users. There's no Macintosh encoder, but the company offers to help Macintosh-based Web authors create files, within reason.

## Vosaic Sound

**http://www.vosaic.com/html/sound.html**

Another in the crowded field of streaming media companies, Vosaic is attempting to get around the problem of low consumer acceptance of plug-ins by offering a Java-based audio player that doesn't require a plug-in or special server support—although obviously it does require Java. A free Windows-based converter is available for Web authors to download.

# COMPUTER-GENERATED AUDIO

You would think that one of the first things to occur to someone using an electronic music synthesizer would be automatic playback: it's not like the personal touch is all that apparent. Yet although music synthesizers have been around for some time, it wasn't until 1982 that a specification was developed to enable generic electronic control of electronic instruments.

The specification, MIDI, was originally intended to merely facilitate communication between the microprocessors embedded in the instruments themselves. However, since MIDI provides for the equivalent of a heavily annotated orchestral score, it soon became apparent that the format would be just as useful for letting a central computer "conductor" handle playback, with no actual MIDI instruments required. Moreover, a MIDI file is much smaller than the file of an equivalent recording of a specific performance of the same piece of music would be.

## MIDI EDITORS AND CONVERTERS

MIDI files are made up of a set of *sequences*, where each sequence is a set of musical events assigned to a particular style of playback. The playback styles are named for real-world instruments, with the expectation that the electronic playback will more-or-less successfully mimic those instruments' sounds. *Sequencer software* is thus software that lets you arrange sequences; that is, lets you create and edit MIDI files.

In this section you'll find pointers to sequencer, conversion and editing software for MIDI files, as well as a wide variety of MIDI utilities and assorted information sources.

### Arnold's Web Page

http://www.planete.net/~amasson/

This unprepossessing little page contains the most popular MIDI utilities for the Macintosh, both by Arnaud Masson. MIDIPlugin is a freeware plug-in for Netscape Navigator and Internet Explorer. The standard QuickTime player and other plug-ins can handle MIDI files, but MIDIPlugin has been praised for its handling of Macintosh peculiarities. Arnold's MIDI Player is $10 shareware that plays any MIDI or karaoke file either on the Macintosh internal speaker or on an external MIDI device. For fellow programmers, Masson provides his MIDIEngineLib MIDI-playing library as freeware.

### Audio Software That Does It All

http://www.hyperstand.com/NewMedia/96/ 05/td/audio/Audio_Editing_Software.html

Another useful comparison review from *New Media* magazine: this one covers commercial MIDI editors that can also handle some editing tasks for recorded digital audio. Both Macintosh and Windows platforms are covered.

### Cakewalk Music Software

http://www.cakewalk.com/

Cakewalk produces a wide range of well-reviewed MIDI and digital audio tools. Its MIDI sequencer Cakewalk Pro is one of the leaders in the field, but beginners might do well with Cakewalk Song Station for only $70, or Cakewalk Home Studio for $130. Besides product information, Cakewalk's Web site hosts pointers to Cakewalk-created music (with reviews), the Tune 1000 catalog of MIDI CD-ROM collections, a troubleshooting FAQ sheet, uncommonly busy, dedicated newsgroups full of technical advice, and downloadable demo versions and product updates.

### The Creative Zone

http://www.creaf.com/

The Creative Zone is the official Web site of Creative Labs, whose Sound Blaster 16-bit cards have become an industry standard for PC sound. The company also produces a range of video capture and compression cards, cards to boost 2-D and 3-D graphics, speakers, modems, and video-conferencing equipment. The usual corporate product listings, press releases, and driver updates are available here, along with technical specifications, FAQs, and a few other additions. The "Music Pub" area includes walkthroughs, tips, and pointers to original compositions created with Creative Labs equipment. The "Online

Newsstand" of annotated links is well-selected but grievously out of date—in fact, many of the most interesting pages on the site appear to have been given up on in early 1996.

### The EMUSIC-L Page

**http://sunsite.unc.edu/mcmahon/emusic-l/**

EMUSIC-L is a mailing list for those who work with electronic music. This, its official Web site, contains background information on the list, a selection of articles that were posted to the list (including pointers on notation software, a keyboards buyer's guide, and many reviews of synthesizers), and a nearly complete archive of list digests, complete with search engine.

### Enhancing MIDI Recordings

**http://www.winjammer.com/ Enhancing_Title.htm**

OK, so you've downloaded or purchased a MIDI sequencer. Now what do you do with it? The WinJammer site hosts this HTML-ization of a brilliant essay on MIDI editing (and, as a by-product, music composition) by Gene Confrey. With all the finicky wit one hopes for but so rarely gets from a Ph.D., Doc Confrey covers the theory and practice behind every possible type of tinkering, all in the service of "reducing or modifying those MIDI events that make us blush. Like multi-struck notes. Awkward hesitations. Banal improvisation. Abrupt endings." (I hope this doesn't count.)

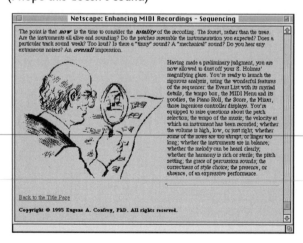

### Future Music

**http://www.futurenet.co.uk/music/ futuremusic.html**

It takes a bit of work to get into the Web site of UK-based *Future Music Magazine*, but if you're serious about making electronic music, it's worth filling out the entry form. Interviews with leading musicians, many reviews and buyer's guides, and general articles such as "Taking Control of Your Synth" are all reproduced from the print version of the magazine.

### Harmony Central

**http://www.harmony-central.com/ MIDI/**

The largest MIDI site on the Web, Harmony Central provides a wealth of material for beginners, advanced users, and engineers. Scott Lehman has organized technical (and not-so-technical) introductions, specifications, software development tools, hardware listings, industry news, and a directory of MIDI collections on the Internet. Directories of software, arranged by computer platform, include demo versions, MIDI players, patch editors, sequencing and notation packages, and more. The online discussion forum contains an unusually high percentage of answered questions. Apropos Usenet newsgroups are archived here with a search facility. There's a very busy classified ads section: if you don't find what you want there, go to the manufacturers and retailers directories. You might also try out the huge buyer's guide, which provides product information, price lists, and contact information. If you're still at a loss, dozens of links to related sites are listed.

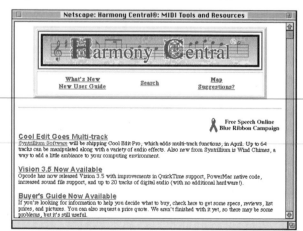

### *Keyboard* Central
http://www.keyboardmag.com/

The home site for *Keyboard* magazine stands on its own as a first-rate spot for musicians, with buyer's guides, reprinted articles, downloadable audio and MIDI files to illustrate those articles, a fine selection of tutorials, a glossary, and even instructional video clips. Don't miss the terrific state-of-the-art overview, "20 Things You Must Know to Make Electronic Music," and its sequels.

### M-Cubed—Macintosh, MIDI, Music
http://coyote.accessnv.com/dhanley/m3/m3.html

This is the Web home of "m3," the Internet Macintosh MIDI user group. As a member of the user group, you're promised the usual array of discounts and special deals. Doesn't sound bad for $10, but I note that the last time any of the group's "Net Resources" were updated was 1995, and that most of the "archives" are bare. Contact the organizer before writing that check!

### The Macintosh MIDI User's Internet Guide
http://www.aitech.ac.jp/~ckelly/mmuig.html

This compact and bustling Web site is the best MIDI resource for Macintosh users. Extensive software pointers are accompanied by practical notes such as "Repeatedly crashed my system" and "these play the wrong Quick-Time instruments." Beginners should welcome the straightforward "Quick Start" section. Software is made available here before it gets to the Info-Mac archives, and the "What's New" section is unusually complete. Links to some excellent tutorials and FAQ sheets are provided.

### The MIDI Archive
http://www.cs.ruu.nl/pub/MIDI/

This MIDI anthology for electronic musicians and computer sound technicians is maintained by Dick Verweij and Piet van Oostrum. The "Other Midi Archives" link will give you a large list of online MIDI collections, gathered from Usenet newsgroups. Skip down to the "tutorials" sections and you'll find not just introductions to MIDI but great collections of tips, techniques, and troubleshooting guides. Copies of documentation files, patch files, and software are all stored in a local archive. (At the time of this writing, the music-samples archive was closed down due to copyright worries.) Newcomers beware: even the "Web" version of the archive is set up FTP-style, with bare displays of Unix directories and files. If you're lucky, you may find a one-line description that matches what you want by reading through a directory's "INDEX" file; otherwise it's best to come here with a specific need in mind.

### MIDI Composers' Exchange
http://www.mindspring.com/~s-allen/picks.html

If you'd like to get a little free publicity for your MIDI compositions, if you'd like to avoid making your own home page, or if you'd just like to see what sort of original MIDI compositions are being put on the Web, come to Steve Allen's MIDI community service. Note that these compositions remain copyrighted by their creators: if you decide that you can't live without one, contact its composer by e-mail. All MIDI files are stored in PC format, but there's a "how to" here for Macintosh users as well.

### The MIDI Farm
http://www.midifarm.com/

One of the most-pointed-to sites in audio, the MIDI Farm's commercial status makes it particularly strong on special offers, product updates, and current press releases. Its file archive contains 4,000 pieces of public domain music. A private newsgroup provides Q&A space, and there's also an IRC for interactive chat.

### MIDIfy Your Pages

http://www.ysba.com/midplug_midify_
index.html

Besides manufacturing synthesizer hardware, Yamaha also produces software support for MIDI, giving users far richer sound than is available with standard MIDI software on either Windows 95 or the Macintosh. This tips and techniques page is part of its browser plug-in area. The "MIDI Basics" are all too basic, but the "Online Tutorial" is reminiscent of some of the more ambitious tips sites for Photoshop: loaded with examples, walkthroughs, and troubleshooting checklists, it covers every conceivable use of MIDI on the Web, including embedded background music, MIDI sound effects, random play (via JavaScript), interfacing with Java, and creating original MIDI files.

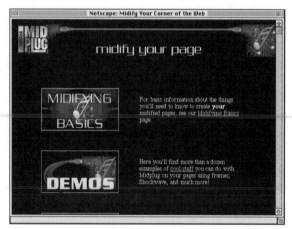

### The Site and Sound of MIDI

http://www2.heidsite.com/heidsite/hotmedia/
hotmedia0397.html

Jim Heid provides this introduction to MIDI for Web authors on his Heidsite multimedia site. It includes a pointer to a *Macworld* column on the subject, a sample page, and an excellent introduction to the workings of the MIDI format and to MIDI sequencers.

### Sites & Sound Links

http://www.servtech.com/public/koberlan/
main.htm

A large directory of links for musicians and composers, Kirk A. Oberlander's Sites & Sound contains many entries for MIDI and other aspects of electronic music, including samples and patches.

### Twin Cities MIDI

http://www.cs.umn.edu/~fischer/Midi/

Twin Cities is another electronic-music resource directory. The much linked-to tutorial here is well worth reading—if you can read it, that is; you might want to turn off background image-loading in your browser before visiting this site. The other original content on the site is an excellent guide for Macintosh users in a Windows-centric MIDI world. Links to MIDI file archives are helpfully annotated. There's a long list of site-visitor profiles; you can add your own with an HTML form.

### WAVmaker

http://www.abc.se/~m9303/

WAVmaker for Windows is a shareware program that converts MIDI files to WAV files—or, to capture the mood of the product a bit more accurately, permanently records a beautiful performance of your MIDI composition, freeing you from the need for specialized hardware, and making your creations available to users who lack MIDI playback capabilities or who can only play MIDI with that cheesy system-standard organ sound. The site offers the program itself for downloading, along with a rich set of add-ons, including a mouse-driven sample creator and a real-time MIDI renderer. Registered WAVmaker users receive 10 diskettes full of instrumental samples.

### WinJammer Software

http://www.winjammer.com/

The popular WinJammer MIDI sequencer for Windows comes in two flavors: WinJammer Professional (for which only a demo is downloadable; it's $200 for the real thing) and the reduced-functionality WinJammer Shareware ($50 if you choose to keep it). Both versions record, play, and edit standard MIDI files with mixers, multiple tracks, and wave events. Once you've entered a basic melody by keyboard, MIDI instrument, or the "virtual keyboard" that comes with WinJammer, you can edit with your mouse: drag notes to a different spot, or modify their volume, pitch, and length. You can even do pitch bends. Other features include a musical "spell checker" for wrong notes and other glitches, and musical-score editing aids, including high-quality printing.

### Yamaha MIDPLUG

**http://www.ysba.com/midplug_index.html**

Both Internet Explorer and Netscape Navigator have default approaches to playing MIDI files on Windows and Macintosh systems, even without explicit MIDI hardware support. That's the good news. The bad news is that without explicit hardware support, the standard software implementations of MIDI produce audio quality that falls somewhere below that of a Casio watch. Yamaha, a major player in the musical-instrument and synthesizer hardware world, has come more or less to the rescue with an alternative software implementation of MIDI instruments, complete with browser plug-ins and ActiveX controls. The difference in quality is noticeable even on my cheap Windows laptop's speakers. So why do I qualify my praise with "more or less"? First, the browser plug-ins for this MIDI implementation have an expiration period, meaning you have to be prepared to lose them or to hope for an updated download from Yamaha. Second, they expire because they're beta software: some versions haven't worked for me at all.

## MODS

The most obvious problem with synthesized sound formats like MIDI is their, well, synthesized sound. When a machine interprets a score, the results will most likely be mechanical and generic.

One approach to fixing that problem is to provide special, customized sound samples for the computer to use as a reference when following the score's instructions. Thus, instead of adapting a "standard trumpet" sound to play a tune, the computer might be instructed to adapt a sample of "Booker Little's trumpet." Of course, the more extensive the sample, the more the end result becomes like a straightforward recording, complete with file-size problems; the less extensive the sample, the more the end result becomes as lifeless as MIDI. Moreover, the hybrid nature of the format demands considerably more CPU power than pure samples or pure MIDIs do.

In the digital audio world, a "module" is a hybrid format that combines sound samples and sequenc-

ing information. Since the word "module" is so popular (and ambiguous) in the world of computer jargon, files in this format are usually called *mods:* conveniently enough, the original and still most-common file format for mods is called MOD and has a file extension of "MOD."

### alt.binaries.sounds.mods FAQ

**http://www2.gvsu.edu/~behrensm/absm-faq/Welcome.html**

This site collects frequently asked questions (with answers) from the alt.binaries.sounds.mods Usenet newsgroup; like all the best FAQs, it serves as a great introduction as well as a reference. Supplied as part of the FAQ are mapping of mod types to file extensions, notes on obtaining samples and on distributing your own mods, sources of existing mods, and pointers to MOD players, editors, and converters for each major platform. Don't miss the appendices: they include a nice "MIDI vs. mods" summary, lists of favorite mods and favorite creators of mods, pointers to a Top 100 list, an index of mods sound-effect codes, and "answers to unanswered questions," including the fairly central one, "How is MOD played back correctly?"

### The MOD Page

**http://www.teleport.com/~smithtl/modpage/modpage.htm**

This is a vast repository of information about MOD files, created by Tim Gerchmez and now maintained by Joaquin Lopez. It includes an excellent introduction to

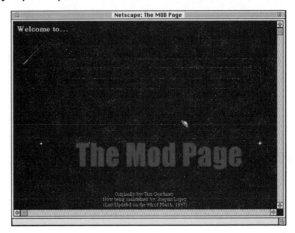

the format, freeware and shareware editor and playback recommendations for major platforms (with a special emphasis on Windows), an archive of the entertaining e-mail zine *Signals* (which, alas, ceased publication in 1993), pointers to mods traders, and honest reviews of mods resources on the Internet.

### PlayerPRO

http://www.quadmation.com/pphome.htm
Antoine Rosset's PlayerPRO is a mods editor for the Macintosh, for Windows, and even for cross-platform programmers: a developer's library is provided for free use. Of course, to be a good mods editor, a program has to handle both digitized recorded music and MIDI. In other words, it must be a complete music editor. Player-PRO accordingly handles many of the functions of both a digital-audio editor and a MIDI sequencer. Downloads are free; for $100, you can buy the program on a CD-ROM filled out with 4,000 MIDI instruments and samples.

# GENERATED MUSIC AND COMPOSITION AIDS

If all you want is some random background sounds, why not explicitly use random background sounds? That would avoid issues of copyright and talent rather neatly—although not, it must be admitted, issues of interest or annoyance. Besides, programmatic instructions to a computer can be even more compact than a MIDI musical score.

Those of us who are fond of quasi-random-process contemporary music (often referred to by friends and co-workers as "that horrible racket") may have a slightly easier time finding research material, but even soothing noises can be generated automatically.

If you'd like a little more control than random-process offers but can't quite manage to get that scholarship to Berklee, you might want to look into software that helps non-musicians compose music without having to bother with notation or performers.

Both types of applications are listed below. If you find the idea of making your own sounds intriguing, you should also look into MIDI directories like Harmony Central: there you'll often find composition programs like Band-In-A-Box and Cybernetic Composer available for downloading.

### Autoscore

http://www.wildcat.com/Pages/Autoscore.htm
Wildcat Canyon's Autoscore (available for Windows and the Macintosh, although in slightly different configurations) is a much-praised composition tool for non-composers. Rather than using a keyboard or another MIDI instrument to enter melody lines, you simply sing them (or play them on a non-MIDI instrument) into a microphone. Option menus give you enough control over the melody-recognition process to overcome most cases of tone deafness. The Windows version comes with its own multi-track sequencer; Macintosh users have to export individual melody lines and import them into an editing program obtained elsewhere. The program retails for $150; you can order it on-line here.

### Be Your Own Band

http://www.zdnet.com/complife/rev/9611/band.html
This article by Randy Alberts originally appeared in print in the November 1996 issue of Ziff-Davis's *ComputerLife* magazine. It's a step-by-step guide to composing and recording music on your home computer, outlining what equipment you'll need, how to set it up, and how to use it. Keyboards, sound cards, sequencers, and software are all covered, but the heart of the article is a walk through the actual composition of a new piece.

### Computer Music Tutorials

http://ccrma-www.stanford.edu/CCRMA/Software/clm/compmus/compmus-tutorials.html
If you're comfortable with computer programming, these two sets of tutorials might help you develop your own music composing software. The first set uses examples written in the Common Lisp Music package to explore techniques of audio synthesis (for example, combining

several carrier/modulator pairs to mimic the sound of a tubular bell). The second tutorial describes some techniques of algorithmic composition, using the Common Music programming environment and ending with an example of code that morphs together two Glenn Miller tunes, "In The Mood" and "Tuxedo Junction." Oh, for an embedded audio file!

## Electronic Muses

**http://www.webcom.com/hurleyj/music/ links.html**

Electronic Muses is a collection of links to sites related to electronic or experimental music, although many of the references are also of more general use. The directory is especially strong on the Csound system and composer-specific links.

## The Fractal Music Project

**http://www-ks.rus.uni-stuttgart.de/people/ schulz/fmusic/**

Most of us have encountered images generated by fractal algorithms: they were the Op Art of the 1980s. As it turns out, the same mathematics can be applied to sound, producing similarly 1980s-like results (in this case, the comparisons would be Philip Glass and New Age music). This page collects links to fractal-based music sources, including a mailing list, and provides a few very nice examples of what can be produced.

## Internet Music Kit

**http://www.wildcat.com/Pages/ Internet%20Music%20Kit.htm**

Wildcat Canyon, continuing to operate on "the principle that you don't have to be a professional musician to use music software," has produced the Internet Music Kit, competing somewhat with its own Autoscore program. The Internet Music Kit attempts to be an all-in-one MIDI-based product for Web authors to add original or adapted background music to their pages in a three-step process. Music composition software from Roland Corp., DoReMiX, is used to glue new compositions together from existing phrases. When the composition is finished, it needs to be converted to a proprietary streaming format, WebTracks. Finally, an "embed wizard" inserts HTML code that will position the WebTracks plug-in and

cause the new composition to start playing when readers load the page. In a sense, the program is impressively idiot-proof. In another sense, however, it may be just too idiot-friendly: How likely is it that jaundiced Web surfers will download a specialized plug-in specifically to hear a limited range of amateurish music? For that matter, why is "automatic play" the only option pushed by the company? Wildcat's Web page answers such questions with the claim that the Internet is "boring," and that adding the sort of jingles that play "in the background of almost all advertisements... at sporting events and in malls" is the only solution. I can't say that I've heard many Web users agree with that sentiment. Still, the Internet Music Kit is downloadable with a 30-day money-back guarantee; if you're intrigued, give it a shot.

## Jammer

**http://www.soundtrek.com/**

Representing the more commercial end of music composition and generation software is Soundtrek's Jammer (available in three models costing from $40 to $200), which can be used by amateurs to thrash out marginally original tunes, or by professionals to provide a fully synthesized backup band. Jammer has an array of "virtual recording studio" features: on the generation side, the program handles drag-and-drop arranging, automatically "improvised" variations on an extensive library of standard parts, user-controlled blending of instrumental styles, and automatic chord progression, harmony, and effects composers. Besides the usual product feature sheets, save-disabled demos of the two higher-priced models of Jammer are available for downloading. Some

short sample compositions are provided in the showroom area; more extensive examples of Jammer-generated music can be found among the company's songwriting contest winners.

## Koan
**http://www.sseyo.com/**
SSEYO's Koan format and applications are designed to generate background music at real-time speeds in a small package. On-site samples include a five-minute-long composition that only takes up 8K of space. The results will never be mistaken for Billie Holiday, but they might be mistaken for Brian Eno—in fact, Eno has supplied a blurb for Koan Pro. At SSEYO's busy site, you'll find plug-ins and ActiveX controls, helper applications, sample Koan pieces, MIDI translations of portions of the samples and, most impressively, a free version of the Koan music-authoring software, which lets you generate new pieces by mixing existing templates. (There are also pointers to the company's more powerful commercial-authoring systems, of course.) With the Java-enabled LiveConnect plug-in, your users can interact with the music; a page walks you through the process. The biggest problem with the format may be that there are no Macintosh players or plug-ins available: it's a Windows-only format.

## Microsoft Music Producer
**http://www.microsoft.com/musicproducer/**
Music Producer automatically generates compositions in MIDI format based on the user's choice of style, instrumentation, tempo, stereo mix, key, compositional shape, and length. Since the program outputs MIDI files, you can use the automatically generated compositions as input to other music-editing programs. The official Microsoft site contains product information, a MIDI FAQ, sample outputs, and occasional beta downloads. As usual with this sort of program, the results are pretty bland, but suitable as background music.

## music@passport
**http://www.passportdesigns.com/cgi-bin/ homepage.pl**
Passport Designs produces a number of software products for music composition, including professional notation programs. On the amateur end of the scale, the company offers an all-in-one Windows 95 package called music@passport, which not only handles notation, composition, and conversion duties, but also includes automatic publishing! When you buy the product, you obtain access to this special area of Passport's Web site, where you can upload the files you've created with the program. Tutorials, archives of MIDI files, and a directory of external links are also available at the music@passport site.

## MusiNum—The Music in the Numbers
**http://www.forwiss.uni-erlangen.de/ ~kinderma/musinum.html**
Beginning from the premise that music is based on whole numbers rather than real numbers, Lars Kindermann leaves fractals and chaos theory behind. On this oddly entertaining page, he instead uses one particular integer series to create melodies. Users of his software have gone on to combine generated melodies into compositions in a variety of moods and styles. You can try generating melodies yourself by filling out an HTML form or, if you're a Windows user, you can download the free software for local music-generation.

## Software by YAV
**http://www.yav.com/docs/Software.html**
Scroll past some add-ons to the Macintosh-authoring package SuperCard, and you'll find two music-generating shareware programs by Christopher Yavelow. PushBtn-Bach will "keep generating new minuets in the style of Bach as long as you can keep pressing the Compose button." CyberMozart performs similar mimicry of the early Classical period.

## Symbolic Composer
**http://www.xs4all.nl/~psto/**
Symbolic Composer appears to be the leader among commercial music-generation software, but I can't say it's a very crowded field. The basis of the program is a complex musical programming language with 300 functions built on Lisp for the Macintosh. Visualization tools provide opportunities for graphically based composition. Lisp programs tend to be easy to extend, and a set of plug-ins for Symbolic Composer is available for downloading. Prices range from $500 to $150 for various versions of the program.

# SOUND CLIPS

"Nasty insistent little tune."

"Extraordinary how potent cheap music is."

—Noel Coward and Gertrude Lawrence, "Private Lives"

There may not be quite as many sound-clip libraries on the Web as there are image libraries, but the number is still a bit overwhelming. As you search for a background sound or an ingredient for your own assemblage, remember that many of the archives are "for personal use only," not for international publication on the Web, so be sure to check permissions. Record companies tend to have expensive lawyers.

## Aristo-Soft Sounds

http://www.aristosoft.com/ftp/Wired/Sounds/

This FTP site's interface won't be winning any awards, but access to these archives is worth a little unfriendliness. If you're putting together a Shockwave animation (or any other sort of animation) and need some sound effects in a hurry, this may be just the spot to strike your chimes: I counted ten different "bells" effects alone.

## Bird Songs from Cornell

http://www.envirolink.org/orgs/wqed/bird_songs.html

The downloadable sound clips on this delightfully specialized site are courtesy of the Cornell Lab of Ornithology. If you need a preview before making the trip, the forward-thinking birds perched on the Web bandwagon at time of writing were the American bittern, the American robin, the barred owl, the yellow-headed blackbird, the blue jay, the Eastern bluebird, the Eastern meadowlark, the hooded warbler, the indigo bunting, the Northern cardinal, the Northern oriole, the ruffed grouse, the scarlet tanager, Steller's jay, Swainson's thrush, and the wood thrush. Photos of the musicians are included, just like in IUMA.

## The Classical MIDI Archives

http://www.prs.net/midi.html

The most-honored (four pages of awards!) and most-linked-to MIDI collection on the Web, Pierre R. Schwob's "Classical MIDI Archive" offers a huge number of classical snippets transcribed into MIDI format and arranged alphabetically by composer's name. (Before you sigh, "Farewell, unkind," take heed that composers born before 1600, including my beloved John Dowland, have their own special ghetto.) A search engine is provided, contributor's e-mail addresses are available for permission-seekers, and a special graphic indicates clips that are especially strong. (In Schwob's words, "I am pleased and regret to say that some of these sequences are quite beautiful while others are rather atrocious...")

## The Digital Kitchen

http://www.dkitchen.com/

The Web site of this leading commercial sample-provider is not much more than a storefront with a few demos, but the demos are sufficient to show the quality of the work. Whether your listeners would prefer dancing to a loose funk bottom or to an ear-splitting industrial grind, Digital Kitchen's license-free, royalty-free CDs may be worth checking out.

## Gerd's MIDI Pages

http://stud1.tuwien.ac.at/~e8925292/midi.htm

Gerd Reichinger, the maintainer of this site, hasn't made any changes in almost a year, but it remains one of the better MIDI anthologies on the Web. The "Very Best of GUS MIDI" page is the highlight here, collecting Reichinger's rather middle-of-the-road favorites into seven .zip archives: classical, piano, two pop collections, and three miscellaneous update archives. Christmas music and TV and movie soundtracks get their own special collections.

## Hollywood Edge

**http://www.soundelux.com/sdx/sounds/sounds.htm**

Soundelux, a sound-editing coalition founded by Lon Bender and Wylie Stateman, has produced 83 commercial CDs of sound effects under the umbrella title of Hollywood Edge. The company's Web site offers over thirty high-quality samples for free downloading. Available effects include such motion picture favorites as "357 Magnum," "Tire Skid," "Female Scream," and "Frog Ribbit." (The script almost writes itself, doesn't it?)

## Johnny V's Music & Sound Extravaganza

**http://ww2.netnitco.net/users/jrv/msound.htm**

Skip to the "Links" section and you'll find the meat on this site: large and enthusiastically annotated directories of links to "real files you can actually download," arranged by format: MIDI files, mods, or WAV sound bites. Smaller lists of bands and of record company sites are also provided.

## Midi File Central

**http://www.tst-medhat.com/midi/noframe.html**

This gigantic repository of MIDI files from around the Internet (and from the alt.binaries.sounds.midi Usenet newsgroup in particular) features wildly varying quality, but undisputed quantity. You may have to exercise a bit of imagination before karaoke-ing to your Bon Jovi favorites. Still, how many other sites can ship simulacra of both "Metallica" and "Amy Grant" to you in such tiny files?

## The Movie Sounds Page

**http://www.moviesounds.com/**

This frequently updated page contains film one-liners and longer stretches of dialogue, available for downloading in uncompressed WAV files and streaming TrueSpeech format. Unfortunately, the emphasis here is squarely on the catch-phrase-driven hits of the 1970s, 1980s, and 1990s, rather than on the faster-moving dialogue of 1930s and 1940s Hollywood. (Speaking personally, I could easily fill my Web server with clips from *His Girl Friday* alone.) Still worth a visit, if only to remind the budding screenwriter how large a portion of her audience will chortle whenever she has an sweet-old-lady character use the F-word. The site is kind enough to give pointers to a Cary Grant collection and to The Balcony's "Classic Cinema Quotes."

## Multi-Media Music: Sound Effects

**http://www.wavenet.com/~axgrindr/quimby2.html**

If you can ignore the compiler's O. J. Simpson obsession, this is a nice little directory of sound bites on the Web, with an emphasis on commercial background music and sound effects. Usefully generic backgrounds in the "Music Loops" collection, which also resides on this site, include "Rave Loop," "Mello Logo" ("for the new age client"), and the "Classic Pause."

## Multimedia Soundtracks

**http://www.kenmusic.com/**

Kennerly Music Production's Multimedia Soundtracks is a $100 CD-ROM collection of royalty-free music suitable for multimedia presentations or Web background sounds. On the company's site, you can listen to a one-minute snippet or download a 1.8 megabyte selection from the CD-ROM. The full collection contains 16 "original themes" and 34 different tracks. Every track is available in seven audio formats, and the CD itself is cross-platform.

## RoarShox Home Page

**http://www.roarshox.com/**

Targeted at Web and multimedia developers, RoarShox is a $130 royalty-free cross-platform CD-ROM collection of over 200 original music loops and clips, many with MIDI versions. At the RoarShox site, you can use a Shockwave application to preview one free sample file from each of eight music categories.

## Rob's Multimedia Lab (RML)

http://www.acm.uiuc.edu/rml/

Rob began this public scrapbook back in 1993. It now takes up two gigabytes of local copies of AU and WAV audio files, GIF image files, and MPEG, QuickTime and AVI video files. No annotations, just file names: you'll have to use your imagination and patience here. There is also a breathtakingly miscellaneous list of links to other sites with notable audio, image, or video content.

## Sites with Audio Clips

http://www.geek-girl.com/audioclips.html

As it straightforwardly states in its opening sentence, "This page provides links to digitized sound archives available on the Internet." And how. The "Miscellaneous Sounds" section includes clips from nature, soundtracks and computer history; the "Music" section splices classical archives to hip-hop tributes; "Voice Repositories" quotes politicians and other show-biz celebrities. The list is certainly large, but given the vast resources of the Web, not quite authoritative—it's probably best used as an occasional browsing point.

## SunSITE Japan Multimedia Collection

http://sunsite.sut.ac.jp/multimed/

This site houses collections of audio files in WAV, MIDI, and AU formats (with AU dominant), along with large collections of GIF, JPEG, and video files. The sound clips cover the usual Computer Science undergraduate range, from cartoons and other TV soundbites to animal sounds, but the karaoke section is larger than those found in most US-based archives.

## Standard MIDI Files on the Net

http://www.aitech.ac.jp/~ckelly/ SMF.html

Now *this* is what I call authoritative: a list of over 1800 sites that contain standard MIDI files. Wisely, maintainer Charles I. Kelly "optimizes for speed": he's arranged for multiple mirror sites, he suggests downloading the full list as a .zip archive, he provides frequent update pages to reduce the number of times a full download is needed, he supplies tips for efficient use of search engines, and there's no decorative nonsense cluttering up his HTML.

Kelly also provides excellent advice for how to use MIDI on the Web, sensible HTML style tips, and some original compositions designed specifically to loop as Web soundtracks.

## The Ultimate TV and Movie MIDI page

http://www.primenet.com/~mrdata/midi2.htm

This site purports to be the largest collection of MIDI-ized TV and movie theme songs on the Web, and indeed it's hard to imagine a larger one. I personally owe it a great deal for giving me my first opportunity ever to hear the opening of "The Andy Griffith Show" covered by a sleazy lounge trio. The directory of external links is extensive and well-chosen.

## Ventana Sound Bytes

http://www.vmedia.com/commodity/ soundbytes/

Ventana has donated a very nice collection of 20-kHz 16-bit sound effects to the Web for free use. Categories include animal sounds, engines, industrial noise, kitchen appliances (for some reason, the clink of coins counts as a kitchen appliance), and musical instruments. All sound bites are supplied in WAV, AU, and Macintosh SND formats.

## Vikram's MIDI-Fest

http://www.midifest.com/

Vikram Pant is a teenage Web celebrity, and his original collection of favorite MIDI files has blossomed into a full-fledged reference site, complete with the official alt.binaries.sounds.midi FAQ. The center of the site continues to be his MIDI anthology, however, with standard classifications (TV themes, movie themes, and pop) that are augmented by special collections: Americana, video games, the complete Beatles, Japanese anime, Broadway, national anthems, and those rabble-rousing numbers that get pumped out by cheesy organs at sports stadiums—finally, music that's specifically tailored to your computer's cheesy built-in MIDI!

## Worldwide Internet Music Resources
**http://www.music.indiana.edu/music_ resources/**

This ambitious site ("a service of the William and Gayle Cook Music Library, Indiana University") aims to provide links to every form of music resource on the Internet, including sound clips. Link classifications include individual musicians or groups, composers, genres, research, commercial entities, and journals. Not yet authoritative, but an impressive stab in that direction.

# CHAPTER 7
# ANIMATION AND VIDEO

**IN THIS CHAPTER, YOU'LL LEARN HOW TO BRING MOTION INTO YOUR WEB PAGES. WE'LL COVER THE FOLLOWING TOPICS:**

### ☞ Knowing when (and when not) to use video or animation.

As always, you don't want to waste your hard work. Technical glory aside, there's not much point to presenting a clip from *Citizen Kane* if it has the picture quality of a circa-1940 TV screen and the download time of the complete works of Shakespeare.

### ☞ Choosing a motion picture format.

There are a head-throbbing number of ways to create the illusion of motion. Whether you call it "animation," "video," or "multimedia presentations," they all end up producing more or less the same thing. We'll look at the choices and suggest ways to make the final decision.

### ☞ Animation tools.

It's easier and cheaper to create animation today than at any other time since the birth of film, largely thanks to the software tools covered in this section.

### ☞ Creating an animated GIF.

The GIF89a format is the simplest, least expensive approach to motion display, both for the author and for the user. We'll examine several different approaches to GIF animation.

### ☞ Video production.

Whether you start from an analog source such as videotape, or work with digital video right from the beginning, you'll almost always need special software to edit your film into a reasonable form.

### ☞ Choosing video rate and compression settings.

Even more than with still images, Web authors working with video find themselves in a painful squeeze between the demand for quality and the need for reasonable file sizes.

### ☞ Converting video to a format appropriate for the Web.

As it is with audio, the number of video format choices can be overwhelming at first. We'll show you how to choose, as well as what to use to convert a movie clip to your selected format.

### ☞ Using streamed video.

We'll also have a go at those video formats that try to give your users something to look at during the long downloading minutes.

### ☞ Using Shockwave to produce interactive animations.

Macromedia Director is the most popular multimedia production software in use today. If you're already a Director expert, you'll have no trouble showing off your skills to the Web audience.

### ☞ Setting up your own Web cam.

You, too, can sacrifice all your privacy (not to mention bandwidth) for the sake of international notoriety! On a more practical level, you can monitor your prized collection of weather instruments—right from your office cubicle.

### ☞ Working with virtual reality.

We'll take a brief trip into the surprisingly limited world of "virtual reality": a form of graphical navigation in which the user can seemingly "move" forward and backward as well as up, down, and sideways.

# WEB MOVIES IN CONTEXT

Just as it's much easier to include color illustrations in a Web publication than in a print publication, it also takes far less effort to put motion pictures (using the widest definition of that term) on a Web page than on a printed one. On the other hand, less effort doesn't necessarily guarantee that the task is either particularly easy or particularly rewarding. There are a few reasons for this contradiction.

Keep in mind that moving visual elements distract from the rest of the page. Tests show that adjacent animations in particular make reading much more difficult. (The proliferation of animated advertising banners is one reason I turn off image loading before going to a news or reference site.)

There's also the fact that, no matter how compressed you make them, multiple pictures always take up more space than a single picture.

In addition, digital video consumes a relatively substantial amount of money, time, and server room. And if you want your video to start playing while your audience is still looking at your page, you'll likely experience some amazingly extravagant server-side expenses, as well.

Having said all that, I don't mean to discourage anyone from trying their hand at original animation or video. It's never been easier or cheaper than it is today. And, after all, the Golden Age of animation came to pass when technically demanding short subjects were being made by profit-hungry corporations even though such work didn't bring money directly to the studios: a paradoxical situation not that far from the Web's own peculiar economic model.

Despite the expense to you and to your readers, graphics that achieve the illusion of motion are well worth making when the following are true:

- **It's the most natural treatment of your content.** If you're covering a visually vivid action, it would make sense to cover it at least partly through video. In this case, rather than being unpleasantly surprised by the sudden slip into QuickSand technology, your users will likely be primed for the download. For example, a page dedicated to the annual Burning Man Festival included one of the most popular early Web videos: a time-elapsed clip of the flaming finale. Analyses of movie shots, descriptions of insect metamorphoses, or comparisons of sorting algorithms are other examples of video-ready topics.

- **It's the content itself.** An experimental filmmaker (such as Zoe Beloff, with her remarkable QuickTime serial and CD-ROM project *Beyond* at *http://www.users.interport.net/~zoe/*) can reach a wide audience at a low cost by using QuickTime or AVI. Amateur animators can show off their work with a GIF long before they make it to one of the international festivals.

- **You're a professional Web author** and you've been ordered by your client to "add animated buttons" so that "the site will be more compelling." What can I say? It happens.

# CHOOSING A MOTION PICTURE FORMAT

There are almost as many competing approaches to video as there are to audio, and no one video format has achieved the ubiquity enjoyed by RealAudio. For any given combination of source material and authoring platform, however, it's usually not that difficult to decide on a format that will be playable across browser platforms. Consider the following issues.

1 For small, short, silent, and simple animations based on flat colors or line drawings, make a GIF animation. Yes, those seem like stringent restrictions, but they include most of my favorite examples of motion on the

Web. If your source material is photographic or contains a large number of colors (3-D shading and gradients are common villains in that regard), it probably won't translate well into the GIF format and therefore won't translate well into a GIF animation. If the image is too large or the animation sequence is too long, playback will be (sometimes literally) grindingly unpleasant: The GIF89a format is not exactly optimized for temporal compression! As for the "simple" characteristic—well, browser programmers have historically had a tough time dealing with all the controls officially supported by the GIF89a standard. Complicated looping and timing instructions may very well be ignored. Ideally, you should be able to picture your material as a flipbook, or as jumping between only a few frames.

Having said all that, I should emphasize that if you *can* use GIF animation, you *should* use GIF animation. It's the format that's easiest for you to produce. It's also the easiest for your users to view because it's the only completely "built-in" format: It doesn't require any special MIME typing by your host Web server; nor does it require any plug-ins or helper applications on your user's system.

**2** If you need sound, or your source images are photographic or captured from video, or if the animation sequence is fairly long (and "long" in the world of the Web can sometimes mean more than ten frames!), you're better off using a digital video format.

**3** Do you need a more complex user interface than "play-loop-stop"? For example, do you want to have your animation react to a mouse click or to take the user to a new link when they drag a moving object? Welcome to the world of multimedia programming! Here the choice of

formats becomes more dependent on your budget and on which items have already eaten into your funds. If you can program Java and you don't mind requiring that your users run Java, that may be the lowest-cost approach. On the other hand, if you've already paid for and sweated over Director, you should try to fit your project within a Shockwave context.

**4** Do you want the illusion of a movable or walkable 3-D imagemap? Do you want it a lot? In that case, it might be worth the considerable effort of looking into QuickTime VR or VRML.

Whichever approach you take, don't expect the user's experience to be seamless: Except for GIF animations, all of these technologies involve noticeable splits from the world of standard HTML.

### Guidelines for Multimedia on the Web

**http://www.useit.com/alertbox/9512.html**

User interface scholar Jakob Nielsen wrote this style guide for Web animations, video, and audio back in December 1995, but most of what he says still holds true. Unlike most Web pundits, Nielsen has actually put serious thought into the implications of a document with embedded motion. His advice on when (and when not) and how to use animation and video makes great background reading.

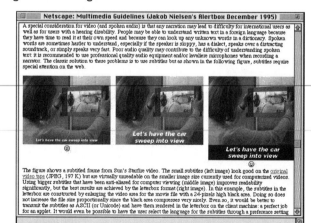

☞ Despite the seeming diversity of motion picture formats, they all do pretty much the same thing in the end: They show a succession of still images to create the illusion of motion. Remember that, and you can take advantage of cross-tool synergy in a number of ways.

- Get your original animation work off to a quick start, with stop-motion video from a QuickCam. I've never done full-fledged stop-motion animation, but a series of still photos depicting an object in motion is a great way to bootstrap painted animation. Just import the QuickTime video output as separate images into a graphics program—Fractal Design Painter handles this automatically—and paint right over the photos. (As far as I know, this trick started with the artistically challenged geniuses at Fleischer Studio and their "Out of the Inkwell" cartoons.)

- Conversely, if you can't afford a full-fledged video effects package, look into using image-editing tools and techniques on video output. At the low-frame rate typical of Web video, hand painting can be a reasonable option. Some inexpensive video editing tools give you capabilities such as image masking and substitution; you can use these functions not just to clean up a jittery background but also to add new effects.

## Multimedia—What Is It?

http://www-dept.cs.ucl.ac.uk/staff/jon/dummy/

Although Jon Crowcroft's page is not much more than a very long sheet of (sometimes cryptic) classroom notes, this material is surprisingly useful, especially the first third or so. In an attempt to cover video, audio, graphics, and video conferencing, the notes achieve a kind of conceptual symbiosis not found in more specialized references.

## Web Animator's Toolbox

http://www.zdnet.com/macuser/mu_0297/features/webfea/webmain.html

*MacUser* originally published this overview of Web animation techniques and Macintosh utilities. Author Lynda Weinman gracefully covers all the usual formats (GIF animation, QuickTime, Shockwave, Sizzler, and Java) with unusual attention to practical details such as plug-in popularity and stability of tools. Tables compare the different approaches and explain the HTML to use for each. A large flowchart can be used to streamline decision making. Weinman even includes recommendations for graphics utilities that are especially suited to animators. Sidebars include detailed reviews of Dancer and FutureSplash.

# ANIMATION

From flipbooks and zoetropes onward, the gleeful looseness of animation has only been attainable through the sort of hard, dull, long labor that makes the industry ripe for computer assistance. Although achieving slick animation *still* involves hard, dull, long labor—and extremely expensive computers, to boot—animation software at least puts the more primitive (and in some ways more interesting) forms of the art within the reach of one-person studios.

## GENERAL ANIMATION TOOLS

### Animation Production Tour

http://www.art.uiuc.edu/local/anle/ANIMATION/ANIMATIONTGAL.html

This breezy site provides a quick overview of basic commercial animation concepts and terminology, heavily illustrated by Disney stills. It's a little like one of those company-produced "behind the scenes" pseudodocumentaries, but there's no denying that the material goes down easily.

### Infini-D

http://www.specular.com/products/infini-d/

Specular's flagship product, Infini-D, is Macintosh (and, more recently, Windows) 3-D software with an emphasis on animation. Besides the usual repositioning and revolving of objects and light, modeled objects and textures themselves can be morphed over time in Infini-D. Animation assistants help you increase the realism of velocity and other natural movements. Not only can QuickTime movies be used as textures, but their movement can be coordinated with changes to their object's shape. The official Web site of the product lists features, points you to ecstatic reviews, and lets you download updates and a demo version.

## John Warnock Gets Animated with GIF

**http://www.adobe.com/studio/tipstechniques/ GIFanimation/main.html**

Vector-based image editors like Adobe Illustrator are especially useful for animation because, unlike bitmap-based image editors, the concept of separate, movable, deformable component objects is built in. Once you've created separate objects, you can move, rotate, deform, or re-layer those objects, saving a "snapshot" of each new configuration to create the next frame in an animation. This article from Adobe—to be more specific, from John Warnock, cofounder of the company—walks through the creation of an original animated GIF. He starts from drawings in Illustrator, using some simple but sophisticated techniques to create the frames, moves frames into Photoshop for some final touch-ups, and then glues together the frames using GifBuilder. Although the emphasis is on GIF animations, the GIF format only appears in the last step. The basic techniques are applicable to virtually any type of non-"generated" animation, and are rarely so clearly illustrated.

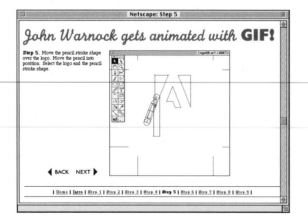

## PaceWorks ObjectDancer

**http://www.paceworks.com/_products/_ overview/overview.html**

For the Macintosh, ObjectDancer is a Web animation authoring tool that can produce Java applets, animated GIFs, or QuickTime movies—even including support for the rarely seen QuickTime sprites. ObjectDancer is particularly strong on sound synchronization (including MIDI music), motion control, and text manipulation. Its object-oriented approach provides layering benefits. Currently, the program lists for $270; a demo version is available for downloading.

## PhotoCell

**http://www.secondglance.com/photocell.html**

It's not that Adobe Photoshop's layers are languishing for lack of utility, but the feature does seem to be exquisitely well suited to animation. Layers are easily copied; they're linked together in an easily revised sequence; they have variable transparency; they handle automatic clipping… It's a perfect setup for painting motion with the technique called *onion skinning* (i.e., tracing a slightly changed drawing on semitransparent paper over the previous versions of the drawing) and for positioning moving objects against a static background. For some reason, Adobe itself hasn't taken advantage of the opportunity, and so Second Glance Software has stepped in with this Photoshop plug-in. PhotoCell lets you drag layers to a filmstrip and drop them in. Multiple layers can be combined in a single frame, allowing for background cells. You can preview animations with a QuickTime player interface and save them as either QuickTime video or a GIF animation. The $60 price seems a little steep to me, but then, I'm cheap. For the curious, a free demo is available for downloading.

## PixelPutty

**http://www.pixels.net/**

PixelPutty is a Power Macintosh 3-D graphics-generation program that lets you define limitations on the movement of joints in a model, helping considerably with realistic animations of humans and animals. At time of writing, the company's Web site was a little light, but it did include a downloadable beta of the next version of the program.

### Ray Dream Studio
http://www.fractal.com/products/rds/

Among the most popular of the $500-and-under 3-D animation programs, Ray Dream Studio has won praise for its rare combination of power and an intuitive interface, including its scene and logo "wizards." Animation previews are also well handled. Ray Dream Studio can directly output AVI video and VRML, among many other formats. The official site includes a directory of commercial plug-in effects for the program.

### Specular 3D Web Workshop
http://www.specular.com/products/3dww/

3-D graphics-generation specialists at Specular International have assembled a Macintosh bundle of several of the company's own low-end 3-D utilities along with Adobe PageMill and 1,500 pieces of clip art, including many animations. The LogoMotion tool is especially well suited to text-based animation, with extrusion modeling and a simple set of effects and lighting controls. A demo version can be downloaded from this site.

### 3D Animation Workshop
http://webreference.com/3d/

Robert Polevoi wrote this serially published tutorial on 3-D graphics and animation for the *webreference.com* site. The lessons move at a very leisurely pace, and at time of writing still had quite a distance to travel to the topic of animation. But if the series is successfully completed, it should stand as one of the easiest and most thorough introductions to the subject.

### WebPainter
http://www.totallyhip.com/

There was a day when animators couldn't generate spline curves for their characters to rollercoaster down, nor could they automatically morph Daffy Duck into Winston Churchill. Instead, they had to draw all the moving parts by hand. To ease their labor (and to keep supposedly stationary elements from jittering with each new frame), animators in the mid-1910s developed a technique called *cel animation,* in which drawings on transparent material (usually celluloid) would be layered. Only the changing portions of individual objects needed redrawing; everything else (background and props, for ex-

ample) only had to be shifted. Totally Hip Software has efficiently computerized traditional cel animation with their WebPainter program, providing support for background layers and onion skinning, as well as simple, useful graphics-editing utilities like skewing and scaling. In fact, WebPainter is probably the most straightforward, immediately useful animation tool on the market. All it's sacrificed for its simplicity are built-in cliché effects, and the sort of antialiasing and color-blending abilities that interfere with the GIF format's strengths. WebPainter exports to PICS, QuickTime, GIF animation, and the company's own streaming Sizzler format. It's available for both Macintosh and Windows for $100. If you don't own any other graphics software and want to experiment with Web animation, this is a good program to cut your teeth on.

## GIF ANIMATION

The cheapest and most thoroughly browser-integrated approach to animation is supplied by the once little-known multiple-image capability of the GIF89a specification. GIF animations support "normal" image features such as transparency and imagemaps. They require no special software (other than a graphical browser) to view. And they can be produced using freeware. It's true that they don't support synchronized sound—but considering the difficulty of effectively compressing sound, it's sort of nice to have a reason to avoid it. All in all, GIF animations are a great format whose major flaws are lack of video-optimized compression (movie clips don't usually work well!) and lack of player control.

Unless you want large files and a snow-storm look, don't use dithering when producing the source still, GIF images that will be glued together into an animation. The human eye might be (slightly) fooled by dithering in a still image, but real-time random shuffling of speckles is just as difficult to compress and much more impossible to ignore. Either restrict yourself to flat colors or make sure that the reduced-color background remains static from frame to frame.

## Amazing animated GIFs—in about an hour!

http://www.adobemag.com/PDFs/howtoPDF/hour.html

This article is basically an Acrobat-formatted reprint from *Adobe Magazine* embedded in a frame. Adobe fan Kurt Murphy walks through his use of power tools (in this case, After Effects—the $700 Photoshop and Premiere video add-on utility) to hammer a nail (in this case, a GIF animation). I wouldn't necessarily recommend buying After Effects exclusively for this sort of thing, but the ideas behind many of the animation techniques are generally useful, particularly for users of painting programs that support masks.

## Club Unlimited—Animated GIFs

http://www.wu-wien.ac.at/usr/h95a/h9552688/local.html

If there's a larger GIF animation collection than this, I don't want it put on *my* Web server. Gerwin Beran has organized 2,600 (and counting) files into 30 categories. Note: Although Beran says that all these files are "to the best of his knowledge" public domain, his approach seems to be to grab the GIF and wait for someone to complain. Browsing here makes for lightweight amusement but, speaking purely for myself, I'd be a bit cautious about using some of these images.

## Funky animation without fancy tools

http://www5.zdnet.com/zdwebcat/content/garage/gif89a/

Part of Ziff-Davis's invaluable ZDNet site, this page collects GIF animation articles and product reviews from publications such as *MacUser* and *PC Magazine*.

## GIF Animation on the WWW

http://member.aol.com/royalef/gifanim.htm

GIF animation pioneer Royal Frazier's massive tribute to the GIF89a standard includes overviews (both nontechnical and extremely technical) and an extensive tutorial (based on GIF Construction Set, although the reader tips and much of the introductory page cover more general ground). The bugs page and the coverage of animation tools are both too out-of-date to be of much use, but the "1st Internet Gallery of GIF Animation" continues to grow. Unlike many archives of Web media, this one provides full credits for the material, including the artists' e-mail addresses and whether permission is needed to re-use the images. Modem users beware: Both the collection and the GIF files themselves are large.

## GIF Animation Station

http://web2.airmail.net/nicktg/moving/

If you want to get an overview of the state of the GIF animation art, or you want to know what clichés to avoid, or if you're just in the mood to use clip art that bounces, take a pass through this anthology of nearly 300 animated GIFs collected from around the Web, most of them weighing in at under 20K. Plenty of spinning earths, flying envelopes, and flaming texts make their home here, but I was most impressed by the rolling-eye Groucho (a petite 1.7K!).

## GifBuilder

http://iawww.epfl.ch/Staff/Yves.Piguet/clip2gif-home/GifBuilder.html

Yves Piguet, my hero. His Macintosh GIF animation building program, GifBuilder, is flexible and rock solid, has a clear interface, and is absolutely free. GIF, PICT, TIFF, Photoshop, QuickTime, FilmStrip, and PICS files are all accepted as input for your new animated GIF file. You can easily control frame position, disposal method, transparency, interframe delay, and looping. You can force the GIFs to use the "browser-safe" palette, or have the program calculate an optimized palette to be shared by all frames. On top of all that, GifBuilder is completely scriptable, meaning that you can rig up even a very complex conversion procedure and process GIF animations en masse. (Piguet's own page demonstrates an AppleScript program that uses GifBuilder to draw an animation from scratch—without use of any external graphics files at all!) All this, and the program is still only at version 0.5. I can't imagine what it'll be like by the time it reaches whole numbers.

## GIF Construction Set

http://www.mindworkshop.com/alchemy/
gifcon.html

From Alchemy Mindworks, GIF Construction Set was one of the first Windows shareware programs to assemble a sequence of GIF files into an animation. More recent versions have distinguished the program by adding an Animation Wizard to simplify the creation process. (In the words of the company, it requires "less effort to master than many brands of soap.") Ten transition effects can be applied to your source images, and text-handling and banner-creation tools are built in. The cost is $20.

## GiffyView

http://www.totallyhip.com/hipstuff/giffy.html

Even more than with still images, the positive or negative impact of animated GIFs depends on downloading time. If it takes too long, your reader may be off to another page before even realizing that an animation is there; if the file loads very quickly, you may have to delay frames or loop a few times. Short of keeping an array of modems attached to a switch box, how can you preview your GIF animation in a realistic way? This little Macintosh tool demonstrates how a GIF animation will play at various download speeds, and provides diagnostics such as frame count and frame delay. It's straightforward, useful, and free.

## Gif·glf·giF

http://www.cafe.net/peda/ggg/

Gif·glf·giF is a simple $28 shareware program designed specifically to create optimized, animated GIFs that demonstrate working software. Automatically timed screen captures collect the basic frames of the animation; the final format conversion reduces file size by taking advantage of the high proportion of overlapped images between frames. The program's authors at Pedagoguery Software freely admit that Gif·glf·giF is not useful as a general-purpose tool; however, they've also made a utility called A Smaller GIF, available at this site. A Smaller GIF tries several methods of optimizing a GIF animation in a nondestructive way and automatically applies the one that's most successful. The program can also view animated GIFs and edit animation settings such as frame duration. A Smaller GIF costs $22. Both programs are available for Windows and Macintosh.

## GIFmation

http://www.boxtopsoft.com/GIFmation/

BoxTop Software specializes in Photoshop plug-ins for the Macintosh, and the look of this GIF animation tool is reassuringly Photoshop-like. It cleverly combines a layer-style interface and a movie-player interface with image-alignment and transparency tools. More powerful than GifBuilder, the program is also more expensive: $25 at time of writing, with a projected increase to $50 to co-incide with the eventual release of GIFmation 2.0.

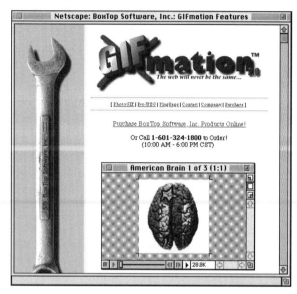

### gifx

**http://www.interdim.com/products/gifx/**

InterDimensions Corp. uses this site to promote gifx, its GIF-animation creation tool for Windows and Power Macintosh. The gifx product distinguishes itself from other GIF animation builders by letting you apply automatic effects to a static image, automatically generating a sequence of animation frames. At time of writing, available effects include fade-in and fade-out, rotation, blending, and rippling. The resulting images don't begin to approach the kind of quality achievable with a graphics editor like Photoshop, but the convenience of gifx may make it worth its $35 cost to you.

### Grassroots Tech

**http://www.webreview.com/96/02/09/tech/ edge/index.html**

Andrew Leonard's article from *Web Review* is interesting not only because it provides some background information on GIF animation, but also as an example of how technology advances on and through the Internet: unpredictably, uncontrollably, and thanks to an otherwise unrelated set of enthusiastic individuals.

### How To Get Animated

**http://www.cnet.com/Content/Features/ Howto/Webanim/**

This sensible, easy-to-follow introduction to GIF animation is from c|net's "How To" series. Although several of the recommendations aren't followed by c|net itself, they're still good advice. The article uses GIF Construction Set for its walkthrough, but most of the text applies to any tool or platform.

### Microsoft GIF Animator

**http://www.microsoft.com/imagecomposer/ gifanimator/gifanin.htm**

Microsoft continues its assault on Web shareware with this free Windows utility, currently bundled with the company's free graphics editor, Image Composer. Microsoft GIF Animator is a simple, easy-to-use animated GIF builder that uses a drag-and-drop interface to import GIF files, clipboard images, or AVI video. The user is given control of loops, transparency, color palettes, and frame rates. You can download a copy of the program, walk through creation of an animation whose basic frames come from Image Composer, and view some not very enthralling samples starting from this page on Microsoft's site.

### PhotoImpact GIF Animator

**http://www.ulead.com/products/ ga_main.htm**

This much-praised utility seems to be the GIF production choice of Windows-based graphic artists. It's well organized, optimizes color palettes beautifully, and supports

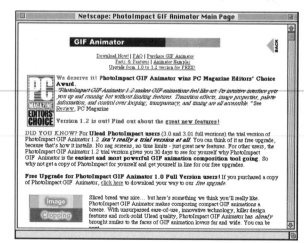

drag-and-drop of images (or even AVI video files) from outside the program. Special built-in features support scrolling text, a variety of transitional effects, and even "color animation" (in which the perceived motion is generated by changes in the color map). The price is $30, but you can download a 30-day trial version for free. The program is also bundled into the Ulead PhotoImpact with WebExtensions product.

## Smart Dubbing

**http://www.xs4all.nl/~polder/**

Smart Dubbing is a Macintosh program that converts QuickTime video to animated GIFs. Now, why would anyone exchange a compressed, full-color audio-video format for a silent, color-restricted format? Transparent embedding, that's why. If your animation is meant to be a distracting illustrative element against a distractingly busy background, then the movie-player frame that's always around a QuickTime video clip just won't cut it. (It's also worth noting that the GIF format can compress animations with extremely restricted color—such as black-and-white line drawings—about as effectively as most video compressors.) On the very good chance that you want a distracting background sound to automatically play while your animation unreels, Smart Dubbing is also able to export AU or AIFF sounds suitable for embedded play. A free minimal version of Smart Dubbing and a demo of the Pro version are both available for downloading; it costs $25 to register the Pro version.

Even if you're not interested in the tool, you might want to stop by this address: At time of writing, the Smart-Dubbing site served as an exquisite example of the kind of havoc that can be wreaked on performance through overuse of animated GIFs, frames, and marching-text banners.

## Tips and Tricks for GIF Animation

**http://www.teleport.com/~cooler/MMMM/ making/tips/index.html**

Instead of treating animated GIFs like severely constrained videos, this engaging essay shows how to take advantage of two special features of the format: variable size and position of frames, and variable delay between frames. Using an Adobe Acrobat document for the central text and HTML pages for examples, the writer walks through ten specific applications. This is part of the Micro-

Movie MiniMultiplex; elsewhere on the site, you'll find a set of GIF animations free for your reuse. There's also a Shockwave interface to a large directory of sites with animations the compiler considers particularly interesting.

## VideoCraft GIF Animator

**http://www.andatech.com/vidcraft/demo.html**

Andover Advanced Technologies cleverly morphed its product PhotoMorph into this $30 GIF-animation utility for Windows. VideoCraft GIF Animator emphasizes special effects—most notably the automatic creation of multiple frames that transform one image into another, but also fades, wipes, rotation, warps, and even alpha channel compositing. A number of image-editor-like filters are included to handle tasks such as blurring, sharpening, and scaling. Where this product reveals its origins is in its weak handling of the GIF animation format itself: You get no preview of the animation in action, and you can't use it to edit existing animated GIFs. A downloadable demo version can be used for 30 days before registration. A more powerful commercial version of the program, which can create AVI video as well as animated GIFs, lists for $120.

## WebImage

**http://www.group42.com/webimage.htm**

Group 42's $40 WebImage program is a drag-and-drop animated GIF constructor for Windows. It's also a general graphics utility for the Web, with palette optimization, filters, format conversion to JPEG and PNG as well as GIF, transparency setting, and even imagemap creation. It comes bundled with the I Spy program, an image-file librarian that lets you browse directories and convert in batch. You can download a ten-day free trial from this page.

## OTHER ANIMATION FORMATS

Resting somewhat uneasily between the thoroughly browser-integrated format of GIF animation and the more generally useful digital video and Macromedia Director formats are a number of Web-specific, plug-in types of animation. Although they may provide efficient playback, they lack widespread support from users and from authoring software: Caution is advised.

### Flash

http://www.macromedia.com/
software/flash/

FutureWave Software's FutureSplash was by far the most praised of the dark horse, non-Macromedia animation plug-ins. Its authoring package, FutureSplash Animator, could do double duty by exporting GIF animations. Wisely, Macromedia purchased FutureWave Software and has re-released FutureSplash under the name Macromedia Flash. That's good news for developers—with the marketing power of the new owners behind it, Macromedia Flash is much more likely to be widely installed. Flash features include a select collection of drawing tools, a well-designed timeline, and, that rarity, truly effective streaming playback. Vector-based graphics can be used instead of bitmap graphics, helping to cut way back on file size. Much as MIDI instructions tend to take less space than do recordings of performed music, the computer drawing instructions of vector graphics typically consume much less space than do the final rendered graphics contained in a JPEG or GIF file. Although Macromedia Flash doesn't include a powerful (and complex) programming language such as Director Lingo or Java, it's fairly easy to construct buttons, imagemaps, and animation players. Courageous designers can use Netscape's LiveConnect to interface to JavaScript, or Microsoft's ActiveX controls to interface to VBScript. Flash is $250, but a 30-day free trial version is available for downloading. Useful (if indistinct) FAQ sheets and technical notes can be found in the "Flash Developers Center" area of Macromedia's Web site.

### mBED Interactor and mbedlets

http://www.mbed.com/

mBED Software has developed a new multimedia language and text-based file format specifically for handling Web animations. Like HTML, the mBED language depends on tying together existing multimedia components, but unlike HTML, it's oriented toward streaming media and graphics-based user interaction. It also communicates easily with CGI programs, VBScript, and JavaScript. The downloaded text files, called *mbedlets*, must be interpreted by the mBED plug-in. For nonprogrammers, the company provides a Windows authoring tool, Interactor, for $100; a trial version is available for downloading. The ideas behind mBED seem sound, but it's not clear that another new multimedia language has much of a chance in the current crowded (and well-funded) field—especially now that giants Macromedia and Progressive Networks are working together.

### PlanetFX

http://www.imagefx.com/main.html

ImageFX takes an unusual approach to animation with its PlanetFX ActiveX controls. Rather than building a frame-by-frame animation yourself and sending it to the viewer, you pass a starting graphic to the PlanetFX components along with a set of requests for special effects (including wipes, rotation, rolls, and more than a hundred others) and text effects to be applied to a static image. An interesting idea—too bad the audience is limited to users running Internet Explorer with ActiveX controls enabled.

### PowerMedia

http://www.radmedia.com/

Rad Media's PowerMedia is designed to accelerate the creation of Web pages in a corporate presentation style. It has a slide-show look and organization, smart cursors, simple transition effects, and so on. The authoring system is available for Windows ($200) and UNIX ($500) systems; plug-ins and demo programs are supposedly available somewhere on the company's clumsy, overweight Web site. If you're in sales, have trade shows coming up, and command a healthy expense account, PowerMedia may be worth a look; artsier types will feel more comfortable elsewhere.

## PowerPoint Animation Player

http://www.microsoft.com/mspowerpoint/
internet/player/

Speaking of corporate presentation authoring systems, the big daddy of them all, Microsoft PowerPoint, can be adapted directly to the Web with Microsoft's PowerPoint Animation Publisher. Pick the Export for Internet option, and HTML pages are generated, graphics are compressed, sound is converted to RealAudio format, and slides are turned into imagemaps. The output can be viewed by your power-pointing, power-tie-wearing power users with the PowerPoint Animation Player ActiveX control or helper application. PowerPoint Publisher and Player are only available for those power operating systems, Windows 95 and Windows NT.

## Sizzler

http://www.totallyhip.com/Products/
Products.html

Totally Hip's streaming animation format, Sizzler, has had a tough time competing with Macromedia Shockwave, but it's approach is unique: Much like an interlaced GIF, it begins roughing in frames before all the details of the frames have been downloaded. (Note that a GIF animation does not work in the same way; in fact, it's a bad idea to interlace the individual images contained in a GIF animation.) Totally Hip has recently added the ability to link sound with the animation; unfortunately, the sound doesn't stream to match the start of the animation, so the end result isn't particularly convincing. Plug-ins and a free conversion tool are both available for free downloading from the company's site.

## WebAnimator

http://www.deltapoint.com/animate/

DeltaPoint's WebAnimator is another plug-in/authoring system combo aimed at producing those corporate presentations that salespeople find so exciting and the rest of us find so mind-numbingly mundane. Sound and text effects are well handled, a large number of easy-to-use templates are supplied, and the company's samples seem considerably more impressive than those produced by, for example, PowerMedia. Nevertheless, this package isn't about to make you the Tex Avery of the new millennium. Plug-ins are available for the Macintosh and Windows. An evaluation copy of the Macintosh-only WebAnimator authoring system can also be downloaded here; registration after 30 days costs $50.

# VIDEO PRODUCTION

In the early days of the Web, doing digital video involved a difficult choice between QuickTime (rarely seen outside Macland) and MPEG (which could only play silently on Macintosh systems). Format converters and multiple copies of movies were the order of those days. In some ways, life is easier now, because QuickTime, AVI, and MPEG all have well-supported players on all major platforms.

Production tools, however, are a different matter: You'll definitely be swimming against the freeware and shareware tide if you try to produce an AVI file from scratch on a Macintosh, or a QuickTime file from scratch on Windows. Even if you decide to go with a streaming or quasi-streaming format, you'll probably have to handle video capture and editing in one of those standard formats.

My advice is to produce AVI or MPEG if you're on Windows, and QuickTime if you're on the Macintosh, and to avoid unnecessary format conversions—because each transformation is likely to discard some image quality.

Despite wide player support, the video world remains a bit more difficult to navigate than the audio world. For the most part, audio compression schemes have settled down within recognizable audio-file formats. However, some of the most popular video formats support a variety of compression schemes, each enabled with a system software or hardware extension called a *codec* (for compressor-decompressor). If the codec used by your video file isn't present on your audience's machines, no video will show up. But the file extension won't tell you which codec is needed.

Even some audio compatibility problems get dragged into movie files because codecs also exist for audio tracks. For example, if an author uses a Macintosh system to compress QuickTime movie audio with MACE, the audio will probably only be successfully uncompressed on a Macintosh.

## SETTING VIDEO FRAME RATE, FRAME SIZE, AND COMPRESSION

Once you've decided on a digital video format, your troubles really begin. First, you have to get your source material into the chosen format. Next, you must tinker with the resulting file to achieve the best balance of quality and file size. You may find that no acceptable balance is possible, in which case you'll end up going back to your source material and starting the whole process over. Digital video production is not for the impatient or easily discouraged.

What you're aiming for is a reduction of what's called the *data rate* of the video: the number of bytes per second that must make it through all the meandering byways of hardware and software for the film to play correctly. The following check list should help.

- **Can you do without sound?** Sure, you want it, but sound is a massive contributor to the data rate and can create synchronization problems too obvious for even a generous user to ignore. Try taking the soundtrack off your source material and viewing the results. Forget "ideal"; "ideal" is not an option in Web video. The real question is whether the material is still worth seeing.

- **How low can your frame rate go?** The frame rate stored on videotape is about 30 frames per second (fps)—enough to give a smooth illusion of motion. But given the strictures of production, transmittal, and playback on a computer, the best rate you can reasonably hope for is 15 fps. (I've had to be satisfied with

much less.) Remember that movie playback performance is heavily dependent on hardware support. When movie players can't keep up to the movie's frame rate, they'll usually skip noticeably. So, to provide a pleasant experience for the largest possible number of users, keep trying lower frame rates until you reach the absolute minimum that you're comfortable with.

- **The Web is a multiplex, not a movie palace.** Reduce the dimensions of your frames as much as possible. If what you want to show can be seen in a postage stamp, swallow your widescreen dreams and show a postage stamp. By the way, most video software has a "preferred" set of dimensions that will be handled more efficiently than "odd" dimensions. For example, some compression options work best if width and height, measured in pixels, are both multiples of 16. Plan ahead!

The first step in video compression is deciding on a compression type. As mentioned just above, the software needed to interpret a particular type of compressed media is called that type's codec, and you can't expect to find all codecs on all systems. In particular, make sure that you're not inadvertently using a hardware-based codec (which you may have as a default if you obtained your source material from a video capture card). Such hardware is very unlikely to be found on your users' machines, although your users won't find this out until after they've already gone through the trouble of downloading your movie.

The most widely supported high-compression software codec is called Cinepak; for the moment, I highly recommend that you stick to that one. A newer codec, ClearVideo, gives very promising results for Web video, but it's not yet as widely distributed as Cinepak.

Although you want to make your movie file smaller, you do need to anchor down some uncompressed frames to keep the visuals from getting too fuzzy as they drift away from uncompressed reality. These uncompressed frames are called *key frames*. The standard rule of thumb is to set one key frame per second; so, for a 10fps video, you would ask for every tenth frame to be a key frame. Make sure that the first frame after a cut and the final frame of the movie are also key frames; your video-editing software may very well take care of that automatically.

Don't be shocked if, after a few time-consuming rounds with your compression software, you realize that you must go back and make some modifications to the source material, starting the cycle all over again. That's why it's so important to keep the original material around.

With careful selection, you may be able to fit something worth seeing into less than 500K. Be sure to note the file size beside the link: If it's large, your readers will appreciate the warning; and if it's small, they're more likely to give it a try. Above all, don't get too ambitious, or the only motion your users will wait long enough to see is the long, slow movement of the browser's download progress bar.

### RECORDING YOUR SOURCE MATERIAL

You may have obtained source material from an existing clip, or from graphics output by a painting program like Photoshop or a drawing program like Illustrator. In this case, you'll simply use a conversion tool. But if you're recording your video from a video camera or a QuickCam, here are some special tips to ease the later stages.

Unfortunately, video compressors are optimized for motionlessness (kind of counterintuitive, isn't it?). **Plan ahead to reduce visual complexity and movement.** Every art nouveau flourish on your wallpaper is one more bit of ugly noise when the images are shrunk; every shifting curtain or fidgety actor or fluctuating light source will disrupt smooth video compression. If possible, try to arrange just one or two moving objects against wide flat backgrounds.

**Provide plenty of light.** It's not always the easiest thing to orchestrate in an office or apartment—which is where a QuickCam is likely to be stationed—but that's what most video hardware and software is optimized for.

You've probably noticed how a television screen looks like when it's shown on TV, or tried the old spy-movie trick of putting a telephone speaker next to another telephone's receiver. So you have some notion of how video and audio degrade when shuttled through too many processing steps. The rule is the same whether you're working with a scanned image in Photoshop, adding effects to a sound track, or putting together a Web video: **Keep the work at the highest possible quality until the very last step of production.** This may be even more important with video than with still images. Lower-quality video tends to have more noise, and noise makes it harder to compress the video. Cutting corners at the beginning of the process might lead to twice as large a file at the end.

Since quality degrades with most video compression methods, **don't compress until the very last step.** One way to get some slack is to restrict the size of your initial recording as much as possible. If you're planning to show a talking head, don't frame the whole torso; if you can add sound afterward, record the video track silently; if you'll be working with black-and-white images, don't shoot color.

Many more general tricks are called for when capturing video on a computer. Check the documentation for your video card, or video production notes on the Web.

## Adobe Premiere

**http://www.adobe.com/prodindex/premiere/**

Best known as a QuickTime editor, Adobe Premiere handles AVI input and output as well. In fact, one of the major advantages of Premiere is its handling of many different formats, including still images and audio files. Until Macromedia's Final Cut is established, Premiere lacks many competitors in its own weight class. But the program is showing its age, and you might be better off assembling a suite of more specialized tools unless you obtain Premiere in one of Adobe's bundles. Like much of Adobe's Web site, their Premiere pages needlessly overemphasize the company's proprietary Acrobat format. Even press releases, which by definition are layout independent, are ludicrously embedded in PDF files! On the saner side of the site, you'll find product updates, a huge downloadable demo version of the program, and pointers to third-party plug-ins and hardware.

## Cinepak Secrets

**http://www.Macworld.com/pages/march.96/Column.1862.html**

Although aimed at QuickTime and CD-ROM producers, this *Macworld* article explaining how to get the optimum combination of file size and visual quality from digital video compression is of much broader interest. It's best to plan for reasonable output sizes from the initial shoot. After summarizing issues of video quality, lighting, and camera movement, the article goes on to provide tips on video capture settings, editing and production, and on the compression step itself.

## The comp.sys.ibm.pc.hardware.video FAQ

**http://www.heartlab.rri.uwo.ca/vidfaq/videofaq.html**

PC-compatible owners looking to upgrade their systems with a new monitor, graphics accelerator, or video capture card can do some preliminary homework here at Michael Scott's FAQ sheet.

## Corel Lumiere

**http://www.corel.com/products/lumiere/**

For only $100, Corel offers Windows 95 and Windows NT users a video editor, a bitmap image editor, 3-D animation generator, and a collection of royalty-free film and sound clips. Lumiere uses the multiple-track timelines familiar to Adobe Premiere owners and, like Premiere, isn't the easiest application to ramp up on. On the other hand, that price and that list of features make the Lumiere bundle seem irresistible to video beginners, despite its lack of MPEG support. Alas, at time of writing, Lumiere seems to be considered a poor cousin on the Corel Web site; even the product's official page is oddly bare, consisting of not much more than a press release.

## The Cross-Platform Page: Movie/Animation Formats

**http://emb121.rh.psu.edu/xplat/xplat.movie.html**

This is the video section of Eric Bennett's invaluable cross-platform site. Every major media format is briefly described, and players and converters of that format are listed for every principal operating system. Like the other sections, this one has a strong anti-Microsoft slant, but if they can ignore the editorializing even Windows users will find useful information here. MPEG, AVI, QuickTime, and QuickTime VR are covered.

## The Damn Fool Digital Playhouse

**http://www.execpc.com/~cwhite/what.htm**

Charlie White set up this site to archive his own digital video articles and product reviews. An article on compression emphasizes JPEG and MPEG, making it an excellent companion to the Cinepak-oriented compression overview listed earlier.

## DDClip

**http://www.softlab-nsk.com/Pro/DDClip.html**

DDClip is Windows 95- and Windows NT-based AVI editing shareware. Its particular strengths lie in the speed with which it mixes audio tracks. A demo version is available for downloading; the full version costs $200.

## Digital Video: A Primer for Hobbyists

**http://www.raley.com/video.htm**

Ken Raley's introduction to digital video production on PC compatibles is distinguished by its hype-free common sense, its tenderness concerning budget, its goal-oriented structure, and its wildly erratic typing. Whether you just want to polish home movies or you want to create the most enthralling soap opera ever broadcast on the Web, this article should be required reading before you sink money and time into video production.

## The Digital Video Primer

**http://webreview.com/97/02/14/feature/**

*Web Review* may have published this fast-paced overview of video production, but the article is not completely Web oriented. It assumes a traditional "from scratch" style of video making, complete with video capture card, Adobe Premiere, and a video camera, adding up to "a moderate investment" of at least $1,500. We're definitely not in QuickCam territory anymore! But if you're interested in more advanced digital video creation, this is about the most compressed walkthrough you'll find, despite the page's distracting "tall and skinny" format.

## FOOTAGE.net

**http://www.FOOTAGE.net/**

If you're looking for stock footage or historical film clips, this searchable directory of online stock footage catalogs should probably be your first stop. If the search engine doesn't find what you're looking for in the online databases, you can go through the source directory listings and make some phone calls. Or, if you're working on a commercial project, you can fill out a form and automatically pipeline your request to a couple of dozen archives and researchers. Not quite sure what you want, or just want to see some clips on line? Head for the Screening Room.

## Jump Cut

**http://www.raley.com/jumpcut/**

A "digital-only magazine," Jump Cut is dedicated to digital video production for the consumer market. To date, there's only been one "issue," but it was a good enough one to keep the site on my reference list. There's a Q-and-A column, practical introductions to chroma keying, proper use of transitions, sound editing, and the first (rather horrid) generation of streaming video formats.

## QuickCam

**http://www.quickcam.com/**

Digital video once implied expensive special cards, cameras, software, and hook-ups, and so Connectix started a bit of a revolution when they introduced the QuickCam line in 1994. It comprises small, low-cost desktop cameras that can record video through a normal computer port, with no other hardware needed. The original $100 grayscale model filled the Web with grim and unflattering self-portraits; it boosted video conferencing and Web cam to absurd heights of popularity. The company later introduced a $250 QuickCam that handles color, faster frame rates, better resolution, and sharper focus. There's no way anyone could mistake QuickCam output for professional digital video—but then no one could mistake *any* Web-delivered movies for professional digital video! The reason for QuickCam's popularity may be that it was the first video hardware designed for the low quality of the

Web, rather than its tackling of a job for which it was grotesquely overqualified and overpriced.

The QuickCams double as digital cameras for still images; in fact, the image quality is so much better when used in snapshot mode that you might prefer to assemble frames for stop-action animation that way, and save "real" video recording for conferencing and other live action. To that end, QuickCam software can be instructed to take pictures at regular intervals and save them in an auto-numbered series. The official Connectix QuickCam site contains announcements, product descriptions, a directory of online reviews, software updates, samples, pointers to video conferencing products, and a third-party developers' page.

## Snappy
**http://play.com/pages/snappy/**

Although this chapter is about animation and video, I can't resist mentioning one tool designed to produce still images. (I won't really be straying that much from the subject at hand, because these are still images derived from video equipment.) Play, Inc., cuts through most of the pain and expense involved in getting high-quality video signals to a Windows PC with its product, Snappy. Priced at $200 and the size of a remote control, Snappy plugs into a standard parallel port and passes along data from a camcorder or VCR. Using a preview window, you adjust your settings and click when you see the still you want. With a VCR, you can get just the right still from *Tilly's Punctured Romance* to illustrate your online diary. With a camcorder, you have a surprisingly sharp digital camera capable of 1500x1125 resolution. At the official Snappy site you'll find the usual product announcements, FAQ sheet, and sample images, including a pretty interesting Picture of the Month page.

## Synesthesia Media Connections
**http://www.cel.sfsu.edu/msp/Instructors/rey/ABT_RY.HTM**

Artist and instructor Rich Young put together this digital video site. He admits that the Digital Video Basics page is "very condensed" in a class notes style, but it manages to cover all the basics on its run through the field. Young prefers creating transparency masks with the Adobe product After Effects rather than using the old chroma key approach or Premiere's transparency tools, and I found his walkthrough most convincing.

## Terran Interactive
**http://www.terran-int.com/prod/**

Terran Interactive's Movie Cleaner Pro garnered ecstatic reviews for its ability to ease the usually onerous task of adapting QuickTime video to the constrictions of CD-ROM playback. A forms-driven wizard led beginners to good compression settings with a minimum of effort; the statistics reports, image masking, and preview windows make the program just as valuable for more ambitious producers. So it was natural for the company to move on into the even more constricted environment of the Web. Terran's Web-Motion add-on has received the same level of applause for its easy and educational interface, and its Web-friendly optimized cross-platform "fast-start" QuickTime output. The $270 price of the two products together, however, may put them outside the reach of a beginning Web author. A free "lite" version of Movie Cleaner is available on the site, and I've found it useful even though it's not specifically aimed at Web production. At time of writing, the company had released a preview beta of a new product, MediaCleaner, which can export to the Progressive Networks streaming RealMedia format.

## Videomaker
**http://www.videomaker.com/**

The official site of *Videomaker* magazine is the premiere video production reference on the Web. A wide selection of articles, product reviews, and columns (notably the Getting Started collection of tips for beginners' issues such as choosing a camcorder) is reprinted from the magazine. The extensive and clearly answered FAQ sheets, covering the entire process of video production and distribution, put Usenet to shame. The glossary is of similarly high quality, and well worth downloading for local reference.

A special area on the site is devoted to digital videotape. Tucked away here you'll also find a wealth of information on digital video-editing and production tools, including overviews of hardware and software for the Macintosh and Window platforms, and the color differences between computer monitors and broadcast video.

Downloadable for free use are color bars, some common title mattes, and sound effects such as telephone rings, applause, and thunderstorms. A collection of downloadable MPEG files include prizewinning clips from *Videomaker*-sponsored contests and, most impressively, two dozen demonstrations of video production techniques including lens effects, reflectors, common camera moves, and 3-point lighting.

Another section of the site focuses on distribution, covering many Internet issues. Even the industry news summaries are first rate.

## VideoShop

**http://www.strata3d.com/products/
VideoShop/VideoShop.html**

Originally developed by Diva and then passed on to Avid Technology, VideoShop left anagrams behind when it was taken over by Strata Inc. in 1996. As a simpler and more economical alternative to Adobe Premiere, the program is especially popular in academia, where it's a mainstay of multimedia courses. (You'll find many class notes referring to it on the Web.) Its multitrack composition support and previewing functions are superb, and over 200 special effects are built in. AVI or MPEG producers take note, however, that this is a QuickTime-only, Macintosh-only product.

## VidWatch

**http://rampages.onramp.net/~kolban/
vidwatch/**

This $15 Windows shareware program is designed to create efficient and smooth time-lapse AVI video. Rather than operating on a strictly time-based schedule, which might lead to many dull frames and possibly miss important transitions, VidWatch only captures frames that have changed by a configurable amount.

### QUICKTIME

Although it's the market leader, Adobe Premiere doesn't have quite the stranglehold on the Macintosh video production market that Adobe Photoshop holds over graphics production, and a variety of shareware and freeware tools are available to work with QuickTime video. Just remember not to throw that source material away after completing the QuickTime file!

If you're working from a group of existing QuickTime movies, a primitive but free digital video editor can be found hidden inside the official Apple Movie Player (the standard QuickTime playback software). You can select a portion of a movie by pressing Shift as you drag or single-step across the time bar. Copy that selection and paste it into your new movie.

After you're done assembling your material, if you want to make any changes to the movie, save it as a self-contained file. But if you're completely satisfied and just want to move on to the compression step, you can save your edited file "allowing dependencies." Your compression program will find the video in the original QuickTime source files, picking up just the selections you've indicated. (For more complicated edits, such as layering a separate sound track, you'll have to turn to a more powerful editor than the Movie Player.)

If you're starting from a collection of still graphics for the individual frames and a separate sound file, you can't beat the shareware program MooVer.

Whatever your approach to editing, try to save your edited movie in an uncompressed format before moving on. You don't want to take the risk of losing all your work if the machine hangs or crashes during the long compression step.

☞ After the initial capture or conversion, you're likely to want to continue working in the QuickTime format. After all, the flexibility of the format is what makes it so appealing. However, freeware or shareware help with transitions and special effects is hard to find. If you want to avoid paying for a specialized program, bear in mind that some commercial still-graphics programs can handle double duty: Not only do I use Fractal Design Painter to produce source material for animation, I also sometimes use it to paint directly onto existing QuickTime frames. Another possibility is to rent time on a system that has video editing software installed.

### Fast-Start

Standard QuickTime movies have to be completely loaded before playing—not surprising, given the flexible user control that is typical of this format. *Fast-start* QuickTime files rearrange some components to allow display of an initial frame and start playback before the file is *completely* downloaded. Microsoft's ActiveMovie and InterVU's MPEG Player are other fast-start video options.

You'll sometimes see fast-start movies called *streaming video,* or you'll see it implied that the viewer will get an uninterrupted viewing experience starting after just a second or two. These claims are, however, exaggerated. It's true that the viewer will see an initial frame sooner and can choose to play the portion of a "fast-start" file that has arrived. But when the player reaches the end of that portion, the player will stop. The user can then choose to interrupt the transfer, or wait for more to arrive and play it again. These are indeed valuable options, but they're not quite the same "live broadcast" experience as true streaming video. On the other hand, the quality can be much higher than true streaming video.

### Apple QuickTime Home

http://quicktime.apple.com/

Apple corporate Web addresses have a way of coming and going, but this one—the official home of Quick-Time—should stick around for a while. This is the spot where you can catch up on press releases and product announcements. In the Developer World section of the site, you'll find an extensive directory of links to Quick-Time utilities from Apple and third parties. The Quick-Time Webmaster's Page is also here; it contains a FAQ sheet, QuickTime plug-in information, and recipes for creating and embedding fast-start QuickTime movies.

### The Little QuickTime Page

http://www.bmug.org/Services/qt/

The best source of QuickTime news is this page operated out of BMUG (the Berkeley Macintosh Users Group). And it's not so little—it's updated every week with a few paragraphs of news and pointers, and often supplies a "how-to" tip on the side.

### MovieClips

http://www.digerati-multimedia.com/

If you own a Macintosh and are just starting out in digital video, and Adobe Premiere is too big or too pricey an editor for you, MovieClips from Digerati Multimedia is a simple, fast, and relatively inexpensive alternative. Movie-Clips uses a drag-and-drop interface to assemble multi-layer movies from component video and audio parts. A single MovieClips project can contain up to six video layers and three audio layers. An effects layer is associated with every additional content layer, giving you substantial editing flexibility before committing to the final production—somewhat like the layered effects available in Photoshop. If you know what transition effects you'll want for your finished film, you can even have it all assembled automatically when you drag a set of component clips into the application. MovieClips doesn't handle much in the way of conversions from non-QuickTime formats, but there are plenty of other tools to cover that. The lack of audio editing features is a bigger problem; nevertheless, MovieClips beats the bigger products in its quick previews. A "light" version, supporting fewer layers and effects, is available for $50; the full version is $250. The company Web site contains a FAQ sheet, a features list, and sample movies, as well as a demo version free for the downloading.

## MovieScreamer

**http://www.digigami.com/moviescreamer/**

Windows and UNIX users can play QuickTime files, but Apple has been slow to provide QuickTime creation or conversion facilities for non-Macintosh users. Digigami has stepped into the gap with MovieScreamer, a $200 Windows and LINUX utility to convert QuickTime files into fast-start format. (Non-LINUX UNIX systems are supported, but for $800 more per platform.) Since no other compression or conversion is done by this product, the price may be a little steep unless you are doing a great deal of batch processing on those platforms.

## New Tools Give QuickTime Muscle

**http://www.hyperstand.com/NewMedia/97/ 01/td2/New_Quicktime.html**

Another valuable *NewMedia* overview, this summary of QuickTime tools from the January 1997 issue covers Movie Cleaner Pro, Web-Motion, MovieStart, Movie-Tools, and MovieScreamer.

## The QuickTime FAQ

**http://www.QuickTimeFAQ.org/**

Apple's own Charles Wiltgen manages this site, a necessary stop for any QuickTime user. His FAQ is less a Q-and-A sheet than a full-blown user's guide to QuickTime. The list of common codecs and their uses is one of the best introductions you'll find, although at time of writing he still hadn't updated it to cover MPEG standards. Other highlights are the chapter on quality settings, compression, and key frames; the guide to suitable Cinepak settings for a variety of target environments; and the list of keyboard shortcuts in the MoviePlayer.

The two biggest problems with the document may be related. First, it's not updated very often. (Readers should especially beware of the horrendously out-of-date software list. Instead, go to the site's well-maintained QuickTime Resources page.) Second, this text-and-tables-heavy document is inexplicably published not as HTML, but only as one huge Adobe Acrobat PDF file (and in a tiny font that probably looked great on a laser printer). This considerably reduces its usefulness for online reference, as well as making it more difficult to maintain. Elsewhere on the site, Wiltgen maintains a select collection of very useful QuickTime utilities, some of them only available here—including the QuickTime Streamliner (which automatically makes QuickTime files cross-platform and optimized for Web and CD-ROM use) and the Sanity SaVR (which helps create QuickTime VR panoramas).

## QuickTime Technicalities

**http://www2.heidsite.com/heidsite/video/ qttech.html**

Jim Heid's splendid introduction to issues facing QuickTime creators is excerpted from the *New Complete Mac Handbook*. First, Heid covers the various resources that limit the speed with which digital video can be played: CPU, storage access speed, and video card. Next, he explains compression and key frames. Finally, he brings the threads together into some practical suggestions for QuickTime settings.

## QuickTime Tips

**http://www.terran-int.com/QTInfo/ QTInfo.html**

Terran Interactive, the makers of Movie Cleaner and Web-Motion, has produced a terrific set of general QuickTime pages here. The long tutorial, Making Multimedia Movies, may be the best introduction to digital video production available anywhere. It covers the most efficient approaches to filming original material, capturing video on a Macintosh, editing and adding effects, compression (the first spot where company propaganda sneaks in), and final clean-up for distribution. There are single-page sections offering a unique guide to making QuickTime work well with Director; the most seasoned description of QuickTime-AVI conversion I've seen; welcome advice on the choice between Indeo and Cinepak compression; and statistics on usable CD-ROM data-transfer rates on a variety of Macintosh platforms. Elsewhere, the site contains a telling comparison between the Cinepak codec, JPEG, and Iterated Systems's Clear

Video (the new pretty face on the compression block—and it wins by an unblobby, undistorted nose).

## Radius Digital Video Information Server

**http://www.radius.com/Support/DV/ MainDV.html**

Sure, there's a definite slant towards Radius products in these compact pages of tips, walkthroughs, and trouble-shooting, but there's also plenty of useful background on digital video settings and advanced QuickTime problems. And besides, given their ubiquity in the video production world, it's not all that bad to have a slant towards Radius products.

## TRMOOV

**http://www.downrecs.com/software.htm**

The San Francisco Canyon Company produced this simple Windows freeware, which handles conversion between QuickTime and AVI formats more reliably than most alternatives.

## MPEG

The MPEG standards, defined by the Moving Pictures Experts Group, have become the most widely used approaches to 30fps (frames per second) video compression—although Cinepak probably remains the most common codec for 15fps video. MPEG-1 was designed to serve audio and full-sized video from a CD-ROM. MPEG-2 is designed for digital transmission or broadcasts, and therefore is optimized for a wider range of video quality. Although MPEG-2 isn't seen much yet on personal computers, it's the standard supported by DVD and HDTV and so should start appearing more often, especially since MPEG-1 is compatible with MPEG-2 engines.

MPEG is one area in which the Macintosh's cross-model hardware compatibility worked against it. Too computationally intense to be decoded on most older Macintosh CPUs, the format was left to the sizable number of PC compatibles having hardware support from dedicated graphics cards. For years, the only software solution for Macintosh owners was a silent shareware player called Sparkle, references to which you still see on older Web pages. Finally, in 1996, Apple brought out a software MPEG-1 extension for QuickTime, and at least some MPEG movies can finally be seen and heard across the Web.

## Astarte MPEG Exporter

**http://www.astarte.de/mpeg_exporter/**

This free Macintosh system extension from Astarte lets QuickTime editors apply MPEG-1 compression to video tracks. I'm not sure why Apple didn't provide this capability, but it's nice that somebody did.

## A Beginner's Guide for MPEG-2 Standard

**http://www.ee.cityu.edu.hk/~edap064/mpeg/ BeginnersGuideForMPEG2Standard.html**

Victor Lo, of the City University of Hong Kong, explains the convoluted workings of MPEG-2 video compression algorithms. He uses well-chosen graphics (apparently borrowed from C-Cube's terrific MPEG-1 overview), helping the mathematically insecure through some of the more difficult stretches.

## InterVU

**http://www.intervu.com/**

For the multitude of video streaming problems, InterVU offers a combined solution: It provides the server software, hosts the servers, and hands out the browser plug-ins. Currently only Windows users are fully supported, but both Windows and Macintosh users can obtain a plug-in for streaming MPEG playback. Note that since the MPEG quality is not reduced to match the capacity of the user's connection, there are likely to be many stops and starts. The first run-through will count as more of a preview than an actual performance; however, after the entire file has been transmitted, the user can replay it at a normal rate.

## MegaPEG

**http://www.digigami.com/megapeg-encoder-info.html**

MegaPEG is a Windows utility to convert existing video to MPEG-1 or MPEG-2 format without the aid of special hardware. The program has some nice features, including batch operations, image correction, and thumbnail GIF creation. It also costs $500. As Smokey Robinson's mama told him, "You'd better shop around."

## MPEG—All Systems Are Not Equal

**http://www.datx.com/drwp.html**

Although this is a white paper from the Director of Product Marketing for Data Translation, Inc., it contains no company propaganda. Instead, it stands up as a well-written and informative introduction to MPEG as a digital video system. The history of MPEG standards, the various levels of MPEG audio, the basics of MPEG video compression techniques, distribution mechanisms, and comparisons to other compression approaches are all covered in a clear, direct fashion.

## MPEG and multimedia communications

**http://www.cselt.stet.it/ufv/leonardo/paper/isce96.htm**

Leonardo Chiariglione was one of the originators of the effort to define MPEG standards. In this white paper, he explains the motives behind the current MPEG-4 effort and, on the side, provides a wealth of acerbic insights into the importance (or lack thereof) of standards and into multimedia's history and future. "After years of multimedia hype, there is no sign that multimedia communications will happen in the way media gurus had anticipated, i.e. by convergence of telecommunications, entertainment and computers, all adopting digital technology … much as the professions of barber, butcher and cobbler have not moved a single inch to a convergence point through the millennia in spite of all sharing the common 'knife' technology." From his point of view, the major feature that tailors MPEG-4 to distributed multimedia is not the "range of quality settings" mentioned by most sources, but its two-way communication and adaptability to the user, including dynamic loading of new coding schemes. Worth more than a year's subscription to *Wired*.

## MPEG Archive

**http://www.powerweb.de/mpeg/**

Maintained by Frank Gadegast, the MPEG Archive is a collection of tools for MPEG authoring, conversion, and viewing. The standard MPEG FAQ sheet is locally maintained here; it seems particularly strong on MPEG audio. Unannotated archives of MPEG-1 files are also on the site. Special note to my fellow Americans: The MPEG-Archive is located in Germany, and downloads can take a while. For faster local access, you can order CD-ROMs containing the archives.

## MPEG 1 or MPEG 2?

**http://hyperstand.com/NewMedia/97/01/td/MPEG1_MPEG2.html**

This article by Jeff Sauer is typical of the informative material on the *NewMedia* site. It covers the differences between the two formats and explains a "compromise" format called *half-resolution MPEG-2*. Sauer discusses the possibility of editing video that's been stored in MPEG-compressed format, and the results of comparative tests performed on a range of MPEG products for Windows and Macintosh systems.

## MPEG.ORG

**http://www.mpeg.org/**

MPEG.ORG is light on original content. Instead, it operates as an easy, all-in-one set of listings and search engines for MPEG technical documents, news stories, product reviews, DVD information, video and audio clips, and software at other Web sites. In that, it does a good job: This is the most extensive and up-to-date MPEG directory I've found. Ambitious programmers will rejoice in the site's free, source-code-included MPEG-2 codec.

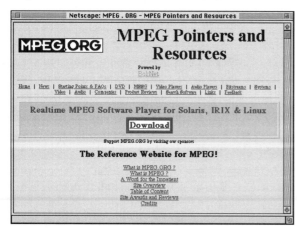

## MPEG Overview

**http://www.c-cube.com/tecno/mpeg.html**

The best introduction to the inner workings of MPEG-1 is this superb page from C-Cube Microsystems. It cleanly and clearly explains the general process, the structures of the video and audio streams, synchronization, and the various forms of compression. If you're curious about just what exactly is going on while your computer looks frozen, this is the place to start learning.

## MPEG Plaza

**http://www.visiblelight.com/mpeg/**

MPEG Plaza is a commercial site especially geared to business information. The commercial hardware and software products list has a strong bias towards PC compatibles; nonetheless, it is extensive, including much high-end gear. The company directory runs to hundreds of entries. A directory of links to MPEG archives is helpfully annotated. The matching directory of online references is impressively long, but disappointingly out-of-date. Links to the associated FTP site provide access to small and not always current sets of downloadable MPEG software for a variety of platforms. For the computer historians among us, there's an archive of press releases.

## MPEG-2 Archive

**http://www.mpeg2.de/**

The exciting sequel to Frank Gadegast's MPEG Archive offers a similar mix of technical documents, introductions, and FAQ sheets, as well as some mysteriously unexplained software and samples.

## MPEG-2 FAQ

**http://bmrc.berkeley.edu/projects/mpeg/faq/MPEG-2-FAQ.html**

Chad Fogg's lively take on MPEG actually covers both MPEG-1 and MPEG-2, despite the humble title. He includes historical background and a very interesting list of debunked myths. You'll find an overview of the specification documents and a pair of competing interpretations of steps in a standard's life span (e.g., the "WD" step either means "Working Draft" or "We're Drunk"). There's a huge amount of technical information, and The 6 Steps to Claiming Bogously [sic] High Compression Rates, which answers the intriguing puzzle of why some people say MPEG obtains 100-to-1 compression, while others say it's closer to 10-to-1.

## OTHER STREAMED AND QUASI-STREAMED VIDEO FORMATS

More recent digital video formats have been developed specifically in response to the special requirements of Web distribution:

- Since video files are so huge, the audience is likely to wander away before a download is complete—thus the need for streaming (and quasi-streaming) formats. Traditional digital-video players require that a file be fully loaded.

- Since the size restrictions of Web video usually lead to fuzzy, small images, the medium seems better suited to "live broadcast" content than to "produced" content. It's not surprising that live multicasting has been one of the most popular uses of video on Web. Traditional digital-video formats can't handle real-time broadcasts, for the same reason that they can't handle streaming.

The streaming and quasi-streaming approaches have their own problems, of course, beginning with their relatively high expense. These are proprietary formats and tend to be priced accordingly. Also, as proprietary formats they often severely restrict the range of applicable authoring tools, as well as the range of your audience. Still, if you have a fairly long movie to distribute on the Web, you'll probably find streaming video too attractive to pass up.

## ActiveMovie

http://www.microsoft.com/imedia/learn/
mediacontrols/movie.htm

Microsoft's ActiveMovie is an ActiveX control that plays video with quasi-streaming. The video doesn't start playing right away, and the server doesn't coordinate data transfer with the client's playback, but video *will* usually start before the entire file is downloaded. (Apple offers the same capability with QuickTime but calls it *fast-start*; Microsoft prefers to use the less precise but easier-to-market term *streaming*.) ActiveMovie seems intended as a generic wrapper around video and audio in a variety of compression formats, and as such might be construed as a direct competitor to Apple's QuickTime format and plug-in. If so, QuickTime currently has the advantage—if only in being playable from both the Netscape browser and from Internet Explorer.

## Microsoft NetShow

http://www.microsoft.com/netshow/

If Progressive Networks can have its RealMedia and Netscape can have its Media Server, then clearly Microsoft must have its own streaming audio and video server. Perhaps in consideration of the corporate presentation market, NetShow also supports a third type of streaming media, *illustrated audio* (aka slide show). NetShow can handle live broadcasts and on-demand downloads and can use a wide variety of compression schemes. Although its performance to date hasn't knocked out the reviewers, NetShow is free. And (given Microsoft's recent record with Web utilities) it's likely to improve. The

product's home site lets you download the server and player software (including simple conversion and editing tools), provides a user guide, and lists NetShow events. At this writing, only Windows 95 and Windows NT platforms are supported.

## RealVideo

http://www.real.com/

Progressive Networks seems to have leveraged its early success with RealAudio streaming media spectacularly well. Not only did the company dramatically improve RealAudio's iffy sound quality, but it also produced RealVideo, a streaming video format which works remarkably well even at 28.8K modem speeds. (Of course, at this point "remarkably well" can still mean frequent pauses, fat-pixeled and artifact-heavy visuals, buggy playback, and extremely low frame rates.) Still, I haven't seen a streaming format handled better at lower speeds. And at higher speeds, RealVideo takes advantage of Iterated Systems's excellent ClearVideo compression.

RealVideo includes multiple compression schemes optimized for various transfer rates and content types, and hot spots that will take the user's browser to Web pages. A stand-alone encoder supplied by Progressive Networks is Windows only (so far), but an export plug-in for Macintosh Adobe Premiere is supplied. Third parties such as Terran Interactive have already begun bringing out their own RealVideo conversion and authoring tools. As with RealAudio, the servers required to stream RealVideo cover a wide range of price and capacity.

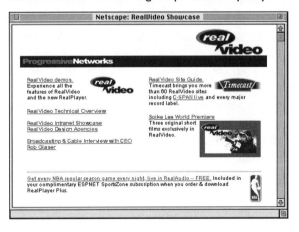

### StreamWorks

**http://www.xingtech.com/**

Xing Technologies's StreamWorks format uses MPEG compression and scalable data rates to provide streaming video and audio. Like its competitors, Xing supplies free plug-in players and appears aimed to make a profit from rather expensive streaming servers. At time of writing, however, they were running far behind competitors in market share and video quality.

### VDOLive

**http://www.vdolive.com/**

VDOnet was an early winner in the streaming video world, working the usual combination of free plug-ins and commercial server. The VDOLive format converts easily from AVI video, giving it a wealth of material to choose from. It performed comparatively well among first-generation streaming formats, but audio and video quality have some catching up to do when compared to the most recent crop of competitors.

### VivoActive

**http://www.vivo.com/**

VivoActive is a rare non-server-based approach to streaming video being tried by Vivo Software. As usual, the company's VivoActive Player is a free browser plug-in or ActiveX control, but VivoActive files are designed to be distributed by the same Web server that handles HTML files and static graphics, rather than by specialized servers that have strict limits on the number of supported users. Where Vivo hopes to make money is in its $500–$800 compression and formatting tool, VivoActive Producer, which can batch-convert AVI and QuickTime source files. The audio isn't knock-out, however. And lack of the two-way communication available with a dedicated server means that the server can't adapt to the bandwidth, and that users have limited control of playback. But the relative ease with which VivoActive files can be distributed may more than make up for those deficiencies. Players and evaluation copies of the authoring system are available for Windows 95, Windows NT, and Power Macintosh systems.

### Vosaic

**http://www.vosaic.com/**

Vosaic Corp. jumped in between the first and second generations of streaming video and audio formats. Taking the RealAudio approach, their plug-ins are free; but the video format can only be streamed from Vosaic's own commercial server software. In the publicity arena—and, judging from my most recent viewing, in the 28.8 modem arena as well—Vosaic will have a tough time competing with Progressive Networks, except for UNIX users.

### VXtreme Web Theater

**http://www.vxtreme.com/**

VXtreme's second-generation streaming video format, Web Theater, just might be able to hold its own against RealVideo. The image quality is similar, and VXtreme's servers are considerably more adaptable. Instead of having to produce multiple video files for different client connection speeds, the Web Theater server can scale a single video file to match the client's bandwidth. The scaling is dynamic enough that the server can even adapt transmission to match current, transient conditions, whereas RealVideo streams have to pause when there's temporary congestion on the network. At time of writing, the player was available only for Windows 95 and Windows NT, although the company promises to release versions for Macintosh and Sun systems. VXtreme also provides a Web Theater Producer authoring tool designed to blend HTML, Java applets, streaming video, and a programmable timeline into "corporate presentation" video-enhanced Web pages.

## WEB CAMS

Nothing better exemplifies the Web's native Aesthetic of Uselessness than the Web cam phenomenon: blurry, randomly composed photographs that are periodically updated. If you have something interesting to track, such as a scientific experiment or a satellite picture, or if you just want to join the party, you'll find a wide assortment of inexpensive tools here to help set up your Web cam.

## EMULive

**http://www.jcs-canada.com/contents.html**

EMULive is the umbrella for a family of Windows 95/NT-based Web cam programs. They range from the $20 EMULive (transferring several frames per second to a central server), to the $300 EMULive PRO (managing live video with built-in postprocessing), to the $400 EMULive 5 STREAM FSx Server (handling streaming broadcasts), and beyond.

## FrameServer

**http://reddwarf.wmw.utwente.nl/pub/www/ persons/vertegaal/software/ aboutframeserver.html**

FrameServer is free, simple Macintosh Web server software (for noncommercial use only) that produces a knocking-on-the-door sound at the site of the target URL and, two seconds later, grabs a snapshot of you, the startled Web author. Good sport Roel Vertegaal not only wrote this software; he lets you annoy him with it.

## ISpy

**http://www.ispy.nl/**

The irresistibly named Charlotte Internet Stuff is responsible for this $90 Windows 95/NT shareware program. It lets you snatch JPEG images from QuickCam or other hardware, with flexible time and caption settings. The unusually informative Web site includes the user guide and a FAQ sheet.

## MacWebCam

**http://www.rearden.com/webcam/ default.html**

MacWebCam is $35 Macintosh shareware that handles the usual scheduled snapshots. It also gives you a choice of PICT, GIF, or JPEG formats; lets you merge graphics and timestamps; and will run AppleScripts to upload the new images to your Web site or handle postprocessing. If you have a Macintosh-based Web server, you may also be able to stream live video (slowly).

## SnapCAP

**http://www.halcyon.com/artamedia/snapcap/**

For Windows 95, SnapCAP is $80 shareware that turns the wildly popular Snappy video-capture tool into a timed Web cam. You can set the snapshot interval and save as JPEG, BMP, or GIF files. Even more impressively, the program handles HTTP serving and FTP access automatically.

## SnapNSend

**http://www.snapnsend.com/**

This Windows shareware can operate a wide variety of video capture methods, including Snappy and VideoBlaster. SnapNSend can store to GIF, JPEG, or AVI formats; and it can automatically dial into a connection and use FTP to transfer new files to your Web server. Uniquely, SnapNSend can also automatically send pan, tilt, and zoom commands to a Pelco remote control driver. (The emphasis on camera control isn't surprising, given that one of the SnapNSend developers is Carl Sutter, who worked on some of the earliest Web-controlled robots.)

## WebCam Central Links

**http://www.cris.com/~jdholley/ wcc/links/**

WebCam Central is one of the largest and most frequently updated directories of sites that contain Web cam pictures. Its extensive link pages provide pointers to cam-oriented software packages (for Windows, Macintosh, and UNIX systems) and hardware add-ons.

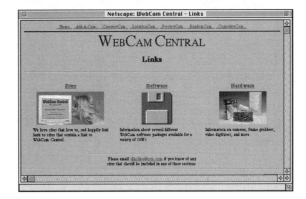

## WebCamToo

**http://www.mmcorp.com/~binky/webcamtoo/**

Macintosh freeware WebCamToo is a general Web server with special capabilities to serve live video and capture snapshots, using the normal HTML <IMG> tag to embed updated images. If you like the program, you might want to check out the same author's WebCamTurbo, a live-video streamer that handles multiple streams.

## WebShot

**http://www.cinecom.com/**

WebShot is a Windows 95 program that automatically captures live images and transmits them as JPEG files to your Web server. It's produced by CINECOM, best known for its CineVideo family of video phone, conference, and broadcast software. Unfortunately, at time of writing, the CINECOM Web site had little information about the program aside from its availability for downloading.

# SHOCKWAVE

Macromedia Director is probably the most popular single tool for creating interactive multimedia on CD-ROM, and when Macromedia decided to move into Web distribution, the company was guaranteed a measure of success.

Although Macromedia hasn't abstained from the occasional outburst of competitor-killing hype, it deserves credit for the good work put into the cross-platform Shockwave format. Shockwave files and playback engines are fairly stable; they are more successfully cross-platform than Java applets; they can stream; they're surprisingly well compressed; and they even support HTML page linking. Having successfully brought the most intriguing of their upstart competitors, FutureSplash, under the Shockwave umbrella, and with recent releases of Director focusing largely on additional Web features, Macromedia and Shockwave seem well set up to continue their bandwidth onslaught.

Since Director's Lingo programming language gives a great deal of flexibility to the developer,

Shockwave might more logically be included along with Java, JavaScript, and ActiveX in the chapter on client-side programming. However, since it's so common for Director multimedia programs to be called "movies" or "animations," I'm including Shockwave here instead.

> 👉 **By the way, experienced Director developers might note an important underpublicized benefit gained from the Web's popularity: It prompted Macromedia to finally provide truly cross-platform Director files. Standard "Director movie players" use different formats for Windows and the Macintosh, and the software that produces the extra format requires an extra payment to Macromedia. Shockwave is sweet relief to amateur multimedia authors who can only afford one computer or one software license.**

## Director Web

**http://www.mcli.dist.maricopa.edu/director/**

One of the best things about working with Director is Director Web, the non-Macromedia-sponsored site from the Maricopa County Community College District. It's highly likely you'll find straight answers faster here than at Macromedia's hype- and buzz-heavy corporate site. Start with the Director FAQ, which is obligingly broken up into reasonable HTML sections; it also offers a search function and downloadable archives. It's slightly out of date, but that's par for the course with FAQs. For up-to-the-minute news (and tips, warnings, and techniques), consider the Direct-L mailing list, a multimedia authoring tradition.

Beginners are likely to find the traffic on Direct-L overwhelming, but there's no need to actually subject your own mailbox to the clobbering: The Director Web site keeps a searchable archive and posts daily bundles. (Even when I'm working with products other than Director, I often drop into the current Direct-L digest page just to check on what's making the most waves.) Excellent tips, tutorials, and walkthroughs are stored on the site, arranged by category.

Even more impressive is the searchable collection of Director plug-ins (called XObjects and XTras). The annotated links directory is a model of its type; speaking of links, at time of writing there were already close to 1,000 online Shockwave examples listed.

### Dr. Diego's F.A.Q. about Macromedia Director and Lingo

**http://www.xtramedia.com/lingoTips.shtml**

An impressively long list of tips and techniques (particularly relating to Director's programming language, Lingo) is presented here in a well-indexed question-and-answer format. Unlike some Director advice archives, this one is kept current to match the latest releases of the program.

### Multimedia Authoring Systems FAQ

**http://www.tiac.net/users/jasiglar/ MMASFAQ.HTML**

If you're curious about alternatives to Director in the interactive multimedia world, Jamie Siglar's FAQ sheet will get your research off to a fast start. The questions and answers themselves may be too concise and jargon-ridden for the comfort of nonprogrammers. If so, scroll down to the annotated list of multimedia authoring products, arranged by platform.

### Shockwave Download Center

**http://www.macromedia.com/shockwave/**

Come here to pick up Shockwave plug-ins—you'll need them to look at much of anything on Macromedia's Web site. This hard-line attitude may have created a little embarrassment for Macromedia when Shockwave security holes were discovered, but there's no doubt that the approach has gained the company's proprietary formats even wider coverage.

### Shockzone

**http://www.macromedia.com/shockzone/**

The official Macromedia Shockwave area, Shockzone is itself thoroughly based on Shockwave, and so you need the plug-in before you can find out much about the format. Besides providing plenty of links to examples of Shockwave on the Web, Shockzone also has links to Macromedia pages for Web authors who wish to develop their own programs.

### Working with Shockwave

**http://www.macromedia.com/support/ director/how/shock/**

At this writing, this is the central spot for Director users who wish to develop Shockwave files—but things change quickly at the Macromedia Web site, and pages are often hidden in the shuffle. This site includes pointers to the Afterburner conversion utilities and to extensive documentation of proper Afterburner use, new Web-oriented Lingo commands, embedding Shockwave in a Web page, Shockwave streaming audio, server configuration, and techniques to improve Shockwave compression.

# THE VIRTUAL REALITY EXPERIENCE

"I don't get it. What makes *this* virtual reality?"
—A Friend

It's true: *Virtual reality* is sort of an inflated name for what's just another way to make graphics respond to user interaction—and one that doesn't add all that much to the magic of drag-and-drop. But, due to a three-way collision of marketing forces with literary and computer history, virtual reality (VR) is the name we're stuck with.

In virtual reality systems, the mouse (or magic glove or body suit, depending on your budget) controls your view of a three-dimensional space. What you see is exactly what programmers using 3-D graphics-generation tools get to see! (Well, that statement sounds better when William Gibson says it…) Common effects generated by mouse drags and clicks include rotating the view for a panorama effect, rotating an object that's floating in space, zooming in to and out of a space, and clicking on blurry, jagged links rather than boring two-dimensional links.

I suppose my own skepticism is all too obvious in this case. I believe that few computer users enjoy scrolling, and so offering them new ways to scroll isn't much of a conceptual breakthrough. Even after trying to set aside my prejudices, the best piece of advice I can offer to Web authors is to not believe the hype—if you end up doing this for a living, your clients will be glad to supply more than enough hype on their own! Know what the tools can do, and use them for what they're best at.

Sometimes (not always!) a rotating 360° view really is much more interesting than a series of face-front stills. VR is ideal for working with material that naturally adapts itself to panoramas or "walks," such as landscapes or architectural studies.

And, like the similarly limited "point of view" hand-held camera in horror films, the VR interface works well at building up suspense or fear. Slow, clumsy exploration of a mysteriously defined space doesn't do a lot for reference work, but it intensifies the atmosphere in a kill-the-monsters or a find-the-clues game.

The most impressive use yet of any "virtual reality" system I've seen has been from filmmaker Zoe Beloff (Figure 7.1). She gladly admits that Quick-Time VR is reminiscent of nineteenth century gad-

gets such as panoramas and stereopticans, but then goes on to say how much she enjoys panoramas and stereopticans. That sane attitude goes a long way to explain her success.

## VRML AND QUICKTIME VR

Put simply, QuickTime VR is well suited for photographic source material. VRML tools tend to use computer-generated 3-D instead. To put it another way, VRML makes it much easier for the viewer to "travel" into and among objects in a scene, but those objects and that scene are likely to be less interesting than the "flatter" graphics of QuickTime VR.

This dilemma of photograph vs. computer image is a more extreme twist on the decisions between digitized sound vs. MIDI, and bitmap graphics vs. vector graphics. Providing a new frame for each new view of an object (as QuickTime VR does) lets authors keep all the computational work on their end of the wire, allowing them to provide beautiful,

**Figure 7.1**
Zoe Beloff's very personal approach to virtual reality, as seen at *http://www.users.interport.net/~zoe/main.html*

non-"mechanical" art. On the other hand, a huge amount of data has to be squeezed across the wires (individual frames for QuickTime VR; samples for digitized sound). Providing a description of what an object looks like (as 3-D tools and MIDI do) reduces the amount of data sent across the wire and makes that data much more adaptable. It also, however, produces a "mechanical" look (or sound) and pushes the job of computation onto the user's machine.

The two types of technology—VR and VRML—have already begun to converge with the animated textures of some VRML 2.0 systems. Ideally, the merging process will continue, eventually overcoming some of the deficiencies (and, alas, probably some of the benefits) of both systems. Unfortunately for this ideal, VRML browsers have from the beginning diverged even more widely than HTML browsers did.

## VRML

VRML stands for Virtual Reality Modeling Language. The final *ML* that the acronym shares with HT*ML* is no coincidence. VRML was specifically initiated by Mark Pesce to be a Web language; in fact, in was intended as the HTML of 3-D interfaces.

Like HTML, VRML is not a programming language. Rather, it's a text description of a layout, which must be interpreted by a piece of client software. As with HTML, the client software used to interpret the text description is called a browser. Also like HTML, VRML's control of layout and display is decidedly primitive—which may be a bigger obstacle to the creation of convincing animation-based navigation than it was to the creation of convincing text-based navigation! But, instead of describing potentially hyperlinked text and static images as HTML does, VRML describes potentially hyperlinked 3-D shapes and environments.

Since VRML's descriptions are of abstract 3-D objects, it's easy to design those objects using a 3-D graphics generation program, which means that, besides the VRML specialist programs, a growing number of commercial products are able export VRML files. As another plus to the description approach, VRML files can be loaded progressively, one object at a time, reducing viewer frustration. For that matter, VRML browsers can choose to discard some of the more complex aspects of 3-D generation, sacrificing image quality for speed and simplicity, as Netscape's Live3D plug-in does.

This freedom points out a major problem for the VRML author: the uncertainty of what any given VRML world will look like on any given VRML browser. Even if one manages to avoid the multitude of VRML "extensions" to be found in any survey of VRML tools, each tool seems to interpret specifications somewhat differently.

VRML 2.0 overcame one of the biggest problems with the 1.0 specification: its static nature. Animation, scripting, audio, and some user interaction with objects are all now possible, although availability of VRML 2.0 browsers is lagging. Of course, there's also the likelihood that increasing the complexity of VRML worlds will further complicate achievement of predictable results across browsers.

### A Beginner's Guide to VRML
**http://www.netscape.com/eng/live3d/howto/ vrml_primer_index.html**

This primer from Netscape might more accurately be described as "An Incomplete Beginner's Guide to Netscape Live3D 1.0." Live3D is a fairly popular plug-in that introduced a number of features to VRML 1.0, most of which have been taken into account in the VRML 2.0 specification, albeit in different ways. Like many Netscape documents, the page seems to have been dropped while "under construction," but its heavy use of examples makes it worth reading.

## comp.lang.vrml Frequently Asked Questions

**http://hiwaay.net/~crispen/vrml/faq.html**

This FAQ sheet for the comp.lang.vrml Usenet newsgroup is meant as a supplement to the "official" VRML FAQ (described in an upcoming listing), but this one is so much more recent that it may be appropriate as a replacement. The page is largely a collection of links to specs and software, but the discussion of whether or not to use a general-purpose 3-D modeler is especially well handled.

## Introduction to VRML 2.0

**http://www.sdsc.edu/siggraph96vrml/**

This is an online collection of slides (with links) used for an introductory course taught at the computer graphics conference SIGGRAPH 96. As usual with slides, the pace is both slower and more cryptic than a real text might be, but I still found its slicing of the specification into bite-sized pieces eminently digestible.

## Liquid Reality

**http://www.dimensionx.com/products/lr/**

VRML 2.0 allows Java scripts to be attached to objects as behaviors. Nothing if not ambitious, Dimension X has gone one better by writing a complete VRML 2.0 platform in Java. The Liquid Reality package includes a set of 3-D Java classes for programmers and a "sample application" VRML browser. At time of writing, the company's Web site included a downloadable beta, along with descriptions of the program, sample outputs, and a FAQ sheet.

## Microsoft Supports VRML

**http://www.microsoft.com/vrml/default.htm**

The emphatic page title is likely meant to combat the impression left by Microsoft's early, somewhat cavalier attitude toward the VRML standardization process. The company lately is devoting an appreciable percentage of its vast resources toward VRML 2.0. Although the Microsoft VRML browser is still in production, these VRML-dedicated pages already contain a large directory of free models (originally created by Viewpoint Datalabs International, with a heavy emphasis on weaponry) and links to external sources.

## New Dimensions in VRML Authoring

**http://www.hyperstand.com/NewMedia/96/16/td2/New_VRML_Authoring.html**

A fine group review typical of *NewMedia* magazine, this one covers VRML creation software for the Windows and Macintosh platforms. Only VRML 1.0 tools were available when the review was written, but many of the insights, warnings, and external links should remain useful for some time.

## ParaGraph International

**http://www.paragraph.com/**

ParaGraph produces 3-D generation and VRML software under the Internet3D umbrella—notably, the entry-level $30 Virtual Home Space Builder, which produces VRML 2.0 worlds with a wide collection of prebuilt spaces for Windows or Macintosh systems. (Such multiple platform support is a rarity among VRML authoring tools, but I note that the plug-in needed to view ParaGraph's multimedia extensions is available only for Windows.) Besides the usual download center and collection of samples, the ParaGraph site includes an informative online tutorial and a collection of tips. Higher range products from ParaGraph include Internet3D Font Magic and the much-praised Windows-only Internet3D Space Builder (which supplies extensive 3-D primitives, object editing, and texture tools).

## Texture Mapping in VRML

**http://www.ywd.com/cindy/texture.html**

Cindy Reed-Ballreich has supplied one of the best VRML references with this texture-oriented set of pages covering VRML 1.0, VRML 2.0, and texture images themselves. The introductory Understanding How Textures Work page will be of interest to beginners in any 3-D graphics technology.

## The Vertex

**http://www.thevertex.com/**

Set up by Dimension X (makers of Liquid Reality), the Vertex database collects downloadable VRML object models and textures, and lets you browse them by directory or search by name. If you'd like to return the favor, adding to the database is relatively easy.

## Virtual Reality Modeling Language (VRML)

### http://hiwaay.net/~crispen/vrml/

Bob Crispen, author of the comp.lang.vrml FAQ sheet, put together this excellent introduction to VRML, covering both versions of the standard as well as Netscape's Live3D extensions. Here you'll find a good mix of original content and pointers to other sources, including tutorials, tips, tools, background history, and reviews of VRML browsers and authoring systems. (Macintosh users, note that the emphasis is squarely on Windows and UNIX systems.) The directory of information (and rantings) about multiuser virtual worlds may be worth a visit, as well.

## The Virtual Society

### http://www.sonypic.com/vs/

Behind the generic name of this site, you'll find Sony Corp., which has supplied some of the better VRML software for Windows systems. Naturally, you'll find links here to Sony's VRML browser, Community Place; to its Java-aware VRML authoring tool, Community Place Conductor; and to its multiuser server, Community Place Bureau, which attempts to bring the VRML world a step closer to the fantasy of shared cyberspace. Also available for downloading are useful specialized tools for converting VRML 1.0 files to VRML 2.0 format and for easily switching between competing Netscape plug-ins. A series of tutorials for VRML authors include VRML 2.0 features such as animation interpolators and scripts.

## VRML FAQ

### http://vag.vrml.org/VRML_FAQ.html

This is the official frequently asked questions and answers sheet for VRML, but it often gives up in frustration or points to other sites. On the other hand, that's not such a bad strategy for avoiding obsolescence, especially since the page hasn't been updated in over a year. The content that's left is useful and straightforward, given that it was written before VRML 2.0 was finalized.

## The VRML Forum

### http://vag.vrml.org/www-vrml/

For those of you who can't get enough near-term history, this site archives the verbose goings-on in the www-

vrml mailing list that was largely responsible for both VRML standards. No index and no search functions are available for the archives, which is too bad because 2 or 3 megabytes of e-mail stacks up each month. But at least the archives are available. If you've browsed a bit and think you have something to contribute, you can subscribe from this Web page.

## The VRML Repository

### http://www.sdsc.edu/vrml/repository.html

This site, maintained by the San Diego Supercomputer Center, is Virtual Grand Central Station on the Web. Even the VRML FAQ sheets point you here. The repository contains the largest available directories of VRML browsing software, helpfully sorted by both platform and level of specification support. You'll also find authoring tools, servers, tests, books, guides, and specifications, as well as libraries of objects, textures, and worlds.

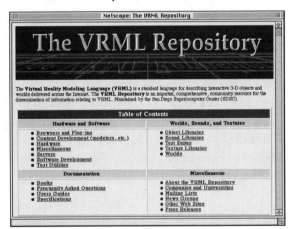

## vrml.sgi.com

### http://vrml.sgi.com/intro.html

Silicon Graphics was more or less the instigator of VRML, and the company has forged ahead to produce this, the most extensive commercial site on the subject. Special on-site public-relations releases cum articles cover VRML conferences, and subjects such as Java and VRML, with an enthusiastic lack of journalistic detachment. Cafe VRML contains a searchable index of commercial VRML resources ranging from consultants to browsers, and provides information on job opportunities and industry events in the VRML world. An unusually selective gallery points out the best VRML worlds on the Web. Best of all is the content developer section, with a wealth of information about VRML 2.0, and well-organized and annotated links to tutorials, tools, and libraries.

## VRMLSite Magazine

http://www.vrmlsite.com/

VRML authors will want to make the Web home of VRMLSite Magazine a frequent stop. Articles focus on real solutions to real problems, such as implementation of concurrent object behavior. The unusually honest news section provides analyses rather than simple reprints of press releases.

## The VRML 2.0 Specification

http://vag.vrml.org/VRML2.0/FINAL/

Just in time to settle disputes in your Web trivia games, here's the official description of VRML 2.0. Unsurprisingly, the specification itself is a little dry, but the associated Overview page is an excellent introduction to VRML 2.0's new capabilities.

## VRML Update Newsletter

http://cedar.cic.net/~rtilmann/mm/vrmlup.htm

Richard Tilmann, administrator of the Mesh Mart collection of 3-D objects, updates this Web-based newsletter every two weeks with new links to news stories, articles, and tools.

## The Web Goes 3-D

http://www.pcmag.com/iu/features/1519/_
open.htm

*PC Magazine* published this excellent introduction to VRML, coupled with a group review of five world builders and eleven VRML browsers. The only problem is that its focus is on the relatively underpowered VRML 1.0 specification; the more useful 2.0 specification had only just been finalized at time of writing.

## What Is VRML?

http://livedv.com/Whitepapers/VRML.html

This page answers the initial question about VRML's identity but then goes on to whip up some enthusiastic propaganda for the VRML format. (Example: "...the majority of people will only get on line if it works like the real world." Or, in my paraphrase, they'll only go on line if the Web is full of unrealistically lit plastic polygon constructions.) As enthusiastic propaganda goes, it's not bad; the section on possible approaches to keeping VRML bandwidth down is especially interesting. On the other hand, the section on Chinese tourists' instinctively reverent reactions to the interior of Notre Dame is a definite low point.

## QUICKTIME VR

Sometimes there are benefits to using a proprietary format. Even in its early incarnations, QuickTime VR was more stable than VRML browsers, with more predictable performance and appearance—very likely due to its centralized development. Speaking of proprietary, though, perhaps the biggest strike against this format is the requirement to lay out $500 for a specialized, complicated, programmer-oriented, Macintosh-only program if you want to create hyperlinks.

The combination of "unfriendly interface" and "Macintosh-only" seems like a recipe for a poison pill. Nevertheless, many artists and educational multimedia creators have found the combination of natural (rather than artificial) source material and quest-and-turn interface irresistible.

## Apple QuickTime VR Home

http://quicktimevr.apple.com/

The official Web site for QuickTime VR is the place to go for announcements and pointers to new software, including add-ons for third-party software. A large directory of online QTVR examples is hosted here, though it doesn't track all the uses being made of the technology by artists. If you want original QTVR, a directory of savvy and equipment-stocked firms is provided. For those who are roughing it on their own, fewer resources are available. Some important tools are available for downloading, the QuickTime Webmaster's guide gives some help, and the page on how to try to compress a QTVR file for Web distribution is revealing.

☞ A normal movie is defined as a sequential (or linear) series of frames. Internally, QuickTime VR is really nothing more than a non-linear movie; that is, it consists of a series of frames that aren't just sequential. Instead of always playing in one direction (forward in time), the QuickTime VR user can make the frames play in a variety of different directions. Although QuickTime VR's nonlinear movie format has been marketed for the 3-D simulations of virtual reality, it can also be used for very non-VR purposes. For example, rather than panning up or panning left, you could make a directional mouse drag to increase temperature, or tie a knot, or massage a back. Rather than using controls for zooming in or zooming out, you could use them to increase and decrease the metamorphosis of a placid face into a more vehement expression, or to valiently thrust a sword into and out of your opponent's yellow-bellied torso.

## Joel's QTVR Workbook and Notebook

http://solutions.apple.com/pub/quicktime-vr/jcannon/Workbook.html

http://solutions.apple.com/pub/quicktime-vr/jcannon/notebook.html

These pages merely consist of quick jottings about ongoing work, but Joel is the hardest working QuickTime VR fiend around (or, perhaps, *was* the hardest-working QuickTime VR fiend around; there haven't been any entries for a while). But even his jottings are useful to those who want to learn more about the format.

## QuickTime VR Digests

http://206.51.25.106/

This site provides a basic search facility for archived digests of the quicktime-vr mailing lists. It's not set up for browsing, unfortunately, but it's better than nothing.

## QuickTime VR Realities

http://www2.heidsite.com/heidsite/hotmedia/hotmedia0197.html

http://www2.heidsite.com/heidsite/hotmedia/hotmedia0297.html

Here's a practical guide to QuickTime VR creation; it's a two-part series by Jim Heid that combines articles from *Macworld* with directories of related links. The first part focuses on panoramas, starting from choosing a camera and collecting software and moving through the actual panorama shoot. The second part covers the less discussed but arguably more unique QuickTime VR feature, *object movies*. It explains how to create the illusion of revolving objects using photographs or 3-D generation software as source material.

## Sumware QuickTime VR Tools

http://www.home.aone.net.au/sumware/

Sumware produces several utilities for QuickTime VR creators—including PanoMatic, a version of Apple's own Make QTVR Panorama tool, enhanced to support hot spots, tiling, and controls over pan, tilt, and zoom. Pending release at time of writing were VROOM (an object-movie creator) and Quiver (for general QuickTime VR authoring with hot spots).

## www.qtvr.com

http://w3.qtvr.com/qtvr/index.html

The centerpiece of this site is a searchable (and international) database of service bureaus and photographers that specialize in QuickTime VR. In addition, there's also a searchable archive of messages from the QuickTime VR developers mailing list (slightly crippled by lack of timestamps), and somewhat exasperated work notes on

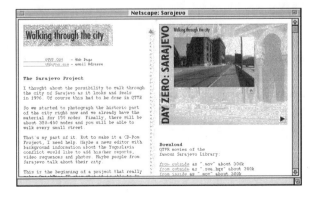

embedding QuickTime VR into Director applications. Just in case you were wondering whether VR panoramas were somehow restricted to showing KPT Bryce-like dream landscapes, check out the beautifully crafted photo of the Sarajevo Library interior.

## OTHER INTERACTIVE 3-D FORMATS

Anyone who's dreaming William Gibson dreams is bound to be galled by VRML's and QuickTime VR's glaring lacks. A number of companies have decided that, unhampered by the delays of standardization (or the even worse delays of working in a large corporation), they might be the ones to reach that appealing goal.

As usual with niche formats on the Web, in this group you may find just the mix of features you're looking for but always at the price of audience share. Not only will your audience need to download the format's browser plug-ins or helper applications, but also will have to be running the right type of computer.

### Meme
**http://www.immersive.com/**

Immersive Systems's Meme is a Windows-only virtual reality system designed for interactivity and multiuser networking. It includes client software and an interpreted programming language that, in addition to the usual 3-D geometry, handles cross-object communication.

### OLiVR
**http://www.olivr.com/**

OLiVR uses fractal wavelet compression to produce streaming, progressively rendered 3-D views that allow early user interaction. You may be playing with something a little fuzzy, but at least you can play with it. The format is like QuickTime VR in emphasizing photographic sources rather than computer-generated images. In fact, Apple has announced plans to incorporate the OLiVR work into future releases of QuickTime VR. Plug-ins are free for downloading from the OLiVR site. The company has announced that an authoring system will eventually be sold for $500, and an OLiVR server (not

needed, but it "adds major back-end functionality") for $2,500. At time of writing, a Windows 95 beta of the authoring system was downloadable at no charge.

Although streaming sounds like a good way to reduce reliance on fast connections, early versions of the OLiVR software have sometimes been less conservative with other system resources: The download page for the alpha version of the Macintosh plug-in suggested using 100M of virtual memory!

### The Panoramic Imaging Zone
**http://ourworld.compuserve.com/homepages/radia/**

The Panoramic Imaging Zone is a general site for the sort of simulated full-surround views you can get with QuickTime VR or Surround Video. It includes a few pointers to panoramic cameras, tips on making a panoramic photo-montage, book and mailing list recommendations, and brief summaries of existing software.

### RealVR
**http://www.rlspace.com/**

RealSpace's RealVR format combines VRML 2.0, QTVR-style panoramic views and rotating objects, and embedded video and audio. The interface quality is still a little ragged, but performance is reasonable even across a modem—all in all, it's a promising start at bringing together the different strands of virtual reality. Browser plug-in players are available for Windows 95, Windows NT, and Power Macintosh systems. A Macintosh-only program

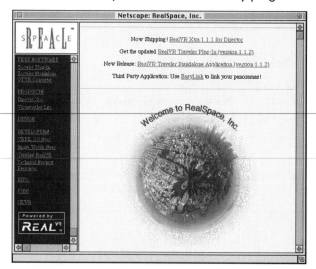

that converts QuickTime VR files to RealVR format is also available for downloading. At time of writing, the only commercial product sold by RealSpace is a bundle, combining a panorama-stitching program with a Director Xtra that embeds RealVR scenes into Shockwave applications; the price is $300.

## SmoothMove and Real World Navigation

**http://www.smoothmove.com/**

SmoothMove is a format developed by Infinite Pictures Inc. Somewhat confusingly, the Windows 95 product line that views and creates SmoothMove files is called Real World Navigation. Like QuickTime VR, SmoothMove supports photograph-based panoramas, hot spots, and foreground objects; video and audio actions can be built into the scenes. Stand-alone authoring tools are available, as well as export plug-ins for 3D Studio Max, LightWave 3D, and Macromedia Director. Free off-line viewers and browser plug-ins can be downloaded from the site.

## Surround Video

**http://www.bdiamond.com/surround/surround.htm**

Created by Black Diamond Consulting, Surround Video specializes in displaying 360° panoramic images or video. Clearly a competitor to the "rotating camera" aspect of QuickTime VR (although not to the "revolving object" aspect), Surround Video has been incorporated into an ActiveX control by Microsoft, and the product's files can be embedded into Microsoft's Office 97 documents. The Surround Video SDK includes a panoramic image editor, a Windows API for programmers, a link editor for hot spots, and the ActiveX control. You can download a copy for evaluation and register it for $500. A Netscape plug-in is also available for downloading.

# CHAPTER 8
# SERVER-SIDE SCRIPTS, EXTENDED HTML, AND FORMS

IN THIS CHAPTER, WE'LL BEGIN TO EXPLORE THE FURTHER REACHES OF WEB-SITE PROGRAMMING. YOU'LL SEE SOME WAYS TO EXTEND THE CAPABILITIES OF YOUR SITE, WAYS THAT RELY ON "REAL" PROGRAMMING RATHER THAN THE SIMPLER HTML TAGS AND DESIGN CONCEPTS THAT HAVE BEEN THE SUBJECT OF EARLIER CHAPTERS. WE'LL COVER THE FOLLOWING TOPICS:

☞ **CGI Scripting.**
Common Gateway Interface scripts that let Web browsers send and receive dynamic documents to and from Web servers. We'll look at some CGI basics and explore sites where you can learn more.

☞ **Server-Side Includes and APIs.**
These alternatives to CGI have their own advantages and demerits.

☞ **Extended HTML.**
Microsoft and Netscape have their own special HTML extensions, and third-party developers such as HeiTML are coming up with even more ways to stretch HTML.

☞ **Forms.**
Forms are the most common type of CGI scripts on Web pages. Find out about form design and form tags here.

☞ **Perl and Other Programming Languages.**
You can use your favorite language to create forms and other CGIs. If you don't have a favorite, Perl is one that you might want to explore.

☞ **Cookies.**
These amusingly named bits of info can be exchanged between client and server computers behind the scenes, with many implications for Web-based businesses and users.

**THE THRILL OF HAVING** the world's data at our fingertips still resonates, but we want more. Static media is just not enough for a generation raised on live action and audio, not to mention interactive chat systems and computer games. We want to interact with media and breathe life into it somehow. That's what the whole idea of adding programmed segments—live data feeds, interactive forms, animated sequences, and more—is all about.

Incorporating programs into your Web mix allows you to create sophisticated sites with added appeal to customers, clients, and casual Web-surfers. Do you have access to corporate intranets? Experiment with using programming links to integrate Internet sites more closely with applications that may eventually be delivered via the Intranet, or even over the Internet itself. Among the business applications for scripts are interactive database applications, or even server-based programs in any software genre that can be accessed by remote users over the Net.

Of course, most server-side programming is much more mundane. Typical server-side operations include adding fields that allow users to return information to the server via forms, and automatically sending visitors to another page.

Web designers who want their sites to more closely resemble broadcast media will find that the client-based programming options have persuasive advantages for multimedia data delivery. Take a look at Chapter 9 for information about Java, JavaScript, VBScript, and ActiveX. In that chapter you'll also find several examples of how client-side "push" technology is evolving as a way to deliver news and entertainment to the online community. The same client-side methods used by companies such as PointCast to facilitate their commercial applications can be adapted to perform many of the same functions now relegated to server-side programs, with security and performance advantages.

Server-based scripts can be written in any programming language that works with HTML. Some people prefer the efficiency of C, C++, and other compiled languages; others (particularly those with a UNIX programming background) like to work in interpreted languages such as Perl. Still others want to let professional programmers do the hard work, and themselves write nothing more than the HTML code that calls up prewritten scripts from the server. Canned scripts are available today that carry out all of the most typical server-side operations. The archives listed in this chapter offer code that you can adapt to enhance your own pages.

## CGI SCRIPTING

Common Gateway Interface (CGI) scripting is the most basic form of programming used within HTML documents. Gateway programs let client-computer users send requests for data or activity to servers, and the servers to return the requested information to the client. The CGI script interacts with the client, the browser, and the server at various stages of this communications transaction.

You've already seen dozens of CGI scripts in action as you've browsed the Web—from visitor counters to search engines that query databases of URLs held on a Web server, to interactive forms that send your information to a server for storage and compilation in a database. The simplest CGI script is probably the ubiquitous feedback request, which allows users to automatically compose and send e-mail via a Web page. This e-mail is sent to the recipient through a link to a CGI mail gateway. Unlike static Web documents retrieved from the server, CGI programs are executed in real time upon retrieval.

Calls to CGI scripts use simple commands that are no more complex than other advanced HTML operations. Since the calls are fairly easy to write (or, more accurately, to cut and paste) you don't have to be a "real" programmer to make use of basic CGI scripting. Here's a sample CGI script that creates a test page with the traditional "Hello, world!" message:

```
#!/usr/bin/perl
print "Content-type:text/html\n\n";
print <<EndOfHTML;
<html><head><title>Test Page</
    title></head>
<body>
<h2>Hello, world!</h2>
</body></html>
EndOfHTML
;
```

Programs that carry out most of the familiar CGI functions are available in online repositories for free, or as shareware. Your Web-authoring package probably has a few built in, such as the mailto command. Collections of advanced commercial CGI programs are also available or can be commissioned. Just put these ready-made programs in an appropriate directory on your server, and follow the accompanying instructions to add the appropriate code to your HTML pages and to ensure that your server is set up correctly to use them.

☞ If you are using a server at an ISP rather than at your site, you may have to check in with the ISP's management about proper CGI etiquette. Some service providers limit the use of bandwidth-robbing CGIs on their system, particularly if you're adding CGIs to a site that generates heavy traffic. On the other hand, most ISPs have their own collection of acceptable CGIs that you can call up, taking a load off the server that vends your Web pages and avoiding a fuss.

## CGI Tutorials

Want to learn how to write your own CGIs, or at least find out how to reuse the ones others have written? Try one of the following tutorials. Also, check out the sections on "Perl Tutorials" and "Forms"; related instructional sites can be found there.

### CGI Programming Class
**http://www59.metronet.com/dev/class/**
If you know HTML but don't have any programming experience, Jacqueline Hamilton's CGI class will teach you the basics of CGI scripting in Perl. All of the lessons are on line here, and the "teacher" is available via e-mail if you have additional questions about the text, sample code, and exercises provided.

### The CGI Resource Index
**http://www.cgi-resources.com/**
One-stop CGI shopping is on line at this Web site, which brings together tutorials, archives, magazine articles, and even job ads for CGI experts. Browse and get educated.

### CGI Resources
**http://www.halcyon.com/sanford/cgi/index.html**
This index to CGI resources includes tutorials for beginning and intermediate CGI programmers. There's a full explanation of how CGIs work, a Perl CGI tutorial, and some advanced material as well.

### CGI Scripting with AppleScript
**http://www.comvista.com/net/www/lessons/CGIScripts.html**
Those writing CGIs for Mac Web servers such as WebSTAR (the featured system here) can follow this nicely written tutorial by Jon Wiederspan. It includes AppleScript samples that you can modify to perform various functions on your server.

### CGI Scripting with Perl
**http://www-genome.wi.mit.edu/ftp/pub/software/WWW/cgi_docs.html**
This site provides a tutorial on using CGI scripts and a Perl module to call up Perl 5.* programs. Explanations about working with Perl under Windows NT and other non-UNIX platforms are included.

# SECURITY CONCERNS IN SERVER-SIDE SCRIPTING

Whenever you allow users access to your server, whether it's with CGIs or the SSI and API methods discussed in this chapter, you could be setting yourself up for disaster. What sort of disaster? Well, the worst a greenhorn could do is accidentally crash your server. Determined hackers, on the other hand, know all about the weaknesses inherent in set-ups that use server-side scripting, particularly CGIs—and can exploit those weaknesses to do such things as e-mailing themselves your password files.

There are steps you can take to protect yourself. (Note that many of the following cautions use terms specific to UNIX, but they apply to all HTTP servers.)

- **Disable the exec option**. Don't let hackers activate this option to take control of your server. Disable the exec option on any directory that you want to keep fully secure.

- **Watch out for eval statements**. Perl and other languages provide an eval command that lets users construct a string that can be executed by the interpreter. This can set up unauthorized access to your server, or simply disrupt it.

- **Watch out for misbehaving clients**. Clients with evil in mind can confuse your script with special characters that it can't interpret. Voilà—unauthorized access. Or at least a confused, dysfunctional server.

- **Turn off SSIs for script directories**. Tricky clients can use Server Side Includes to gain entry by piggybacking on scripts that directly output whatever they've been sent.

- **On UNIX servers, don't run your Web server as root**. This is an "easy in" for a hacker.

- **Limit access to the server**. Keep tabs on anyone who has a login account to the Web server. Limit the number of login accounts, and be sure to delete old, unused accounts promptly.

- **Improve your password protection**. Make sure that all login accounts are protected with strong passwords, not easy-to-guess ones like "password" or the name of the local baseball team. If you need to give a password temporarily to a consultant or temporary user, make sure that you change the password when the job is done.

- **Unload extra Net services**. Get rid of FTP daemons, finger, and any other leftover Internet daemons that don't have to share your Web server.

- **Get rid of unneeded shells and interpreters**. For example, if you don't run Perl CGI scripts, you don't need to keep the Perl interpreter on the server.

- **Keep your eyes open**. Log files are useful, but only if you actually look at them now and again. Check yours (both Web and system) frequently for signs of attempted entry, such as someone trying several different passwords.

- **Set permissions**. If your server package or OS provides built-in protection for sensitive files, folders, and programs, use it. Setting it up may be a hassle, but it could save you days of wasted time later on. You'll want to pay particular attention to any areas where interlopers might access an exec file.

- **Pay attention to physical security**. This is one area that trips up even those who install firewalls and security software. The easiest way to mess with a machine is to do it in person, so establish controls on who has access to your server(s). And make sure that nighttime staffers, assistants, and others know the access rules.

- **Beware of "social engineers."** Contrary to public perception, hackers rely more on sheer brainpower than on secret codes and fancy tools. Posing as a repair technician or new employee, for instance, they may try to get passwords or other useful information over the phone. Make sure everyone in your Web workgroup is careful about the people they talk to, in person or by telephone.

- **Get wise—go client-side**. If you can switch to a client-side way of doing the same thing, *do it*.

For more information about CGI security on UNIX Web servers, see Michael Van Biesbrouck's CGI Security Tutorial at http://www.csclub.uwaterloo.ca/u/mlvanbie/cgisec/

## An Instantaneous Introduction to CGI Scripts and HTML Forms

http://www.cc.ukans.edu/info/forms/forms-intro.html

Complete with line-art illustrations, this primer on creating CGIs is well done. The emphasis is on basic scripts and forms, with examples provided. It's not as hands-on as some of the other tutorials, but the visuals may be very helpful to some readers.

## Introduction to CGI Programming

http://www.usi.utah.edu/bin/cgi-programming/counter.pl/cgi-programming/index.html

If you're starting from scratch with CGI scripting, start here: This carefully written tutorial on CGI scripting will walk you through the process of writing simple CGI calls step by step. This tutorial assumes a basic knowledge of C programming and UNIX.

## NCSA CGI Tutorial

http://hoohoo.ncsa.uiuc.edu/cgi/

It makes sense to start at the NCSA when you're looking for CGI info. Not only does this CGI-centric site include a basic tutorial, it also serves up wide-ranging discussions of security issues and how to handle them, among other related topics. You'll definitely want to peruse the huge library of prewritten CGI scripts in a variety of programming languages.

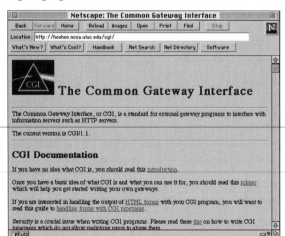

## NYSERNet Workbench: CGI Library

http://nysernet.org/workbench/cgi.html

Offerings here include a CGI primer, an excellent tutorial called "CGI for the Non-Programmer" and a large library of canned CGI scripts in C, Perl, and other languages.

## The WDVL: Common Gateway Interface

http://WWW.Stars.com/Authoring/CGI/

Not only does this site provide an advanced look at CGI scripting, it's got a pretty snazzy interface to boot. Tutorials here explain the basics of CGI creation and give examples of using such scripts to your advantage.

## Web Engineer's Toolbox: CGI Library

http://lightsphere.com/cgi/

More CGIs for your use are stored here, all written in Perl.

## Windows CGI Interface

http://website.ora.com/wsdocs/32demo/windows-cgi.html

For Windows 95 and Windows NT users, this tutorial provides a platform-specific introduction to CGI use and creation. There's an emphasis on Visual Basic CGIs, of course. It was created especially for users of the WebSite server, but the lessons within are generic.

## The World Famous Guestbook and CGI Shop

**http://www.lpage.com/**

Examples and tutorials abound at this interactive site for would-be CGI programmers. You can grab free source code for a guestbook, and check out the instructional offerings as well.

## CGI LIBRARIES

Quite a few commercial packages are available that will simplify creating custom CGI scripts. Easier still is leveraging on scripting that's already been done by another programmer! To find up-to-date libraries of CGI programs that you can call up with your Web pages, as well as related files of use to CGI programmers, see the libraries attached to some of the tutorials referenced in the preceding section. Also, check out the following sites on a regular basis.

## cgic: An ANSI C Library for CGI

**http://www.boutell.com/cgic/**

Experienced C programmers can find samples and tools for building CGIs in C at this library site.

## CGI-Perl Library

**http://WWW.Stars.com/Authoring/CGI/ Process/cgi-lib.html**

Perl programs for use with CGIs from two libraries can be accessed via this page, which also contains very readable instructions on how to download and activate the scripts.

## Jon Wiederspan's CGI Database

**http://host.comvista.com/Internet.tfm**

Along with tons of other resources for Netheads, Com-Vista's Jon Wiederspan has collected a huge number of CGIs and related files here. A special CGI search engine is built into the bottom of the home page.

## libcgi++

**http://www.ncsa.uiuc.edu/People/daman/ cgi++/**

Recently revamped, libcgi++ is a C++ class library that decodes CGI-encoded data and allows other applications to use it. Any program that requires CGI input (typically through an HTML form) can use the functionality provided by the classes in libcgi++.

## Mac Chat CGIs

**http://www.starnine.com/development/ extendingwebstar/chat.html**

StarNine keeps a list of CGI options for adding chat and Web-news capabilities to your Mac-based Web server. Many of the plug-ins are specifically for StarNine's Web-STAR servers, but some are available in other flavors as well (including PC and UNIX possibilities).

## NCSA CGI Library

**ftp://ftp.ncsa.uiuc.edu/Web/httpd/UNIX/ncsa_ httpd/cgi/**

CGI scripts in several programming languages are archived here, courtesy of the NCSA. The archive is not updated as often as Selena Sol's, however (see description coming up).

## Resources for CGI Scripting

http://www.web-nation.com/village/
scripts.htm

An exhaustive catalog of CGI script archives and related resources can be found here, courtesy of Web Nation. A wide variety of languages is represented in the choices available, including Ada95 (!), AppleScript, Perl, C/C++, and Visual Basic.

## The Scripts Home

http://www.virtualcenter.com/scripts2/

With one of the most stylish interfaces I've seen lately, this site collects and gives away CGIs and Perl scripts for use on your Web server.

## Selena Sol's Public Domain CGI Script Archive

http://www.eff.org/~erict/Scripts/

Everything here is free of charge for noncommercial users, and quite a selection there is! Sol also provides a discussion forum where you can post and answer questions about the finer points of scripting. This archive has long been an invaluable resource for many a Web programmer, thanks not only to its nicely maintained selection — but also to the fact that Sol personally ensures that everything here is legal for reuse.

## Teleport CGI Library

http://www.bluewaterp.com/support/
webweave/cgi/

Thanks to the crotchety reviews, this collection is fun to visit *and* to pillage. You can't beat that for a great combination.

## UNIX CGI Scripts

http://www-swiss.ai.mit.edu/wtr/cgi-unix.html

Philip Greenspun's collection of UNIX CGI samples is nicely put together and fairly extensive. It includes some simple Perl tools for tweaking your own scripts.

## OTHER CGI RESOURCES

You can extend your CGI knowledge with these sites and products.

## The CGI Book Web Site

http://www.cgibook.com/

William Weinman's *The CGI Book* is probably the most complete printed reference for CGI programmers. He has built a companion Web site that includes tutorials, tips, and downloadable code to complement the volume. (And, of course, to convince you to go out and buy it— which is not a bad idea!) There's also an interactive Web forum for CGI discussion attached.

## CGI Newsgroup

comp.infosystems.www.authoring.cgi

If you're doing Web-specific CGI programming, here's the place to talk with your peers. The **www.authoring.cgi** newsgroup covers the development of CGI scripts as they relate to Web-page authoring. Possible subjects include discussion of how-to's on handling the results of forms, generating images on the fly, and putting together other interactive Web offerings.

## CGI-Perl List

cgi-perl-request@webstorm.com

Send a message with body "info" to the above address for a FAQ and subscription information. This mailing list is for people interested in using Perl to write CGI scripts.

## FastCGI

**http://www.fastcgi.com/**

Compared to CGIs, Web server APIs increase application performance. However, they are vendor-specific, complex, language-dependent, difficult to maintain, prone to security risks, and inherently unstable. (For more about APIs, see the next section.) FastCGI is an extension of current CGI technology that adds increased security and makes servers operate more efficiently as they deliver dynamic pages to clients. According to its vendor, Open Market, FastCGI delivers performance increases that match those realized with APIs, but without the compromises mentioned. Oh, and it's free, too.

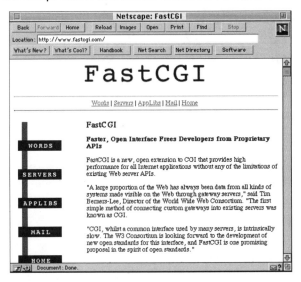

## htmlscript

**http://www.volant.com/**

Created by Htmlscript Corp., the htmlscript package runs on Web servers and operates as a preprocessor for CGIs by interpreting HTML and htmlscript tags. This product reads the htmlscript document and looks for tags that it recognizes; all other tags are output as they are found. It is browser and server independent, and can be installed by ISPs that want to support its extended library of commands to enhance clients' Web sites. HTML and htmlscript code are used the same way and can be mixed in a Web document.

## Scripts Mailing List

**http://www.virtualcenter.com/scripts2/**

Sponsored by The Scripts Home archive (see listing in section on "CGI Libraries"), the Scripts Mailing List is an interactive forum for sharing ideas about building better interactive Perl CGIs. Traffic is fairly light, and there are many experts available through the list who can help you improve your CGIs.

## Understanding the SGML Declaration

**http://luna.bearnet.com/sgmldecl/index.html**

If you plan to delve deeply into CGI programming, you may want to bookmark this guide. It's written in outline form.

☞ **CGI, SSI, and API Info for Windows 95 and NT**

Despite the growing popularity of the Windows platform for Web servers, there's a severe shortage of canned server-side programs for Windows. That's because Microsoft has not given much official support to CGIs and SSIs, and its ISAPI API for the Internet Information Server is still fairly new. Instead, the company is pushing ActiveX scripting as a client-side alternative.

If a server-based approach is better for your application, however, or if you want to leverage on your company's investment in existing applications written as Object Linking and Embedding (OLE) servers, Microsoft is beginning to offer some options. Take a look at "Options for Creating Dynamic Web Content" at http://www.microsoft.com/syspro/technet/boes/bo/iiserver/technote/iiscgi.htm for a very thorough introduction to CGI, SSI, and API programming as it applies to Windows Web servers.

# Server Side Includes and APIs

You can also make your server deliver dynamic documents to Web clients via two competing methodologies: Server Side Includes (SSIs) and Application Programming Interface (API) programming. Server commands using the SSI system can be embedded directly in an HTML document, but the method as a whole is underwhelming, according to most experts. API extensions run right on the server and provide more powerful possibilities than either SSI or CGI, without taxing the processor as much.

Unfortunately, APIs can also be a server-management nightmare. They plug into your Web server software. That's great in terms of extending the capabilities of your current package, but changing APIs means digging into server code. And if you screw up your server code, you've got major problems. Canned API extensions can be obtained, of course, and your server-software vendor should be able to point you in the right direction.

Because SSIs rely on server command lines within HTML documents, it's easier and faster to change how these particular bells and whistles are used.

## A Word About Security

Like CGIs, SSI and API programming can have serious security drawbacks. These methods allow users to make calls to your server, calls that can either be misused by knowledgeable crackers or allow clueless bumblers to do damage. Many systems operators simply forbid the use of SSIs on their machines. (You're probably aware of this issue if you use an Internet Service Provider to get server space.) In fact, the default setting on your Web server software almost surely locks out the use of SSIs. At the time of this writing, Microsoft's Internet Information Server package supports only the #INCLUDE SSI directive, for example. You may be able to override this setting—but do you really want to?

See the earlier section, "Server-Side Scripting and Security," for more details about security when using any server-side technology within HTML documents.

## Comparing the Options

Here's a table developed by Robert B. Denny to help Webmasters visualize the benefits and trade-offs of CGIs, SSIs, and APIs.

| Factor | SSI | CGI | API |
|---|---|---|---|
| Flexibility and power | Low | High | High |
| Level of required developer expertise | Low | Medium | High |
| Development and testing time needed | Low | Medium | High |
| Adaptability to change | High | High | Low |
| Life-cycle cost | Low | Medium | High |
| Operational risk | Low | Low | High |
| CPU overhead* | High | High | Low |

\* Exclusive of the work required to generate the content; called "null overhead."

If you'd like to see how he came up with these value judgments or explore the differences between the three server-side technologies in greater depth, read Denny's article "SSI, CGI or API? Choosing the Right Tool for the Job" in *Web Site Professional* at http://solo.dc3.com/wsdocs/extending.html

Just remember this warning as you make your plans: If security is an important goal to you, nothing's foolproof—except keeping users as far from your server's inner workings as possible.

## SSI Format

What does an SSI look like? Here's an example borrowed from the JemTek SSI Tutorial listed in the "SSI Tutorials and Info" section. The script:

```
Hello from us at <!--#echo
var="SERVER_NAME"--> to you at <!--
#echo
var="REMOTE_HOST"-->.
The local date is <!--#echo
      var="DATE_LOCAL"-->.
You are viewing the file <!--#echo
      var="DOCUMENT_NAME"--> which
      is
<!--#fsize file="tutorial.htm"-->
      in size and was last modified
      on <!--#echo
var="LAST_MODIFIED"-->.
```

The output:

```
Hello from us at www.camtech.com.au
to you at ip-pdx07-09.teleport.com.
The local date is Saturday, 05-Apr-
      97 00:01:52 CST.
You are viewing the file
      tutorial.htm which is 12K in
      size and was last modified
on Monday, 05-Aug-96 16:51:32.
```

SSI directives are formatted as SGML/HTML comments. If the document is delivered to the client unparsed, the directives will not be displayed. All directives have the same format:

```
<!--#command argument="value"-->
```

Table 8.1 lists SSI directives. You can quickly see how some of these could be misused. In the table, the value "relative path" specifies a file relative to the directory of the current document; a "virtual path" is a pathname relative to the base directory of the Web server.

**Table 8.1: SSI Directives**

| Command | Argument | Value | Description |
|---------|----------|-------|-------------|
| config | errmsg | "error message" | Sets message sent to client, and server log if an error occurs while parsing the document. |
| | sizefmt | "bytes abbrev" | Formats display of file sizes to either bytes or kilobytes/megabytes. |
| | timefmt | "conversion string" | Formats display of dates. (Identical to UNIX strftime conversion specification.) |
| echo | var | "environment variable" | Displays the value of an environment variable. |
| exec | cgi | "virtual path" | Executes CGI script or program, with all subsequent output included in the document. |
| | cmd | "command" | Executes shell command, script, or program, with all subsequent output included in the document. |
| fsize | file | "relative path" | Prints size of a file. |
| | virtual | "virtual path" | Prints size of a file. |
| flastmod | file | "relative path" | Prints date when file was last modified. |
| | virtual | "virtual path" | Prints date when file was last modified. |
| include | file | "relative path" | Inserts text of another file. |
| | virtual | "virtual path" | Inserts text of another file. |

# SSI ARCHIVES

Looking for a specific SSI script that can perform a needed function? If you're sure you want to go that route, check with your vendor first about server-software-specific SSIs.

SSIs are often free for the grabbing. If you like an SSI-based function that you see in use, ask the site's Webmaster if it's okay to reuse it yourself. There are also a few archival sites for SSIs; following is my list of a few favorites. Other archives are attached to the tutorials listed later in this section.

> ☞ I do urge caution when experimenting with SSIs, however, both because of the security concerns discussed previously and because of the potential for really bollixing up your server. This is one area where discussing your options with an experienced SSI programmer, perhaps via a newsgroup or other online forum, will be time well spent.

## New Breed Software's Server Side Includes

http://zippy.sonoma.edu/kendrick/nbs/unix/www/ssi/

Many free SSIs can be snatched up here, most of them written specifically for UNIX-based Web servers.

## Mac SSIs

http://www.starnine.com/development/extendingwebstar.html#ssi

If you're running a Mac Web server, you're in luck: The WebSTAR folks have provided a long list of Mac-OS SSIs. Each entry has a short description and a hyperlink back to the vendor or repository. The offerings include a number of commercial extensions.

## SSI TUTORIALS AND INFO

Want to know more about using and choosing SSIs? Here are the Web sites where the experts hang out, and some guides and introductions to this useful Web scripting technology.

## ApacheWeek Guide to SSIs

http://www.apacheweek.com/features/ssi

Although it does feature some info on Apache-specific guidelines for using and making SSIs, this article is a good introduction for users of any UNIX server. And since *all* Web servers are at their bottom line about UNIX, that probably means you.

## JemTek SSI Tutorial

http://www.jemtek.com.au/jemtek/ssi/tutorial.htm

Easy as pie to read and featuring tables of all the SSI directives and commands, this tutorial from an Australian computing firm covers all the basics.

## Server Side Includes

http://www.webcom.com/~webcom/help/inc/include.shtml

Web Communications clears up the mystery of what *shtml* means in a URL: It indicates that SSI calls are in use to deliver dynamic documents. The SSI intro at this site explains how to write SSI server calls. There's also a guide to SGML (server-parsed HTML) comments and proper syntax.

## NCSA HTTPd Server Side Includes

http://hoohoo.ncsa.uiuc.edu/docs/tutorials/includes.html

Tutorial segments graded from beginner to advanced are offered up here for your use, accompanied by links to a collection of canned SSIs.

## NCSA HTTPd Discussion

http://union.ncsa.uiuc.edu/HyperNews/get/www/ncsa-httpd.html

SSIs and other aspects of dynamic HTTP (HTTPd) are on tap here, with high-level questions receiving high-level answers. You can simply read through the material on the Web page, or you can subscribe to be notified via e-mail whenever a topic of interest has been addressed. See the bottom of the main Web page for subscription information.

## Server Side Includes FAQ

http://www.ecn.purdue.edu:80/ecn/FAQ/html/httpd/ssincl/

Purdue University supports this (fairly short) FAQ. One of its most useful bits is a list of known HTTPd bugs found in SSIs.

## SSI+ 2.0

http://webquest.questar.com/reference/ssi/ssi+20ref.sht

Look here for information about SSI+, a standard in the making for extended SSI functionality. The information is provided by Questar, whose WebQuest95 server for Windows 95 features built-in support for SSI+. Templates and such are also available here.

## Setup & Configuration for SSIs

http://www.sigma.net/tdunn/ssi/setup.html

Tim Dunn's single-page guide to configuring your server to work with SSIs is as well written as they come. Links from here lead to information about specific types of SSIs.

## API RESOURCES

All API routines are both server- and software-specific, so you'll need to contact your hardware and software vendors to get hooked up with the appropriate resources there. You may also want to look for independent Web archives dedicated to your equipment, including the libraries listed below.

API programming can be tricky, and many Web designers choose to outsource the job. It may pay off to find someone with a very thorough knowledge of both the server and software in question, not to mention the standards issues that may crop up (see the *MacWEEK* article referenced below for some examples of these). If you plan to add an off-the-shelf API to your server mix, take all appropriate precautions. Starting on a test server is a must.

Now here are a few more sources of API info, including sites that cover the three major APIs.

## "Stalking the Deadly 404: Avoiding Broken Link Headaches With ISAPI Filters"

http://www.avatarmag.com/columns/serverside/default.htm

This article from *Avatar* magazine is a tutorial in disguise. Learn how to create and apply ISAPI filters that can carry out a variety of functions to help your server work more efficiently.

## Java API Overview

http://javasite.bme.hu/doc/java/platform/APIOverview.html

This page presents an overview of the various Java APIs, each of which is specifically tailored for a particular task or function, including the JEEVES API for servers. Specifications and code are linked in where applicable. (See also the Java Beans sidebar.)

### Java Beans Alert

One API that's getting more attention than the rest is JavaSoft's recently released Java Beans specification. The Java Beans APIs define a portable, platform-neutral set of APIs for software components. Components created with Java Beans APIs can be plugged into other component architectures, including OpenDoc (if it still exists by the time you read this), Microsoft's OLE/COM/ActiveX architecture, and LiveConnect from Netscape. According to JavaSoft, it will be easy to use application builders to link up a string of discrete Java Beans into an application or active document. For example, you could use an application-builder package with a simple point-and-click interface to drag a live data feed into an HTML page.

For developers, the best news is that Sun is working overtime to build bridges between Java Beans and other component architectures, such as ActiveX. That means you'll be able to take existing objects and convert them into Java Beans with a minimum of fuss.

And although Java Beans can be used to build any type of application, not just server-side stuff, this reusable component architecture seems particularly well suited for the fast-paced world of Web-site creation, where you want to add and extend functionality without having to do a lot of custom programming.

Want to know more about Java Beans? See the long list of Java resources in Chapter 9, and also take a look at JavaSoft's info at http://splash.javasoft.com/beans/

### Java Servlets

**http://jeeves.javasoft.com/products/java-server/**

Here you can learn more about Java Servlets, which are server-side applications created with Java's JEEVES API.

### JEEVES Mailing List

**http://jeeves.javasoft.com/products/java-server/interest.shtml**

JavaSoft sponsors an official mailing list for those interested in server-side API programming with JEEVES. List subscription information is available at this Web address.

### Mac API Controversy

**http://www.macweek.com/mw_1037/gw_web_api.html**

Standards are just one of the problems caused by the proliferation of APIs as substitutes for CGIs, SSIs, and client-side scripting. The well-written story from *MacWEEK* at this site will give you a heads-up on how these conflicts are manifesting themselves on Mac Web servers. And believe me, the problems described here are only multiplied in the PC and UNIX worlds.

### The Netscape Server API

**http://live.netscape.com/newsref/std/server_api.html**

This lengthy paper presents full documentation for Netscape's NSAPI API, including a comparison of NSAPI programming and CGI scripting, a technology backgrounder, and all the basic info you'll need to grasp the concepts of NSAPI.

### Vijay Mukhi's API Tutorials

**http://www.neca.com/~vmis/**

Who would've thought it possible? API tutorials written in plain English! Well, actually, Mukhi's English is anything but plain—here's a sample: "The second glitch is that computer technology has begun to move faster than anything else… which brings us to the amorphous blob of the Internet and the vast scaffold of the World Wide Web." Not only will you learn a lot here, but you'll get a kick out of it, too. Server-side API creation and use is explained for Microsoft's Internet Information Server (ISAPI), Java server (JEEVES), and Netscape server (NSAPI).

## "Taking the Splash: Diving Into ISAPI Programming"

**http://www.microsoft.com/mind/0197/ isapi.htm**

In this article, written for Microsoft's Interactive Developers program, author Christian Gross presents an introduction to server-side programming using ISAPI. It's written with an intermediate-to-advanced audience in mind, and includes a basic tutorial, code samples to work with, and high-quality information on all aspects of the process. There's also a linked-in list of Windows-based servers that accept ISAPI filters and extensions.

## W3C Libwww Library

**http://18.23.0.23/pub/WWW/Library/**

Libwww is an extensible API written in C that you can use as a basis for your own projects. Certain copyright restrictions do apply and are described in this library. A new API written in Java is expected in late 1997. Like other World Wide Web Consortium projects, Libwww is intended for experimental use and for extending the reach of existing technologies.

# EXTENDED HTML

Some Web-page creators prefer to keep all their jazzy programming within HTML. That may mean stretching it like a rubber band, and running the risk of alienating users of one browser or another.

Regardless of what you may think of their disregard for standard HTML, both Microsoft and Netscape have certainly had success with the HTML extensions they've developed—look at Netscape's frames extensions, for example. Like frames, some HTML extensions have acquired such a following among Web designers that their eventual inclusion in future HTML standards is inevitable. Others are somewhat more annoying, as is any Web elements reliant on HTML tags that don't have industry-wide support.

Regardless, employing some form of extended HTML generally represents a more user-friendly so-

lution than implementing Java—at least for typical, small applications such as counters. Browsers will generally skip over HTML segments that they don't understand, but will crash when confronted with Java, JavaScript, and ActiveX segments.

The HTML Tag Reference (Table 3.1) presented in Chapter 3 lists and explains these exclusive tags—at least the ones that are current this week. Chapter 3 also includes a catalog of Web sites concerned with current and proposed HTML standards, including HTML 4.0 and Cascading Style Sheets info.

In addition to Netscape's and Microsoft's gifts, several companies have come up with extended HTML software of their own. Check out HeiTML (Extended Interactive HTML) in the resource listing that follows; you'll find some of the possible permutations of HTML coding "on the edge." And don't fail to look into htmlscript, which is discussed in the earlier CGI section.

## EXTENDED HTML RESOURCES

### BrowserCaps

**http://www.browsercaps.com/**

Tests and comparisons are posted here about whose browser supports what, and how well. So before you

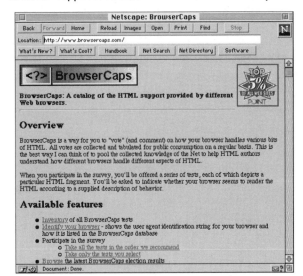

implement that nifty new tag, at least take the time to check in here to see which browsers can handle it, and find out what will happen if it's encountered by one that doesn't. Alternative methods for achieving the same effects on different systems are also discussed here at BrowserCaps. And for the purists among us, the latest *standard* HTML specifications can be downloaded.

### Browser-Optimized Content Delivery
http://www.webreference.holowww.com/dev/automatic.html

All sorts of possibilities for extending basic HTML pages are presented by Andrew B. King at this interesting (if smallish) site. Although some of the material could use a bit of updating, it's a reasonably good guide to those tags beloved of Netscape and/or Microsoft alone.

### HeiTML Introduction
http://www.h-e-i.de/stheitml/

The HTML-based HeiTML programming language from the German firm H.E.I. GmbH is one of several commercial HTML-helpers. This CGI alternative lets Web designers add interactivity to their HTML documents via extensions to HTML that reside on the server. Uses include SQL database applications, animations, dynamic forms, windowing, and more.

The H.E.I. site provides a tutorial, a library of extensions, and many examples of how HeiTML can be used to enhance Web pages without using client-side operations that may tax some users' machines or browsers. How well does it work? Well, I have to admit that the pseudoanimations and windowing displayed here function quite well, even in older versions of Navigator. In fact, the site is cluttered as can be with all sorts of Java-made contraptions! The company's work hasn't received much publicity stateside, and I think that's a shame. So go take a look already.

### WebTechs HTML Test Service
http://www.webtechs.com/

Not sure if the HTML code you've just written is "street legal"? WebTechs, a Texas consulting firm, provides a free code-validation service at this site. Included are browser-specific checking and testing of code written to meet evolving HTML specs. You can also click a link here that explains how to set up a validation service of your own on a local server.

## HTML-RELATED MAILING LISTS

If you want to be more in the know about HTML 4.0 and beyond, browser-specific HTML tags, and advanced HTML issues in general, try one of these mailing lists on for size.

---

### BUILDING BETTER PAGES

## A SOAPBOX SPEECH ABOUT BROWSER-SPECIFIC PROGRAMMING

With the browser market in flux and dozens of new technologies nipping at the heels of this month's top contenders, it's truly tempting to pick your favorite browser and exploit it to the hilt.

It's also a really bad idea. And here's why:

**1** Browser-specific programming defeats the purpose of making documents available to the largest number of people possible. It alienates visitors instead of bringing them closer.

**2** It ties Web builders to a specific developer—which could have major repercussions if that vendor's

fortunes fall because of all-too familiar catastrophes such as a highly publicized security blunder, a major public-relations gaffe, or a suddenly successful competitor.

**3** *Nice* Web designers make their sites as universally useful as possible. You can be nice and still create a thing of beauty.

Now I'll get down off my soapbox, and hope that you listened to my plea.

### www-html

**www-html-request@w3.org**

Send an e-mail message to this address with subject "Subscribe" to join this public mailing list for technical discussion about enhancing the HTML standard and building systems that support HTML. It is explicitly intended for the collaborative design of new systems, software, protocols, and documentation of use to the HTML developer community.

### www-style

**www-style@w3.org**

To join this mailing list, send e-mail message with subject "Subscribe." It's for focused, technical discussion on Web Style Sheets only (see Chapter 3 for more on this topic).

# FORMS

Life without forms to fill in is a tempting prospect, but alas, it's already too late to realize this dream on the Web. Forms now abound, ranging from one- or two-line multiple-choice quickies to long, involved questionnaires. And I'll have to grudgingly accept that they frequently serve a useful purpose.

For example, if you are collecting data that will be stored and tabulated in a database—survey responses, for example—it's important to control the form of the data that is entered. By asking users to choose from a limited set of acceptable answers, you'll avoid data discrepancies caused by errant responses.

Forms are the type of CGI script you'll notice most frequently on the Web. Why?

- Forms are tremendously easy to create, from writing the HTML tags to grabbing the ubiquitous prefabricated pieces.

- Most people who are trying their hand at CGI scripting for the first time do so by building a simple form.

- There is a need for forms in almost every area of business, education, and research—from subscription forms to questionnaires.

- Forms provide a simple interface for identifying and interacting with visitors to your site.

Mail-based feedback also has its place, but when you need more than just a subjective comment, forms are the answer. They can help you ensure that respondents answer all of the questions in a series, because you can build in a requirement for full completion before the form is accepted. And finally, forms can provide a simple mechanism for building in feedback about your site, and ensuring that you get the message.

## FORM FUNDAMENTALS

Forms are simple programs that can be written into an HTML script with the FORM tag. You can have more than one form per page, although you can't nest one form inside another. You can put pretty much anything else inside a form, though—from graphics to layout commands.

When users answer your form's questions, their answers become part of a *query* that's sent to a *query server*. When the user hits the Submit button at the end of the form, the data typed in the form is returned to the query server with an ACTION value. The ACTION lets the server know which program it should call up in order to process the data. The server calls up the program, the program chews on the data, and the program then returns the appropriate information in response to the answer or set of answers sent.

## HOW FORMS ARE PROCESSED

When a form is submitted, the names of each INPUT/TEXTAREA/OPTION list are matched up and separated by equal symbols (=). These pairs are strung together using ampersands (&), and spaces are replaced with plus signs (+). For example:

field1=value1&field2=value+2

You have two choices for dealing with this string in your form: the GET method and the POST method.

- **The GET method** appends the string of information to the ACTION URL. The number of characters that can be passed to the script or program specified by the action URL is limited. The GET method places all data on the URL, and it's transmitted to the CGI script via command-line parameters. GET is faster than the POST method; however, because the information is visible in the URL, the GET method is less secure.

- **The POST method** treats the string as standard input and sends it to the CGI script identified. POST is the preferred approach for working with forms because the URL remains unchanged.

With enough programming skills, you can use pretty much any sort of data-gathering tools that you might program into a stand-alone software program. Forms can include a wide variety of entry options, including multiple-choice questions, yes/no questions, fill-in-the-blank questions, and even questions that display the typed answer on screen as a series of asterisks (as for a password entry). Menus of options or scroll-through lists are fairly simple to concoct, as are a vast variety of button styles—from the familiar radio buttons and check boxes to the all-important Reset and Submit buttons.

Forms input can also be linked to coordinates within an inline image, much like an advanced imagemap (for instance, "Click the donkey to choose Democrat; click the elephant to choose Republican; click the gorilla to choose None of the Above").

HTML 3.0 supports the following kinds of fields:

- Simple text fields
- Multiline text fields
- Radio buttons
- Check boxes
- Range controls (sliders or knobs)
- Single-choice menus
- Multiple-choice menus
- Scribble-on image
- File widgets for attaching files to forms
- Submit buttons for sending form contents to the server
- Reset buttons for resetting fields to their initial values
- Hidden fields for bookkeeping information

Future revisions to HTML will probably add support for audio fields, multiple-row database tables, and the ability to extend multiline text fields to support a range of other data types in addition to plain text. Client-side scripts will provide the means to constrain field values and to add new field types. These features are not yet supported in HTML itself, however. Until they are, form-builders who need them will have to look to extended HTML tags, server-side programs, or client-side enhancements such as those using JavaScript or VBScript.

> Building forms is a great way for novices to start honing their Web programming skills. If you haven't programmed before but intend to learn, take advantage of all the prefab parts out there—but also take a look at the source code as you go, and try out some of the tutorials listed below. There are automated ways to create forms, but before you take the lazy way out, see if you can dig just deep enough to find out how canned components do the job.

## CODE EXAMPLES

What does a form look like in code? Take a look at the following example. It's a simple questionnaire that uses the INPUT element for basic text fields, radio buttons, check boxes, and Submit and Reset buttons. The TEXTAREA field is used to add a multiline text-entry field. The form fields are laid out with several paragraph elements and an unordered list. Notice the use of the NAME attribute to name each field.

Here's the code:

```
<TITLE>Sample Questionnaire</TITLE>
<H1>Sample Questionnaire</H1>
<P>Please fill out this
    questionnaire:
<FORM METHOD=post ACTION="http://
    www.hal.com/sample">
<P>Your name: <input name="name"
    size="48">
<P><input name="male" type=radio>
    Male
<P><input name="female"
    type=radio>Female
  Number in family: <input
    name="family" type=int>
<P>Cities in which you maintain a
    residence:
<UL PLAIN>
<LI><input name="city"
    type=checkbox
    value="portland"> Portland
<LI><input name="city"
    type=checkbox
    value="vancouver"> Vancouver
<LI><input name="city"
    type=checkbox
    value="seattle"> Seattle
<LI><input name="city"
    type=checkbox
    value="redmond"> Redmond
<LI><input name="city"
    type=checkbox
    value="sanfran"> San
    Francisco
<LI><input name="city"
    type=checkbox
```

```
    value="sanjose"> San Jose
<LI>Others <textarea name="other"
    cols=48 rows=4></textarea>
</UL>
<P>Nickname: <INPUT NAME="nickname"
    size ="42">
<P>Thank you for responding to this
    questionnaire. We will use the
    results to improve our Web
    services for employees in your
    area.
<P><INPUT TYPE=SUBMIT> <INPUT
    TYPE=RESET>
</FORM>
```

Like the example above, all forms must be enclosed within a FORM element on your HTML page. There can be several forms in a single document, but the FORM element can't be nested.

The browser is responsible for handling the *input focus* (determining which field will currently get keyboard input). Generally users will be able to advance from answer to answer with the Tab and Shift+Tab keys.

Many platforms have existing conventions for forms; for example, the Enter (or Return) key is typically used to submit the completed form. This standard defines and requires support for the HTTP access protocol only. Under any protocol, the submitted contents of the form logically consist of a list of NAME/VALUE pairs, in which the names are given by the NAME attributes of the various fields in the FORM. Each field is normally given a distinct name. Several radio buttons can share the same name, since this is how you specify that they belong to the same control group—but only one button in the group can be selected at any time.

Table 8.2 lists the allowed attributes within a FORM element.

**Table 8.2: Permitted Attributes for FORM**

| FORM Attribute | Definition |
| --- | --- |
| ACTION | A URL that specifies the location to which the form contents are submitted to elicit a response. If ACTION is missing, the URL for the document itself is assumed. Data submission varies according to the access protocol of the URL, and the values of the METHOD and ENCTYPE attributes. |
| METHOD | Specifies variations in protocol used to send form contents. Currently (at this writing) restricted to GET (the default) or POST. The attribute was introduced to inform user agents about supported HTTP methods. |
| ENCTYPE | Specifies the MIME content type to be used for encoding the form contents. Defaults to the string *application/x-www-form-urlencoded*. |
| SCRIPT | Can be used to give a URL for a script. Scripting language and interface with the user agent are not part of the HTML 3.0 specification. |

## HOW FORM CONTENT IS PROCESSED

Unfortunately, HTML 3.0 doesn't provide direct support for constraining the values entered into text fields, or for derived fields whose values are calculated from the values of other fields. Rather than extending the markup to support these features, HTML 3.0 provides a means for associating the form with a script. Support for scripts is not required, however, and the HTML 3.0 specification doesn't cover the scripting languages or the details of their interface with the user agent. This doesn't really make it easy to use add-on scripts, but you may well feel forced to do so because of HTML's current limitations—not to mention the slowness with which changes are being made to the HTML standard. If your data needs require it, you can use multiple-choice forms to constrain input in a different way.

The SCRIPT attribute of the FORM element specifies the script. The user agent downloads the script and interprets it locally. Scripts can handle a variety of messages for individual fields, as well as for the form as a whole. These messages correspond to events, such as

- Entering or leaving the form
- A field's gaining or losing the input focus
- Mouse clicks-and-drags over a field
- Keyboard events

Scripts can examine and set properties of fields. They can also examine a small set of standard user-agent properties, such as the user's name, the time of day, the type of user agent, and so on.

Scripts can't do anything that might jeopardize the user or the host machine. Scripts can't send messages over the network, for example, or read or write files. Library calls are restricted to a very small and well-defined set. These precautions are necessary for untrusted scripts. In the future, script interpreters will likely offer a wider application programming interface to trusted scripts. (The trust issue is resolved by the presence of a digital signature from a trusted third party.) Since trusted signature technology has not yet gained wide acceptance, this feature hasn't been heavily implemented.

## FORMS TUTORIALS AND EDITORS

Building forms is actually one of the easiest things you can do with HTML, once you've mastered its basic page-description commands. With the help of the sites listed here, you'll be surprised at how quickly your skills will grow.

### Web Diner
**http://www.webdiner.com/annexe/forms/**
Here at the Web Diner, you can explore basic forms programming in its most frequently encountered guises: the forms-based menu and the interactive guestbook.

You fill out the sample form on the first page, and then examine how its components were assembled.

![Netscape: Web Diner Menu browser window showing the sample form for the Web Diner Forms Tutorial, with links for Form with Graphics, Sample Guestbook, Sample Guestbook with Graphics, and the Web Diner Menu featuring seating and ordering options]

## Carlos's FORMS Tutorial
**http://robot0.ge.uiuc.edu/~carlosp/cs317/cft.html**

This is short, simple, and spare—just the basics on how to construct and test the most common types of forms. Carlos Pero presents a series of brief, easily digested tutorials that include the code, appropriate visuals, and opinions on what works best. The tutorial concludes with a self-test.

## Fill-Out Forms Tutorial

**http://www.wnmu.edu/html/forms1.htm**

This two-part forms tutorial with source code walks you through the process of creating and testing forms, including commonly used tags, templates, and server information. It's kindly provided on line by the Web Development Team at Western New Mexico University.

### TESTING YOUR FORMS

When you're first building your Web site, chances are that your company's setup may also be in transition. If you need to test your newly minted forms with a server that's ready to roll, two options are available.

The following ACTION lines access query servers that will spit back what your prototype forms submit, with name/value pairs coded and itemized if all goes as planned.

If you are using METHOD="POST", use

```
ACTION="http://
hoohoo.ncsa.uiuc.edu/htbin-post/
post-query"
```

For METHOD="GET", use

```
ACTION="http://
hoohoo.ncsa.uiuc.edu/htbin/query"
```

Of course, ultimately you'll want to have your own test facilities on site for a variety of Web-page features that need regular investigation. Not many of us have an "extra" server hanging around, however, so it's wonderful that the NCSA has seen fit to let the computing public glom onto one of the agency's spares on occasion.

> ☞ If you use the GET method in your form and send more than 200 or so bytes at once to the test server, it may crash and burn. The test server passes your data to a form-processing module via a shell command line that can't handle much input. The NCSA probably won't appreciate it much if you crash its test servers, and you really don't want to do it to yourself either, if you can help it.

### PERL TUTORIALS

Planning to roll your own CGI programs? Perl is a popular choice for this sort of modular programming because of its flexible syntax and ease of use—popular enough, in fact, that I decided to do some of your homework for you. (If you prefer to work in another language, use Lycos or another search engine to look for other language-specific resources.)

Created by ace programmer Larry Wall, Perl (for Practical Extraction and Report Language) was originally devised for processing text. These sites offer many Perl-related resources, as well as tutorials and FAQs.

## The Perl Data Structures Cookbook

**http://brie.cs.sfu.ca/doc/perl-cookbook.html**

This "cookbook" is for programmers who want to build up complex data structures in Perl 5. Unlike the rest of the tutorial pages described in this section, this is not a beginner's resource.

## The Perl Language Home Page

**http://www.perl.com/perl/index.html**

Many Perl fans consider this Web site to be the definitive resource for programmers. It's certainly the most complete. Software, news, ideas, bug reports, Perl training sources, information on setting up a support contract for your site, tons of links … it's all here. There's also a link to a selection of Perl-related mailing lists. These are an excellent, lower-traffic alternative to the Perl discussion on Usenet; they're well suited to those who want to work with a "support group" as they learn new skills.

## Perl Tutorial

**http://agora.leeds.ac.uk/Perl/start.html**

Nik Silver's Perl tutorial differs from the dozen or so others floating around the Net. This one is Web-focused and lets you work through a series of examples. Silver assumes a knowledge of basic UNIX, but other than that his tutorial is a good starting place, especially for beginners. You can walk through everything on the Web, or download the whole thing via FTP from this page.

## Take Ten Minutes to Learn Perl

**http://www.geocities.com/SiliconValley/7331/ten_perl.html**

This tutorial from GeoCities is almost ridiculously easy. And they're not kidding about the "ten minutes" part, either—these examples are short, simple, and eminently masterable.

### PERL ARCHIVES

Along with archives housed at several of the other sites listed in this section, following are two places to find canned Perl scripts.

## SRA Perl Archive

**ftp://sra.co.jp/pub/lang/perl/**

At this Japanese FTP site sponsored by Software Research Associates, a huge number of Perl scripts have quietly taken up residence. You'll find scripts for DOS, Mac, Windows, Windows 95, and Windows NT.

## University of Florida Perl Archive

**http://www.cis.ufl.edu/perl/**

Strictly for the uninitiated, this site's first page provides an in-depth intro to Perl: who created it, what it is, how you can use it, and why you might want to make it part of your programming repertoire. Both beginners and advanced users will derive value from the copious archives here. Items on offer include tutorials, the latest version of Perl, and even a "Perl fun" page.

## OTHER PERL RESOURCES

Once you know how to do a bit of programming in Perl, you may want to explore some of the language's finer points. The following sites hold a mix of resources that include articles, theoretical papers, Perl archives, and links to all sorts of related information around the Web.

### O'Reilly's Perl Page

**http://www.ora.com/info/perl/**

O'Reilly's—the publishing home of Perl guru and author Randal Schwartz—has placed selections from two of its justifiably famous Perl books here. So not only can you see camels on these pages, you can try out some online tutorials, purchase books, and send yourself to related pages.

### The PERL5 Manual

**http://www.its.unimelb.edu.au/manuals/perl5/perl.html**

For ease of access, this manual for version 5 of Perl has been divided into several short sections. There's a built-in search function, too.

### The Perl Institute

**http://www.perl.org/**

Sort of a cross between a support group for Perl junkies and a research organization, The Perl Institute is a membership organization formed to encourage the development and spread of the language.

### The Perl Journal

**http://orwant.www.media.mit.edu/the_perl_journal/**

You know that a language is avidly loved when it merits its own magazine. This journal is a fine source of up-to-the-minute info. It's for subscribers only; check the site to find out more. Incidentally, it's also the funniest programming publication you'll ever read... I don't know what it is about the crowd that's attracted to Perl, but they certainly are a whimsical bunch!

### Perl on Usenet

**comp.lang.perl.misc**

Need to get a quick answer to a Perl question? Post it to this Usenet group and watch the responses roll in.

### Perl Versus...

**http://www.perl.org/CPAN/doc/FMTEYEWTK/versus/index.html**

Want to know how Perl stacks up against alternative scripting languages like tcl, Python, and Java? Several writers give their (mostly pro-Perl) perspectives here, contributing to the ongoing argument about which language is superior to the rest.

### Powered by Perl Pages

**http://www.infohiway.com/~jk/perl/perlindex.html**

This site collects everything from research papers on ways to use Perl with HTML, to software specs, to Perl subroutines, to musings on how to fix broken pipes (the online sort, of course).

### The Programmer's Source: Perl Resources

**http://infoweb.magi.com/~steve/perl.html**

A long list of resources collected here features FAQs, scripts, tips, tutorials, pointers to various archives, and even a little humor.

### The Taming of the Camel

**http://www.cre.canon.co.uk/~neilb/perl/VHLL/slide01.html**

Perl creator Larry Wall dreamed up this combination lecture and slide show (sideshow?) to illustrate how his ideas about programming mutated into Perl as we know it today. Sample scenes are titled "Humble(?)" and "My Irrationalities." You may enjoy the history lesson, and it will give you a different perspective on the language.

# COOKIES

**cookie** *n, pl.* **cookies**   A handle, transaction ID, or other token of agreement between cooperating programs.

"I give him a packet, he gives me back a cookie."

Computer Jargon 3.0

Cookies are controversial data-snacks that are sent to your browser by Web servers. Unless you have changed its settings to refuse cookies, your browser will accept the data; check its length, expiration date, path and domain name; and save it. Cookies aren't programs—after all, they can't exceed 400 bytes in length. But every time you return to a Web site where you were given a cookie, your browser will have a little chat with the server.

What might they be talking about? Well, the benign applications of cookies might include user-set preferences that govern how a dynamic Web page appears when you drop in, or storing of shopping choices that you made previously at an online catalog site. Other, not necessarily benign applications include tracking your movements since your last visit, grabbing information about your computer hardware and software, and more. In fact, Microsoft and some other vendors have taken serious heat about the potential for mischief or invasion of privacy with certain cookies they've promulgated. Published reports even hinted that Microsoft, in an effort to ferret out software pirates, was considering using an Explorer cookie that would return a list of users' hard-drive contents to the company. Just in case you missed the ensuing melee, the company had to duck major bad publicity over this rumor.

As a Web designer, you may be excited about the potential of cookies for delivering customized data to your visitors. You may also want to use cookie technology to track the way people move around on your site—it's a way of taking a survey about what's interesting without bothering the end-users. Cookies can tell one user from another, so you can use them to deliver accurate information to potential advertisers about how many actual people are visiting your pages, as opposed to how many mouse clicks occurred.

That's all neat stuff, but the involuntary aspect of cookies irks privacy advocates and many Web surfers—and rightfully so. Your computer, your ISP, your online movements, and your shopping preferences are not necessarily subjects that you want to discuss with anyone else.

Microsoft has finally put the ability to refuse cookies into the Internet Explorer browser; Netscape Navigator was definitely ahead of its competitor on this one. If many users exercise this choice, cookies won't be particularly useful to you as a page designer. That being the case, you might wish to explore other data-gathering alternatives. Consider initiating voluntary surveys, looking at log files, and distributing counters to various parts of your site to track the number of hits per section.

For something with such potential power as a marketing tool, cookies are actually small and simple. For example, the syntax of the cookie sent to the client by the server under Netscape looks like this:

```
Set-Cookie: NAME=VALUE;
expires=DATE;
path=PATH; domain=DOMAIN_NAME;
secure
```

## COOKIE-RELATED RESOURCES

Simply because they're scintillatingly controversial as well as potentially useful, be sure to browse a few of these sites about cookies. Afterward, you'll be immune to media hysterics, as well as more informed about the real issues involved.

### Andy's Netscape HTTP Cookie Notes
**http://www.illuminatus.com/cookie.fcgi**
Personably presented, this site explains what cookies are, how they're used by browser developers and others, and ways you can get in on the action as a Web site developer. With an accent on the Mac, Andy includes everything from cookie basics to source code. Links lead out to dozens of other cookie-related sites, including security alerts, cookie archives, and official documentation.

### Malcolm's Guide to Persistent Cookies

http://www.emf.net/~mal/
cookiesinfo.html

This very thoughtful and thorough page treats not just the technical side of cookies, but the ethical questions involved with using them. It's got a great set of links for cookie bakers, too.

### Night of the Living Cookies

http://www.hidaho.com/cookies/cookie.txt

Bill Dortch's free script for mucking about with persistent cookies, including tools for killing "vampire cookies that won't die," is archived here.

### Persistent Client State Cookie Specification

http://www.netscape.com/newsref/std/
cookie_spec.html

Netscape's preliminary specifications for persistent cookies are posted at this site.

### Robert Brooks' Cookie Taste Test

http://www.geocities.com/SoHo/4535/
cookie.html

Whose Web sites have cookies? What do these goodies look like, and what do they do? Brooks knows, and he and his faithful informants will answer your questions here.

### Web Marketing

http://www.newtonline.com/HOMEPG/
market.html

Who loves cookies? If we're talking silicon chips, not chocolate chips, the only folks who really, *really* love cookies are online salespeople. Take a look here to see what sorts of promises are being made (and kept) to corporations that want to use cookie technology to learn more about you, the consumer. It's proof positive that not all of the fears about cookies are unwarranted.

Do cookies make you queasy? You're not alone. The Electronic Privacy Information Center (EPIC), the Center for Media Education (CME), and the Consumer Project on Technology (CPT) are all urging people concerned about privacy on the Internet to communicate with the Internet Engineering Task Force (IETC) in support of a proposal already under consideration. This ruling will control the misuse of cookies and give Internet users better command over the collection and use of personal information. Please note that this proposal would not spell the end of cookies but will provide a set of ethical guidelines for the legitimate use of cookies and the data they gather. Some online advertisers are already lobbying against the proposal, so if you want to counter *their* pleas to the IETF, now's the time. For more information and a form letter, see

    EPIC: http://www.epic.org
    CME: http://tap.epn.org/cme/
    CPT: http://www.cptech.org

# CHAPTER 9
# JAVA, JAVASCRIPT, AND ACTIVEX

IN THIS CHAPTER, WE'LL INTRODUCE SOME PROGRAMMING TECHNIQUES THAT ARE SOMEWHAT MORE SOPHISTICATED, INCLUDING THE FOLLOWING:

☞ **Java.**

Sun's Java language has changed the once-static character of Web documents. We'll discuss what it can do for you—and what it can't.

☞ **JavaScript.**

Netscape's JavaScript brings some of Java's functionality to Web design but with less of a learning curve. You can use its scripting tools to automate the process of bringing concepts introduced with Java to work in your HTML pages.

☞ **ActiveX and VBScript.**

ActiveX and VBScript are Microsoft's answer to Java and JavaScript. What's the difference? What are the advantages?

☞ ***Push* Technology.**

We'll get under the hood of the Web's latest buzzword to find out how you can make use of this new information-delivery paradigm.

**NOW THAT YOU'VE HAD** a good look at CGIs, you're well aware of their limitations. Let's be frank: No matter how cleverly you use it, HTML is more akin to a page description language (a la PostScript) than to a full-featured programming language. And that's exactly what HTML is meant to be. Trying to turn into a vehicle for creating animated sequences or interactive options is unfair. This realization led to the introduction of programmed segments embedded within HTML pages in the form of CGIs, SSIs, and API calls.

But servers, too, have limitations. If your server is tied up with delivering an opening screen in which a comet flies across the viewer's field of vision, that comet's going to move at a crawl if more than a few folks are logged on. Worse yet, it could get hopelessly overloaded and crash. And it's not just big files that cause problems. Millions of visitors grabbing the same itty-bitty file by way of a CGI script or other server-based technology can freeze your system just as quickly.

Sun's Java programming language and Netscape's JavaScript, as well as Microsoft's ActiveX, offer you tools for extending Web pages into the realm of true multimedia and real interactivity. These tools also remove the burden from the server of delivering the goods, by letting client computers do the heavy lifting required to deliver dynamic segments. With a modicum of programming expertise, or at least some inspired theft from public-domain sources, Web designers can use these tools to make their sites both more attractive and more functional—and they can do so without straining servers.

You can make these programmed add-ons as complex as any other computer program, although at present Web designers must use caution in exploiting the technology to its fullest. Like forms, frames, and even fancy graphics, programmed segments are not necessarily for general audiences.

They can crash users' computers, leading to annoyance and avoidance.

And although these technologies may technically be supported by the latest browsers, that promise of support is predicated on the availability of plenty of memory on the user side, and by robust technology on the server side as well. Unless your audience is made up of bleeding-edge buyers with high-powered machines, your insistence on pushing the envelope of Web programming may instead push away the very people you want to attract and inform.

That said, there's no doubt that Java, JavaScript, and ActiveX represent the future of the Web. Its a future in which *push* and *pull* technology will play important roles, and in which such programming will be a routine and accepted part of Web site design. So go ahead and experiment, innovate, and attempt what you can—just keep your target audience and its equipment in mind as you do so.

## A CUP O' JAVA

Sun Microsystems has made many contributions to the Internet environment, but none has been as warmly embraced (and hotly debated) as Java. Java is an object oriented programming language, similar to C++. It was not originally developed for Net-based programming—in fact, the mission of the original Java team was to find a way for disparate devices such as game machines and computers to communicate without adding on a jumble of translation devices. Java almost withered on the vine at Sun, but once its applicability to the needs of the then-nascent Internet became clear, the technology adapted so well that it might as well have been tailor-made.

As with any young language, there are still bugs, omissions, and difficulties in standardizing ways of doing things in Java. Nevertheless, many experienced programmers are already enamored of the language. Why? Because Java can be used on a wide

BUILDING BETTER PAGES

## A ROSE BY ANY OTHER NAME...

Want to use Java without driving away your non-Java-using visitors? Here's a simple program by Web programmer/designer/writer Jason Wehling that can cycle through five random images when it encounters a Java-equipped Web browser—but provides one static image (and no crashes) when it is met by an older browser.

```java
import java.awt.*;
import java.applet.*;
import java.net.*;
import java.util.*;
public class HomeImage extends Applet {
        String imageName;
        Image img;
        int imageNum;
        MediaTracker tracker;
        Random randGen;
        public void init() {
        setBackground(Color.white);
        img = null;
        Random randGen = new Random();
        imageNum = Math.abs(randGen.nextInt()%10+1);
        if ((imageNum == 0) || (imageNum == 1)) {
        imageName = "PortlandCity1.gif";
        }
        else if ((imageNum == 2) || (imageNum == 3)) {
        imageName = "PortlandCity2.gif";
        }
        else if ((imageNum == 4) || (imageNum == 5)) {
        imageName = "PortlandCity3.gif";
        }
        else if ((imageNum == 6) || (imageNum == 7)) {
        imageName = "PortlandCity4.gif";
        }
        else if ((imageNum == 8) || (imageNum == 9) || (imageNum ==
10)) {
        imageName = "PortlandCity5.gif";
        }
        else {
```

```
        imageName = "PortlandCity5.gif";
        }
        showStatus("Loading image...");

        img = getImage(getDocumentBase(), imageName);
//      tracker.addImage(img, 1);
//      try {
        //  tracker.waitForID(1);
        //} catch (InterruptedException e) {
        //System.out.println("Error! Image can't load");
        //showStatus("Error while trying to load
image!");
        //}
        }
  public void update(Graphics g) {
        paint(g);
        }
        public void paint(Graphics g) {
        g.drawImage(img, 0, 0, this);
        }
        public void start() {
        repaint();
        }
}
```

This program exemplifies some principles you should keep in mind as you work when you're using Java (or Java-Script or ActiveX, for that matter):

- Don't assume that all visitors will be equipped with software that can handle more than standard HTML.

- Always provide attractive alternate visuals for standard, HTML-only browsers.

- Consider the impact of your design decisions when the results are viewed with both standard-HTML and Java-compliant browsers.

- Avoid the use of Java "alternatives" that come close to insulting the standard HTML-only visitor. For example, stay away from insolent text substitutions for Java animations, such as "You can't see Java applet" or (the worst one I've seen) "Get a real browser!"

variety of computers—it is (or at least it's intended to be) "platform independent." On the Internet, this capability was the key to creating programs usable by any Web surfer whose browser supports Java (marketers call these "Java-enabled" browsers).

Some Java programs are full-featured applications. These are analogous to programs written in any other language, such as Corel Office. Smaller Java applications that are dependent upon browsers or other full-featured programs are called *applets*. Applets are like to plug-ins for browsers; they add some sort of discrete functionality to the larger program.

Applets reside on a server on the Internet, or in a networked environment, where they are compiled into bytecode. Called into action by users (clients) via tags embedded in an HTML document, the applet then carries out its tasks within the client's browser rather than on the server. If a client wants to grab some stock information, its call to the server will bring what's needed to the client computer; that is, both the data and the applet required to view and manipulate it. The applet will actually run its program for data viewing and manipulation on the client computer.

This system lets designers take advantage of client/server computing in the most flexible way possible. For example, it's not necessary for each user to download and store every possible applet to have a specific one available when a Web browser application needs it, because users can access applets dynamically as they interact with servers. Like plug-ins, applets can easily be upgraded and changed with no effect on the viability of client-side technology, as long as advances are supported by browser makers. In addition, servers need not actually run the applications, as they must when CGI programs are called. Indeed, heavy-duty CGI traffic can immobilize a server just when it's needed most. By putting the processing on the client side, Java exploits the increasingly powerful desktop machines in use today.

Which, of course, brings us to the downside of Java. Not all client computers are going to be top-of-the-line, RAM-laden Pentiums, PowerPCs, and workstations. The majority of Internet users are probably somewhat underpowered, and smart Web designers will keep this in mind as they incorporate applets in their Web sites. In fields where institutions are not exactly rolling in dough, such as education, it's unlikely that Java support will reach critical mass anytime soon.

That said, certain functions absolutely demand heavy-duty programming. If your site serves as an advertisement, for example, flash is probably necessary and not at all a luxury. On other sites, Java-enabled features are mere bells and whistles. You'll have to judge the disposition of your particular Java uses and adjust accordingly. It would certainly be wise to provide alternate pages for your non-Java-using visitors.

## A WORD ABOUT JVMs

One other caveat: Java may be hot, but insiders know that it's not "all there" just yet. The culprit: the Java Virtual Machines (JVMs) that reside in the supposedly Java-compliant software.

Unlike other programming languages, Java isn't strictly an interpreted language or a compiled language. It's both—sort of. Compiled languages such as C++ generally execute commands to the computer faster, while interpreted languages retain their English-like syntax until the very moment messages are sent. With Java, commands are first compiled and *then* interpreted by a JVM that resides within the browser or other software program.

Here's the problem: The several JVMs available from various vendors each handle things (or don't...) differently. Moreover, they do not behave identically on Macs, PCs, and UNIX workstations. This can pose major difficulties when your goals include creating standard interface items, including

GUIs for cross-platform software. Netscape is currently hard at work, via its Netscape Internet Foundation Classes library, to create truly workable cross-platform standards utilizing Java. These new Java Foundation Classes should help developers immensely.

If you'd like to know more about the joint JFC efforts currently under way at Netscape and Sun, visit the Netscape DevEdge JFC Central site (Figure 9.1). You'll find it at http://developer.netscape.com/library/ifc/index.html. It's a potent resource for anyone working with Netscape browser or server products, Java, or JavaScript and is particularly essential if you want to keep up with the emerging JFC standard.

What's really exciting about Java isn't its ease of use so much as its portability and the possibility of using it in ways that go far beyond delivering animated pixies to a Web browser. Sun and other companies have grasped the idea that Java programs delivered over a network could take the place of a complex, networked operating system like Macintosh or Windows, and they're pursuing it with a ven-

> If you arent a programmer, please be hype-wise when it comes to Java. Although OOP programming in general does make it possible for rookies to use sophisticated components within their programs, prior programming knowledge is still required to build Java programs. You'll need to understand the rules of syntax and construction, and you'll need to know how to debug and test your creations. Some articles published in the last year have intimated Java is so easy that just about anyone with a little spare time will soon be stringing Java applets together to build database applications and games. But unless "just about anyone" has the added benefit of programming experience, that's not too darn likely.
>
> Without a doubt, however, Java *will* simplify the chores of programmers who use it—just as any other object-oriented system does. And Javas platform-independent ways promise to cut out the time currently spent on painstakingly porting software from one type of computer to another.

geance. Such an "OS" would be endlessly extensible and dynamic, and would allow users to pick the computer platform of their choice and still share applications with others. Internet-based resources could be seamlessly linked to on-site resources.

Unless you like to play beta tester, that's all in the future. But it's something to keep in the back of your mind while you're making decisions about platforms and software. Unless Sun makes a very serious misstep somewhere along the line, I think it's safe to say that Java will maintain an important role in corporate computing—even if it doesn't end up replacing traditional operating systems—for a long time to come.

## JAVA ARCHIVES

Most Java applets have specific purposes, such as calculators and counters. Others provide more specific functions that are intended to be plugged into larger programs. How to compare? The JARS site below is

**Figure 9.1**
Netscape's DevEdge site

one source of reviews. Usenet newsgroups and Java mailing lists can also provide tips.

## Applets From JavaSoft

**http://www.javasoft.com:80/applets/js-applets.html**

Programmers are invited to use and adapt the code in these applets for their own purposes—except, JavaSoft notes, "in programs where a bug could be life-threatening." There's some cool stuff here, but I'd pay attention to that warning if I were you.

## Black Coffee

**http://www.km-cd.com/black_coffee/**

Knowledge Media's searchable accumulation of Java applets, resources, and source code is steadily growing.

## Café del Sol

**http://www.xm.com/cafe/**

JavaSoft isn't the only place at Sun where applets are under construction. This set of snazzy items is from the New Media Marketing Group at Sun, and they are experimental indeed. "The Café del Sol is the first bit of the 'outside world' the applets see," says the anthropomorphising text at the site. "Here they congregate, compile amongst themselves, and finally (with the permission of their creators) venture out amongst the other Kilo-Mega-Gigabytes that whiz by the Café del Sol, Sun Microsystems, and every other place on the Internet."

## The Coffee Shop

**http://patriot.net/~gillette/applets/**

Nifty Java animation stuff, among other items, can be found here. The frames-based interface is a little hard to navigate, but you can always browse through the complete alphabetized catalog.

## Digital Cats' Applet Archive

**http://www.javacats.com/US/search**

Applet categories represented at this site are many; they include Art, Commerce, Desktop Accessory, Educational, Entertainment, and Multimedia.

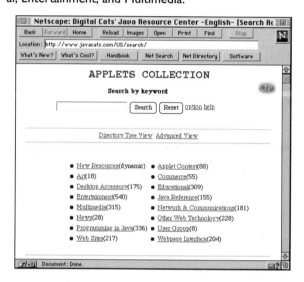

## Gamelan Java Class Libraries

**http://java.developer.com/pages/Gamelan.programming.libraries.html**

Several hundred applets from all Java classes are stored here, with brief descriptions. You'll be able to choose among freeware, shareware, and commercial options. Gamelan's is the best-known and the widest-ranging collection around, particularly when it comes to commercial Java stuff.

## JARS: Java Applet Review Service

**http://www.jars.com/**

JARS is the best source for unadulterated opinions on the efficacy of the newest Java applets. You'll find reviews of an applet here almost as soon as it has been released to the programming public. You can check out the "Top 1%," "Top 5%," and "Top 25%" rankings, or simply browse new and archived reviews of individual products. Be sure to look into the Java news and announcements presented here: JARS avoids the blatant Sun-worship exhibited by certain other sites, and the result is refreshing.

### The Java Boutique

**http://www.j-g.com/java/**

Well over 100 Java applets are available via this snazzy site, along with instructions on how to download them and add them to your HTML pages.

### Java Class Warehouse

**http://www.entmp.org/jcw/**

James Tauber's long-running archive was undergoing a facelift as this book went to press—no doubt James was trying to find room to stuff in everything he's collected. This site is the best place to look for high-level Java stuff.

### Java Gallery

**http://www.sgi.com/Fun/free/java-apps.html**

Everything here is freeware created by those wacky Java nuts at Silicon Graphics Inc. The selection runs toward games and other amusements, including some rather cerebral puzzlers, but among all the playthings await some utilitarian surprises, as well.

### Java URN (User Resource Network)

**http://www.nebulex.com/URN/**

Open up the URN and pour a cupful of Java applets, resources, news, views, and more. This site also has an extensive directory of Java consultants and programmers for hire.

### Yahoo! Applet Index

**http://www.yahoo.com/Computers_and_ Internet/Programming_Languages/Java/ Applets/**

It's a real pain going through the incredibly long list of applets and applet archives and who-knows-what-else that's applet related at this site, but at least it's all here. And I do mean *all*: From automatic "poetry" generators to Java-based MUD clients, this is one complete collection.

## JAVA TUTORIALS

Get smart about programming in Java by perusing and working your way through one or more of these tutorials. Some of them are the sort of thing you'd have to pay several hundred dollars for at your local college, and though you won't get credit for completing the work on line, you'll also have the pleasure of working the examples at your leisure. And you won't have to worry about grades.

### Brewing Java: A Tutorial

**http://sunsite.unc.edu/javafaq/ javatutorial.html**

Elliotte Rusty Harold, the programmer behind Café au Lait (description in the Java Archives section), has created this fine tutorial. Heavily laden with exercises of gradually increasing complexity, this tutorial series eventually became a book, *The Java Developer's Resource* (Prentice Hall). Harold has generously kept it online as well, and continues to update the examples and other content on a monthly basis.

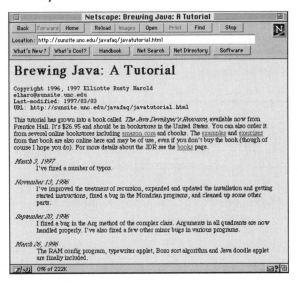

### GSW's Java Tutorial

**http://www.thedswgroup.com/java/tutorial/**

This set of lessons is reminiscent of a college programming class: very organized, very concise, lots of tables, and not much in the way of graphics. Even the section on building GUIs is something less than graphic. On the other hand, with such a lack of distractions it's easy to cover the material quickly.

### The Java Developer: How Do I...?

**http://www.digitalfocus.com/digitalfocus/faq/howdoi.html**

Digital Focus has created a site that's truly useful. All areas of Java development are covered, with the emphasis on real-world applications for Sun's language. Tutorials and advice are available for beginning, intermediate, and advanced Java programmers. Best of all, there's a real spirit of information-sharing in evidence here, facilitated in large part by the Java-based real-time chat areas. Visitors can post questions and get expert replies quickly; many of them pass on their findings through this site.

### The Java Development Environment

**http://www.webconn.com/java/progGuide/tools/index.html**

This tutorial focuses more on tools and processes than on actual programming. How do you manage your project, keep your components organized, and see the job through? Find out here. Caution: The sections on compiling and debugging were still in progress as this book was being written.

### Java Programming

**http://java.developer.com/pages/Gamelan.programming.html**

Hosted by Java developer Gamelan, these pages are frequently updated. They'll be of special interest to anyone who wants to look at Java's "big picture." Internet, intra-

net, and even more advanced applications for Java are well represented. You'll also find information about the latest compilers and add-ons for Java programming.

### Sluuuurp... Java!

**http://www.neca.com/~vmis/java.html**

If you prefer your toil spiced with humor, this beginner's tutorial is for you. As author Vijay Muhki says, it offers "the first few sips of Java (seasoned not to burn your tongue)." Instead of 100-line code examples, you can work this tutorial line by line—definitely a boon for first-time programmers. It's even available in French and Spanish. There are links to lots of useful Java resources, all chosen for their value to the absolute amateur.

### Writing Java Programs

**http://java.sun.com/doc/programmer.html**

This is Sun's official Java tutorial. It walks you through applet basics, explains all the Java terms, serves up all the documentation you can eat, and then hooks you up to more caffeinated resources than you ever dreamed possible.

## JAVA DEVELOPMENT TOOLS

Integrated Development Environments (IDEs), compilers, and debuggers seem to be cropping up at a dizzying rate. Hmmm... wasn't it just last week when every story on Java was full of complaints about the lack of professional-quality tools for programmers? What follows is a woefully incomplete selection, because at the rate these tools are now being released, there's no way to keep up. For news and reviews about new offerings in this product category, check *JavaWorld* and the other online publications referenced later under "More Java Resources."

### Café

**http://cafe.symantec.com/**

Symantec Corp.'s Café is a developer's suite for Java, and is available for the Macintosh as well as for Windows 95 and Windows NT.

## Diva for Java

**http://www.qoi.com/javaside.html#download**

This set of tools for Java is from Quintessential Objects. Formerly known as Javaside, it's a favorite among programmers who were early Java adopters. The latest version (a beta of which was available here at press time) will also edit, compile, and test Perl and HTML files.

## Java Grinder

**http://www.tpex.com/**

Another Java development option for Windows and Windows NT is the Java Grinder from the Paradigm Exchange. It offers point-and-click access to the Sun Java Development Kit in a seamless production environment, with a graphical interface to make your work easier.

## JFactory

**http://www.roguewave.com/products/ java.html**

JFactory is Rogue Wave's cross-platform Java IDE. Also available at the company's site is a variety of other Java programming tools, such as JChart for adding dynamic charts to Java-enhanced pages.

## JWidgets

**http://www.qbss.com/internet/jwidgets.html**

JWidgets complements your IDE by providing common, business-oriented Java-language widgets. These plug-in components can help you build good-looking, intuitive user interfaces, and would be time consuming to create by hand.

## Kalimantan

**http://www.dstc.edu.au/projects/kalimantan/**

Australia's contribution to the Java IDE race is Kalimintan, formerly known as Espresso before the trademark police zapped its sponsors at the Distributed Systems Technology Centre. This offering has been tested on Solaris 2.4 and up for UNIX, and on Windows 95. And the price for the beta is right: free, at least for now.

## KAWA

**http://www.tek-tools.com/kawa/**

The Kawa Java IDE from Tek-Tools Inc. advertises itself as "simple, yet powerful." Tek-Tools is also known for following JavaSoft's JDK (Java Development Kit) development cycle very closely, which means that updated versions of the IDE are delivered rapidly on the heels of a new JDK release. Evaluation copies can be downloaded from the Web site. This one is for Windows and Windows NT only.

## Pizza Compiler

**http://wwwipd.ira.uka.de/~pizza/**

This high-speed compiler hails from Germany and is not for Java per se, but rather for a subset thereof. Pizza compiles programs to ordinary Java bytecode and interfaces with existing Java code, while retaining the broad compatibility of Java. And after you've upgraded to Pizza, you can continue to use all of the old Java libraries as well as your own past code. And it's free!

## Project Percolate

**http://fairfax2.laser.net/~jsmall/percolate.html**

Project Percolate is about bringing together links to lots of Java freeware for programmers, and also about collecting assorted Java-related links. It's definitely a cheapskate's paradise.

## Waking Up the Web

**http://www.pcmag.com/features/1511/ java.htm**

This story from *PC Magazine*'s online version compares and reviews several IDEs as well as the Java Development Kit.

## MORE JAVA RESOURCES

These sites are mostly for Java pros: places to get the latest gossip, follow links to related sites and archives, and discuss developments in the programming field.

## Digital Espresso

**http://www.mentorsoft.com/DE/**

Too busy making applets to bother with all those Java newsgroups and mailing lists? Then stop in here for a taste of Digital Espresso, a weekly Web-based newsletter that brings together the biggest stories from all the forums out there. The editors at Digital Espresso sort through the dross, spam, fluff, and flames so you don't have to.

### Java at Sun

**http://java.sun.com/**

Sun offers Java news, Java views, and an ever-increasing suite of Java-related software here at the company's own site. Available for download are Sun's complete Java Development Kit (JDK). Including software for compiling, debugging, and otherwise fine-tuning Java applets and programs, the JDK will be of interest to anyone who wants to create highly complex Java programs. You'll also find software for creating Java Beans components, which are fully cross-platform; and links to Java drivers, compilers, and debuggers for a variety of platforms; and much more. Sun is, of course, the ultimate source for "official" Java pronouncements and releases.

### The Java Developer

**http://www.digitalfocus.com/digitalfocus/faq/**

This *Dr. Dobbs Journal*-affiliated site features news and views from hard-core programmers. Most of these folks can be heard whining regularly about how JavaSoft is putting the frills into Java before fixing some basic bugs. They're probably right. This site also provides a link to a chat room where you can discuss your Java joys and troubles in real time.

### Java Developer Connection

**http://developer.javasoft.com/developer/index.html**

This JavaSoft-sponsored group is rather like an online users group, and so it's a good conduit for official news, API info, and tips. Registration is free. Benefits include some online training options, technical support, and product discounts. Occasionally there are even free goodies for members, not to mention early access to beta wares and an inside line on new developments.

### Java Jolt

**http://netday.iworld.com/devforum/javajolt.html**

Get your bleeding-edge fix every Friday from this *NetDay* column, which gets the news out about Sun's machinations as well as third-party moves.

### Java Message Exchange

**http://porthos.phoenixat.com/~warreng/WWWBoard/wwwboard.html**

There's plenty of give-and-take on this Web-based discussion board for Java developers. Even newbies might pick up a clue or two, although most of the posts are full of arcane acronyms. You can include code in your message to get comments from others.

### Java Newsgroups

**comp.lang.java**
**alt.www.hotjava**

Serious developers can often be found griping (and sometimes even helping one another) on these newsgroups.

### JavaSoft's Mailing Lists

**http://www.javasoft.com:80/mail/index.html**

Several employees at JavaSoft are sponsoring mailing lists that cover specific Java issues for the developer community. Check in here for the latest selection.

### Java Users Groups

**http://sunsite.unc.edu/javafaq/usergroups.html**

The Web isn't the only place to find out how to program with Java. You can also join fellow enthusiasts from your local area in an actual face-to-face meeting. This regularly updated list of Java users groups, organized by city and country, is worldwide.

## JavaWorld

http://www.javaworld.com/

Computer publisher IDG puts out this Web-zine for "the Java community" (an odd turn of phrase if there ever was one). It regularly features Java tips and tricks, news about new Java-related software, and reasonably unbiased reviews. The practical articles on how to accomplish specific goals with Java are the best part of this publication, if not the most fun—that role would have to go to the industry gossip section of the magazine.

After enjoying the relative impartiality of JavaWorld, you get quite a jolt when you visit its sister publication *NC World* at the same site. *NC World* covers the emerging network computer concept with a breathlessness reminiscent of early Mac magazines.

## Javology

http://www.javology.com/javology/

This online newsletter is available on the Web or by subscription. It's heavy on "breaking news," and also carries profiles of the leading lights of Java programming and reasonably in-depth examinations of Java-related technological advances.

## Making Sense of Java

http://reality.sgi.com/shiffman/Java-QA.html

There's been a lot of hyperbole tossed around on the topic of Java. Silicon Graphics's Hank Schiffman takes on the hype here in a Q&A format and sensibly goes about busting some common Java myths. It's well worth a visit if you're feeling even the least bit confused.

## Online Magazine

http://www.online-magazine.com//index.htm

With the Java-heavy interface to prove it, this magazine is on top of the Java development scene. Its offerings include archived reviews in addition to current articles. Of course, the content goes far beyond Java.

## Programming, Utilities, and Bytecode

http://www.surinam.net/java/util.htm

This is a simple pointer list to some Java programming resources, several of which aren't referenced elsewhere.

## Soup's Up

http://www.phoenixat.com/~warreng/soup.html

This Java e-zine is on the boosterish side—enjoy, if you can. It includes copious links to resources, software, and sites of interest. There are Java samples in actual use here that you can observe and study; some of them will knock your socks off.

## Squatt

http://web.ukonline.co.uk/Members/ge.jones/Squatt/SquattHome.htm

This self-described "Java/JavaScript Netzine" takes a user's-eye view of the Java scene, via a funky interface and a very British perspective. Step-by-step tutorials are included, as are links and downloads aplenty.

## TeamJava's Links

http://teamjava.com/links/#scripts

Constantly updated and heavy on stuff for advanced Java programmers, the menu here includes tools, tips, code, and cutting-edge exploration.

👉 **JAVA-COMPLIANT BROWSERS**
**Which browsers include support for applets written in Sun's Java language? As of this writing, here's the complete list.**

- **HotJava, JavaSoft (Sun Microsystems)**
- **Netscape Navigator 2.0 and later (Netscape Corp.)**
- **Internet Explorer 2.0 and later (Microsoft Corp.)**
- **Spyglass Mosaic (Spyglass)**
- **Power Browser (Oracle Corp.)**
- **WebExplorer (IBM)**

# JAVASCRIPT

JavaScript is modeled on the Java language, but it's not the same thing. That's an important point to make, and one that has unfortunately been lost in the publicity frenzy swirling around both technologies.

Java is a complete programming language that can be used to build word processing programs, database software, and anything else that you might imagine, far beyond little applets that carry out Web functions. Java features static typing and strong type-checking, and utilizes a compile-time system of classes that are built by declarations.

JavaScript, on the other hand, revolves around an instance-based object model. (Don't worry if this technical language means nothing to you—all of these terms get full explanations on the sites listed in this section.) It's a run-time system with a limited number of data types, each of which represents a numeric, Boolean, or string value. It does support the majority of Javas expression syntax and control-flow constructs, but Java is more exacting and programmable than JavaScript.

Basically, JavaScript requires less skill and knowledge from a programmer. For example, although JavaScript does support functions, which can be properties of objects, the functions don't have special declarative requirements.

So what, exactly, is the relationship between the two? JavaScript's built-in functions and syntax are borrowed from its older, wiser cousin. (In fact, Netscape licensed Java from Sun specifically for this purpose.) But JavaScript was never intended for building office-productivity software or emulating an operating system. It was designed specifically to run between the <SCRIPT> and </SCRIPT> tags in HTML documents—nothing more.

In fact, JavaScript is wholly dependent on Netscape Navigator for execution. Its sole purpose in life is extending the capabilities of Web designers by allowing them to use JavaScripts programmable API to build events, objects, and actions that can operate in a cross-platform environment.

As the name implies, this is a scripted language; scripted languages are interpreted languages. That means JavaScript routes around the compiling step that's required with Java. That doesn't make the scripts run any faster, but it does make life easier for programmers—because everything looks more or less like English until the moment of truth when the code is sent to the client computer.

Another benefit is that JavaScript, while nowhere near as flexible and extensive as Java, is much, much easier to learn than Java. This is especially important for those with no previous experience in object-oriented programming (or in programming at all, for that matter). Most of the events and functions needed to build programs delivered on a Web site, from mouse clicks to pop-up windows, are available as modular sets of code that you can plug in to your own framework. All you need to do as a programmer is design the way the modules fit together to carry out your task, and figure out how to call up your creation from within an HTML document. In other words, JavaScript automates the programming process. And if you don't write code just for the joy of it, automation is definitely a point in JavaScript's favor.

Unlike Java, JavaScript insulates you from class issues. Despite that fact, it's got enough juice to do some amazing things. Your JavaScript programs can interact with aspects of a Web page, including forms, frames, and background color, providing a much greater level of control and customization than was possible within vanilla HTML. For example, you can use HTML and a CGI script together to submit a forms input data to a server. By adding a JavaScript script within this process, you can also validate the data between the browser and the server. JavaScript can also interact with Java applets, calling on these more powerful tools to effect even greater control.

## JAVASCRIPT ARCHIVES

Libraries of JavaScript stuff seem to be proliferating faster than Starbucks coffee shops. Some specialize in the tried-and-true; some like to catalog the wildest and most esoteric applications. The choice is yours.

### Café au Lait
**http://sunsite.unc.edu/javafaq/**

Updated daily, this generic-looking site is actually quite exciting. Archives of new Java applets, Beans, and Builders are held here, along with critiques of Java programming trends and ideas for new ways to use the language. El-liotte Rusty Harold's great contribution is creating a safe place for cutting-edge developers to post their just-fin-ished projects. In other words, if you're a Java pro, check it out. If you aren't, it's worth looking at, but be careful what you download—it's here to be tested.

### The Complete JavaScript Library
**http://members.aol.com/insanelife/jvascrpt.htm**

This Library is Complete-ly misnamed—but I like it any-way. Programmer Matt Whitlock has a love for short, simple scripts. "Ive found lots of JavaScripts on the Inter-net, but they're all so long and complex. I just wanted

---

BUILDING BETTER PAGES

# THE RIGHT WAY TO PUT JAVASCRIPT SCRIPT IN YOUR HTML

How do you let incoming browsers know that Java-Script is your scripting language of choice without causing problems for browsers that don't support Java-Script? Put it within the <HEAD> of your HTML docu-ment, in this form:

```
<SCRIPT LANGUAGE="JavaScript"></SCRIPT>
```

Why? Because if you put it anywhere else, it won't be the first thing on the page to load. And if your visitor starts clicking on images or links before the page is fully loaded, you've got a whopper of a conflict that will probably crash the viewer's browser.

Here's how you do it in a way that won't zap users of non-JavaScript-compatible browsers:

```
<HTML>
<HEAD>
<TITLE>Example</TITLE>
<SCRIPT LANGUAGE="JavaScript">
<!-- HIDE FROM OLD BROWSERS
put your code here
// --> STOP HIDING
</SCRIPT>
</HEAD>
<BODY>
put your regular HTML code here
</BODY> </HTML>
```

Easy, isn't it?

something small to put in my HTML. So I created these scripts," he says. And true to his word, they are both functional and elegantly spare.

### Intergalacticnet's JavaScript Outpost

**http://intergalactinet.com/www/javascript/**

This site is so JavaScript-happy it drives me crazy. And it's proof positive that just because you can do something doesn't mean you *should*. That said, this site's frenetic, frames-infested interface can lead to you to content galore, including a large and ever-expanding storehouse of Java applets. Just *try* to ignore the hideous use of rainbow-gradient 10-point type. Its intended to show off the latest capabilities for text coloration in Netscape Navigator, but all I can say is "ugh." And all I can do is turn off my image loading and hope this site doesn't crash my browser before I find what I'm looking for!

### Java Cats' JavaScript Archive

**http://www.javacats.com/us/search/dir010.html**

Finding the JavaScript components you seek is quite simple with the Yahoo!-style hierarchical menus on this site, coupled with a search engine.

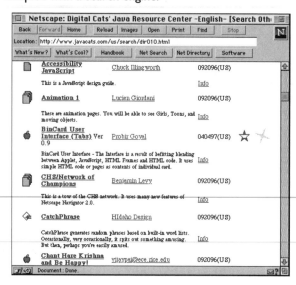

### JavaScript Library

**http://www.sapphire.co.uk/javascript/lib/**

A few functions, a lot of applets, and the odd application are on line at this U.K. site managed by Andrew Wooldridge. Here the accent is on the experimental and the envelope-pushing. Oh, and you'll need a JavaScript-enabled browser just to look.

## JavaScript Tutorials

A good tutorial is worth its weight in gold, or at least gold-plated coffee beans. Here are some of the best tutorials around for those who want to get into JavaScript programming.

### JavaScript 411

**http://www.freqgrafx.com/411/tutorial.html**

Intended as a full beginner's tutorial, this site is woefully incomplete. It does, however, offer a fine introduction to the basic infrastructure of JavaScript programming. If you can handle that paradox for now, keep checking in: You're dealing with a rapidly evolving language here, so this really shouldn't be surprising. The JavaScript 411 Tutorial includes links to FAQs and several well-executed sections, including the traditional "Hello World" exercise. If you've never programmed before, you might want to check in here first.

### The JavaScript Forum

**http://www.geocities.com/ResearchTriangle/1828/index.html**

This site used to run a regular JavaScript authoring competition, currently suspended. It's still a great place to find working examples, sample code, and step-by-step instructions on working with JavaScript.

### JavaScript Tip of the Week

**http://webreference.com/javascript/**

If you're already up to speed on basic JavaScript, schedule a weekly visit here to see the latest applications and ideas in action. These "minitutorials" are a nifty way to keep building your skills.

## TechTools's Hands-On JavaScript Tutorial

**http://techweb3.web.cerf.net/tools/java/ java44.html**

From basic stuff to making your very own scrolling banner (I know you just can't wait…), programmer and author Reaz Hogue has set up a step-by-step tutorial that includes several examples and exercises.

## Very Basic JavaScript Tutorial 1.0

**http://www.cs.newcastle.edu.au/Staff/ bohdan/jscript/tutorial.html**

B.S. Majewski takes the time to explain Java fundamentals and walk beginners through plenty of simple programming tasks. This one's very easy to read and follow.

### JAVASCRIPT RESOURCES

For those who have a yen for JavaScripting, here are some additional resources on the Web.

## JavaScript Authoring Guide

**http://home.netscape.com/eng/mozilla/3.0/ handbook/javascript/index.html**

Here in Netscape's own handbook for JavaScripting, you'll find a surprisingly good introduction to the topic.

Advanced lessons are on call, as well. As this book goes to print, the Authoring Guides emphasis is on educating programmers about the latest developments in JavaScript available in the Atlas beta of Netscape Navigator. Among the things you can look forward to are improved communications capabilities and new security features.

This very complete handbook offers up everything from term definitions to sample code for objects. It's an obvious starting point, particularly for beginners.

## JavaScript FAQ

**http://www.freqgrafx.com/411/jsfaq.html**

This non-Netscape FAQ maintained by Andy Augustine is constantly undergoing revision—especially in the section that covers documented bugs, unfortunately. If you have a JavaScript question and it's not completely esoteric, chances are that the answer is somewhere at this site.

## JavaScript on Usenet

**comp.lang.javascript**

Chatting about JavaScript ad nauseum is the order of the day here.

## JavaScript Sourcebook

**http://gmccomb.com/javascript/**

Gordon McComb, author of *The JavaScript Sourcebook*, maintains this support site. It includes free examples, tutorials, bug reports, and links to his excellent *JavaWorld* column.

## JavaScript Development Tools

By following links from the general Java and JavaScript resource pages, or in the archives listed earlier, you can acquire helpful tools for developing your JavaScripts. In addition, here are a pair of sites that are focused primarily on helping developers, and therefore good sources for tools.

### TeamJava's JavaScript Links

**http://teamjava.com/links/#scripts**

TeamJava is a collaborative group of consultants. Quite a few JavaScript tools are available through this frequently updated index.

### TronGod's Toolbox

**http://www.tnet1.com/trongod/**

Dumb name, but a cool page—tons of tools, tips, and techniques for JavaScript. Make sure you have plenty of memory available when you visit, though, or you'll be shut out. It's definitely applet-intensive.

☞ If you want to delve deeply into JavaScript, one of the best resources available is the JavaScript Pro mailing list. A FAQ and subscription information are available at http://www.inquiry.com/techtips/js_pro/maillist.html as is a handy JavaScript-specific search feature called "Ask the JavaScript Pro." The list, incidentally, is available in digest format for those with less time to read messages.

## Tclets: A Java Applet Alternative

This point in the chapter is appropriate for a mention that the folks at Sun have some other tricks up their sleeves, one of which uses the Tcl/Tk language. Miniprograms for use with HTML can be created with Tcl/Tk as well as with Java; they're called Tclets, and don't *even* ask me how to pronounce that...

It's an idea that has received little attention, having been drowned out by the massive fanfare over Java. But because Tcl/Tk really is easy to learn and use (unlike Java, should you happen to be a total programming novice), the Tclets technique is something that deserves a moment of your time—especially if you are already familiar with the language. Incidentally, Netscape offers a plug-in that supports Tclets.

### Introduction to Tclets

**http://www.neca.com/~vmis/tclets.htm**

This very caustic, very funny intro to Tclets bashes both Java and Perl (not to mention Microsoft) as it evangelizes the use of Tcl/Tk on the Web. Links are provided to Tclets archives, and to all the (free) software you'll need to roll your own.

## ActiveX and VBScript

In terms of data exchange and program linking, Sun and its faithful sidekick Netscape now find themselves locked in deadly combat with Microsoft. Microsoft has spent years developing its technologies in these areas, only to see its efforts threatened by upstarts Java and JavaScript.

But it's a funny kind of war, because Microsoft also supports Java now. The company simply tied it into ActiveX, Microsoft's overall framework for supporting third-party technologies. ActiveX, which includes both server- and client-side technologies, acts as an interface between your Web browser and other applications. For example, it helps to cement links between the browser and desktop applications such as Microsoft Word.

ActiveX has three main pieces: ActiveX Controls, ActiveX Documents, and ActiveX Scripting. The ActiveX Software Development Kit (SDK) is free from Microsoft—see the site description below for a pointer. Like Sun's JDK, the ActiveX SDK is both a cornucopia of code libraries, samples, and documentation as well as a somewhat incomplete set of development tools for creating your own client applications.

ActiveX Controls are the basic bits you'll be using in your Web pages: buttons, search functions, and other scripts that let users interact with HTML pages or other types of active documents on their own computers, using a convenient, consistent Web-browser interface. These controls can also be used within Visual Basic.

The ActiveX Controls are guided in their actions via ActiveX Scripting, which can be done using either VBScript or, in a nod to market realities, Java-Script. (VBScript is a subset of Visual Basic, and Microsoft's choice; see the following section for more information.) Both languages can communicate with ActiveX Controls via OLE Automation, and OLE events can then be fired that will be handled by the ActiveX Script code.

## VISUAL BASIC AND VBSCRIPT

VBScript is Microsoft's challenge to JavaScript. It's a powerful subset of the more complex Visual Basic, which was originally designed to make developing new applications for Windows quicker and easier than programming with compiled languages such as C and C++. Intermediate-level programmers and even some beginners can tap VBScript to create interactive documents and programs. It features a novice-friendly drag-and-drop programming environment.

Microsoft has made VBScript (the Visual Basic Scripting Edition) an integral part of ActiveX. VBScript is specialized for building Internet applications and connections, and because it's a scripted language, its programs can be embedded between the <SCRIPT> and </SCRIPT> tags in an HTML document.

In other words, ActiveX is Microsoft's (incomplete) answer to Java's promise of cross-platform interoperability, and VBScript is its answer to Java-Script.

As I hinted earlier, those of you already familiar with OLE, Microsoft's older system for communicating between programs, will have an advantage over newbies with ActiveX: OLE controls and ActiveX controls are nearly identical, as are their operations. ActiveX just extends the OLE concept and functionality into the more nebulous world of the Web. (That's oversimplifying things a bit, but a close relationship does exist between the two that goes beyond mere compatibility.)

## ACTIVEX/VBSCRIPT TUTORIALS

As Microsoft pushes to be heard above the Java din, and as programmers respond, tutorial offerings are increasing. Following are a few places to begin your search for ActiveX/VBScript skills.

### "Building ActiveX Controls for the Internet"

http://www.vcdj.com/vcdj/oct96/activex.htm
In this seven-part *Visual C++ Developers Journal* article/tutorial combo, author Lon Fisher walks C++ programmers through a few simple experiments in writing their own ActiveX controls. You can download the code, and there are links to more ActiveX resources and a discussion group.

### Microsoft Site Builder Workshop

http://www.microsoft.com/workshop/
Official documentation, tutorials, and examples are on tap here from the ActiveX evangelists at Microsoft. The

interface of this recently redesigned page offers some clues as to what's possible with these tools.

### VBScript Central: Getting Started

http://www.inquiry.com/vbscentral/

Decorated in bright primary colors, this tutorial walks you through your VBScript ABCs. Included are instructions for installing VBScript development software and running the usual beginner-level programs, from "Hello World" on up.

## ACTIVEX/VBSCRIPT ARCHIVES

At these sites, ActiveX and VBScript programmers can find just what they need to tie sites together using Microsoft's framework.

### ActiveX Template Library

http://www.microsoft.com/visualc/v42/atl/default.htm

Look here for a wide selection of prefabricated ActiveX templates that you can use to activate your HTML pages.

### The ActiveX Control Room

http://www.techweb.com/activexpress/control/control.html

Presented by the publishers of *ActiveXPress* (see separate listing coming up), the Control Room offers a searchable database of ActiveX controls in dozens of categories.

Most of these are commercial applications that you can license for use on your site; a few are freebies.

### ActiveX-Files

http://the-pages.com/activex/

No aliens in here, Mulder, just a searchable database of several hundred controls that can be downloaded.

### NetHeads Inc. X-Zone

http://www.netheads.net/alink.htm

As the home page here proclaims, "It's huge!" The full list of ActiveX controls and components, particularly for multimedia applications, is not to be missed. Items are categorized according to function, or you can search the extraordinarily comprehensive list.

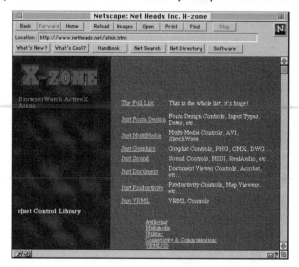

### Softoholic's ActiveX WWW Server

http://www.softoholic.bc.ca/ocxserver/

Freeware, shareware, and commercial options are arranged here for your delectation, including tools for developers using both OLE *and* ActiveX controls. Also present are links to related resources elsewhere.

### Unofficial ActiveX Guide

http://www.shorrock.u-net.com/index.html

The (Unofficial) ActiveX Guide manages to be boosterish without fawning all over Microsoft. That's quite a trick—

as are some of the ActiveX examples youll find in the archives here.

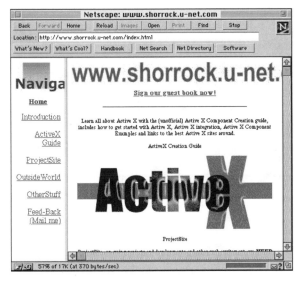

## VBScript Central

http://www.inquiry.com/vbscentral/

Inquiry.com's contribution to spreading the Visual Basic/VBScript gospel is an impressive effort, complete with an interactive Q&A feature ("Ask the ActiveX Pro"). There's a lot of snaggable stuff.

## VBScripts.com

http://www.vbscripts.com/

According to some users, this archive is the ultimate in VBScript collections.

## ZDNet's ActiveX Files for Webmasters

http://www5.zdnet.com/zdwebcat/content/masters/activex/

Aimed specifically at folks like you, ZDNet's ActiveX repository features lengthy articles that explain what ActiveX technology means for Webmasters. Plenty of downloads, too.

## ZWorx ActiveX Controls

http://www.zworx.com/OurActiveX.htm

At this site you can browse a small gallery of Microsoft Internet Explorer-specific ActiveX Controls developed by ZWorx. And you can look at some cool Camaros, too, if you'd like.

## ACTIVEX/VBSCRIPT DEVELOPMENT TOOLS

Aside from Microsoft's offerings—which are hard to resist, since the company has wisely decided to make them free of charge for the time being to encourage ActiveX development—there is a paucity so far of development tools for ActiveX. Please note that commercial Visual Basic compilers and such are available from Microsoft, through any software archive (such as c|net or ZDNet), or from any online software shop.

### Active X Starter Kit

http://direct.gamelan.com/product_100085.html

This book/software combo features a full tutorial on paper for both ActiveX and VBScript, as well as a large selection of development software. You can order it online here.

### "Building ActiveX Controls: The State of the Tools"

http://www.pcmag.com/issues/1516/pcmg0142.htm

For a cautious view of ActiveX tools, see this article from *PC Magazine*. It references the development tools currently available, and notes some areas where there are problems.

### Envelop

http://hjh.simplenet.com/freeware/envelop.html

The freeware Envelop Visual Basic compiler rivals many of its commercial cousins, which is why I'm mentioning it instead of them. Free is a very good price.

### Microsoft's ActiveX Development Discussion

**http://www.microsoft.com/mind/0497/activeXtools/activeXtools.htm**

In this article, Microsoft discusses development tools currently available for working with ActiveX. The emphasis is on well-tested stuff, and it includes links to the tools themselves.

### Microsoft's ActiveX Software Development Kit

**http://www.microsoft.com/activex**

You can link to the Microsoft ActiveX SDK from here. You can also look through the company's huge library of ActiveX controls, and rummage through related bits and pieces. This is not only the "official" ActiveX archive, it's also the most extensive.

### Microsoft's VBScript Stuff

**http://www.microsoft.com/vbscript**

You can go straight to the source for source code and development tools for VBScript at this Microsoft site.

### Softel

**http://www.softelvdm.com/**

This firm sells several low-cost tools for working with ActiveX and Visual Basic on the Web.

## OTHER ACTIVEX/VBSCRIPT RESOURCES

This category is growing rapidly as the use of ActiveX and VBScript spreads throughout the Net. Begin your search for data with these sites.

### The Active Group

**http://www.activex.org/**

This working group is an open, industry association of users and developers. It's dedicated to promoting and guiding the evolution of ActiveX on multiple platforms. New developer-oriented software is usually linked in here, and

it's the best place to look if you want to know more about where the technology is going.

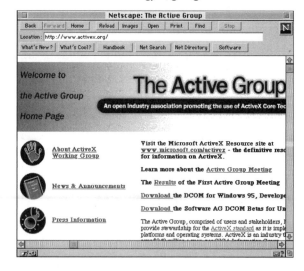

### ActiveX.com

**http://www.activex.com/**

c|net's ActiveX-centered download haven is also home to articles about using the technology on the Web, and other goodies. Since c|net's pretty good about freshening up its offerings, this is a good site to check frequently.

### ActiveX Journal for HTML Writers

**http://www.folkarts.com/journals/activex**

This independent, subscription-only online newsletter will keep you up to date, and connected to other ActiveX developers as well.

### ActiveXPress

AUTHOR'S CHOICE

**http://www.techweb.com/activexpress**

Here you'll find Microsoft-independent news, plus reviews of ActiveX controls, objects, compilers, debuggers and such. The selection is very up-to-the-minute, and broad enough to encompass the relationships between ActiveX and Java Beans, various programming languages, and more. Be sure to click on "Interest Groups" to link into ongoing discussions of ActiveX-related issues.

### ActiveX-Related Newsgroups

http://www.vbonline.com/vbdev/vbnwgr.htm

This listing of Visual Basic-related newsgroups includes many in the Microsoft hierarchy. You can get to them via hyperlinks from this page.

### ActiveX Technologies User Group

http://www.interserver.com/AXTUG/

This online/offline organization for users in search of fellow ActiveX enthusiasts maintains an excellent site, with links to software and other resources as well as self-education aids.

### Scribe

http://www.km-cd.com/scribe/

Billed as a resource site for VBScript users, Scribe comprises over 300 related site pointers. You can add your own, too.

### Visual Basic Developer

http://www.vbonline.com/vbdev/vb.htm

Both the full Visual Basic language and its VBScript subset are covered in this online magazine.

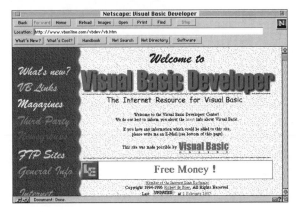

### What Is ActiveX?

http://whatis.com/activex.htm

This page summarizes ActiveX, compares it to Java and Visual Basic, and provides links to other helpful information.

# PUSH TECHNOLOGY

*Push* is a buzzword you've already heard, I'm sure. It seems you can't pick up a computer magazine these days without reading either a vicious screed about the evils of push technology or a glowing tale of the venture-capital megabucks being pulled down by early push vendors.

Just to recap, in case you've been sleeping: What you usually do on the Web is *pull* the information of your choice. You go looking for it (a process that is sometimes random and time-consuming); then you grab it and bring it "home" to your desktop with your Web browser. In contrast, push technology lets servers *push* information at your browser, cutting out both the fun and the pain of the Web-searching process. You make an initial choice by, say, subscribing to a news service that will feed you a steady diet of stories about new Web technologies. Then a stream of data comes (constantly or intermittently) at your machine over the Internet, and continues to emanate from that source until you make it stop.

There are plenty of problems to be worked out when it comes to push technology. Some end-users find it intrusive, and some companies don't want ads being shoved across their networks into the hands of employees. There are various standards and approaches.

And then there's the not-so-minor matter of memory: Most home PCs have less than eight megs of the stuff, which severely limits the amount of data that can be pushed in—especially if you're peppering the information stew with Java-animated advertisements.

But chances are you'll need to know a lot more about pushing in the next year or so, because there are some very compelling, potentially lucrative, perhaps even useful applications for the process. If nothing else, you may be called upon to deal with the bandwidth hogging and time wasting of PointCast and other entertainment/news feeds, should you be so unlucky as to be working on a corporate office network.

The following set of Web sites includes all the major push vendors. Each of these companies is doing something slightly different from the rest, mainly because the technology's still in its infancy. The first one to find a way to use push to its fullest without turning off or overloading end-users will win the prize: a fortune in venture capital and a chance to land on top of a new media bonanza. Who will be the victor? Explore these sites, take a look at the players, and file away your judgment for future reference.

## BackWeb Technologies

http://www.backweb.com/

BackWeb's award-winning push/pull news service currently offers over 40 channels. The company's partnership with Microsoft is sure to make BackWeb the 100-pound gorilla of the industry.

## Cognisoft

http://www.cognisoft.com

Cognisoft's Windows NT product, IntelliServe, can provide customized data delivery and has rated high reviews

in the trade press. When Cognisoft merged with Verity in early 1997, tongues were set to wagging. Paired with IntelliServe, Verity's text-retrieval software could take on new importance in corporate information systems.

## Diffusion

http://www.diffusion.com/

Diffusion's IntraExpress puts the brakes on unmitigated, excessive push by allowing intranet managers to be in charge. And on the content provider side, IntraExpress lets pushers get choosy about who receives their data. IntraExpress is not just about the Web, either—companies can arrange to offer their reminders and news via other media, including fax and pager.

## Netscape

http://www.netscape.com/

Netscape has a number of irons in the fire, from Constellation on the client (see "Netscape Shoots for the Stars," coming up), to Netcaster on the server side. And then there are all those intriguing little deals the company is making with the likes of Marimba and PointCast. Learn more here.

## Marimba

http://www.marimba.com

This product is the darling of forward-looking software vendors, who are visualizing the day when they can upgrade the software on your desktop machine using push technology, or easily download Java applets direct to your desktop when you access a Web site. If you've been following the concept of the low-cost network computer, I'll bet a light bulb just went off in your head. Marimba shares your vision. For now, it offers a Java-based server (Castanet) and client software, as well as its own channels of licensed content a la PointCast.

## PointCast

http://www.pointcast.com/

There are two ways of looking at pushing information, if you're a vendor: Either you can work on pioneering technology that will somehow be incorporated into productivity software, or you can simply use the push concept as a delivery mechanism and concentrate on your data.

PointCast is taking the latter approach, shoving articles (and ads, ads, ads) through your browser 24-7. It licenses content from "names," including the Reuters wire service. The company also has some technology to sell, of course—look here for information about the I-Server, a package that will let your Web site take advantage of what PointCast has learned.

## First Floor

**http://www.firstfloor.com/**

First Floor, the maker of Smart Delivery and other push products, likes to say that it is "delivering on the promise of the Web." The company's approach is not consumer oriented; instead, it targets internal communications solutions such as transfer of critical sales data on the fly, on the Web or over the intranet.

## Lanacom Headliner

**http://www.lanacom.com/**

Like PointCast, Headliner delivers news, sports, weather and entertainment to your desktop. Unlike PointCast, Headliner tries to keep things brief and is slightly more adventurous in the content choices it offers.

## Wayfarer Communications

**http://www.wayfarer.com/**

Wayfarer's Incisa concept takes push and applies it to the intranet. Smart move, since business is without a doubt the bigger market. Buyers can use Incisa to push in-house information (memos, newsletters, software updates) to employees, or it can license ad-free third-party content for intraoffice broadcast.

### MORE PUSH RESOURCES

Following are a few articles and discussion forums where you can learn more about using your Web server to push information.

## Netscape Shoots for the Stars

**http://www.news.com/News/Item/ 0,4,5469,00.html**

Netscape's push-savvy client, Constellation, was still in development as this book went to press. At this site,

c|net offers some opinions on its nascent technology. Is it more than a "me, too" reaction to Microsoft's inclusion of push support in Internet Explorer 4.0?

## Push Me, Pull You

**http://www.slate.com/webhead/96-12-19/ webhead.asp**

From the Microsoft-linked online magazine *Slate* comes this "push-for-dummies" introduction. Of course, Microsoft is up to its eyeballs in this stuff (albeit as a latecomer), so if you want to know the official position from Redmond without having to read a press release, try this. It's gentler on the eyes and stomach.

## When Shove Comes to Push

**http://www.pcweek.com/business/0210/ 10push.html**

In this article, *PCWeek* takes certain push-pushers to task for tossing around the hyperbole, and then guides you through the *real* push story. After reading this, you'll have better understanding of where this technology is headed, and who's likely to make a big finish.

# ONE LAST CURMUDGEONLY WORD

Observant readers will notice that the conclusion to this chapter is about to say nearly the same thing as the introduction. That's because I want to emphasize a point.

Client-side technologies have taken off in a big way over the past year, but sometimes the most important part of a Web site—its content—can be obscured by gratuitous use of "cool" visuals. Every time my browser crashes, simplicity looks even more attractive. I'm beginning to appreciate those sites that showcase ActiveX and Java components tastefully, and despise the ones that have no consideration for the "average" user. I figure that if my reasonably contemporary computer, running Netscape's latest browser and endowed with twice the average amount of RAM, is crashing from excess at least once per session, then Joe and Jane Web-Browser are in *really* bad shape.

And so I'll say it once again: As you stretch your programming abilities, *don't let the excitement and hype get in the way of your common sense.* Unless your site is strictly for the digerati, make sure your audience's computers can handle what you're dishing out. If you're not sure, check out some of the sites listed under "Web Demographics" in Chapter 10 to find out. And always, always, always offer no-frames, Java-free, ActiveX-less alternatives if you possibly can. And include a text-only alternative, too, since a large portion of academic and home users still need it.

The browsing public will thank you for it.

# CHAPTER 10

# MAKING THE MOST OF YOUR WEB SITE

IN THIS CHAPTER, WE'LL TALK ABOUT THE NITTY-GRITTY SIDE OF YOUR LIFE AS A WEB PROFESSIONAL: CHOOSING EQUIPMENT AND SOFTWARE, SITE MAINTENANCE, AND EVEN ARRANGING PUBLICITY AND GETTING ADS. YOU'LL GET SOME SUGGESTIONS FOR KEEPING YOUR AUDIENCE INTERESTED, AND ALSO INFORMATION ABOUT KEEPING YOURSELF INFORMED. THE TOPICS COVERED INCLUDE:

### ☞ Server Hardware.

What's the most important piece of equipment you'll be buying? Your Web server. This section offers helpful hints for buyers, and links to the latest info.

### ☞ Server Software.

Here's the skinny on choosing a server software package, including links to most of the major vendors.

### ☞ Other Tools and Equipment.

What else will you need? What frills might you like to add to your toolkit later on?

### ☞ Outsourcing.

Prefer to have your site run on an ISP's equipment? In this section we'll cover the ins and outs of outsourcing.

### ☞ Working with Consultants.

You *don't* have to do it all yourself. Nor do you have to get taken for a ride by a consultant with second-

rate skills. Here you'll discover how to find and work with reputable outside help.

### ☞ Announcements and Publicity.

Publicizing your site, checking links, setting up site maintenance routines, and installing counters and guestbooks that can help you keep track of your audience—these are the "little things" that make a big difference. This section also includes an insider's primer on how to get your site written up in magazines and books.

### ☞ Getting Advertisers.

If it's appropriate for your site, you may want to put ads on your Web pages. Here's some basic information on advertising practices, with online resources that can help you get started.

### ☞ Keep 'Em Coming Back.

This section explores tried-and-true ways to retain your audience over a long period of time, with examples of sites that do it well.

### ☞ Extending Your Own Skills.

The Web is forever changing, and forward-thinking Websters will keep their skills up to snuff. This part of the chapter provides pointers to resources for staying on top of the game.

**SO FAR IN THIS BOOK,** we've assumed that you already have your computer equipment and software. For beginners, of course, that may not be the case. Maybe your site has been successful enough to tax a starter setup to the limit, and it may already be time to check into alternatives. For all of you who fit one or the other of these categories, this section presents a selection of sites that cover the latest hardware and software.

Also, since this is the final chapter of the book, we've also thrown in a kitchen sinkful of other useful stuff, including information about site management, publicizing your fabulous creation, and building a Web career. You may not need any of this now, but as your online work continues, you'll likely want to return to this information. Take what you need, and save the rest for later.

## SERVER HARDWARE

A Web server is made up of two things: a computer and a Web server software package. We'll get into software in a later section. For now, let's examine the important considerations of platform and specific computer model.

### HOW TO MAKE YOUR CHOICE

Here are some questions to ask yourself before you even start to research different models.

- Are you a complete novice?
  If so, you'll want to look at "turnkey" solutions only. These are Web server packages that include both hardware and software. You'll also want to take a close look at the quality of the vendor's documentation, and the quality and cost of support—you'll be needing it. Apple's Internet Server Solution packages have received high ratings from many novice Web site creators, for example; straight UNIX-based systems are more complex.

- What computer platform do you use now?
  It's smart to avoid adding the task of learning a new operating system to the big job of setting up a Web server. So if you're already familiar with a particular OS, you should give a couple of extra points up front to servers that run that system.

- What computer platform does most of your company run on?
  If you don't have an OS preference, give those extra points to your company's platform of choice.

- If your company's dominant platform is not the one you use, are there compatibility issues?

  If you want to integrate your Web installation easily into the corporate network, as in the case of an Internet/intranet setup, you'll want to make sure that you're not subjecting yourself and your clients or employers to a Herculean effort. And be sure to include the cost of any additional software or hardware needed for integration: don't make the mistake of leaving those costs out of your projections. (There's a lot more about costs coming up in this discussion.)

- What's your total budget for this installation?
  Although the server machine is probably going to be the most expensive part of the picture, remember that there are several other prices to consider, including server software, modem(s), routers, and Internet service itself. Then there are the costs of your site-design and site-management tools to consider. You don't want to buy an underpowered server for a high-volume site, of course, so if money is tight, look for servers that come bundled with applications that you want, or even with additional hardware. This may tip you toward a

UNIX server, for which many free, powerful server packages and utilities are available.

- Are you considering using Java to facilitate cross-platform compatibility?

  If you're looking into Java, make your choice with that direction in mind. Despite the much-vaunted promise of total cross-platform compatibility, not all of the Java Virtual Machines are equal. Choose a server that runs the best.

- What volume of traffic do you anticipate at your site?

  This is a complex question. Often you haven't a clue about volume when you're just getting started! The sites listed in the Web Demographics section coming up can help you get a handle on how high interest might be in your material, and you can also collect traffic data from servers your company may already have on line. In addition, take a look at the counters installed on similar servers (Web sites run by your firm's closest competitors, for instance). Once you have a rough estimate, make sure that the hardware you choose can support not just your projected initial audience, but some growth in the future as well.

- What amount of memory you will need? Multiply it!

  Serving up large Web graphics and running server-side programs devours an enormous amount of RAM. You can minimize the load by designing your site carefully, but as every experienced Web developer knows, you really can't have too much memory.

When it comes to selecting server hardware, the answers to these questions are what you need to get started. I realize this isn't much to go on, but with new equipment coming out daily, there's no way to provide a blow-by-blow comparison between all the

options—not in this book, anyway. Answer the questions listed here *before* even looking at specific servers, and use your answers to build a list of server specifications.

Here's an example of the sort of simple criteria that you might come up with:

1.  Platform: Windows NT

    (You chose Windows NT because you already know the Windows interface, and because other non-Web servers at your company are running Windows NT.)

2.  Budget: $25,000 total for hardware and software

    (A figure sent down from on high, which you're just going to have to work with!)

3.  Volume: 2,000 hits a day from outside; possibly many more internal hits via the intranet link.

    (This is a guesstimate based on traffic on your competitors' Web server.)

4.  A machine with a long warranty, from a company with a good reputation for technical support and quality.

    (These are "other considerations" that are meaningful to your installation.)

There—you have the basic outline of the server you want to buy. From here, start researching machines that run Windows NT. Rule out any manufacturers whose quality and warranty don't meet your expectations, and then cut the list to only those models that meet your price point. If turnkey solutions or package deals are available that mix your desired hardware with some software that meets your needs, great! Packages like these can save you time, money, and hassle.

Once you're down to perhaps three good choices, start checking reviews, talking to users, and examining benchmark scores. You may also be able to obtain evaluation units to test. Call the companies in question and ask to speak to the product manager for the machine you're interested in. Explain that you are interested in doing a hands-on evaluation of their server, with an eye toward buying one or more machines. If you've never tried to do this before, you'll be surprised at how many vendors will gladly send you a server to try before you buy.

Another advantage of working with product managers is that they can provide you with more detailed information about the servers than salespeople in computer stores can. A packet of some sort is generally available that may include reprints of the most recent glowing reviews, benchmark scores, background info on any new technologies used, facts about the warranty and service plan, and more. You don't need this level of info about every single model on your initial list, but you should definitely have it when it's time to pick from the final two or three contenders. Chances are you'll find one machine has some slight advantage to tip the scales in that model's direction.

Product managers may also be willing to provide the names and phone numbers of other users. Any referrals given to you will necessarily be from basically happy customers, but my experience indicates that most are willing to discuss both the negative and positive points of the item they've purchased. The information you get from real-world users will have significant value—you don't need me to warn you about the unreliability of ad copy and trade-press articles (which are themselves based on public-relations material from manufacturers, and limited testing under lab conditions). You may want to post an inquiry on one of the server-related newsgroups listed in the following section, or search for commentary in the archived messages from these groups via DejaNews. Some of the publications listed below (most notably ServerWatch) also carry news tips about problematic machines that you will want to avoid.

## HARDWARE INFORMATION RESOURCES

Do you feel ready to go out there and buy a server now? I didn't think so! With your indecision in mind, I have included some Web-based resources that are well known for providing up-to-date product reviews and tips. The news, reviews, and descriptions found here will help you find the best deal on the right server.

### *New Media*'s Dynamic and Interactive Web Server Comparison

http://www.hyperstand.com/NewMedia/97/03/td/Dynamic_Web_Servers.html

Five of the biggies are rated and reviewed here. Others are discussed by way of comparison.

### Server Watch

http://serverwatch.iworld.com/

Mecklermedia's contribution to the server scene is this online magazine, which excels at delivering breaking news about new models. It's updated almost daily with stories about advances in server hardware. It also carries many stories about software, management, and networking in general.

### inquiry.com

http://www.inquiry.com/

If you're in the market for equipment, inquiry.com features a very searchable index of product info from vendors. You can search by category or platform, or plug in the name of a specific item you've unearthed and want to learn more about. The material you retrieve will generally not include critical assessments, however, so be sure to search out reviews of anything you find here before making a purchase decision.

### MacTech Magazine Online

http://web.xplain.com/mactech.com/

Strictly for the MacGeek crowd, this publication attracts rabid programmers who have this special platform preference. Server software and add-ons are regularly featured, and the reviews tend to be both highly technical and opinionated. If these folks say that it's good (or that it isn't), you can take their word for it.

## MSTM News
### http://mweiser.bus.okstate.edu/mstm/news/hotsites.htm
This university-sponsored site collects URLs for and brief descriptions of Web sites run by hardware companies and software manufacturers. It's a huge list of primarily Net-related products and their makers.

## UNIX Server Price/Description Comparison Chart—and More!
### http://www.zdnet.com/intweek/filters/serverunix.html
Courtesy of the editors of *Inter@ctive Week,* this server comparison looks at the top UNIX models. From the selection bar to the left of this story, however, you can also access server hardware charts for Amiga, DOSNet-Ware, Mac, OS/2, Windows, and VMS. Please note that not all of the options charted are preconfigured as Web servers; other types of network-ready machines are represented, too.

## Web Server OnLine
### http://www.cpg.com/ws/
All the Web server news, all of the time—that's what you'll find in this professionally oriented online magazine. Links include benchmark testing results, product reviews, opinion columns, and news about new equipment. You can register here for a free subscription to the paper version, too.

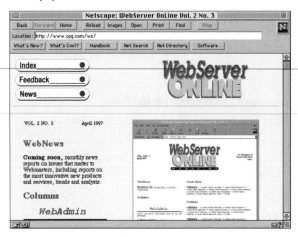

## Yahoo! Benchmark Index
### http://www.yahoo.com/Computers_and_Internet/Hardware/Benchmarks/
If you're testing your own servers, download some good benchmarking software from one of the collections indexed here.

## ZDNet
### http://www5.zdnet.com/
Ziff-Davis, preeminent publisher of computer magazines, has leveraged on its expertise and its respected test laboratories to create this superbusy news-and-reviews site. Plug the name of the server you want to investigate into the search engine, and see what the experts have to say. Incidentally, ZD's benchmark software is of high quality, and provides a good basis for comparisons. You can download it and try it on eval units yourself.

## SERVER-RELATED DISCUSSION
The following platform-specific Usenet newsgroups and mailing lists host spirited conversations about Web-server hardware *and* software.

## Mac Web Server Discussion
### comp.infosystems.www.servers.mac
Macintosh Web servers are the topic of this newsgroup. Possible subjects include configuration, security issues, directory structure, and bug reports.

## Microsoft Windows 95 and NT Servers Discussion
### comp.infosystems.www.servers.ms-windows
This newsgroup features discussion of Web servers running on Microsoft Windows and Microsoft NT. Topics include configuration questions and solutions, security issues, directory structure, and bug reports.

## UNIX Web Server Discussion
### comp.infosystems.www.servers.unix
This newsgroup covers discussion of Web servers for UNIX platforms. Possible subjects include configuration questions, security issues, directory structure, and bug reports.

## Discussion of Web Servers for Other Platforms

**comp.infosystems.www.servers.misc**

This newsgroup discusses World Wide Web servers for other platforms, such as Amiga and VMS. Subjects include configuration questions, solutions to specific problems, security issues, directory structure, and bug reports.

## Webserver-NT Mailing List

**webserver-nt-request@mailserve.process.com**

Send an e-mail message to the above address, with body "subscribe webserver-nt" to get this list. It's also available in hypermail (Web page) format at http://www.pacemail.com/hyper/web-nt/.

Not merely about the merits of Windows NT Web servers, chat topics here can be all over the map. Recent threads have covered personal reviews of HTML editors, storage and backup system questions, and comparisons between Microsoft's Internet server software and its competitors.

## WWW Speed List

**www-speed-request@tipper.oit.unc.edu**

Send an e-mail message with body "subscribe www-speed-request" to the above address to get this list, dedicated to the proposition that the Web is just too darned slow. Participants here believe that some of the Web's key components have inherent performance problems that cannot be corrected without changes to protocols. Find out about performance problems Webmasters are experiencing with their current setups. You'll also pick up some ideas about how to build faster server solutions.

## WWW Server Manager List

**majordomo@lists.stanford.edu**

Send an e-mail message with body "subscribe www-managers" to the above address. The goal of this list is to provide a useful, quick-turnaround forum for managers of Web servers and Web sites. Subscribers can ask questions about setting up and maintaining HTTP servers and clients. No discussions take place on this list. Answers are to be mailed back to the person who asked the question, who then has the responsibility for summarizing the relevant answers and posting them back to the mailing list.

# SERVER SOFTWARE

Okay—you've chosen a platform. You're on your way. Maybe you decided to buy a turnkey solution that comes with everything. If so, get cracking on building that site!

If not, you've still got a long road to travel. And when it comes to software, comparing the dozens of competing programs is an extremely exacting task. My best suggestion is to keep an eye on platform-specific magazines, including the Web-related magazines listed in this chapter, for "server software shoot-out" stories. These invariably include carefully researched charts that compare several packages on the basis of interface, capabilities, price, and other factors. The best of these will provide the results of exhaustive benchmark testing, as is done at ZD Labs (see the Ziff-Davis publications on ZDNet, referenced in the preceding section).

What sort of criteria should be the basis for your comparison? Here are a few basic questions to answer before you start shopping.

- Does this software run on your chosen server? Duh!

- Can it support the number of concurrent users that you expect or want?
  You don't want your server to act as a bottleneck, so make sure it can handle the load.

- Does it support any server-side programming options that you plan to add to your HTML pages?
  For example, some Web server programs, including Microsoft's Internet Information Server, offer little support for SSIs.

- Does it support any client-side programming that you plan to add to your HTML pages?
  Built-in support for Java, JavaScript, ActiveX, and the like is a must if you expect these tech-

nologies to be important to your site, now or in the future.

- Will this software require the use of pricey add-on programs to get the additional functionality that you need?

  Many packages have basic site-management capabilities built in, for example. If money is a concern and these features are adequate for your current needs, the package merits closer consideration.

- If a package cannot handle certain tasks, such as site management or link tracking, are add-on programs available that work well with the software?

  Make sure to check out these choices when you evaluate your main server package. If the add-ons you'll need are poorly integrated or from fly-by-night vendors, you may find yourself hung out to dry.

- Do you like the interface?

  Software that's easy to learn and use will save you time, and time is money.

- Does the vendor promise free or low-cost updates?

  If you're going to be on the hook for expensive upgrades every few months, take that into account.

- Does the vendor offer high-quality documentation and support?

  Web sites don't build themselves. Good manuals, and telephone/online support that's actually available and not just promised, are essential for beginners. In fact, even you experts out there need some hand-holding from time to time. This is one area where it pays to talk to other users—that's a good way to find out if a company's promised support system is real.

## SUMMARIES OF POPULAR PROGRAMS

Just to get you started, here's a short (and far from complete) list of the most popular server-software solutions going, as of this writing.

### Macintosh Server Software

| Package | Vendor | Web Address |
| --- | --- | --- |
| MachTen | Tenon Intersystems | http://www.tenon .com/ |
| NetWings | NetWings | http://www.netwings .com/ |
| WebSTAR* | StarNine | http://www.starnine .com/ |

\* Apple's Internet Server Solutions use WebSTAR.

### Windows 95 Server Software

| Package | Vendor | Web Address |
| --- | --- | --- |
| Commerce-Builder | Internet Factory | http://www.ifact .com |
| Communications Builder | Internet Factory | http://www.ifact .com |
| WebSite | O'Reilly & Associates | http://www.ora .com/ |
| Netscape* | Netscape | http:// www.netscape. com/ |
| Internet Information Server* | Microsoft | http://www. microsoft.com |

\* Both Microsoft and Netscape have several different server-software packages available.

### Windows NT Server Software

| Package | Vendor | Web Address |
| --- | --- | --- |
| Alibaba | Computer Software Manufaktur GmbH | http://www.csm.co .at/csm/ |
| Internet Information Server* | Microsoft | http://www.microsoft .com/ |
| Netscape* | Netscape | http://www.netscape .com/ |
| PowerWeb | PowerWeb Corp. | http://www.netclub .com/PowerWeb/ |

### Windows NT Server Software (Continued)

| Package | Vendor | Web Address |
| --- | --- | --- |
| Purveyor | Process Software | http://www.process .com/ |
| WebSite | O'Reilly & Associates | http://www.ora .com/ |
| WebQuest | Questar Microsystems | http://www.questar .com/ |

\* Both Microsoft and Netscape have several different server-software packages available.

### UNIX Server Software

| Package | Vendor | Web Address |
| --- | --- | --- |
| Apache | Apache Group | http://www.apache .org |
| OpenLinux | Caldera | http://www.caldera .com/ |
| NCSA HTTPd | NCSA | http://hoohoo.ncsa .uiuc.edu/ |

As useful as the sites listed here are, you'll want to make sure your comparison is based on *this week's* information, and you'll need to collect a lot of details to make an informed comparison. Check the Web sites of the companies listed above to learn about their latest software offerings, features, and prices.

Here are several places to look for details, and for information about software from other companies.

## Cybergroup's Server Page

http://www.cybergroup.com/html/ servers.html

This helpful collection of information about server software and setup basics includes pages that list software for Mac, Windows, Windows 95, Windows NT, and UNIX machines.

## InfoWorld Test Center

http://www.infoworld.com/cgi-bin/ displayTC.pl?/reviews/reviews.htm

*InfoWorld*'s hands-on reviews of Web server software and related products, such as database-linkage applications, are pretty darn reliable.

## *MacAddict*'s Macintosh and the Internet Info

http://www.evangelist.macaddict.com/ market_internet.html

Straight from *MacAddict*'s "Evangelist" column, this site features dozens of articles on Web server software for the Mac environment, including reviews, comparisons, official Apple info, pointers to sites using specific packages, and (as usual in this magazine) general cheerleading for all things Apple.

## NCSA HTTPd Details

http://hoohoo.ncsa.uiuc.edu/docs/ Overview.html

Even if you don't plan to use HTTPd as your UNIX Web server package, this selection of FAQs, tutorials, and general information on UNIX servers and the Web is a good starting point. The tutorials here are fairly generic; they cover topics such as creating imagemaps and the fundamentals of setting up your first Web server.

## New Media's Hyperstand

http://www.newmedia.com/

The focus here is on Web server and Web production products that accelerate and improve multimedia delivery. New Media's software tests are well known for their accuracy, so it's worth a look even if you aren't trying to do streamed video and such—they do cover the basics, too.

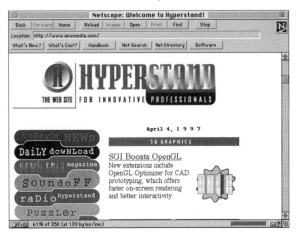

Want to know who's using what? The consulting firm Netcraft runs a monthly survey of Web servers in use, and publishes the results of its poll athttp://www.netcraft.com/Survey/. You may be surprised at what you find there: Heavily advertised packages still haven't outstripped the freebies in popularity.

The Web Server Survey is another list of software packages, arranged by popularity, available at http://nw.com/zone/WWW-9507/www-servers.html.

## Web Server Software Roundup for Windows NT

http://www.winntmag.com/Issues/Sep96/webs.htm

*Windows NT* magazine has compiled a browser-busting compendium of test results, opinions, and facts about all of the Windows NT Web servers they could get their hands on for this story. If you're looking for packages that run on the NT platform, be sure to read what this group has to say.

## Web Compare

http://webcompare.iworld.com/

You can use this site's comparison chart, links, and FAQ info to compare around 50 current Web server packages on the basis of features, platform, scalability, and price. If you want to start building a list of possibilities, this is a good place to do it.

## The Webmaster's Starter Kit

http://www.eit.com/goodies/software/

Created by EIT Software, this Starter Kit is a free collection of software for building a UNIX Web server. What's more, all of it was chosen for ease of use as well as that *very* reasonable price.

## Windows 95 Solutions: Free and Cheap

http://www.windows95.com/apps/servers-websrv.html

Hit this page for an introduction to several freeware and shareware Web server packages that work with the Windows 95 OS.

## Yahoo!'s Web-Server Software List

http://www.yahoo.com/Computers_and_Internet/Software/Internet/World_Wide_Web/Servers/

As always, Yahoo! provides a mass of unrated, almost undifferentiated links to who knows what. But because it's the service that links to everything commercial, Yahoo! is also a good place to look for the latest. You'll find all sorts of related links nearby, from server-specific CGIs to publications.

The best way to ensure that you choose the right server software is to try it before you buy it. Take a look at ZDNet (see the "Server Hardware" section in this chapter), and also at clnet's software libraries (http://www.download.com) for free demo versions of many popular programs.

If you can't find a demo version on line, consider contacting the manufacturer of a package whose reviews and ratings are enticing. Most companies are more than willing to send out a trial version of their software, and all will gladly provide you with more information. Ask for the product manager, or talk to someone in sales.

## OTHER TOOLS AND EQUIPMENT

What else do you need now? Scanners and digital cameras give you input options for paper documents, groovy graphics, and quick snapshots. Fast and dependable modems, of course, are a must.

As for routers, firewalls, and such, see the "Publications for Pros" section at the end of this chapter. *InfoWorld* and *LAN Times* are particularly good sources for news about the latest networking hardware possibilities.

In addition, university users and others in the know will periodically post the results of their benchmarking tests on high-end items, allowing you to take a sneak peak at what goes on in big-time labs (and use it to your advantage). Put your favorite search engine to work ferreting these out.

### Digital Camera Gateway

http://www.sbu.ac.uk/~kerrmw/digital_
camera.html

This one's as simple as it comes: just a dozen or so related links to click, and a built-in search engine to find all your information. It includes links to each of the major manufacturers of digital cameras. One of these cameras is a great addition to your toolbox if you're creating an online catalog, or simply want a quick way to create custom graphics for your site.

### Scanner Comparison

http://www.rlspace.com/rs_live/products/
vistadoc/scanners.htm

Compiled from reports sent in by correspondents around the world, here's a roundup of stats and opinions about some of the big-name scanners.

### Scanner Comparison II

http://www.win95mag.com/archive/11_96/
html/compare.html

With an eye toward finding the best scanner for Win95 users, this roundup does a thorough job and includes output examples in color.

### "Voice, Data and Speed"

http://www.tcp.ca/1996/Apr96/Apr96OL/
Voice/Voice.html

In this article, Jeff Evans of *The Computer Paper* provides a Modem 101 course that will help you to make informed decisions. (As for actual modem comparisons, there are simply too many on line to list. Just plug the names of your favorite models into any search engine, and you're sure to come up with comparison charts galore.)

## OUTSOURCING SERVER SUPPORT

Many Web managers prefer to have their sites run on an ISP's equipment. Sometimes that's simply the best solution. For example, you may not have the technical skills yet to keep a server up and running, or you may be too busy doing fabulous design work to bother learning those skills. Or maybe all your time is taken running a business. If so, outsourcing is definitely for you.

Bear in mind that your site doesn't have to be handed over to someone else lock, stock, and barrel. You will have just as much control over the content of the site as ever, regardless of where the server may be physically located, including the ability to make remote changes as often as you like.

Look for a company with several years' experience in the business. Use your Web browser to check out responsiveness at a few high-traffic sites already living on the servers of each company you're considering. Also, contact the Web managers at some of those sites—you may get an earful (almost everyone has a complaint or two about their ISP). From these folks you'll find out more real facts about the state of service and customer relations at the ISP than the company's hand-picked references could ever give you.

---

☞ **What to Avoid in an ISP**

It's much easier to tell you what denotes a *good* ISP than to offer up the warning signs of a bad one. But here are three sure-fire hints that all is not well:

- **Unresolved service complaints:** Check with your local Better Business Bureau, and run the ISP's name through DejaNews and a search engine or two, to see what people are saying.
- **Unresponsive tech support:** This one's a major problem at several otherwise excellent ISPs. It's usually just growing pains, but you want a company that's dealing well with such issues. Check the hold time in technical support, as well as overall knowledge—*before* you buy.
- **Pushy salespeople:** Certain crummy ISPs make their money by roping unsuspecting customers into expensive packages that include design, maintenance, marketing, and who knows what else. Be prepared in advance with a list of what you actually want. Look for an ISP that is more interested in providing you with high-quality server space and connections than with snagging a new page-design client.

Finding an ISP in your area should be easy unless you're very, very isolated. The easiest place to begin is The List.

## The List
**http://www.iworld.com/**
Well over 5,000 Internet Service Providers from around the world are just a click away through this service-oriented site. It's fully searchable.

# WORKING WITH CONSULTANTS

Working with a consultant to accomplish one or more of your site's design goals can be a frightening prospect. But if you need help, there are ways to avoid being taken for a ride. Unfortunately, that's what happens to inexperienced managers every day. The following list is comprised of points to keep in mind when you look for outside help It is by no means exhaustive, but it will help you get started.

- **Research the project yourself first**. Yes, I know you don't have much free time—that's probably the main reason you want to hire a consultant in the first place. But by doing your homework, you get a clue about customary procedures, time allowances, and hourly rates.

So you'll have something substantive to work with when you're negotiating a contract.

- **Check references—several of them**. Ask for work samples. Ask questions that will get detailed answers. Why? Because this business is still new, and there are individuals out there who think they know more than they do. Simply building a home page is not enough to qualify someone to be a Web designer, no matter what they think. And not everyone who's used e-mail can run a server. It just ain't so. Not only should you talk to former clients, but you should make an inquiry with the appropriate Better Business Bureau office as well.

- **Take care with contracts**. Perhaps the most important thing you can do to protect yourself is having a solid, written contract with your consultant. This contract should cover hourly fees and allowable equipment costs, a firm timetable, and a carefully written description of the job you want done. It's wise to write in penalties for shoddy work and late delivery. (By the same token, don't bring these into play if you know there was an acceptable reason for missed deadlines, such as malfunctioning equipment.)

- **Pay attention to security**. Whenever you provide an outsider with access to your computer network, you do run a risk. Careful supervision, checklists, and a good working relationship with your consultant will ensure that what's yours stays in the office. Checkpoints like these will free you from worrying that your consultant might be up to any monkey business, such as installing a "trap door" program to gain access to your network later on. You'll also want to keep proprietary information locked away unless it's needed for the job. Perhaps the most important thing you can do to enhance your security, however, is to pay your consultants what they're worth, provide the tools and time needed to do the job, and treat them with courtesy and respect. Hell hath no fury like a disgruntled worker with the ability to wreak digital havoc.

The following sites will help you find reputable consultants to assist you in your Web-building chores.

### Expert Market

http://expert-market.com/

This membership-only (but free) site is a directory of consulting firms in a variety of computing disciplines.

### Internet Direct Consultant Database

http://www.consultlist.com/

Experienced Web developers and site-managers-for-hire are just a few of the talents available through this database service.

### Mac Web Consultants

http://macweb.com/consultants/

This large, searchable directory of Macintosh Web consultants has over 900 entries. You can narrow down your search according to the expertise you seek, such as integrating a particular database system into Web sites, or working with specific software.

> ☞ In case your eyes start to glaze over after searching these directories (or, perhaps, after interviewing several nerds-in-waiting), you might get a kick out of a little consultant humor. Try the following address for a good one: http://picard.macs.ripon.edu/~godfreyb/humor/others/UnixConsultant.html.

# ANNOUNCEMENTS AND PUBLICITY

If you thought you'd have time to kick back and relax once your server and site are running perfectly, you were wrong. An unpublicized Web site is much like the proverbial tree falling in a lonely forest: If no one hears it, does it really exist? Your ultimate goal is to bring in people—the right sort of people—and to serve them with information, products, or entertainment.

So how do you find the people? Putting the URL on corporate stationery and business cards won't exactly cut it in the online world. You'll have to put on your publicist's hat and send the word out on the Internet grapevine, among other places.

## INDEXES, SEARCH ENGINES, AND OTHER PROMOTION RESOURCES

Indexes and search engines are your best allies in the task of promoting your site's existence. Once your site's address and description have been submitted, millions of users will be able to pull up this information in response to their inquiries each day.

Once upon a time, site managers had to visit Lycos, Yahoo!, and all the other search sites individually. At each one, they'd have to submit their site's URL and hope that their indexing bots would soon add the new information to their catalogs. Now you can use several services that will send your URL and related information to many places at once.

Here's a list of these sites, along with some other helpful site-promotion resources.

### AddURL

http://addurl.com/

You'll have to subscribe, but there's no charge for the AddURL service. It automates the site-registration process, and has the added bonus of being multilingual in both its interface and its list of resources.

## The Internet Promotions Megalist

**http://www.2020tech.com/submit.html**

Collected here are links to dozens of sites where you can submit your URL, either for free or for a fee. Choices include not just the big names that you've no doubt already thought of, but also lists of regional directories and topic-specific venues.

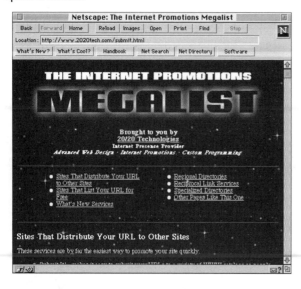

## Register-It!

**http://www.register-it.com/scripts_clean/ states/start.cgi?banner=addurl**

When measured against the value of your time, the fees charged by this commercial service are relatively low. One innovative service offered here submits your site to the Top 50 Web Awards sites—you know, the ones that give you those shiny logos to display on your site that proclaim it to be in the "Top 5%" and such. A free trial membership is available, as are volume discounts for you major producers out there.

## Submit It!

**http://free.submit-it.com/submit.htm**

Scott Bannister has done a great service for Webmasters: All you have to do is fill out a simple form in order to submit your URL to Infoseek, Web Crawler, and other sites. You can choose or exclude search engines from the list of sites receiving your data, or send it to all of them. You can also choose an arbitrary category for your

site that will help to place it in the appropriate category in hierarchical indexes such as Yahoo! In addition, Submit It! has a commercial variant that sends your URL to more sites, carries out directed publicity campaigns, and continues to publicize your site as long as you subscribe.

## MultiSubmit

**http://users.boone.net/yinon/multisub/ default.html**

From this site, your address can go out to 70 major Web search engines, according to your preferences. MultiSubmit is nicely designed and easy to use. The designer created the site in the aftermath of his eighth-grade science project because he was frustrated with how much time he had to spend submitting the project to all those pesky search services. (Eighth grade? Search services? That really makes me realize how old and slow I am!)

## VirtualPROMOTE

**http://www.virtualpromote.com/**

VirtualPROMOTE offers a weekly e-mail newsletter about site promotion, various links to site-submission utilities, a promotions primer, and many other resources to get you started.

## WebPromote

**http://www.webpromote.com/av.shtml**

Proffering promises of guaranteed traffic, WebPromote will submit listings to a wide variety of search services. It can also tailor special marketing programs to work with your content or target audience.

## WebStep Top 100

**http://www.mmgco.com/ top100.html**

This service sponsors this single-interface invitation to submit your URL to 100 search engines or indexes that will list your Web site at no charge. WebStep will do it for you in return for a small fee, or you can work your way through its long, long list of site-submission links.

If you have a specific audience in mind for your material—psychiatrists, Java programmers, or amateur auto-racing buffs, for example—you may also want to seek out specialty search engines and indexes that will catch their eye. There are "meta-index"-style sites available for most academic disciplines, professions and avocations.

## The Three Biggies

If you choose not to use one of these services, be sure to submit your URL to the obvious choices: the three major Web index services operating today.

## Lycos

**http://www.lycos.com**

Lycos long ago moved out of the academic world to become a major commercial player. Precise searches are supported, and submitting your URL is free.

## AltaVista

**http://www.altavista.digital.com/**

One of the most powerful search engines around, Digital's AltaVista lets users search with a high degree of precision. It also accompanies listings with the first few lines grabbed from an archived page—one more reason to carefully consider how your page opens and the words that will appear first to a reader (or to a search engine's robot). There's no charge to submit your URL.

## Yahoo!

**http://www.yahoo.com**

Yahoo! allows visitors to delve through its hierarchical listings in search of sites. According to some site managers, many Web sites receive as many as 70% of their hits directly from a listing in Yahoo! URL submission is free.

> ☞ **Want to automate the process of submitting your URLs to search engines? See http://www.neca.com/~vmis/addurl.htm for a Windows program that you can grab and adapt to fit your needs. It can run on your server and be called into play whenever you want to give a shout-out about your site to your favorite search engines.**

## WORD OF (DIGITAL) MOUTH

The next move in getting the word out is to post a paragraph about your new site to the Usenet newsgroup created specifically for the purpose of such announcements:

### comp.infosystems.www.announce

For guidelines about what sort of announcements are acceptable on this newsgroup and how they should be presented, direct your Web browser to the newsgroup's home page:

### http://boutell.com/~grant/charter.html

If you don't have Usenet access, you can submit your comp.infosystems.www.announce announcement by e-mail to

### www-announce@boutell.com

You can also submit it over the Web via the Deja-News site at

### http://www.dejanews.com/

You should also submit your URL to any topic-specific newsgroups out there—once again, Deja-News is both a good source for finding these groups and a conduit for posting to them with ease. Be sure to check first in the newsgroup FAQ to be sure that it's okay to post this sort of message, however.

Mailing lists on your site's subject are also a good place to crow about your accomplishments. If you know of some where such an announcement would be appropriate, use them.

The next step in the publicity process involves integrating your site into the Web proper. Think about other sites that your target audience is likely to be visiting, and contact those site managers about the feasibility of offering a link to yours. A quid pro quo arrangement is in order here, of course: You should sweeten your suggestion with a corresponding offer to link to their site.

### GETTING PRESS: A PRIMER

If you've never done PR before, take heart: It's not that hard. But you do need to know how the press works and how to get the attention of busy reporters.

As someone who has worked in the computer trade press; placed many, many stories with mainstream, consumer magazines; and been the corporate writer-for-hire in search of a venue for my press release, I've seen the process from all sides. From your point of view, the most important point is that I've been in the shoes of the editor who's deluged with press kits and phone calls from eager-beaver PR people. So I'm going to let you in on a few of the secrets of publicity success. Here's the first of my three PR rules:

1. Figure out who wants to know about your Web site, and find out what they read.

You'll need to know which publications can get information about your site to your preferred audience. If you still don't have a definite picture of your audience (not an unusual situation in the case of a consumer-oriented site with "general audience" appeal), pay close attention to the Web Demographics section coming up. Several companies today are collecting data about who's on line in the "general public," including the average computing layperson, and what sort of sites they visit. You can use this information to adjust your approach.

There are dozens of magazines out there that either cater to a general audience or are read by very broad segments of the browsing public. *Time, Newsweek, US News & World Report,* and *Reader's Digest* are all examples of such publications. By definition, newspapers are geared toward the entire reading population—and many newspapers have a national readership (*USA Today,* the *Wall Street Journal,* the *New York Times,* and *Christian Science Monitor,* for example). And don't forget the large group of magazines that cater to specifically male or female audiences (you can't get a larger subgroup than that!): *Women's Day, Glamour, Working Woman, Men's Journal,* and *Esquire,* to name just a few. These publications carry stories on a very wide variety of topics, including new technologies that offer some sort of benefit to their readers.

If you already know your niche—pathologists, graduate students, C++ programmers, or new parents, for example—then of course it's much easier to target your audience. Hop on down to the public library and search through the pages of *Reader's Guide to Periodicals,* a book published yearly that indexes articles that have appeared in most major magazines.

Do online searches, too, because many special-interest magazines have Web sites themselves. You should treat these online publications just like a print magazine, since they all use the same process for choosing what stories will get written and published. You can probably also benefit from a trip to a good newsstand; libraries these days rarely carry a wide selection of niche magazines, and the annual *Reader's Guide* only indexes a fairly mainstream segment of what's out there.

Buy copies of the magazines or newspapers that you want to target and pay attention to the following items (or, if you must rely on the library, make some photocopies):

- The masthead (the part of the publication that lists the editors and includes a mailing address and contact information)

- A representative feature or two (features are the long stories, which usually appear in the middle)

- Most importantly, any sections that consist of very short stories, such as new product announcements, household or health tips, and the like.

It's best to start with a small selection of publications, because it's not particularly effective to simply broadcast a press release to all and sundry. In fact, here's my second principle of PR success:

2. Successful public relations is based on persuasive personal contact with the right editor.

"Persuasive personal contact" doesn't mean you have to be a super-salesperson. You just need to figure out who's in charge of the section that your site ought to get coverage in, and make sure that they receive your press release—plus a follow-up call or e-mail. Which brings us to the third and final rule:

3. Be persistent, but don't be a pest.

In my capacity as a journalist for various computer trade-press magazines, I work with around 100 different corporate PR people every year. The best of them are the ones who remember my name, know whom I write for and what I write about, and who then send me *only* those press releases that are appropriate.

These paragons of public relations also take the time to put a "spin" on their particular story that's likely to pique my interest. For example, a PR rep for a modem manufacturer, knowing that I write for several multimedia magazines, might send me a personal letter along with the general press kit for her company's new model. Her goal might be to tell me about how a multimedia company is using this model for rapid file transfer.

You can use the same successful tactics to publicize your Web site. If your site is aimed at clients, talk to some of your clients. Then include in your publicity material the tale of how access to your corporate database, sales catalog, or chat area has helped their businesses. This is a story you could pitch to a business magazine or a computer magazine. If you're using a cutting-edge technique for delivering information on the Web, that's a story, too. If your Web site has made your firm's management more responsive, provided timelier information about consumer needs to your sales force, or attracted an unusual audience (a site that's particularly popular with seniors, for instance) those facts can all become stories. And stories are just like free ads, only better, because people really read them.

Pay particular attention to any apropos human interest stories that come your way, such as college friends meeting again by chance in your chat venue. These are the yarns that can get you into general-interest magazines and newspapers with ease.

## A Word About the Computer Trade Press

If your intended audience is computer-savvy, you'll want to target the computer trade press with your publicity campaign. And I include in this category the Internet magazines (*InternetLife*, *The Net*, *Yahoo!*, and the rest) aimed at Web hobbyists, because by and large these Web-zines are owned and operated by the same publishers that do the tech titles (*boot*, *Windows95*, *MacUser*, and so forth). Luckily for you, "selling" your story to the trade press is actually quite easy.

Editors at computer magazines are absolutely deluged with press releases and calls from PR flacks every day. This multiplicity of data forms the basis for almost all news stories that aren't about mergers or stock prices; it's used as research material for features, too. Because of the sheer volume of stuff coming across their desks, however, editors have to filter out most of it. Make sure that your materials are nicely packaged, and that a compelling headline appears on the very first page. Otherwise, your release will wind up in the circular file.

**Magazine Sections** Computer magazines have many different sections, and each magazine is a little different, but certain types of stories are run by almost all of them. Your Web site tale may or may not fit into one or all of these general categories:

- News stories about new products or technological breakthroughs.

- News analyses about a single technology or product category.

- Features that compare (and perhaps rate) several products in the same category.

- Features that show how a product or technology has helped a company (often called "solutions stories").

- "Tips and techniques" articles that show the reader how to do something.

- Profiles of interesting people in the industry.

- Opinion pieces about new technologies or industry issues; these often come from corporate sources.

- Reviews of products or services (sometimes including Web sites).

- Industry gossip.

Now, think about how you could pitch your Web site's story in each of those categories…. You could offer up your company CEO's statements on the importance of the Web to mission-critical operations, or a "how we did it" story. Everybody's got a Web site these days, so that's no longer news. The services or information offered on *your* Web site may be news, though—or tantalizing enough to interest your favorite trade-press gossip columnist. So be creative.

Another venue that you shouldn't overlook is printed Internet directories, particularly books that are specific to your field. There are directories for legal sites, medical sites, business and kid-oriented and African-American sites, and many more. And if you examine a few appropriate titles, you'll know that the writer almost always includes an e-mail ad-

dress for your comments or suggestions. Feel free to send a suggestion: In the two Internet directories I've written, I mentioned almost every site I got e-mail about. It only takes a minute to ask, and these books do get read.

Many of the printed directories also have associated online directories; you may be able to submit your URL and description directly to their Web sites.

## GIVING SOMEONE ELSE THE JOB

If you're working in a corporate situation and the communications value of your site is critical, you may be able to turn non-Web-based publicity chores over to the marketing department or public relations staff. If these folks are clueless about the Web, that may mean you have to set up a miniseminar for them about what the new site offers for potential customers, investors, or other viewers. Also, if it's politically possible within the corporate structure, you should look over any publicity materials written by Web novices. Make sure they're accurate; I've seen some pretty boneheaded releases out there that should have had a technical review.

Some big-ticket, commercially oriented Web sites use outside PR firms to do the work, and that's also an option if your budget will allow. Look for a company that has a proven track record, and try to arrange a relationship with a single PR rep whose persuasive powers are top notch.

> **If you just don't have the time or money to do PR, you might consider contracting with the Internet News Bureau. This single-minded company sends out a targeted press release for you via e-mail to over 1,200 publications. Granted, this qualifies as spam in the eyes of some editors. But in some cases it could be a rewarding strategy. Check out the information on the INS Web site: http://www.newsbureau.com/.**

# TRACKING YOUR AUDIENCE

Chapter 8's section on persistent cookies showcased one rather controversial option for tracking your audience. Of course, you *do* want to know who's hanging out at your site—but cookies aren't the only recipe for getting that data. In this section we'll examine other options.

It's likely that you Webmasters are most interested in the following important information:

- **Audience demographics.** Are your visitors older or younger? Male or female? Rich or not-so-rich? Students, programmers, businesspeople, or retirees? All of these demographic details help you target your information in the most efficient, most attractive way.

- **Numbers**. Exactly how many people are coming to your site each day? This information helps you plan for growth, and it can also be used to attract advertisers. (See the later section "Humans vs. Hits" for more on this topic.)

- **Destinations.** When people visit your site, where do they go next? Once you find out, you can beef up the sections of your site that attract the most interest.

- **Spending habits.** If you're selling products, keep track of what moves and to whom. These facts help you tailor your ordering methods and product stock to match customer demand. This is one type of data that can sometimes be collected via a cookie.

- **Off-site spending habits and more.** You may want to collect information about what your visitors do when they're not surfing your site. Knowing their off-site habits, hobbies, and other not-so-trivial pursuits could help you tailor an online catalog more closely, or identify "fun" features that will attract a lucrative or otherwise desirable audience to your pages.

Using cookies to track a visitor's movements around the Web is controversial, but may work under some circumstances.

## WEB DEMOGRAPHICS

Once you have the goods on your audience, use the following sites to compare them to the general Web-browsing population. You'll be able to pick up hints on how to attract more people, and find out how the Web audience is changing. When you know whom you're reaching, it's easier to make your information to fit their needs.

### "The Accidental Superhighway"
**http://www.info-age.com/support/internet/survey/intro.htm**

*The Economist* has combined demographic data with Net history to create this lengthy overview of the Net audience and growth trends. As always with this publication, the results are pithy and substantive, and even readable.

### Nielsen Media Research—Interactive
**http://www.nielsenmedia.com**

Yep, these are the same folks who do the Nielsen Ratings for television. The Nielsen measures of online audiences include several surveys of Web audience composition, numbers, spending habits, and activities.

### O'Reilly Research
**http://www.ora.com/research/**

These business-oriented Internet surveys, made available by the ever-entrepreneurial O'Reilly & Associates, provide useful information for investors. Naturally, this data is also of interest to those looking at the economic potential of their own Web sites.

### Survey Central
**http://www.cio.com/WebMaster/wm_survey_central.html**

Survey Central presents abstracts of recent Web-related surveys. The analysis has been done for you, and links to the original data are provided.

### COUNTER INTELLIGENCE

Access counters on your pages track how many times each part of the site has been visited since a particular date. Used judiciously, such counters can help you assess the popularity of various areas of the site, see whether promotional efforts have paid off in a measurable way, and find out if visits to your site are becoming more or less frequent.

What counters *can't* tell you is how many people have visited.

That's because counters simply tot up the number of hits that occur. They can't tell you which of those hits are from the same clueless newbie surfing in and out of your site for no discernible reason, or from 25 different people visiting within a half-hour period.

These distinctions are important, because "hits" as a measure of popularity can be pretty meaningless. For example, when I built my first Web site several years ago, I installed a conspicuous counter and checked it daily for the first few days. It quickly racked up a hit score in the hundreds—not bad for a totally unpublicized site, I thought… until I figured out that 99.9% of those hits were from me! As I worked on my site, checking and expanding the page, the counter was clicking merrily away. And the other .01% were from strangers accidentally stumbling in!

Advertisers have also wised up to this flaw in counters—particularly since certain enterprising folks figured out early on that they could inflate their hit figures by spamming their own sites with pseudohits generated by automated scripts. Tsk, tsk… These days, advertisers want to see truly specific data about the actual number of visitors, what sorts of domains they're coming in from, that sort of thing. Mere numbers of hits is not enough.

Regardless, you may want to install a counter anyway for your own purposes, whether it's just to keep a general eye on traffic or to impress visitors with your site's seeming popularity.

Graphical counters abound in archives of CGI scripts; be forewarned, however, that they may slow down performance because they're rendered by the Web server. Some of them are ostentatiously ugly to boot. If you want to add a "plain text" counter that can be placed unobtrusively within your site, try the following simple procedure and program:

1. Change into your public_html Web directory.

   ```
   cd ~/public_html
   ```

2. Create a subdirectory in which to store the page count.

   ```
   mkdir cnt
   ```

3. Make the new directory readable and writable by "nobody" (this is the username under which the Web server operates).

   ```
   chmod 770 cnt
   chgrp nobody cnt
   ```

4. Initialize the counter at zero. You're now creating a file called "counter" within the cnt directory.

   ```
   echo "0" > cnt/counter
   ```

5. Make the counter file readable and writable by the Web server.

   ```
   chmod 660 cnt/counter
   nobody cnt/counter
   ```

6. To actually include the current number from the counter within your HTML page, you'll have to add some commands to your HTML document that will instruct the Web server. Don't change the part inside the < >

brackets, but you can change the sentence outside of the brackets to anything you'd like. For instance:

```
This site has had
<!--#exec cmd="perl -pi -e '$_++'
cnt/counter;cat
cnt/counter"-->
hits!
```

7  To make the counter on your Web page work, you'll have to make your page "executable" by the Web server, giving it permission to run the required commands. So, for a page called index.html (which will display the counter), you'd enter this command:

```
chmod 755 index.html
```

You should now have a functioning counter on your Web pages. This unobtrusive little program is a tasteful substitute for those brightly colored, attention-grabbing counters that are so ubiquitous these days.

> ☞ It's possible to add this counter to each page in a multipage site to track hits per page; just be sure to change the filename counter to something different for each page, such as counter2, counter3, and so on.

## COUNTER CHOICES

The following sites offer counters you can add to your own Web pages. Quality definitely varies, as does usefulness, so *caveat emptor*.

### Access Counter

**http://www.nquest.com/webutils/slide06.htm**

Four choices of counters and a counter tutorial are found here. There are C-based and Perl-based counters and a cool "odometer."

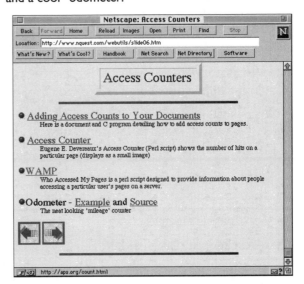

### Sample Access Counters

**http://livewire.ee.latrobe.edu.au/~sjm/ counters.html**

This is just a simple archive where you can see some plain counters—as well as some that are so overdesigned they overwhelm the page. Please, for the sake of eyesight on the Internet, leave some of these where they lie.

### The Web Counter

**http://www.digits.com**

This is a commercial service that will track hits for you. Choose from various plans to fit your site's needs.

### WebHints: PageCounters

**http://www.ross.net/webhints/counters.html**

This introduction to the mechanics of page counters is simply written, but gets into the advanced side of the subject. Topics include invisible page counters and commercial counter services.

## LOG FILE ANALYSIS

All Web servers generate a file that records all hits to its documents. When you analyze this file, you can generate many different types of reports that describe what users are up to on your site, where they're coming from, and even where you can find them later if you want to.

These log entries contain several pieces of information. The specific type of data gathered in your own server's log files can be set using software intended for that purpose. Among the usual items saved are

- Date and time
- Service that caused the entry
- Client address that caused the entry
- Host on which the server runs
- Event

### Log File Analysis Resources

Digging into your Web server's log files is kind of a hassle—there's usually a lot of text, and on simple visual inspection it can be hard to discern patterns. However, software is available, both commercial and public-domain, to do the pattern searching for you. In addition, most commercial Web server packages include some level of customizable log-file analysis and reporting functions, or can accommodate software- and platform-specific add-ons to do so. Check in with your vendor to find out about those options. You may also want to have a look at the following sites.

### Getstats

**http://www.eit.com/goodies/software/getstats/**

Written by Kevin Hughes, Getstats is a versatile (and free) log-file analysis utility. It can take the log files generated by CERN, NCSA, Plexus, GN, MacHTTP Web servers or UNIX Gopher servers, and return a variety of statistics. It runs on Sun Solaris, SGI, VMS, and several other machines.

### ServerWatch Usage Analysis List

**http://serverwatch.iworld.com/tools/usage.html**

Presented as a table, ServerWatch's list of log-analysis packages is divided according to platform, and includes links to complete information on each program included.

### User Tracking Software

**http://www.infoport.com/loganal.htm**

Packages are listed at this site in no particular order, but almost all of them are here. The information is presented in handy table form with the vendor's name, a brief review in several cases, and platform information—as well as a hyperlink to the vendor's Web site.

## WebHints: Management Traffic Tools

http://www.ross.net/webhints/mgt_traffic_tools.html

This list of site-management packages isn't complete, but it comes close. Both commercial and freeware options are listed.

## Webmeister 95

http://www.questar.com/products/webquest/webquest95/webmst95.sht

Windows 95 servers can be managed with this package from Questar Microsystems, which has assembled a rather impressive set of features. Supported tasks include link validation and mapping, plus file- and directory-level encryption and authentication.

## WebTrends

http://www.webtrends.com/PRODUCTS/WEBTREND/QA.HTM

As one of the most extensive log analyzers around for Windows and Windows NT, WebTrends deserves a look. Its customizable reports are particularly powerful. Be sure to check out the very complete FAQ.

## Web Server Statistics Software for Windows 95

http://www.windows95.com/apps/servers-webstat.html

With an interface that makes for easy comparisons, this collection of links to solutions for freeware and shareware statistics is quite useful. Some of these tools are also available for Windows NT and other platforms.

## Yahoo!'s Log Analysis Tools Index

http://www.yahoo.com/Computers_and_Internet/Software/Internet/World_Wide_Web/Servers/Log_Analysis_Tools/

Go look for yourself—log analysis software and info for all platforms and all purposes are listed here.

Why do you want this information? To some extent, it's for your own benefit: You want to see if people like what you're doing, and you want to

---

### ☞ Humans vs. Hits: What's the Difference?

Both "hits" and "visits" are terms used to describe and measure activity at a Web site or on a particular page within a site. However, visit logs provide a much more valuable statistic than anything connected with the vague concept of hits. Here's why:

Hits: Since each of your Web pages has multiple elements (individual graphics, bits of text and links, and so on), that means each time the page loads you'll get a number of "hits" equal to the number of elements on the page. For example, if your page has three graphics and two text files, your Web server log will register five hits when the page loads. Hits can be used to calculate server traffic—and that's something you'll want to track. But they are not an accurate indication of your site's popularity.

Visits: What you really want to know isn't how many files were loaded when your page came up in a visitor's browser, but rather how many people came to see your page—that is, how many visits your page experienced. And figuring out the number of visits will take something more sophisticated than a simple hit counter.

---

know if they're coming back. This information can also be used to add revenue to your site, however.

# GETTING ADVERTISERS

Advertising is not appropriate for every Web site. Indeed, your site may *be* an ad if it's intended as the Web presence for a corporation. In that case, you'll want to think about using advertising techniques to push your own products, but you probably won't want to sell space to anyone else.

Some corporate sites do run ads for partner companies, of course. For example, I've seen computer-consulting firm sites that feature banner ads for the manufacturers of equipment that the consultants recommend or are certified to install. If your firm has some special relationships with other companies, you may be able to capitalize on that fact to bring in a small revenue stream. It's worth thinking about.

On the other hand, if your site is *intended* as a vehicle for advertising, you need to take a different approach. Online publications, search services, entertainment sites, and topic-specific Web attractions are all competing for advertisers, and in many cases the payment you receive for ad space will be less than you might expect. Then again, "some" is always more than "none"—you make the call.

## RATE KITS

Advertisers will almost always want very specific information about whom they'll be reaching with their spot. You'll want to prepare a package that's intended to lure their business. In the print world, this is sometimes called a "rate kit." It's similar to a press kit, but with a slightly different objective. Your rate kit should include the following items:

### 1. A single-page sales pitch targeted at a specific potential advertiser.

This is the most important part of your package, and if you're not a super-persuasive writer, it's the one piece you might want to consider outsourcing to a professional writer or publicist. Your sales pitch should prominently feature the name, address, e-mail address, and telephone number of the person who will handle advertising arrangements for your site. Target one person at one company; form letters will get no response. If you don't know who's in charge of placing ads, call corporate headquarters and ask for the marketing and communications department. Even if they don't make ad buys in house, they'll know who the outside ad agency is.

The sales pitch should sum up all of the most important factors that you think will attract this advertiser. For example, let's say you're pitching your site

to an automobile manufacturer. You might start with the following four points and build your sales pitch around them:

- "Your car company wants to reach forward-thinking, high-salaried people."
- "Visitors to our Web site are the kind of people who buy your cars—and here are the demographics to prove it."
- "We offer a cost-effective advertising option with measurable results."
- "We're really excited about being a partner with your prestigious firm in this exciting new medium… (blah, blah, blah)"

### 2. A one- to two-page description of your site.

You'll want to explain your goals. Tell potential advertisers who your sponsoring company is or, if applicable, who your investors are. Provide a very visual picture of what your Web site does to attract readers.

### 3. Detailed demographics.

There's been much talk lately in the advertising trade press about numbers fudging by Web-based companies—and that makes companies leery. Accordingly, corporate advertisers now expect a lot more than a hit count. Luckily for you, your traffic can be measured and dissected in much more precise ways today.

Use your log analysis software to tease out information about what sort of domains your visitors hail from (corporate, military, education, and so on). Try to gather data, as well, about what parts of your site are the most attractive (see "Tracking Your Users" earlier in this chapter for help with this). Can you prove that you frequently have repeat visits from the same IP address (that is, the same person)? If so, show it here. Finally, use any studies that have been done by professional demographers about the Web audience to add some perspective to your real-world numbers.

**4. Screen shots.**

The Web is a visual medium, and if your site has great design, that's a selling point. Take one or two screen shots that show off your interface, and print these at full-page size. Color printing is a good idea.

**5. Corporate backgrounder.**

If you're working for a big company, chances are that a background piece has already been written and can simply be adapted to fit. This item is generally several pages long and provides the details of what your company does, how long it's been around, who its important officers are, and where it's going.

Even if your Web company is just you, or just you and a couple of pals, you'll still need a backgrounder. You're going to have to come up with something comparable to what the biggies use, but true to your own smaller-scale appeal. Tell your potential advertisers how long you've been in business, mention any awards you've won for your work, and brag a little about your illustrious background and professional affiliations. It's a bit like an extended resume. This piece, unlike the short sales pitch, can be reused without changes in each rate kit you send out.

**6. Ad rate card.**

This is going to the hardest part. In the print world, there is a whole set of standard expectations about ad rates and audience size. These do not necessarily apply on the Web, however. So how do you make sure your rates are not too high or too low? You do competitive research. Contact sites that are similar in appeal to yours and ask for *their* ad rates. You may even have to pose as a potential advertiser—though it may seem underhanded, this is typically how it's done in the print world when magazines won't let their competitors know what they charge.

Information about ad rates and practices can also be found in advertising magazines: *AdWeek* and *Advertising Age* are probably the most widely read, and the articles they run can be real eye-openers. Their online versions are listed in the later site descriptions, along with other resources that can help you learn about what sites are charging and how the online advertising business is going.

Most print publications offer special incentives to advertisers. Typical come-ons include a lower rate for your first ad, a complimentary ad for every X number of ads purchased, and long-term advertising packages that offer a discount for committing to (and paying for) three, six, or 12 months of continuous advertising. These incentives are based on many years of experience in the business of attracting and holding advertisers, and they are very much applicable to Web advertising.

## Ad Kit Appearance

Like well-designed Web pages, the materials in your ad kit should have a consistent look. Use letterhead where appropriate, and pay attention to typeface and design.

When all of your materials are assembled, choose a snazzy folder in which to put your brand-new ad kits—get the kind that allows you to include a business card on the inside flap (these folders are available by the dozens at your nearest office supply store). Mail it off in a nice envelope with a printed label, and wait at least a week.

## FOLLOWING UP

When you are sure that your package has arrived on the appropriate desk, make a follow-up call (or have your company's ad salesperson call).

- Keep a sales-pitch outline in front of you if you've never done this before—it does wonders for nervousness.

- Have a couple of ideas in reserve to sweeten the pot for your potential advertiser, should your target seem less than enthusiastic. For example, if the advertiser argues that they don't have an appropriate ad designed for the Web, you might offer to design one—for free, if that'll clinch the deal. (In fact, some Web designers have offered to design a home page for non-Webified companies, as well as the ad itself.)

- Mention those incentive packages discussed above. And tell the company how you'll help measure ad response through reports culled from your log file, via click-throughs to its corporate site (see the TIP that follows), by setting up a system for e-mail inquiries, or any other idea that you can think of.

You may have to make a couple of phone calls to cement the deal. You may have to set up an in-person meeting. You may have to send flowers. But once you've got the ad, make sure that you don't stop there. Keeping advertisers happy requires constant attention and regular care. If you have promised to make periodic reports about ad response, site traffic, or new features, do so. And give your faithful advertisers an unexpected reward now and again, whether it's a copy of your latest software, a box of chocolate chip cookies, or a free ad "just for being such a wonderful supporter."

## WEB ADVERTISING RESOURCES

This list of online publications, articles, and related Web sites should help you get up to speed on the topic of online advertising. Be sure to also browse related stories in general-interest Web and Internet magazines—particularly *WebWeek*, which is listed later in this chapter under "Publications for Pros."

☞ For advertisers, the important issue will be measuring performance. Some typical measures are

- *Click-throughs:* Customers who click on the ad and are transported to the company's own Web site or to additional information about the product or service that's housed on your own Web site.

- **Percentage of actual sales:** A figure gathered by calculating actual online sales, or by somehow figuring out that a particular ad campaign moved consumers to buy more in the store. This latter statistic reflecting customer decisions may be derived through polls or focus groups, or by analyzing changes in spending habits as they relate to the presence of a new ad campaign.

None of this is an exact science... but you'll want to understand the terms that you'll hear. Read conscientiously the magazines listed in this section, and you can't help but be more knowledgeable.

## Advertising Age
http://www.adage.com/

Daily news updates, along with almost the entire contents of the hefty print version of this mag, are posted here. *Advertising Age* is the bible of the ad business. Articles cover the activities, tactics, and revenues of major ad firms and, incidentally, of major advertisers. If you need an education about how the business works, you'll have to learn a bit of industry jargon. But it will be well worth your time if you have any intention of playing in the big leagues.

## AdWEEK Online
http://www.adweek.com/

The online editions of *AdWEEK* and two other well-respected ad industry publications include much news of new-fashioned media, including the latest about advertising trends on the Web.

## DoubleClick

**http://www.doubleclick.com**

The DoubleClick network helps advertisers place customized messages based on user demographics. Its site is highly informative to providers of ad space as well, because it helps you find out what demographic elements are most attractive to advertisers, and who's buying where.

## Link Exchange

**http://www.linkexchange.com/**

Link Exchange members can get statistics and demographic profile information, updated daily, and have access to ad placement services. This group is best known for working with smaller, single-topic, targeted-audience sites. Not only can you use Link Exchange as a mechanism for getting ads placed on your site, but it might be able to provide the kind of cost-effective advertising tools you need to get readers to visit your site. Members also have access to three newsgroups and a mailing list to exchange advertising ideas and strategies.

## NetMarketing

**http://www.netb2b.com/**

NetMarketing is an *Advertising Age* spin-off that does a very thorough job of covering the emerging advertising market on line. You can find out how sites are getting advertisers, what ad sales techniques are working for what sort of sites, and more. Highly recommended—especially if this is your first foray into the ad world. It's also a good forum for hooking up with companies that can sell ads for you.

## Web Ad Rates

**http://www.sisoftware.com/ whatitco.htm**

Subtitled "What It Costs and What You Get," this is a compilation of ad rates arranged according to the type of site: major search engine, major content site, small targeted content site, or "new models that break the mold." It's updated every couple of months to reflect changes in the market. If you're getting ready to set your ad rates, this is a good list to compare with to make sure you're in the ballpark. In addition, you'll find ratings, "best buy" recommendations, and insider info about many major ad venues. You can compare what you're doing with your ad incentive program, measurement scheme, and more.

## The Web Ad Space Registry

**http://www.fwy.com/ADVERT/**

This free service can be used by anyone who's buying or selling ad space on line. Check through the database and add your own listing.

### WebConnect

**http://www.webconnect.net/**

Possibly the biggest current trend in online advertising is the growth of firms that act as ad brokers. These organizations help advertisers find the right sites on which to place their ads—and, conversely, also help sites find the right advertisers. WebConnect is one of the biggest and best. And even if you choose to do it on your own, this site's information on measuring ad response and statistics about Web advertisers will be interesting to read.

## Site Maintenance and Link Checkers

As vendors of Web server packages attach more and more new features in a competitive frenzy, an enhancement becoming quite typical is rudimentary site-maintenance capabilities. There is much work involved in keeping your site on track, so these tools are greatly appreciated. You'll need to stay on top of a lot of things, including

- **External links**. Are they still valid? Have linked sites moved or been rearranged?

- **Internal links**. As you change your site, be sure to check internal links regularly to avoid leading visitors on a path to nowhere. Most Web authoring programs now have the ability to ensure that when the name of a page is changed, any references to the old name on other pages are also changed.

- **Removing dated references**. Get rid of references to events already held, "upcoming" products that have long since shipped, and old news. This housecleaning is one thing that software *can't* do for you.

- **Adding fresh material**. It's important to freshen up your site as often as possible, even if all you have time to do is swap in a new opening graphic now and then or add a few more external links. (See the Java programming example

earlier in this chapter for an interesting way to rotate graphics automatically.)

As noted earlier, all of the major server packages—and most HTML authoring packages as well—offer some internal and external link-checking tools. If yours doesn't, chances are there's an add-on or a freeware program that will fill the bill. Give your vendor a call to see what your options are.

You can even let somebody else do the job on the Web.

### NetMechanic Link Check

**http://www.netmechanic.com/link_check.htm**

This site's snappy robot will check your site for broken links. Testing large sites may take several hours; you'll get an e-mail when the process is done.

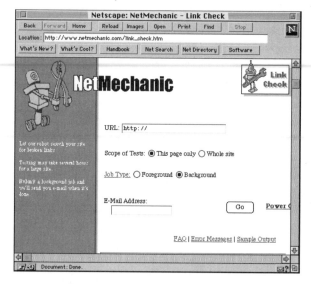

## Keep 'Em Coming Back

There's more to maintaining your audience's interest than occasionally freshening up your text and graphics. If repeat visitors are what you need to satisfy your employer or your advertisers, take a look at what other sites are doing to keep the same people coming back for more. Options include automated e-mail updates, BBS-style discussion forums where visitors can post questions or witty repartee, interactive chat boards, "ask an expert" features, and even games and contests.

The following sets of sites are road maps to the possibilities. Visit them with an open mind—the high-bandwidth glitz of some may not be right for your topic or audience, but you might get inspired to try something similar, if more subdued.

## E-MAIL LINKS

Here are two ways to use e-mail to give your users something extra.

### Orange County Democratic Party
http://www.orangedems.org/email.html

This California political group uses e-mail as a vehicle for delivering an online newsletter to visitors who ask for it. It's a low-cost way to get the word out and maintain contact, once an elusive and rare Democrat from Orange County actually surfaces!

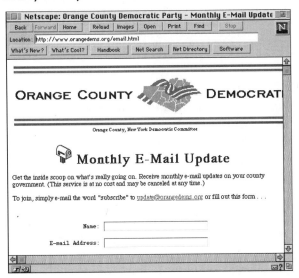

### PowerMac Pac
http://www.macpac.com/

How do you get readers to come back to a site that's essentially a catalog, if they don't buy something on the first round? This Oregon computer store specializes in mail-

order, and they know about creating repeat customers. If potential buyers click a link on the front page, they'll receive regular e-mailings about special offers.

## DISCUSSION FORUMS

These two sites add value with well-managed chat forums.

### Neurology WebForums at Massachusetts General Hospital
http://neuro-www.mgh.harvard.edu/

The extensive set of chat boards and interactive chat rooms found at this site, including an experimental Java-based chat system, attract a large audience. It's professionally managed by Webmaster John Lester, and tremendously helpful to a worldwide audience of parents and patients dealing with puzzling neurological disorders and injuries.

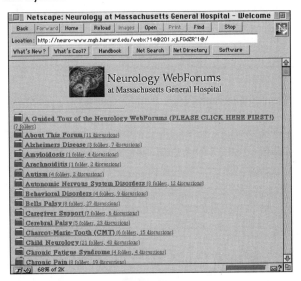

### Salon's Table Talk
http://tabletalk.salon1999.com/webx

Conversation here isn't always as refined as the interface might lead you to expect, but it's certainly thought provoking. And it's a feature that attracts repeat readers, as those who post messages and quips come back to see how their words have fared. It's definitely a freewheeling environment.

### "ASK AN EXPERT" FEATURES

Do you have a resident expert available who could answer the occasional question? These two sites have leveraged on the availability of such people to good effect.

### Ask the Pros

http://www.inquiry.com/

Along with its index of vendor-penned product plugs, in-quiry.com serves up answers to your questions on several topics. Current pros on hand cover ActiveX, C++, Java, Oracle PowerObjects, networking issues, and more. Answers to previous questions are housed in a searchable archive. This is an invaluable resource, and it took only a small investment of brainpower and computer space to create it.

### ParentsPlace.com

http://www.parentsplace.com/genobject.cgi/readroom/dr_answers.html

Using a CGI program and the services of several experts, the Websters behind this nicely designed site for parents will let you query a doctor, dentist, midwife, lactation consultant, or nutritionist. Answers to past questions are cataloged in a database, so this isn't just a "one-to-one" service. And it's *exactly* the sort of thing that will keep people coming back, as attested to by the site's traffic statistics.

### GAMES AND PUZZLES

Everyone loves a good puzzle, and games and such are surprisingly excellent ways to get readers to stick around for a while. While they play or try to get the solution to the puzzle, you can bombard them with your ever-changing ads and perhaps ensure that they bookmark your site.

### *National Geographic* Kids

http://www.nationalgeographic.com/kids/maina.html

For now, only relatively simple online games can work for users who have current Web browsers and typical home-computer configurations. That's something to keep in mind if home users are your target audience. The online version of *National Geographic* Kids does a good job of working within these limitations while delivering games that are both fun and educational.

### Period.com Puzzles

http://www.period.com/puzzles/puzzles.shtml

This entertainment-oriented Web site uses puzzles to draw in new customers. Its puzzles run as SSIs, and some are quite complex.

### Scott Kim's Puzzler

http://www.hyperstand.com/Search/search.html

New Media readers already know how devilish this monthly printed feature can be. Now try your skills against its interactive counterpart. Definitely addictive!

### CONTESTS

Contests are really no big deal to set up, and they can generate a huge volume of visits. Prizes can be cheap (coffee mugs, T-shirts, mouse pads) or swanky (Hawaiian trip for two, new computer, cash). In fact, you might even get more mileage and word-of-mouth by offering a silly novelty item than an expensive one. A graphics firm could give away Etch-a-Sketch toys, for instance; a company trying to make the impression that its technology is "hot" could offer up jars of superfiery salsa. Creativity counts if you want to get noticed, and could even help you get your contest written up for free.

That said, you will need to check the appropriate state and national laws before running a contest—on line or elsewhere. All those lines of fine print found on contest entry blanks derive from regulations that prohibit one sort of competition or another. For example, certain states insist that a contest, by definition, be based on some element of skill. You may even need to find out about international rules. The good news: If you take a look at the fine print found at the sites listed in this section, you should be able to glean most of what you need to know.

Here are a few sites that play the contest game well.

## Disney.com

http://www.disney.com/

Disney, of course, is the all-time champion of self-promotion. This mega-organization can even get you to *wear* an ad for its products, not to mention selling you ad-laden foods, toys, and software. Contests are a regular feature at this site, so look here to see how the pros do it.

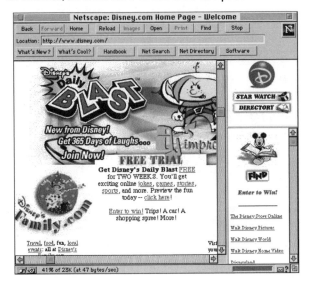

## MathSoft Keeps Visitors Puzzled

http://www.mathsoft.com/prize/details.htm

Who said math is no fun? (Well, I probably did back in Calculus class—but obviously these folks don't agree!) The MathSoft company runs regular contests with creative and inexpensive prizes, such as a radio-controlled model plane. Not only must contestants use their math and history skills to find the right answer, but they get extra points for presenting their results elegantly.

### FREEBIES

Everybody likes free stuff. Online giveaways are so popular that sites have sprung up just to index places to get freebies. A case in point:

## VIVID Workplace Solutions: Building Better Nerdware

http://www.ub.com/product/solutions.html

How do you drag network managers over to your site to look at cool Ethernet stuff? Offer them a free T-shirt as an enticement. Some online PR types might question the approach taken here—forcing readers to fill out a survey to get a crack at the freebie—but for a smaller company that's trying to build a mailing list, it seems like nothing less than a smart move.

### SITES FOR SORE EYES

One last word about refreshing your site's appeal: Be sure to continue calling up your site in all of the major Web browsers as they evolve. Changes in the ways browsers handle specific types of data and scripting are something you definitely want to keep abreast of.

You also want to explore new techniques for grabbing your audience's attention. The following sites cover the latest in "cool" Web site technology. Keep these in mind and in your research, but let the bleeding-edge types perfect them before you try them out yourself. (Be sure to see the section on push/pull technologies in Chapter 9 for more along these lines. And also cruise around the major Java, JavaScript, and ActiveX sites listed in that chapter—that's where most of the action is right now.)

### Cool Java Applets

**http://techweb3.web.cerf.net/tools/java/ java2.html**

Eye-popping examples of what Java applets can do for (to?) your site are happening here. Take this virtual tour, but be sure to wear your "cool" shades.

### FEED

**http://www.emedia.net/feed/**

FEED—everybody's favorite overdesigned Web-zine—takes each new design trend to extremes. And that's exactly what's good about this site.

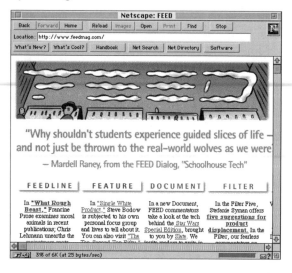

### Said Chat Page

**http://www.said.com/**

At this site, programmer Cabel Sasser experiments with JavaScript and frames, coming up with nicely designed, even classy results.

As browsers become more extensible and desktop computers grow more powerful, who knows what directions our Web sites will take? "Less static and more dramatic" seems to be the most likely guess.

Luckily, the Web's ever-evolving nature means that the online resources listed in this book will change right along with the trends, staying up to date and continually bringing you information about the latest products and procedures.

## EXTENDING YOUR SKILLS

It's critical that you keep your Web authoring skills up to pace. As with any computing career, that means making time in your schedule for seminars, trade shows, and formal training. It also means getting involved with formal and informal networks for Webmasters and designers. These organizations can include online newsgroups, computer users groups, and professional associations.

### SEMINARS AND TRADE SHOWS FOR WEB-HEADS

The sites listed here will keep you informed of the principal annual and regional events for Web designers and techies. Classes are frequently a part of what's on tap at trade shows, and these study groups often prove to be of much more value than the boring CEO speeches and hall prowls.

> 👉 Incidentally, some of the best educational stuff is often available on line. You might even be able to get the information you seek by browsing the conference's Web site instead of trudging the aisles!

### International World Wide Web Conference

**http://www.w3.org/pub/Conferences/ Overview-WWW.html**

Occasionally held in exotic locales, this is the one to go to if (a) your boss is paying your way; and (b) you're interested in Web theory and futurology. All the big names will be there, because it's sponsored by the W3 Consortium.

## Internet World

**http://events.iworld.com/**

"World" is not a misnomer here: This traveling trade show is an international phenomenon, landing everywhere from Jerusalem to Chicago to Tokyo. Event schedules, registration information, and supporting documents are available here.

## NetWorld +Interop

**http://www.interop.com/ index.html**

This Ziff-Davis production is the biggie of Net-related trade shows, almost *too* big for one attendee to handle without a tour guide. It used to be strictly for the hub-and-router crowd, but that probably means you now, doesn't it? The Web site's a good year-round resource, incidentally, and NetWorld +Interop shows take place around the globe. Be there, or catch the keynote speeches via cybercast at this site.

## Java Developers Conference

**http://sbjdc.xweb.eds.com/**

If you're pursuing a career as a Java programmer or developer, this Sun-centric meet is shaping up as *the* place to be. Developers from around the world will converge yearly in San Francisco to gab and grab.

## Trade Show Central

**http://www.tscentral.com/**

If none of the shows listed above sounds right for you, go search the database of 30,000+ shows, conferences, and seminars listed here at Trade Show Central. You'll find what you're looking for.

## TRAINING

What more do you need to know? Probably a lot—and it's highly likely your job will expand in ways that you don't expect, such as handling more of the infrastructure planning for your company, or creating custom graphics. Be sure to check into the groups listed under "Professional Organizations" just below. Many of them offer classes, seminars, and referrals to reputable instructors.

Vendors can also point you toward product-specific expert trainers. Community colleges as well as universities are good sources for training that comes with college credit.

Trade schools can be more problematic; I recommend that you insist on seeing the equipment you'll be working on at any of these schools. Some of them have a reputation for overselling courses that turn out to have you running last year's apps on outdated equipment. You might be better off with a tutorial on the Web!

## PROFESSIONAL ORGANIZATIONS

Others who share your passion are just a meeting (or an e-mail) away. The following are groups that can put you in the mainstream of the online-media community. They're invaluable sources of camaraderie, assistance, shoulders to cry on, and practical assistance. Several of them (notably the Society for Technical Communication and two trade unions that organize multimedia writers and coders) are also good places to look for work when your current position has lost its glamour.

## International Society of Internet Professionals

**http://www.webpro.org/**

ISIP boasts several thousand members and provides a number of useful benefits. This is a nonprofit organization dedicated to promoting professionalism in the Internet career marketplace.

 ### International Webmaster Association
### http://www.irwa.org/

You work in an international medium, so why not link up across borders? IRWA offers international job listings, information about certification and work requirements around the world, and news about software internationalization efforts. Students as well as current professionals are eligible for membership.

 ### National Writers Union
http://www.nwu.org/

The NWU is a United Auto Workers-affiliated union for freelance and contract writers—and in this case the term "writer" applies to those who write code as well as words. The NWU's Business, Instructional, Technical, and Electronic (BITE) campaign agitates for better contracts, educates its members, and even has a union "hiring hall" in the form of a job hotline for technical writing and multimedia. Other benefits include group health insurance and a grievance system for dealing with employers who don't pay or who abuse the hired help.

## Network and Systems Professional Association
### http://www.nascom.com

NaSPA used to be pretty much just for systems administrators and their ilk. As more of these folk move into managing Web servers, however, and as more site managers find that their jobs increasingly resemble systems administration, NaSPA is beginning to provide other services of interest.

## Society for Technical Communications
### http://www.stc.org

The path from technical writer to Web page builder or Web content provider is a clear one these days, as companies put their technical reports, manuals, and white papers on line. STC has been instrumental in educating tech writers for these new duties. This organization now has chapters active in almost every metropolitan area and can be a great avenue for networking.

## Users Groups on Yahoo!
### http://www.yahoo.com/Computers_and_Internet/Organizations/User_Groups/

There's no better single interface for finding an appropriate users group on line than this one. (You may also find easier-to-navigate links to local groups at vendor Web sites.)

## The Webmaster's Guild
### http://www.webmaster.org/

This national, professional organization for Webmasters seems like a good idea. There are currently about four active chapters meeting in the major US urban markets. Its Web site offers access to "The Thread," the Guild's newsletter, as well as to job postings and career tips.

## Writers Guild of America
### http://www.wga.org/

With the advent of movie-linked multimedia, this organization has acquired new members other than garden-variety screenwriters. Many HTML writers now belong, as well as multimedia types who work for big media corporations such as Time-Warner. Freelancers, too, are eligible, if their employer has signed one of the special single-project agreements that the Guild is using in the multimedia industry. The Guild's Web site is also an excellent source for inside news about the multimedia industry, including Web and game development.

## PUBLICATIONS FOR PROS

Throughout this book we've mentioned several dozen on- and off-line magazines. Here are a few "leftovers" that could contribute to your self-education as a Web designer and/or Web site management professional.

## Avatar Magazine
**http://www.avatarmag.com/**

With bold, eye-catching graphics, Avatar certainly practices what it preaches. This publication's articles cover issues of interest to those designing interactive media. Typical subjects: the use of color on Web sites, and how to get search engines to index your site.

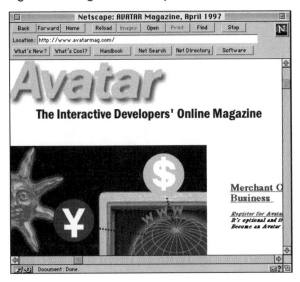

## InfoWorld Electric
**http://www.infoworld.com/**

This magazine for IS professionals and network gurus is just the ticket if you're nervous about the increasingly technical nature of your Web duties. For individuals who came into this arena from the desktop publishing, promotions, design, and/or writing side, *InfoWorld*'s well-

written features and news stories will likely be educational. Even if you already have the hardware savvy, you'll want to visit here just to keep on top of the news.

## Inter@ctive Week
**http://www.zdnet.com/intweek/**

This is *the* trade magazine of the multimedia/Web confluence. Like ZD's *MacWEEK* and *PCweek*, *Inter@ctive Week* caters in equal parts to industry insiders and high-end users. More honest business coverage can be found here than you'll see in strictly consumer-oriented Internet magazines.

## iWorld
**http://www.iworld.com/**

Mecklermedia's entrant in the daily Net-news race is iWorld, which after a slim start is beginning to shape up as a contender.

## LAN Times
**http://www.lantimes.com/**

It's not just about local area networks anymore. In fact, this magazine has been on the front lines of coverage for the convergence of computers and telephony; of high-end networking topics of interest to large-site managers; and more.

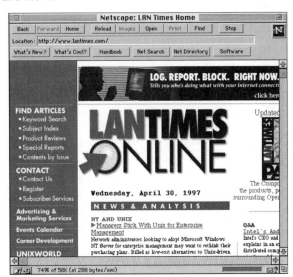

### *NetscapeWorld's* Net News Central

**http://www.netscapeworld.com/ netscapeworld/netnews/netnews.index.html**

The Net News Central feature of this online magazine from Netscape is a boon for busy Websters. You'll find abstracts of interesting articles from a variety of sources. The articles are also hotlinked, of course. And the rest of the e-mag is worth reading, too.

### Online World

**http://www.idg.widewest.com.au/ online.world/news.html**

This weekly newsletter is geared toward the Web developer. It's based in Australia but very much on top of the scene.

### Web Developer

**http://www.webdeveloper.com/**

Billing itself as the "#1 Technical Magazine," *Web Developer* maintains its own informative FAQs on subjects ranging from VRML to text editors. Of course, there are articles, too—including weekly news updates every Thursday.

### Webmaster Forum

**http://www.cio.com/aforum/forums/aca/ dispatch.cgi**

This Web-based chat forum is for discussing professional concerns (salaries, certification issues, that sort of thing) and tricks of the trade with other Webmasters. Registration is required.

### WebMaster Online

**http://www.cio.com/WebMaster/**

WebMaster Online's business orientation means lots of articles about the care and feeding of corporate intranets, as well as Web-related news and reviews. A "breaking news" e-mail update service is also available by subscription.

### WebWeek

**http://www.webweek.com/**

This news weekly covers the business side of the Web more than software and hardware, although you'll also find news analysis on what new products may do for the Web. There are job ads, and current news that lets you in on your competitors' latest moves. Sample headlines: "Pathfinder Licenses Pop Culture Content," "USA Today Expands Online Classified Ads."

## A FEW LAST WORDS

Well, that's it. We've force-fed you just enough information to get you going (yes, there *is* more out there). Hopefully, the rapidly changing information that you can access through the Web site listings herein will ensure that you find out about the latest practices and products.

I hope you enjoy playing a part in the fast-paced, fascinating environment that is today's World Wide Web, and that you contribute something to make the Web a more interesting and useful medium.

# Appendix A
# Tips for Using Lycos to Search the Web

**TO SEARCH THE LYCOS CATALOG,** just enter one or more words (better known as a "search query") in the text entry box on the Lycos home page or search results page. Next, press the Enter key (or click the Go Get It button). Lycos will display the results. If you need to customize or refine your search, however, Lycos provides an easy way for you to "fine-tune" your search.

The Customize Your Search form is a tool that Lycos provides to make searching its index easy for you to do. It's especially helpful if you need to do any of the following:

- Make your search wider or narrower
- Have the search match ALL words in a query rather than ANY single word (which is the default setting)
- Search for special variations of a given term (for example, to search for several possible spellings of a word AND some other word)

Most of the time you won't need to use this search form at all if you only want to perform "wide" searches of the Web. However, Lycos gives you other Search options which you can change if you want to search for different types of information, such as

pictures, sounds, and sites that have been categorized by subject.

You can also "refine" your search by making it narrower or wider. You can have the search match ALL words in your query rather than the default ANY word. You can also search for a number of terms which are DIFFERENT from the number you entered (for example, to search for several possible spellings of a word AND some other word).

The search form gives you two ways to control your search: *Search Options*, and *Display Options*. You'll notice that both Search Options and Display Options are pull-down menus. Simply click the down-arrow in each of these pull-down menus and look at the selections that are available.

## Using Search Options to Set Terms to Match (Boolean)

You might wonder why you can't do Boolean searches on Lycos. You might also want to know what exactly a Boolean search is. Boolean searches are those queries that let you search the Web for very specific combinations of words. For example, you might want to see all instances of peanut and butter together, but only where they appear without jelly.

Although you can't perform true Boolean searches on Lycos, you can come very close by using the Search Options features. Just keep these simple guidelines in mind:

- AND searches are possible by selecting the match all terms (AND) option and then entering whatever words you want in the search box. In the above example, you'd simply enter peanut butter.

- NOT searches are a bit trickier. You may currently prepend (that is, begin) a term with a hyphen to make it a negative indicator, like this: -jelly. This will only reduce the score for sites containing the word jelly, not remove them entirely. The good news is that the first set of results you get will most likely give you what you want: peanut butter without jelly.

By default, Lycos will find all documents matching any word you type in your query (except for certain words like "a" and "the" which are generally not meaningful in a search). If you type "jeep cherokee" as your query, Lycos will find all documents containing either "jeep" OR "cherokee." This is the match any term (OR) Search Option, and is what you get when you type a query into the form on the home page, or if you select the match any term (OR) option on the Customize Your Search form.

Sometimes you might want to find only documents which match ALL the words in your query. This is the match all terms (AND) option. Try it on the form and then see what Lycos returns for "jeep cherokee" when you use the "OR" option and when you use the "AND" option.

# SYMBOLS YOU CAN'T USE IN YOUR SEARCHES

You can't use + in search terms. A common instance of this is the term C++, which gets stripped down to C. Unfortunately, this leaves a single letter which, being shorter than three characters, is ignored. This behavior can be annoying, but Lycos is in the process of choosing the best solution to solve it (and related problems) without affecting the speed and performance of conducting searches. For now we suggest you search for related terms: Instead of C++, for instance, you might try programming languages. Hopefully, Lycos will fix this soon.

You also cannot search for numbers. The current version of Lycos strips out all numbers at the beginning of words. This causes problems if you search for 3DO, 4AD Records, or any other letter-number combination.

The problem is that numbers are a whole different breed of cat from letters. Lycos is trying to teach its retrieval engine to determine for itself which sequences of letters are words and which are not; once they do, you'll be able to make these searches.

# SYMBOLS YOU CAN USE IN YOUR SEARCHES

At the present time, you can use the following symbols in your search queries:

- (-) As we mentioned earlier, you can use the - symbol to help narrow down your search. For example, to search for bank, but without river turning up in the search, you would type bank -river in your search query. This is similar to the NOT Boolean search term.

- (.) Use a period at the end of the keyword to limit it with no expansions. Bank. will bring up only results with the keyword "bank" and ignore expansions like "bankers" and "banking."

- ($) Put this symbol after the keyword to make the search engine expand it. The search term "gard$" will bring up results like "garden" and "gardenias." This feature is great if you don't know how to spell a word, or if you aren't sure what you're looking for.

## LIMITING YOUR SEARCH TO A SPECIFIED NUMBER OF TERMS

You might also be wondering why you need "match 2 terms," "match 3 terms," and so on. These options give you more flexibility in your search. Suppose you wanted to find references to Sarajevo and Yugoslavia. But you're not sure whether Sarajevo is spelled "Sarajevo" or "Sarayevo." So you enter your query "Sarajevo Sarayevo Yugoslavia." To get the best results, you can use the Search Options.

You can't use match all terms (AND) because that would give you only documents which contain both spellings of "Sarajevo" AND Yugoslavia, and there probably aren't any of those. You could use match any terms (OR), because that would return all documents that contain any of these three terms, but you would also get lots of documents you don't want in the list.

Here's what you do: Enter "Sarajevo Sarayevo Yugoslavia" as your query, and choose match 2 terms. This selection will match at least two terms in each document. Since it's quite unlikely Sarajevo will be spelled two different ways in the same document, the results returned will have references to BOTH one of the two spellings of Sarajevo AND Yugoslavia.

## USING THE SEARCH OPTIONS TO SET THE SELECTIVITY OF THE SEARCH

You can change the Search Options to adjust the selectivity of the Lycos search engine. When set to "loose match," you will get more documents, but they will tend to be less relevant to the query you've made. Often, particularly when you are beginning a search and wish to cast the widest possible net, this is exactly what you want.

If you want the Lycos search engine to be more selective, change the Search Option from loose match to "strong match." Lycos will return only documents which have a very high relevance to your query. If you are on a slow dial-up connection, setting the selectivity to "strong match" can save you time by reducing the number of irrelevant hits downloaded to you.

You should try out the effect of changing various selectivity settings on the form. Try some searches with various selectivity settings to get a feel for how it affects your results.

## SETTING THE DISPLAY OF THE RESULTS PAGE SIZE

Lycos always gives you all the results or "hits" matching your query, even if there are hundreds or thousands of documents. If the number of hits is large, however, Lycos does not display them all at once, so you don't need to wait a long time for the whole page to come to you. By default, Lycos displays 10 hits on each results page. Once you've looked at those 10, you click on the "Next 10 hits" link at the bottom of the page to get the next 10 hits, and so on until all the hits are displayed.

To change the default from 10 hits displayed on each page, you can set the number in the Display Options pull-down menu. Simply choose another value from 10-40 results per page.

## SETTING THE AMOUNT OF RESULTS DETAIL YOU WANT DISPLAYED

You can also control the amount of information you want Lycos to display about each result. There are three levels of detail you can choose from:

- Standard (the default)

- Detailed (all information displayed)

- Summary (the minimum amount of information is displayed)

## INTERPRETING THE RESULTS OF A SEARCH

The percentage numbers are simply Lycos's way of showing you how close it thinks each site will match what you're looking for, based on the words you asked Lycos to search for.

When the Lycos search engine compares each page to your query, it gives higher scores to pages that contain the words as you typed them in. It also looks for pages that mention these words early on, rather than far down in some subsection of the site. The page with the combination most like the words you typed in is ranked at the top and assigned the number 1.000. Other sites are ranked below and assigned numbers based on how much or how little they resemble your search terms.

This means that if you asked for Hungarian goulash, then a site titled The Hungarian Goulash Recipe Page will end up above sites that mention Carpathian goulash, salad, and Hungarian bread or some less precise combination.

The percentages are in no way a rating of how good Lycos thinks any page is. They're simply a tool to help you narrow down your choices.

# Appendix B
# Using the CD-ROM

**THE CD-ROM** that's packaged with this book includes software for you to use. The software will not only allow you to explore the Internet and search the Web, but will also allow you to view a fully hyperlinked HTML version of the printed book, also contained on the CD-ROM. Before you can use the software, you will need to install it on the hard drive of your computer. This is a simple procedure that will take only a few minutes.

## What's on the CD-ROM?

The CD-ROM includes the following software and other items that can be installed on your computer:

- Microsoft Internet Explorer Web browser for PCs and Macs
- MindSpring Internet connection software for PCs and Macs
- A fully hyperlinked HTML version of the book for PCs and Macs, which you can view using your Web browser
- Lycos Affinity Browser (Microsoft Internet Explorer 3.02) for Windows 95/NT

## Viewing the Hyperlinked HTML Version of the Book

The CD-ROM contains the fully hyperlinked text of the book, including thousands of Web sites and Internet addresses, including live links to Women's Wire and Lycos, the search engine. Although you can use the CD and view the HTML book version without a live Internet connection, every section of the CD allows you to select an Internet address and instantly connect to the actual site. To connect directly to these Web sites, however, you'll need an Internet connection.

## Using the CD-ROM

To view the hyperlinked version of the book, you will need to use a Web browser. Simply follow the steps below.

### Running Most Web Browsers (Including Netscape Navigator)

1 Place the CD-ROM in your CD-ROM drive.

2 Launch your Web browser.

3 Choose **Open File** from the File menu.

**4** Select your CD-ROM drive. For PC users, this is usually drive **D**. Mac users, double-click on the **CD-ROM icon**.

**5** Double-click on the file named **Welcome.htm**.

### Running Microsoft Internet Explorer

**1** Place the CD-ROM in your CD-ROM drive.

**2** Launch **Internet Explorer**.

**3** Choose **Open** from the File menu.

**4** Click the **Browse** button.

**5** Select your CD-ROM drive. For PC users, this is usually drive **D**. Mac users, double-click on the **CD-ROM icon**.

**6** Double-click on the file named **Welcome.htm**.

**7** Click on **OK**.

### INSTALLING WEB BROWSER SOFTWARE

If you do not have a Web browser currently installed on your computer, we have included Microsoft's Internet Explorer on this CD. The steps for installing Internet Explorer are described below.

### Recommended PC System

- 486 Processor (Pentium Processor preferred)
- Windows OS (3.x, 95, or NT)
- 8MB of RAM (16MB preferred)
- 8MB free space on your hard drive (16MB preferred)
- 2x CD-ROM drive (4x recommended)

### Macintosh System Requirements

- Apple Macintosh or Power Macintosh (or clone) running System 7.0.1 or later

- Apple Open Transport or Mac TCP and Thread Manager
- 8MB of RAM (16MB preferred)
- 8MB of free space on your hard drive (16MB preferred)
- 2x CD-ROM drive (4x preferred)

### For All Systems

A modem (14.4bps or faster is recommended for optimum performance)

### INSTALLING INTERNET EXPLORER

### Internet Explorer Version 3.01 for Windows 95

You must be using Microsoft Windows 95 to run Microsoft Internet Explorer 3.01. Locate the Win95 folder in the MSIE directory on the CD. Create a temporary directory on your computer. Copy the MSIE301M.EXE file from the Win95 folder on the CD and paste it in the temporary folder on your hard drive.

Double-click on the file. Follow the instructions that appear on your screen to complete the installation.

### Internet Explorer Version 2.1 for Windows 3.1

You must be using Microsoft Windows 3.1 to run Microsoft Internet Explorer 2.1. Locate the Win3.1 folder in the MSIE directory on the CD. Create a temporary directory on your computer. Copy the DIMINI21.EXE file from the Win3.1 folder on the CD and paste it in the temporary folder on your hard disk.

Double-click on the file. Follow the instructions that appear on your screen to complete the installation.

### Internet Explorer Version 3.01 for Windows NT 4.0

You must be using Microsoft Windows NT 4.0 to run Microsoft Internet Explorer 3.01. Locate the WINNTI31 folder in the MSIE directory on the CD. Create a temporary directory on your computer. Copy the LENT351X.EXE file from the WINNTI31 folder on the CD and paste it in the temporary folder on your hard disk.

Double-click the file. Follow the instructions that appear on your screen to complete the installation.

### Internet Explorer Version 2.0 for the Macintosh

Double-click the Internet Explorer installer icon, located in the MSIE directory, to install. Follow the prompts that appear on your screen to complete the installation.

**Note:** Eudora Light is an Internet Mail client application that is included in Microsoft Internet Explorer 2.0 for the Macintosh. Documentation for Eudora Light is not included. To download the Eudora Light Manual separately, visit the Microsoft Internet Explorer Web site at: http://www.microsoft.com/ie/iedl.htm#mac.

### INSTALLING MINDSPRING

On this CD-ROM we have included a software package from an Internet Service Provider (ISP). This software from Mindspring called PipeLine+ will allow you to gain full access to the Internet. The following information tells you how to load this software and get connected to the Internet. Please review all of the following information before you start to load this software.

### Minimum System and Software Requirements

The PipeLine+ software requires the following minimum system configuration to run properly:

- Windows 3.1, 3.11, or Win95 on a 486 processor
- Macintosh: System 7.1 or higher on a 68020 processor
- 8 MB of RAM or memory
- A 14.4 or faster modem capable of hardware handshaking
- PC users need a serial port with a 16550 UART
- Macintosh users need a hardware handshaking cable

### Installation for Windows

1  Insert the CD into your CD-ROM drive.

2  Run:[your drive]:\minds\setup.exe.

3  Follow the instructions at the prompt.

4  Complete forms for registration.

5  Select your monthly usage plan.

6  We will check for your modem, verify the mailbox name that you requested, and return confirmation of a UserID, your mailbox name, and your password. Please write down your password!

7  You will be asked if you want to restart your computer. You must restart your computer for the installation to be complete.

8  Click on the PipeLine+ icon on the desktop.

9  Click on the Connect button to MindSpring. Some subscribers may experience a short delay in establishing their first connection while MindSpring activates their new account.

- ***When prompted, please enter the 8 character CD KEY:MACM-7577

### Installation on Macintosh

1 Insert CD into your CD-ROM drive.

2 When the CD appears on your desktop, double-click on it.

3 Open the MindSpring folder and double-click the Install icon within the folder. Installation will begin automatically.

4 Complete your forms for registration.

5 Select your monthly usage plan.

6 We will check for your modem, verify the mailbox name that you requested, and return confirmation of the UserID, your mailbox and your password. Please write down your password.

7 You will be asked if you want to restart your computer. You must restart your computer in order for installation to be complete.

8 Click on the PipeLine+ icon on the desktop.

9 Click on the Connect button to connect to MindSpring. Some subscribers may experience a short delay in establishing their first connection while MindSpring activates their new account.

- *** When prompted, please enter the 8 character CD KEY: MACM-7577 (all caps).

### Windows Product Overview

MindSpring's PipeLine+ software has been designed to make your Internet experience easy and enjoyable. During the installation process, you will be prompted for the necessary information to start your account with MindSpring. All of the Internet client applications included with our package will be installed and configured automatically.

Here is the list of applications included in the Windows 3.x and Windows 95 packages. The clients marked with "*" are shareware. The clients marked

with "**" are licensed by MindSpring for distribution. The remaining clients are freeware.

**TCP Pro 32bit Winsock—Connect, Console

**Netscape Navigator software for Windows 3.x

**Microsoft Internet Explorer for Windows 95

**Eudora Light—e-mail

**WsFTP—File Transfer Protocol (FTP)

Free Agent—Newsreader for Usernet

WsTalk—one-on-one text chat client

Ping-NTSI—for checking to see if another machine is online

WinCode—uuencoder-decoder

Ewan—telnet

*WinZip—compression utility

*LviewPro—graphics viewer

*WsIRC—Internet Relay Chat

### Macintosh Product Overview

MindSpring's PipeLine+ for Macintosh is a self-installing software program that provides an interface for connecting to and disconnecting from the Internet as well as a suite of Internet client applications.

All set up configuration is handled during the installation process, including modem type, user ID and selecting your local dial-up phone number. Once installation is complete, the PipeLine+ Access panel provides MindSpring-specific information such as a "Message of the Day," monthly usage statistics and e-mail notification.

Frequently used applications, such as FTP, WWW browser, e-mail client, newsreader and chat client, are preconfigured on a Launch It! toolbar which also allows you to add or remove any application, utility, or document. All other applications provided with MindSpring PipeLine+ for the Mac, such as JPEG View, are located within the PipeLine+ folder.

## A Notice about Licensed Products and Shareware

Do not distribute the Netscape Navigator or Internet Explorer applications—they are not shareware or freeware. In addition, do not distribute the shareware clients for which MindSpring has licensing arrangements such as Fetch, Anarchie, or Newswatcher.

Notice: MindSpring encourages you to pay the shareware fees for any programs which you decide to keep and use. We've included these programs in this package because we think they are the best ones available for the respective jobs. There are other Internet client programs available, and you may prefer to use one of them rather than registering the offered shareware programs.

### Contact Information
MindSpring General Office
Local (Atlanta, GA) (404)815-0770
Toll Free (800)791-4660
Facsimile (404) 815-8805
Web Address: http://www.mindspring.com

## MindSpring Technical Support

Our technical support is free, and we make it available to our customers in several ways. Technical support is available 24 hours a day, 7 days a week to answer any technical questions you may have. We encourage you to contact MindSpring using the medium that best suits you and your particular problem.
Email support@mindspring.com
Usenet newsgroup mindspring.help
Telephone Local (404)915-9111
Toll Free (800) 719-4660

## MindSpring Billing or Customer Service

Customer service is available to answer any questions you might have about pricing, upgrades, billing or other charges to your account from 9:00 a.m. to 9:00 p.m., Monday through Friday (EST).

# Index of Site Names